Oral Roberts

THE NEW TESTAMENT COMES ALIVE

A Personal New Testament Commentary

VOLUME TWO
ACTS-PHILEMON

Table of
Contents

The
Acts
of the Apostles

The
Acts
of the Apostles

As we begin the book of Acts I have never been more excited in my life, for we are going to see the power of Jesus Christ manifested as if He were still on earth. We will see Him even in greater power because of His ascension and glorification and because of the sending of the Holy Spirit, working through His disciples who are His followers. It is as if Christ had never gone away. Through the one Christ, now there are many "little Christs" rising up doing the same works of Jesus Christ.

Many believe that the Church was born on the day of Pentecost as described in the second chapter of Acts. Luke, a noted historian, medical doctor, and a co-evangelist with St. Paul, gives us the running account of the work of God through the disciples. Luke wrote this book about A.D. 62, some 30-35 years after the death of Jesus. It might be better to call "The Acts of the Apostles," "The Acts of the Holy Spirit." Luke builds his account of the work of the new Church primarily around two of the original apostles, Peter and Paul.

The book of Acts seems to have no logical ending. It ends abruptly with Paul in jail in Rome, indicating that the Acts of the Holy Spirit are not over, are not finished, but continue in us today and are to become mightier and mightier.

Acts1:1-3

The former treatise have I made, O Theophilus, of all that Jesus began both to do and teach, Until the day in which he was taken up, after that he through the Holy Ghost had given commandments unto the apostles whom he had chosen: To whom also he shewed himself alive after his passion by many infallible proofs, being seen of them forty days, and speaking of the things pertaining to the kingdom of God . . .

3

Preparation for the Spirit

Jesus, after His resurrection, was on the earth for 40 days. He appeared several times to various groups of His disciples. He personally showed himself in His resurrection body by many infallible proofs. He appeared in their presence as a means of preparing them for the coming of the Holy Spirit into their lives.

Acts 1:4,5
> And, being assembled together with them, commanded them that they should not depart from Jerusalem, but wait for the promise of the Father, which, saith he, ye have heard of me. For John truly baptized with water; but ye shall be baptized with the Holy Ghost not many days hence.

A Distinct Difference

Jesus is referring to John's baptism of water, a baptism unto repentance, but of His own baptism Jesus said it would be a Spirit baptism. Jesus was making a distinct difference between water baptism and Spirit baptism — the baptism with the Holy Spirit.

Acts 1:6
> When they therefore were come together, they asked of him, saying, Lord, wilt thou at this time restore again the kingdom to Israel?

Trusting the Spirit

The apostles still accepted to some extent the general Israelite belief that the Messiah would restore the political kingdom of Israel. Even His closest apostles had not quite understood that was not His purpose. To the apostles it appeared as if their Lord and Master, their protector, their Messiah, was returning to the Father in heaven and they were being left alone in a hostile world. They faced the cruel Roman Empire, the prejudice and hatred of the Roman people, and the Jewish nation.

The apostles were reaching out for protection. Jesus had just told them what He was going to do. He was going to baptize them with the Holy Ghost and fire. Yet they were unsure about what this baptism would mean.

How was Jesus able to go on through with His ascension? He was leaving everything in the hands of these few men who did not understand what was going on. There are two reasons why Jesus could ascend unto the Father. One of them was that He had to trust the Holy Spirit — the Divine Paraclete, the other Comforter. He had told the disciples that the Holy Spirit would bring all things to their remembrance whatsoever He had said. He told them the Holy Spirit had been with them but would be in them.

It is of great importance to us today to understand how much Jesus trusted the Holy Spirit.

Second, He trusted them. He trusted the apostles! Jesus knew that upon receiving the Holy Spirit they would allow the Holy Spirit to do His mighty work through them.

Acts 1:7,8

> And he said unto them, It is not for you to know the times or the seasons, which the Father hath put in his own power. But ye shall receive power, after that the Holy Ghost is come upon you: and ye shall be witnesses unto me both in Jerusalem, and in all Judaea, and in Samaria, and unto the uttermost part of the earth.

Obey the Spirit

The Christian's concern is to do what God tells him to do. Christians should receive the gift of the Holy Spirit and then start witnessing about Christ. For the apostles, they were too. "Start witnessing in Jerusalem and going throughout all Judaea and in Samaria and unto the uttermost part of the earth." Jesus is telling the apostles to get their priorities straight, to receive the Holy Spirit, and then to go about the work they were called to do, witnessing unto Jesus Christ, the Son of God.

Speaking personally, I am asked many times, What will happen to Oral Roberts University and the City of Faith Health Care Center which God has led me to establish — what will happen to it when I am gone? Here is where I have received my greatest comfort and guidance. I, too, must trust the Holy Spirit. Since my ministry was raised up by the Holy Spirit and God told me to build Oral Roberts University on the Holy Spirit and on His authority and to establish the City of Faith Health Care Center upon the power of the Holy Spirit — to merge His healing streams of medicine and prayer — then the only one I can trust is the Holy Spirit. But, second, I trust the people who will be obedient to the Holy Spirit to carry on this ministry greater than I have been able to carry it on. If I did not believe that, I would be upset all the time. As I come nearer and nearer to His calling me away, I want to be able to depend upon someone greater than I am, the Holy Spirit himself, and also upon Holy Spirit-filled people. I believe that God raised it up with His plan. He has a plan to keep it going until His second coming.

Acts 1:9

> And when he had spoken these things, while they beheld, he was taken up; and a cloud received him out of their sight.

The word "cloud" is not just condensed vapor — it speaks of a shekinah glory, or the presence of God. He was taken up and the presence of God received Him out of their physical sight.

Acts 1:10,11

> And while they looked stedfastly toward heaven as he went up, behold, two men stood by them in white apparel; Which also said, Ye men of Galilee, why stand ye gazing up into heaven? this same Jesus, which is taken up from you into heaven, shall so come in like manner as ye have seen him go into heaven.

This is the point where the visible and the invisible are separated. The angels tell them that this same Jesus, just exactly as He was then going up into heaven, is going to come back from heaven in the same manner as they saw Him go up. He will come to the same spot — the Mount of Olives. This passage is speaking of the second coming of Jesus.

Acts 1:12-14

> Then returned they unto Jerusalem from the mount called Olivet, which is from Jerusalem a sabbath day's journey. And when they were come in, they went up into an upper room, where abode both Peter, and James, and John, and Andrew, Philip, and Thomas, Bartholomew, and Matthew, James the son of Alphaeus, and Simon Zelotes, and Judas the brother of James. These all continued with one accord in prayer and supplication, with the women, and Mary the mother of Jesus, and with his brethren.

His Brethren Believers

The apostles returned to an upper room where they continued in prayer and supplication. In addition to the apostles, there were women who were present, including Mary, mother of Jesus. This is the last time that Mary, the mother of Jesus, is mentioned in the New Testament.

Jesus' brethren in the flesh also were there. You recall in the Gospels that at times they came to Him with cynicism and doubt. They did not believe in Him at that time, but now they are believers and they are there on the day of Pentecost in the upper room to receive the Holy Spirit.

Acts 1:15,16
> And in those days Peter stood up in the midst of the disciples, and said, (the number of names together were about an hundred and twenty,) Men and brethren, this scripture must needs have been fulfilled, which the Holy Ghost by the mouth of David spake before concerning Judas, which was guide to them that took Jesus.

When Peter stood up and called them men and brethren, that was the normal way that both men and women in a gathering were addressed.

Acts 1:17
> For he was numbered with us, and had obtained part of this ministry.

Many have asked such questions as: "Why did Jesus choose Judas?" "Was Judas a spiritual man?" "Was he a man who had been changed by Jesus Christ?" "Was he a man who was worthy to be an apostle?" The answer is yes. Judas was worthy until he transgressed. He was numbered with the apostles. He had a part of the ministry and the apostleship. He transgressed from it and through transgression, or sin, he fell away from the Lord.

When people reject Jesus Christ as the Son of God, having once known Him, then they remove from their existence the only one who can save them. This process is called apostasy.

Acts 1:18
> Now this man purchased a field with the reward of iniquity; and falling headlong, he burst asunder in the midst, and all his bowels gushed out.

Almost Saved, Almost Lost

Matthew 27:5 records the death of Judas. It is believed he tied one end of a rope around his neck and the other around the limb of a tree. He jumped off. His body was too heavy for the rope and it broke. His body hurtled down the side of the mountain, hit the rocks, and burst open. Judas was almost saved, but lost. The apostle Peter knew how Judas felt, for he was almost lost through his denials

7

but was saved, whereas Judas, having every opportunity, was almost saved, but lost.

Acts 1:19

And it was known unto all the dwellers at Jerusalem; insomuch as that field is called in their proper tongue, Aceldama, that is to say, The field of blood.

Love of Money

The 30 pieces of silver for which Judas sold Christ was the amount of purchase for a burial plot for a stranger who died in Jerusalem. It was not the amount of money that Judas had in mind. He that loves money does not depend on the amount of it. Whether it is large or small, it is just money, and the love of it caused Judas to transgress against God.

Acts 1:20

For it is written in the book of Psalms, Let his habitation be desolate, and let no man dwell therein: and his bishoprick let another take.

That is a reference to Psalms 69:25, Psalms 109:8.

Acts 1:21,22

Wherefore of these men which have companied with us all the time that the Lord Jesus went in and out among us, Beginning from the baptism of John, unto that same day that he was taken up from us, must one be ordained to be a witness with us of his resurrection.

The Resurrection Evidence

One of the twelve, Judas, was now gone and he must be replaced. Judas' replacement must be a person who had been with them from the very beginning until the very day He was taken up. That person must have been a witness of His resurrection.

This is the first reference to resurrection in the book of Acts. Jesus' resurrection is the turning point of all Christendom, of all God's kingdom upon this earth. It is the number-one fact of history by which the work of God is infallibly true and will endure forever. The resurrection of Jesus was the one single thing that no power on earth or beneath the earth or any other place could prevent. The resurrection is the indisputable evidence that Jesus is alive forevermore. And that is what the word "resurrection" stands for, "Christ alive forevermore." Therefore, the apostle who would take the place of Judas must have been a witness of the Christ who is alive forevermore.

Acts 1:23-26

> And they appointed two, Joseph called Barsabas, who was surnamed Justus, and Matthias. And they prayed, and said, Thou, Lord, which knowest the hearts of all men, shew whether of these two thou hast chosen, That he may take part of this ministry and apostleship, from which Judas by transgression fell, that he might go to his own place. And they gave forth their lots; and the lot fell upon Matthias; and he was numbered with the eleven apostles.

Let God Guide

In their prayer they asked God to show them who was to be chosen. Then apparently they put some names in a container and one put his hand in and pulled the name out. Today, we would do that by voting. But whichever method is used is a dependence upon God, that God himself will see that the right person is chosen. Once again the full number of the 12 is established.

Acts 2:1

> And when the day of Pentecost was fully come, they were all with one accord in one place.

The day of Pentecost is the feast of weeks, or the waiving of the sheave of the first fruits. The day of Pentecost occurs 50 days after the Passover, after the death of Jesus. This feast goes back to the Passover in Egypt and 50 days later when they came to Mount Sinai where Moses went up in the mount and received the Ten Commandments.

It was on Mount Sinai that the light of God shone, and the place was shaken by fire and lightning. The Lord revealed himself in mighty power. There was a launching forth of these people to be a people who would take the Promised Land. This was a tremendous occasion in the life of Israel.

The day of Pentecost fell 10 days after Jesus' ascension. Prior to His ascension, Jesus had shown himself alive 40 days. After the ascension, the followers of Christ were in the upper room waiting for the precise moment when the day of Pentecost would have fully come.

Acts 2:2

> And suddenly there came a sound from heaven as of a rushing mighty wind, and it filled all the house where they were sitting.

Pentecost Power

This was a sudden happening: a pushing, rushing, gushing wind of such force that it was almost like a blast or clap of thunder. The whole house was filled with the noise and the vibrant power. Some believe that the noise was heard throughout the city.

Acts 2:3

> And there appeared unto them cloven tongues like as of fire, and it sat upon each of them.

Tongues Like Fire

Forked tongues, not of fire, but like as a fire, sat upon their heads.

Acts 2:4

> And they were all filled with the Holy Ghost, and began to speak with other tongues, as the Spirit gave them utterance.

In Old Testament time, prophets, kings, and great leaders were filled with the Holy Spirit. Now Jesus' promise is coming to pass. Jesus told His following they were to be baptized with the Holy Spirit. They were to be filled with the Holy Spirit, and they were.

That is very important to understand. There is a baptism of the Holy Spirit that is different or in contrast to the infilling of the Holy Spirit. At the moment they were filled with the Holy Spirit, they began to speak with other tongues as the Holy Spirit gave them the power, or gave them the utterance, or the ability to speak in a tongue or language that they had not learned.

Acts 2:5

> And there were dwelling at Jerusalem Jews, devout men, out of every nation under heaven.

The "Devout Men"

These people probably included many who were part of the

dispersion. Others who were pilgrims had come to this feast in Jerusalem. But the fact is that they dwelt there. They had established themselves in Jerusalem. Apparently they were a very special group of people because Luke takes pains to mention it. In some way they are different from the regular "run-of-the-mill" Jewish people.

Acts 2:6-13
> Now when this was noised abroad, the multitude came together, and were confounded, because that every man heard them speak in his own language. And they were all amazed and marvelled, saying one to another, Behold, are not all these which speak Galilaeans? And how hear we every man in our own tongue, wherein we were born?
>
> Parthians, and Medes, and Elamites, and the dwellers in Mesopotamia, and in Judaea, and Cappadocia, in Pontus, and Asia, Phrygia, and Pamphylia, in Egypt, and in the parts of Libya about Cyrene, and strangers of Rome, Jews and proselytes, Cretes and Arabians, we do hear them speak in our tongues the wonderful works of God. And they were all amazed, and were in doubt, saying one to another, What meaneth this? Others mocking said, These men are full of new wine.

When this noise from heaven filled the room and the Holy Spirit filled the disciples, they began to speak in other tongues as the Spirit gave them utterance. This was an event of such power and significance that it was noised abroad in the city. The whole town was aware that something extraordinary, earth shaking, was going on in an upper room. These Galileans who had not been trained in the higher councils of Judaism were now supernaturally endowed with power from on high. The word for power is dunamis. We get our word "dynamite" from this Greek word. This power from on high signifies that the Holy Spirit had come to indwell the disciples and to make their bodies a temple of the Holy Spirit.

The disciples were speaking in the various dialects of the Jewish people who had come from 16 different nations. These Jewish people were astounded when they heard this for they said, "We hear them speak in our tongues the wonderful works of God." Many people say that the reason that tongues accompanied the gift of the Holy Spirit was so they could speak the Word of God and preach in the language of all these different people. However, that is not what these Jewish people said. "We do hear them speak in our own tongues the wonderful works of God." The disciples were praising and magnifying God. They were honoring and glorifying His name. They were releasing the pent-up emotions they had had for those three years of Jesus' lifetime when they were with Him day by day. They had been a motley bunch in a way. They had risen to great heights and descended to the lowest levels, up and down, in and out. On top, now on the bottom. And the Lord has had mercy upon them. They finally believed in the resurrection after doubting it.

The disciples finally got together, came into unity. They were of one mind. The high priestly prayer of Christ in John 17 is partially answered, "That they may be one in Him." Now ... they are bursting forth with this new language which is given them by the Holy Spirit. They are releasing the joy that at last, at last, they are full believers. Their concern was not primarily with those people who came to see or hear them. Those people came after they heard about it. The 120, including Mary the mother of Jesus, had already experienced the Holy Spirit and the speaking in tongues. They were giving vent to the glory of God, praising the Lord for His wonderful works. Those people who came were eavesdroppers. They heard it all. They were struck by it because it seemed impossible that uneducated Galileans could speak in so many different languages. Can you imagine how impressed they were? Yet there was a group among them who doubted and mocked the disciples. This group said, "Ah, they are just drunk."

Acts 2:14,15

> But Peter, standing up with the eleven, lifted up his voice, and said unto them, Ye men of Judaea, and all ye that dwell at Jerusalem, be this known unto you, and hearken to my words: For these are not drunken, as ye suppose, seeing it is but the third hour of the day.

Drunken Myth Dispelled

This was nine o'clock in the morning. It was also the prayer time at the temple. The Jews had three prayer times each day: nine in the morning, twelve noon, and three o'clock in the afternoon. Peter was saying that the most unbelieving Jews would not desecrate the hour of prayer by drinking. He is saying it is but the third hour of the day.

Acts 2:16-18

> But this is that which was spoken by the prophet Joel; And it shall come to pass in the last days, saith God, I will pour out of my Spirit upon all flesh: and your sons and your daughters shall prophesy, and your young men shall see visions, and your old men shall dream dreams: And on my servants and on my handmaidens I will pour out in those days of my Spirit; and they shall prophesy ...

Eternal Dividing Point

The last days were a reference to the Messianic era. Joel said that God would pour out His Spirit upon all flesh. In the four Gospels one of the things Jesus had to contend with was the belief of the Jewish people that they were an exclusive people, whereas their father, Abraham, the father of all who have faith, was told by God that he was to be a light to the Gentiles, to all the nations of the earth. In the Messianic era Peter is referring them back and saying, "The Spirit of God will be poured out upon all flesh."

This is the eternal dividing point from that hour on that God's Spirit is poured out upon all flesh. The Spirit of God will be poured out upon you, upon every member of your family, upon every person who will ever be born. That does not mean that we will accept it or will respond to it, but it means the faithfulness of God will touch every human being.

Then Joel specifically says, "Your young men shall see visions. Your old men shall dream dreams." The Sadducees did not believe in the resurrection, or angels, or visions and dreams. The Pharisees did, but merely in an outward sense. They did not really believe in their hearts. God had been trying to recapture that, to restore it to His people. The coming of the Holy Spirit meant the return of visions, dreams, and prophecies. It meant the unloosing of the supernatural powers of God to affect the dreams of people, to inspire visions, to reveal prophecies of the other world as those prophecies impact the world that we live in.

Acts 2:19,20

> And I will shew wonders in heaven above, and signs in the earth beneath; blood, and fire, and vapour of smoke: The sun shall be turned into darkness, and the moon into blood, before that great and notable day of the Lord come . . .

God's Agent Shapes Destiny

Joel is speaking directly here of the second coming of Christ — of Armageddon. The outpouring of the Holy Spirit has to do with us being infilled personally and it has to do with the events of the entire human race. The Holy Spirit is the power that will produce the Armageddon. The Holy Spirit will bring forth the revelation of our Lord Jesus Christ coming back in the clouds of heaven through which He ascended to His Father. Jesus will be with His saints whom He has raised from the dead and translated from among the living.

13

Jesus will be coming with them to reestablish himself upon the earth, only this time He will take over all the political kingdoms. He will amalgamate all nations, including Israel, into His own kingdom which shall be an eternal kingdom of peace and righteousness. Do not denigrate the outpouring of the Holy Spirit. Know that the Holy Spirit is the agent, the executive of God's people after our Lord's ascension to heaven. He is the manager and administrator of our lives and of the future events of our civilization.

Acts 2:21

> And it shall come to pass, that whosoever shall call on the name of the Lord shall be saved.

Opening the Kingdom

Peter had said that God will "pour out of My Spirit upon all flesh," which is the great dividing point. Now he adds to that by saying, "Whosoever," "Whosoever shall call on the name of the Lord shall be saved." Taking it out of a nation that seemed to be exclusively possessors of the kingdom of the ordinances and the commandments of God, He says that from this point on it is "whosoever," taking in all the Gentiles and everybody else who will call on the name of the Lord. When they do, they will be saved. This is an awesome moment in history. This is heaven bending low and kissing the earth. God takes off the wraps and opens up the whole kingdom of God to all people and to every individual who will take action to call upon the Lord.

Acts 2:22-24

> Ye men of Israel, hear these words; Jesus of Nazareth, a man approved of God among you by miracles and wonders and signs, which God did by him in the midst of you, as ye yourselves also know: Him, being delivered by the determinate counsel and foreknowledge of God, ye have taken, and by wicked hands have crucified and slain: Whom God hath raised up, having loosed the pains of death: because it was not possible that he should be holden of it.

Peter's Transformation

Look at Peter as he stood there at the trial of Christ when the little maid and the others said, "You are one of them," and he said, "No, I do not even know His name. I am not one of Jesus' disciples."

Then see him now, filled with the Holy Spirit, baptized with the Holy Spirit, energized with power from on high. He is not the same man who was denying. He is now the man who is affirming. He is the man who looks them straight in the eye and says, "Ye men of Israel, I'm talking to you! This man Jesus Christ was approved by God and God approved Him by the miracles and wonders and signs which He gave Him. You saw them in the midst of you and you know them. That man was delivered up by the determination of God, by His foreknowledge of Him as the lamb slain from the foundation of the world. You took this Jesus of Nazareth, and you had Him crucified. Now God raised this man, Jesus of Nazareth, from the dead, and He raised that dead body from the tomb. It was not possible for death to hold Him."

Acts 2:25-27

> For David speaketh concerning him, I foresaw the Lord always before my face, for he is on my right hand, that I should not be moved: Therefore did my heart rejoice, and my tongue was glad; moreover also my flesh shall rest in hope: Because thou wilt not leave my soul in hell, neither wilt thou suffer thine Holy One to see corruption.

Peter Points Out Prophecy

Peter was saying that this man, Jesus Christ, whom you killed and put in the tomb, was raised by God so that His body did not experience corruption, which is a fulfillment of the prophecy of the king and prophet David in Psalm 16:10.

Peter continues quoting David.

Acts 2:28

> Thou hast made known to me the ways of life; thou shalt make me full of joy with thy countenance.

Now he changes back from quoting David to speak directly to these people again.

Acts 2:29,30

> Men and brethren, let me freely speak unto you of the patriarch David, that he is both dead and buried, and his sepulchre is with us unto this day.
>
> Therefore being a prophet, and knowing that God had sworn with an oath to him, that of the fruit of his loins, according to the flesh, he would raise up Christ to sit on his throne . . .

David's Descendants of Flesh

David, as a prophet of God as well as the king of Israel, had forseen the resurrection of Christ. God had sworn to David with an oath that of the fruit of his loins, according to his flesh, he would raise Christ to sit on his throne. David did not beget spirit beings. He beget children-of-flesh beings. The fruit of his loins speaks of flesh beings, not spirit beings, but flesh beings of soul, mind, and body.

Acts 2:31-37

He seeing this before spake of the resurrection of Christ, that his soul was not left in hell, neither his flesh did see corruption. This Jesus hath God raised up, whereof we all are witnesses. Therefore being by the right hand of God exalted, and having received of the Father the promise of the Holy Ghost, he hath shed forth this, which ye now see and hear.

For David is not ascended into the heavens: but he saith himself, The Lord said unto my Lord, Sit thou on my right hand, Until I make thy foes thy footstool. Therefore let all the house of Israel know assuredly, that God hath made that same Jesus, whom ye have crucified, both Lord and Christ.

Now when they heard this, they were pricked in their heart, and said unto Peter and to the rest of the apostles, Men and brethren, what shall we do?

Appeal to Peter

Compare Peter's speaking in the Gospels with his speaking on the day of Pentecost and you see an entirely different man. Paul was later to say in II Corinthians 5:17, "If any man be in Christ, he is a new creature: old things have passed away, and all things become new." I think this is one of the greatest examples.

It goes back to when Christ first met Peter, who was brought to Him by his brother Andrew. Jesus looked at him and saw that he was like a reed fishing pole blown by the winds, shakable, without deep convictions, but knew He would make him a rock. Here is a man unshakable in His convictions. Here is a man who knows what He knows and says, in effect, "I know that I know that I know." Here is a man who has received power from on high. Here is a man who, although he was not educated in the higher councils of Judaism, was able to connect the most difficult prophecies of the Old Testament and bring them into a oneness, and a nowness, and a direct application to the crucifiers of our Lord Jesus Christ.

When Peter finishes speaking, his hearers are pricked or cut in their hearts. They are convicted as if by a higher tribunal. It occurs to them, "We have killed the only hope we have. We did it. Now we are cut off. We have no other way to be saved." They cried to Peter and the other apostles, "Men and brethren, what shall we do? Where will we turn? How are we going to get out of what we have done?"

Now, for the first time, we are going to see the use of the Christians' power of attorney, because Peter had the right answer.

Acts 2:38-40

> Then Peter said unto them, Repent, and be baptized every one of you in the name of Jesus Christ for the remission of sins, and ye shall receive the gift of the Holy Ghost. For the promise is unto you, and to your children, and to all that are afar off, even as many as the Lord our God shall call. And with many other words did he testify and exhort, saying, Save yourselves from this untoward generation.

Receiving the Gift

That last phrase, "save yourselves from this untoward generation," means "this crooked generation." When Jesus gave us His name, that whatsoever we would ask in His name He would do it, He was giving us the power of attorney. When these people wanted to know what to do, Peter used the power of attorney. Peter said to "repent," which in the Greek means "to change your mind and turn around." They were told to make an abrupt about-face — having been going one way, turn around and go in the opposite direction — having had the spirit of hatred, of blasphemy, of murder, having killed the Son of God, turn opposite from that — that is the meaning of repent The next thing he said to do was to "be baptized every one of you in the name of Jesus Christ for the remission of your sins." To do that, Peter said repent, make an about-face, and be baptized in a name: the name of Jesus Christ. This is a far cry from John the Baptist baptizing people with water. Peter is talking about the name of Jesus Christ. He meant that they no longer would be members of the faith of Judaism or a part of the political kingdom of Israel. They would walk out and become new creatures. They would become Christians, disciples of the Lord Jesus. Their people would cut them off, but in contrast to that they would have their sins remitted, which in God's view is the number-one thing of importance in every human's life.

When these people repented and were baptized in Jesus' name they received the gift of the Holy Spirit all in one simultaneous act.

17

There was no period of time that had to elapse between their repentance and receiving the gift of the Holy Spirit. It was all one continuous act. What does that mean to us today? It means we are all going to have to rethink the doctrines that the various Christian groups have come up with through the hundreds of years.

There is one group that believes that upon coming to Christ you receive the Holy Spirit but you do not speak with tongues and there are no visions, dreams, prophesies, or supernatural outpourings. They would leave this unsaved world bereft of the continuance of the miracles of Jesus.

Then there is a group that pulled away around the opening of the 20th century from this group and believed that there was a baptism of the Holy Spirit subsequent to conversion. This group had not observed, in their time as Christians in the churches, what Peter had talked about on the day of Pentecost. They had already accepted Christ, but had not spoken with tongues. They then tarried before the Lord and were able to release tongues because they already had the Holy Spirit. They did not know they already had the Holy Spirit; they thought they had to receive the Holy Spirit. The truth was, all they did was to release the tongues that had been in them since the Holy Spirit had brought Christ into their lives.

The eighth chapter of Romans informs us that the way we know we are saved is by the witness of the Holy Spirit. Unless we have the Spirit we do not have Christ. It is the Holy Spirit who first convicts us of sins, who leads us to repentance and baptism in the name of Jesus and who comes in himself to become the agent and executive of God upon this earth in our lives. Because the Holy Spirit is a person — He speaks, He thinks, He acts, He is living within us, He is in perfect communion with the Father. As He lives inside us, He speaks to the Father in prayer and praise 24 hours a day as He lives in us and we, by our will, simply tap into the Holy Spirit's language. We speak as the Spirit gives us utterance.

Peter says, "Repent, and be baptized every one of you in the name of Jesus Christ for the remission of sins, and ye shall receive the gift of the Holy Ghost." No ifs or ands or maybe sos, but you shall! It does take an act of the will to bring forth the tongues or the prayer language of the Spirit.

I suggest that you restudy this so you can consider what I perceive to be a revelation of God to me, after 35 years of study, meditation, prayer, and of preaching and teaching the Word. If you can get just one or two thoughts that will cause you to think and pray and seek God, perhaps God will reveal something to you greater than what I have said. If you have been studying this and have not yet allowed Christ to come into your heart, if you have not repented of your

sins and received the gift of the Holy Spirit, let me lead you now in
a prayer of repentance and of receiving the Lord Jesus Christ by
the power of the Holy Spirit. Would you pray along with me:

> *Oh, Lord God, I need to repent, to change my mind and to turn*
> *myself to God. Lord, I am sorry for my many sins and I truly,*
> *honestly repent, and from the innermost part of my being I*
> *receive You, Lord Jesus. I receive You into my heart. I receive*
> *You as my personal Savior and I receive the gift of the Holy*
> *Spirit to release my prayer language, to pray in the Spirit and*
> *with the understanding, to follow Christ, to obey Him, to witness*
> *for Him, and to live for Him forever and ever. Amen and amen.*

Acts 2:41,42
> Then they that gladly received his word were baptized: and the same
> day there were added unto them about three thousand souls. And
> they continued stedfastly in the apostles' doctrine and fellowship,
> and in breaking of bread, and in prayers.

The Lifted Burden

These people to whom Peter was preaching then gladly received
his word. They were thrilled to get out from under the burden of
their sins. That is where this world is now, under the burden of its
sins. I remember the time when the Spirit convicted my heart of sin,
how glad I was to get out from under the burden of that sin. Now
they were baptized in Jesus' name, they received the Holy Spirit,
and there were about 3,000 of them that day who did that. Luke says
the converts continued steadfastly. They developed a new
determination to follow in the Christian faith, to know the doctrine
that the Holy Spirit was revealing to the apostles. They were
determined to have fellowship one with another, to take the holy
communion and then to really have an earnest prayer life.

Acts 2:43
> And fear came upon every soul: and many wonders and signs were
> done by the apostles.

Christian Recognition

Fear, reverential awe, touched many people in Jerusalem, for
suddenly the Christian faith stood side by side with Judaism. It is

no longer Jesus dumping the plans of world conquest upon the shoulders of these 120 by trusting in the Holy Spirit. It is His faith coming to pass.

Many wonders and signs were done by the apostles. There was the continuation of the same approval of God upon His Son Jesus Christ, which was an approval by miracles, signs, and wonders. That same approval was upon the apostles. This is important to you and me because the approval of our work is on the basis of the wonders and signs that we do through the name of Jesus by our faith in Him. Peter meant what he said when he declared through prophecy that the incoming Holy Spirit would bring visions, dreams, and prophecies, indicating the opening up of the supernatural realm to us in this natural realm.

I, for one, believe it with all my heart and have based my ministry upon the name of our Lord Jesus Christ, depending on the Father and the Holy Spirit to make Him real in me and through me to lost and suffering humanity.

Acts 2:44-47

> And all that believed were together, and had all things common; And sold their possessions and goods, and parted them to all men, as every man had need. And they, continuing daily with one accord in the temple, and breaking bread from house to house, did eat their meat with gladness and singleness of heart, praising God, and having favour with all the people. And the Lord added to the church daily such as should be saved.

Don't Enclose God

These 120 disciples had won 3,000 souls to Christ, most of whom were cut off by their Jewish brethren and were thrust upon this tiny band of Christians who had sold their possessions and divided them so that everybody could eat. A little later we will speak of that. This is not communism, because the Lord Jesus was the head. He was still the theocratic form of government that was in the Old Testament where God was the head.

Meanwhile, they continued daily in their unity and fellowship and love, daily taking the holy communion, not in a church or a cathedral but in their private homes. Jesus taught us where two or three are gathered together in His name, there He is in the midst of them.

I am an ordained elder in the Church, in the Body of Christ. I go to the church sanctuary. I support it with my tithes and offerings, my presence, my faith, and my life. I love it. But in no way do I restrict the work of the Church to some building or some cathedral or some organization upon this earth. It is far greater than that. We can take holy communion wherever two or three of us are gathered together in His name. Let's not try to put God in a mold and build four walls around Him and say, This is the way it is. God is bigger than all that.

Acts 3:1

Now Peter and John went up together into the temple at the hour of prayer, being the ninth hour.

Equity in Christ

This is the third prayer period during the day for the Jewish people. This was three o'clock in the afternoon. Peter and John went up together. Neither is wanting preference over the other. They went together as praying men, men in the New Kingdom, men as followers of Christ.

Acts 3:2-6

And a certain man lame from his mother's womb was carried, whom they laid daily at the gate of the temple which is called Beautiful, to ask alms of them that entered into the temple; Who seeing Peter and John about to go into the temple asked an alms. And Peter, fastening his eyes upon him with John, said, Look on us. And he gave heed unto them, expecting to receive something of them. Then Peter said, Silver and gold have I none; but such as I have give I thee: In the name of Jesus Christ of Nazareth rise up and walk.

Better Than Gold

We are about to see the second use of the power of attorney that Jesus has given His followers. As the man looked on them, he expected to receive something material of them. Then Peter, looking at that Beautiful gate adorned with silver and gold, just put his hand out and said, in effect, "We do not have silver and gold like that to give you. In fact, we are not here for that purpose — to give you silver and gold to perpetuate the condition that you are in — but we have something better than silver and gold, something that we can give you that, when we give it, will change your life. We have the name of Jesus. He has empowered us from on high and given us His name as the power of attorney. He has told us whatever we

21

ask in His name, He would do it. Sir, in the name of Jesus Christ of Nazareth, in whom all the Godhead bodily dwells, I say unto you, 'Rise up and walk.'"

Sometimes it is much easier to give money than it is to give the name of Jesus. But it is better to give the name of Jesus because the name of Jesus has life in it, healing power, restorative power so the person can be healed and work for himself. Peter said, "In the name of Jesus Christ of Nazareth, rise up and walk." With the power of attorney, Peter and John were acting through Christ's name. When the lame man gave heed unto them, it suggests that he asked them what they meant. They explained the background upon which they were speaking in the name of Jesus. Based upon that, he was expecting to receive something of them, but Peter said, "Silver and gold have I none." The literal rendering of Peter's statement is, "It is not my purpose to give you silver and gold, but such as I have give I thee."

Many people say that Peter and John had no money. They use this to say that Christian people should be poor. But can you imagine the King of Glory would not supply money to His two top leaders — Peter and John? I personally believe they had money. I just do not believe that that is why they were there. Begging was not something that was in harmony with the kingdom of God. Peter and John were not going to contribute to this kind of thing. They had something better, is what they were saying.

Acts 3:7

> And he took him by the right hand, and lifted him up: and immediately his feet and ankle bones received strength.

Healing: A Process

Peter identified himself with the man at the point of his need. This is the way Christianity began, with the disciples being like their Master who met people at the point of their need. Here are men following Jesus, doing the greater things in His name that Jesus said they would do once the Holy Spirit had come upon them. Peter gave him the right hand of fellowship and then he lifted him up.

Many times when I pray for people in wheelchairs to be healed, or others who are badly crippled and who can scarcely move a muscle, I say to them, "When I speak in the name of Jesus for your healing, move something. If it is only a finger or a toe or a foot or an arm, move something. Get into action."

Peter had to reach down and start pulling him up before the lame man's healing began. I am pointing this out to you that God is not going to arbitrarily just lift you out of your chair, or pull you out of a wheelchair, or cause you to rise up out of a bed. There is something YOU have to do.

I want you to understand that healing is both an act and a process. There is that moment when the healing is immediate, but there is also that process during which things have to be done before the precise moment of immediate healing. This process can take seconds or minutes, hours, days, or even weeks and months before the immediate act of healing begins. Many people used to come to hear me preach in the big tent and did not want to hear the message of faith: they wanted me to stop and touch them, get their healing, and rush back to their homes and forget all about God. I refuse to do that. I told them that healing was a process and I say it again today. It is a process in which you go through what this lame man did.

He gave heed to what they said. He received the hand of fellowship. He really was entering into the kingdom of God. He had to look for something else which was in the name of Jesus.

We have to look to God, look to our source and know that God works through supernatural means. He also works through material means. He works through prayer. He works through the word of faith. He works through medicine. He works through aerobics or exercise. He works through good nutrition, but He is the source of our healing.

Acts 3:8-11

And he leaping up stood, and walked, and entered with them into the temple, walking, and leaping, and praising God. And all the people saw him walking and praising God: And they knew that it was he which sat for alms at the Beautiful gate of the temple: and they were filled with wonder and amazement at that which had happened unto him. And as the lame man which was healed held Peter and John, all the people ran together unto them in the porch that is called Solomon's, greatly wondering.

Healing Draws a Crowd

This man was so gloriously, supernaturally touched that he leaped up and began jumping up and down, shouting at the top of his voice, praising God. All the other Jewish people nearby saw him and they knew who he was and they said, "How in the world could this have happened to him?"

Then the Word says the lame man got hold of Peter and John and held them. He must have had super strength because he held Peter and John until the people ran together on Solomon's porch. This was an area of the temple about eight hundred feet long and it would contain thousands of people. They attracted a crowd.

Acts 3:12-16

> And when Peter saw it, he answered unto the people, Ye men of Israel, why marvel ye at this? or why look ye so earnestly on us, as though by our own power or holiness we had made this man to walk? The God of Abraham, and of Isaac, and of Jacob, the God of our fathers, hath glorified His Son Jesus; whom ye delivered up, and denied him in the presence of Pilate, when he was determined to let him go.
>
> But ye denied the Holy One and the Just, and desired a murderer to be granted unto you; And killed the Prince of life, whom God hath raised from the dead; whereof we are witnesses. And his name through faith in his name hath made this man strong, whom ye see and know; yea, the faith which is by him hath given him this perfect soundness in the presence of you all.

Faith in Jesus Healed

When the people ran together, Peter did the scriptural thing. He immediately told them that it was not he nor John who had healed this man. They were not to give them the credit, but Jesus of Nazareth. It was faith in His name — the name of Jesus which gave the power of attorney. Through faith in His name, this man was given wholeness in his body.

Don't you see now how we are to have the miracles of God through the name of Jesus? We are to bring healing to people by faith in that name, that name of Jesus whom God has raised from the dead. He is alive!

Peter said, "We are witnesses of His resurrection. We saw Him. We handled Him. We looked at Him. We know He is risen from the dead. It is His name that has given this man, through faith, this marvelous healing."

Acts 3:17,18

> All now, brethren, I wot that through ignorance ye did it, as did also your rulers. But those things, which God before had shewed by the mouth of all his prophets, that Christ should suffer, he hath so fulfilled.

Prophecy Fulfilled

What is Peter saying? He is saying that they and their rulers acted out of ignorance, they did not really know. No doubt Peter was recalling the words of Christ upon the cross when He said, "Father, forgive them for they know not what they do." Peter said that God had foretold all this by all of His prophets beginning with Samuel, the first prophet, through all the prophets of Israel who had prophesied that Christ should suffer and that all things should be fulfilled.

Acts 3:19-26

> Repent ye therefore, and be converted, that your sins may be blotted out, when the times of refreshing shall come from the presence of the Lord; And he shall send Jesus Christ, which before was preached unto you: Whom the heaven must receive until the times of restitution of all things, which God hath spoken by the mouth of all his holy prophets since the world began.
>
> For Moses truly said unto the fathers, A prophet shall the Lord your God raise up unto you of your brethren, like unto me; him shall ye hear in all things whatsoever he shall say unto you. And it shall come to pass that every soul, which will not hear that prophet, shall be destroyed from among the people. Yea, and all the prophets from Samuel and those that follow after, as many as have spoken, have likewise foretold of these days. Ye are the children of the prophets, and of the covenant which God made with our fathers, saying unto Abraham, And in thy seed shall all the kindreds of the earth be blessed. Unto you first God, having raised up his Son Jesus, sent him to bless you, in turning away every one of you from his iniquities.

Talking Their Language

Peter is now surrounded by a great multitude of people who are enraptured by this tremendous miracle. It is as though Jesus Christ were still here on the earth. Truly He is in those disciples, giving them the power of attorney of His name. They are performing miracles through that name.

Peter is explaining to these people what is going on. At that time, these Jews' sins could only be rolled back for the previous year for which they had come to the temple. They stood outside as the high priest went into the Holy of Holies and there put the blood upon the mercy seat as a sacrifice, a substitute for them. Then they had to come back a year later and do the same thing. Now Peter is saying, "Through Christ your sins will be blotted out. They will be gone. You will have times of refreshing from the Lord." He said that "Jesus right now is in heaven and He will remain there until sin has been fully dealt with, until its results have been wiped from the earth, until the restoration of all things from the beginning will take place. All that Adam lost through his fall will be restored and ye yourselves remember that your prophets spoke of these things from the very beginning. Moses told you of a prophet greater than he was that God would send. You were to hear Him and if you did not hear Him your soul would be destroyed."

Peter was talking their language. All of them knew that when Moses spoke of that prophet like unto him, that he was referring to the Messiah. So Peter is telling them again of the things they already knew and reminding them that the prophets had foretold all these things. Then he got right down to the nitty-gritty, saying, "My brethren, you are the offspring of the prophets of God and of the covenant that God made with our forefather Abraham in which He said that through Abraham's seed all the kindreds of the earth shall be blessed. You people here are the descendants, the seed of Abraham. You are supposed to be so close to God, receiving the fulfillment of His prophetic Word. Receive Christ as your Messiah so that God can use you to bless all the people of the earth." Then in Verse 26 he said, "Christ came unto you first. God having raised up His Son sent Him to bless you."

I can imagine the tears were streaming down Peter's face when he said that "God remembers you, His own people, the people that He called out from all the others" — the tiniest of people in the smallest of nations so that they might be a blessing to the kindreds of the earth. Think now of the Jews — how they have been scattered throughout the world. What a blessing they could have been, and they could be right now, by opening their hearts to receive the prophet like unto Moses.

It seems as if the Jewish people have looked at Christianity and said, "No, that is not for me." They have looked at Christ and said, "He is an impostor." No wonder Paul was to later say that he could wish himself accursed if that would bring his Jewish people back to God.

Acts 4:1,2

And as they spake unto the people, the priests, and the captain of the temple, and the Sadducees, came upon them, being grieved that they taught the people, and preached through Jesus the resurrection from the dead.

Prophecy Denied

The Sadducees were the strongest group, and they believed that there was no resurrection. They were grieved along with the chief priests and others that Peter and John and these other disciples are preaching to the people that Jesus is risen from the dead. He is the living embodiment of all the prophets said about the resurrection. This preaching that He is risen from the dead is knocking Jewish doctrine into a cocked hat. They have lost their stroke. They are grieved about it. They think more of their little doctrine than they think of what the prophets taught.

Acts 4:3,4

> And they laid hands on them, and put them in hold unto the next day: for it was now eventide. Howbeit many of them which heard the word believed; and the number of the men was about five thousand.

Miracles Approved

Right in the midst of their preaching which followed the healing of the lame man, they made invitations for the Jewish people listening to receive Christ. Five thousand of the men did. The number of believers was then at least 8,000, for there were 3,000 who accepted Christ, were filled with the Spirit at the day of Pentecost. Now 5,000 others repent in the name of Jesus Christ and receive the Holy Spirit.

It is amazing how, in the midst of opposition and persecution, people still come to Christ, at least when they have an opportunity to hear the Word of God which is confirmed by miracles. Let us not forget that in his sermon on the day of Pentecost, in Acts 2, Peter stated plainly that God had approved Jesus with miracles. Now these men are approved by miracles. Do you think that we can operate in God's work as Christians with anything less than God's approval by miracles?

Acts 4:5,6

> And it came to pass on the morrow, that their rulers, and elders, and scribes, and Annas the high priest, and Caiaphas, and John, and Alexander, and as many as were of the kindred of the high priest, were gathered together at Jerusalem.

Sanhedrin Meets

The Sanhedrin came together, the 70 leaders of the nation called the Sanhedrin, or the highest court in the land.

Act 4:7
> And when they had set them in the midst, they asked, By what power, or by what name, have ye done this?

License Questioned

This is the same question that they asked Jesus Christ. There is a repetition among the people who are genuinely following Christ of those things that happen through Jesus Christ when He was upon the earth. But there is no repetition unless we are like Jesus. When the Sanhedrin asked Peter and John by what power or by what name had they done this, they were referring to the fact that they had to grant license to people for religious work. In effect they were saying, "Who licensed you to do this? We did not. Who did?"

Acts 4:8-14
> Then Peter, filled with the Holy Ghost, said unto them, Ye rulers of the people, and elders of Israel, If we this day be examined of the good deed done to the impotent man, by what means he is made whole; Be it known unto you all, and to all the people of Israel, that by the name of Jesus Christ of Nazareth, whom ye crucified, whom God raised from the dead, even by him doth this man stand here before you whole.
> This is the stone which was set at nought of you builders, which is become the head of the corner. Neither is there salvation in any other: for there is none other name under heaven given among men, whereby we must be saved. Now when they saw the boldness of Peter and John, and perceived that they were unlearned and ignorant men, they marvelled; and they took knowledge of them, that they had been with Jesus. And beholding the man which was healed standing with them, they could say nothing against it.

Good Evidence

Peter begins his statement by being filled with the Holy Ghost. That is the key. Had he not been filled with the Holy Ghost, or had he not been imbued with power from on high, that dunamis, that power of a dynamo, he would have wilted as he stood there. Instead, he said, in effect, "We got our license, or our power and authority, through Jesus Christ of Nazareth, the one you crucified, the one that God raised from the dead. It is through His name, His power, that this man who stands before you whole was delivered. It is Jesus who is the stone, who has become the cornerstone. You talk about licensing people to do God's work but let me tell you, there is no other name under heaven given among men whereby you must be saved. He is the one who does the licensing, the ordaining, and the commissioning." When they saw the boldness of Peter and John, and as they looked at that man standing there, they could not say anything against it. I can imagine this healed man standing there would just shift from one foot to the other. About the time they got their minds off him, he would shift to another foot to remind them that he was the evidence. He was standing there saying, "That's right, that's right, I'm the one, I was healed, I'm a living miracle. Yes, they have been with Jesus, I'm testimony of it. I am the witness, I'm the evidence." You cannot have faith unless you have evidence for it. Here was sufficient evidence for them to throw up their hands and say, "Thank God the Messiah has come, let us receive these men, let us honor God for healing this lame man who has been sitting at the gate of our temple day after day for years asking us alms, let us praise God." But let us see what happened.

Acts 4:15-22

But when they had commanded them to go aside out of the council, they conferred among themselves, saying, What shall we do to these men? for that indeed a notable miracle hath been done by them is manifest to all them that dwell in Jerusalem; and we cannot deny it.
But that it spread no further among the people, let us straitly threaten them, that they speak henceforth to no man in this name. And they called them, and commanded them not to speak at all nor teach in the name of Jesus.
But Peter and John answered and said unto them, Whether it be right in the sight of God to hearken unto you more than unto God, judge ye. For we cannot but speak the things which we have seen and heard. So when they had further threatened them, they let them go, finding nothing how they might punish them, because of the people: for all men glorified God for that which was done. For the man was above forty years old, on whom this miracle of healing was shewed.

Christian Faith Spreads

When Peter and John took their stand and showed their evidence, which was this healed man standing in their presence, these people could not deny the miracle. They conferred among themselves and said, in effect, "The real thing has happened and everybody in Jerusalem knows it. If we go out and deny it we will get in trouble; so, let's just call these men back in and threaten them."

Something marvelous happened then in fulfillment of what Christ had promised through the Holy Spirit. When you are called before the heads of state and other leaders, do not worry in advance about what you are going to say. The Holy Spirit will give you what to say. Thus, Peter said, "Whether you think it is right or not to speak in Jesus' name is up to you to decide. But do not bring us into your decision. Here is what we know. We are not going to lie. We saw the man. We know Him. He is risen from the dead. We just spoke in His name and there is a miracle right in front of your eyes. Don't you men understand there is something bubbling up within us? We cannot help it. As long as we know what we know, we cannot help but speak."

Many people in the Church really do not believe that Jesus is risen from the dead. They do not believe He sends the Holy Spirit to fill His disciples today. They do not accept the fact that people are healed through the name of Jesus; they reject the power of attorney of His name. But I am here to tell you in the words of Peter that they can judge whether it is right or wrong. We have our appointment from God and it is our responsibility to obey God. After the answer Peter gave, these leaders could only threaten him because they could not withdraw a license, never having issued him one. What they really were frightened of was that Christianity had risen and taken a place of substance and caliber in the city. Many people were believing. If they kept on believing, these leaders who had been responsible for the death of Jesus would be left with nothing.

Acts 4:23-30

> And being let go, they went to their own company, and reported all that the chief priests and elders had said unto them. And when they heard that, they lifted up their voice to God with one accord, and said, Lord, thou art God, which hast made heaven, and earth, and the sea, and all that in them is: Who by the mouth of thy servant David hast said, Why did the heathen rage, and the people imagine vain things?
>
> The kings of the earth stood up, and the rulers were gathered

together against the Lord, and against his Christ. For of a truth against thy holy child Jesus, whom thou hast anointed, both Herod, and Pontius Pilate, with the Gentiles, and the people of Israel, were gathered together, For to do whatsoever thy hand and thy counsel determined before to be done.

And now Lord, behold their threatenings: and grant unto thy servants, that with all boldness they may speak thy word, by stretching forth thine hand to heal; and that signs and wonders may be done by the name of thy holy child Jesus.

The Secret of Boldness

What do you think you would have done had you been in Peter's place, or John's? When you have been threatened within an inch of your life? They were told not ever again to mention the name of Jesus or to pray in His name or to expect a miracle. What they did was go to their own company. They went to believing believers and told them all about it. When they heard, the entire company of believers lifted their voice as one voice and they began to extol God for His mighty creative acts. Then they said, in effect, "And now, sovereign Lord of heaven and earth, behold they are threatening us. They are threatening You, Lord. They are using us to get at You. Grant unto thy servants that with all boldness they may speak thy Word."

The very thing that the chief priests and the Sadducees had commanded them not to do, they asked God for boldness to do. They knew it would take the boldness of God, and to insure that boldness they said, "Lord, give us this boldness by stretching forth thine hand to heal. (Incidentally, "stretching forth thy hand" — when you see that phrase in the book of Acts or other books of the Bible, it refers to the power of God to perform miracles.) So they said, "Give us this boldness by stretching forth thine hand to heal so that signs and wonders may be done by the name of thy holy child Jesus."

We wonder today why people say, "Do not expect me to say anything about Jesus, I do not know what to say." Why do they not have boldness? Because they have not called upon the Lord to stretch forth His hand to heal and to do signs and wonders by the name of His Son Jesus of Nazareth who was born of the virgin Mary. They do not know that Jesus Christ is the Son of God. They believe that the Bible was written just like some other kind of book, that it was not written by inspiration. They are not going to have the boldness because the boldness comes through God's power being poured out through them.

31

I want to affirm something today here in Acts, Chapter 4, Verse 30: This is the prayer that I pray more often than any other. I pray, God, grant unto me that with all boldness I may preach Your Word, by anointing me to pray for the sick that You may heal them, and that miracles will be done by the name of Your holy child Jesus. I am not ashamed or embarrassed to tell you that, because I believe without the healing and miracle-working power of Christ in you and me today as Christians, there will be no boldness. The boldness originates in the Holy Spirit, but the Holy Spirit in us must be encouraged so that He can do His mighty works through us. I also want you to notice in Verse 24 that when John and Peter came back to their own company and reported the evil things done to them, the people, the Christians as a group, came together in one accord. They did not begin to say, "If you had not been out there you would not have gotten in this trouble." Peter and John had just been in jail overnight! So many so-called Christian people today say, "Well, if you had not done that you would not have had that bad article written about you, or people would not be opposing you." But just suppose we all came together in one accord and we were proud of the work of God, that we were honoring the Lord because of His healing power. Christian people today must get together in unity and pray for the leaders who are standing up for Jesus, who are bringing healing to the people as Jesus did.

Acts 4:31
> And when they had prayed, the place was shaken where they were assembled together; and they were all filled with the Holy Ghost, and they spake the word of God with boldness.

Prayer Initiates Action

Their prayer shook the place up. When real, genuine Christian people get together in one accord and pray, something happens. They received a new infilling of the Holy Spirit. The baptism of the Spirit was to bring the Holy Spirit, but the infilling of the Spirit was to be a continuous thing. These people were present on the day of Pentecost. They were leaders in it, Peter and John. They, along with all those who had met in one accord to pray with them, were filled with the Holy Spirit, given a new infilling, and through it the boldness of the Lord came upon them so that they spake the Word of God in Christ's name again with great boldness. I feel as if I have had hundreds of fresh infillings of the Holy Spirit. It seems to me I can never get enough. I want more and more.

32

Acts 4:32

> And the multitude of them that believed were of one heart and of one
> soul: . . .

Unity Example

There was a multitude of Christians present. Not only the 3,000
who had accepted Christ and were filled with the Spirit on the day
of Pentecost, or the 5,000 that were mentioned, but people were
continually, daily, being added to the Church. There were now
thousands upon thousands of these people in Jerusalem. Their
primary meeting place was Solomon's porch, which was about 800
feet long and could accommodate thousands of people. They were
with one accord. Do not tell me we cannot have unity. Do not tell
me that we Christians cannot lay aside whatever denominational or
other differences we have among us. Jesus Christ is the sovereign
Lord. He is the one who saved us. Our denominations did not save
us. Our leaders are not saving us. Jesus Christ is our Redeemer and
we can come together.

Acts 4:32,33

> . . . neither said any of them that ought of the things which he possessed
> was his own; but they had all things common. And with great power
> gave the apostles witness of the resurrection of the Lord Jesus: and
> great grace was upon them all.

Resurrection Belief Vital

These apostles gave a powerful witness of the resurrection of
Jesus Christ. That was the theme of their preaching. If He were not
risen from the dead they had nothing to preach about. Maybe that
is what is wrong today — nothing to preach about. People really do
not believe that Jesus Christ is risen from the dead. They are not
filled with the Holy Spirit. They are not bold.

I would like to include myself in this. I do not feel that I have
arrived in the ministry. Yes, I have seen multitudes saved and
multitudes healed, but my soul still hungers and thirsts for more of
God, for greater boldness, to give a more powerful witness that Jesus
Christ is alive today.

Acts 4:34,35

> Neither was there any among them that lacked: for as many as were

possessors of lands or houses sold them, and brought the prices of the things that were sold, and laid them down at the apostles' feet: and distribution was made unto every man according as he had need.

Christianity Not Communism

This was not a commune. These people were living in different places in Jerusalem. This was a special need because so many people, in accepting Christ, were thrust out of Judaism. They actually lost their place in the Jewish nation. Other Christians who had possessions often would sell them or would share what money they had so that these people could be tided over that particular circumstance. They did not just have one massive sale and pool everything together. When the communists take this scripture and say, "You see there, Christianity is like communism," they are lying because Christianity has a head, it has a sovereign Lord, and the power comes down from above. Even the power of the Holy Spirit is power from on high. This was not a common practice, except when special needs arose.

Acts 4:36-5:10

And Joses, who by the apostles was surnamed Barnabas, (which is, being interpreted, The son of consolation,) a Levite, and of the country of Cyprus, having land, sold it, and brought the money, and laid it at the apostles' feet.

But a certain man named Ananias, with Sapphira his wife, sold a possession, and kept back part of the price, his wife also being privy to it, and brought a certain part, and laid it at the apostles' feet. But Peter said, Ananias, why hath Satan filled thine heart to lie to the Holy Ghost, and to keep back part of the price of the land? Whiles it remained, was it not thine own? and after it was sold, was it not in thine own power? why hast thou conceived this thing in thine heart? thou hast not lied unto men, but unto God.

And Ananias hearing these words fell down, and gave up the ghost: and great fear came on all them that heard these things. And the young men arose, wound him up, and carried him out, and buried him. And it was about the space of three hours after, when his wife, not knowing what was done, came in. And Peter answered unto her, Tell me whether ye sold the land for so much? And she said, Yea, for so much. Then Peter said unto her, How is it that ye have agreed together to tempt the Spirit of the Lord? behold, the feet of them which have buried thy husband are at the door, and shall carry thee out. Then fell she down straightway at his feet, and yielded up the ghost: and the young men came in, and found her dead, and, carrying her forth, buried her by her husband.

Choice of Repentance

Barnabas, a very wealthy man who was devoted to God and a man of great compassion, sold some large possessions. He took the money and brought it to the apostles to use in the work. He was honored for it. Then there came a couple, Ananias and Sapphira, who wanted the same honor but did not want to do what Barnabas did. They sold what they had but withheld part of the price.

The Word says that the devil put it in their heart. These two people, husband and wife, were seeking an earthly honor and that is the spirit of the devil. They also were tempting the Holy Spirit and were lying. When Peter accosted them, he said, "Did someone command you to do this?" No. "Even after you sold it, did they command you to give the money to us?" No. "Well, why have you lied? Satan has filled your heart. You have tempted the Holy Spirit." And the shock of it was so great that both of them fell down dead.

Remember, each of them had his own chance. Ananias came in first and about three hours later his wife Sapphira, who had not known what happened, came in and went through the same thing. Both of them had their own chance. Both of them lied. Both of them let the devil have his way with them. Both of them tempted the Holy Spirit and the shock was too great.

A Holy Ghost-filled person like Peter, like any of us today, has the power of discerning of spirits. We have the ability to speak the word of knowledge as the need arises and the Holy Spirit chooses. When Peter discerned Ananias, Ananias could have repented. When he discerned Sapphira, she could have said, "I disagree with my husband, we should not have held back part of the price." Peter gave them both the opportunity and they suffered the consequences. Each of us who as a Christian commits anything to God, that is our choice, no one is dictating that to us. It was a voluntary thing.

This was not the tithes and the offerings. This was not seed-faith unto God. This was something these people were doing to receive self-honor or the praise of other people. They found out that when they dealt with a church that was filled with the Spirit and with leaders who were filled with the Spirit, they could not get by with it.

Acts 5:11

And great fear came upon all the church, and upon as many as heard these things.

35

The Church Forms

This is the first time that the word "church" has been mentioned in the book of Acts. The Greek for it is ecclesia, or "the called out ones." God has called them out to be a new people. The Church begins to take form here in the fifth chapter of Acts.

Acts 5:12-16
> And by the hands of the apostles were many signs and wonders wrought among the people; (and they were all with one accord in Solomon's porch. And of the rest durst no man join himself to them: but the people magnified them. And believers were the more added to the Lord, multitudes both of men and women.) Insomuch that they brought forth the sick into the streets, and laid them on beds and couches, that at the least the shadow of Peter passing by might overshadow some of them. There came also a multitude out of the cities round about unto Jerusalem, bringing sick folks, and them which were vexed with unclean spirits: and they were healed every one.

Wanted: Bible Believers

This was as common to the Christian Church as breathing. This was the norm, not the exception. Many times I am asked, "Will God heal all people? Is it God's will that everyone will be healed?" I usually say, "We have not had the opportunity to find out because there are so few of us praying for the healing of the sick."

If every one of us understood that we are to be approved by signs and wonders through our witness for Christ, if every one of us had compassion and released our faith in the name of the risen Lord, if every one of us — preachers, lay people — every one of us would come together in one accord, then we would know the extent of God's healing power. Too few are praying for the sick. One thing about medicine that is so powerful is that every doctor knows he is to try to cure the sick.

Every doctor works on sick folks. And every time they have any success, they keep records. They build a body of knowledge. Doctors do not have theological hang-ups — whether God wants sick people healed. Our seminaries today need a genuine Holy Spirit revival. In effect, we need to start over and go back to the Bible as the number-one book. How many have I talked to who have graduated from theological seminaries who told me that the Bible was not the number-one book in the seminary, that they studied books about the Bible far more than they did the Bible itself?

We are producing a type of so-called "Christian" today who, in too many instances, does not believe the Bible. He does not think it is a Bible for the now. He does not think God is speaking in the now. We have got to get back to the Bible, to the risen Christ.

People are hurting today. When people really get genuinely converted and filled with the Holy Spirit, under men and women who are anointed of God, and they begin to reproduce through the power of the Holy Spirit the greater things that Christ talked about, we are going to have an impact upon this human race unparalleled in history.

I tell you this, the Bible is the number-one book at Oral Roberts University and the Holy Spirit is the number-one teacher!

Time and time again I have heard the professors in the Oral Roberts University Graduate School of Theology say that while they are going to expose their students to all the theological knowledge that is available, in the final analysis they are going to build their lives around the Word of God, around the risen Christ and the power of the Holy Spirit operating in the now. They are turning out a new breed of preachers, evangelists, teachers, and other workers in the Church of our Lord Jesus Christ. But not only in the seminary but in the rest of Oral Roberts University — the School of Arts and Sciences, the other graduate schools — and we are not ashamed of that. We are proud that our Lord counts us worthy to have His call to build Him a university.

Acts 5:17-21

> Then the high priest rose up, and all they that were with him, (which is the sect of the Sadducees,) and were filled with indignation. And laid their hands on the apostles, and put them in the common prison.
>
> But the angel of the Lord by night opened the prison doors, and brought them forth, and said, Go, stand and speak in the temple to the people all the words of this life. And when they heard that, they entered into the temple early in the morning, and taught.
>
> But the high priest came, and they that were with him, and called the council together, and all the senate of the children of Israel, and sent to the prison to have them brought.

An Unscheduled Act

They thought they were still in jail. They did not know that there was an unscheduled act of the Holy Spirit in sending an angel to set them free.

37

Acts 5:22-33

But when the officers came, and found them not in the prison, they returned, and told, saying, The prison truly found we shut with all safety, and the keepers standing without before the doors: but when we had opened, we found no man within. Now when the high priest and the captain of the temple and the chief priests heard these things, they doubted of them whereunto this would grow.

Then came one and told them, saying, Behold, the men whom ye put in prison are standing in the temple, and teaching the people. Then went the captain with the officers, and brought them without violence: for they feared the people, lest they should have been stoned. And when they had brought them, they set them before the council: and the high priest asked them, saying, Did not we straitly command you that ye should not teach in this name? and, behold, ye have filled Jerusalem with your doctrine, and intend to bring this man's blood upon us.

Then Peter and the other apostles answered and said, We ought to obey God rather than men. The God of our fathers raised up Jesus, whom ye slew and hanged on a tree. Him hath God exalted with his right hand to be a Prince and a Saviour, for to give repentance to Israel, and forgiveness of sins. And we are his witnesses of these things; and so is also the Holy Ghost, whom God hath given to them that obey him. When they heard that, they were cut to the heart, and took counsel to slay them.

Acts of the Spirit

The statement that they were cut to the heart is not the same as being pricked in the heart as was true at the end of Peter's sermon on the day of Pentecost. Then the hearers were pricked in their hearts of their sins and wanted to be saved. These people were cut to the heart with jealousy and anger, and they wanted to murder them.

Religious people without Christ can be the meanest people in the world. It is a shame and a disgrace today that so much evil is done in the name of God.

Can't you just see these soldiers going out to the prison to get Peter and John and the others and to bring them out before the council? They go inside to find them and they are not there. The soldiers stand there with egg on their faces. At the same moment the apostles and the others are out preaching and teaching because the Holy Spirit had gone into prison through His angel and delivered them. Surely the book of Acts is the book of the acts of the Holy Spirit.

Acts 5:34-42

Then stood there up one in the council, a Pharisee, named Gamaliel, a doctor of the law, had in reputation among all the people, and commanded to put the apostles forth a little space; And said unto them, Ye men of Israel, take heed to yourselves what ye intend to do as touching these men. For before these days rose up Theudas, boasting himself to be somebody; to whom a number of men, about four hundred, joined themselves: who was slain; and all, as many as obeyed him, were scattered, and brought to nought. After this man rose up Judas of Galilee in the days of the taxing, and drew away much people after him: he also perished; and all, even as many as obeyed him, were dispersed. And now I say unto you, Refrain from these men, and let them alone: for if this counsel or this work be of men, it will come to nought: But if it be of God, ye cannot overthrow it; lest haply ye be found even to fight against God.

And to him they agreed: and when they had called the apostles, and beaten them, they commanded that they should not speak in the name of Jesus, and let them go. And they departed from the presence of the council, rejoicing that they were counted worthy to suffer shame for his name. And daily in the temple, and in every house, they ceased not to teach and preach Jesus Christ.

Worthy to Suffer

Gamaliel was probably the most respected doctor of the law of Moses of that time. Saul of Tarsus, who became Paul, the great apostle, studied under Gamaliel. As the Jewish Sanhedrin was judging these men, Gamaliel stood up and reminded them that they were overlooking other people who had risen up in the name of God and claimed to be such and such and perished. So, he said his counsel was to let these men alone. If their work was of men, it would come to nought. But if it were of God, then the Sanhedrin would be found even to fighting against God.

They agreed with him except in one thing. They agreed to let them go, but first they wanted to beat them. They just could not control their rage and jealousy. They took them, beat them, and when they got through they said, "Now you go on but do not speak again in the name of Jesus." We are told that they left. They were praising God, with bloody backs and with words that tried to cut them to the heart and with the command not ever to mention Jesus' name again. They were praising God, saying, "Lord, I just thank You that You count me worthy to suffer shame for the name of Jesus." We are told that every day they went to the temple and they went from house to house among themselves and taught Jesus Christ. They ceased not to preach and to teach in His name.

Acts 6:1

> And in those days, when the number of the disciples were multiplied, there arose a murmuring of the Grecians against the Hebrews, because their widows were neglected in the daily ministration.

Favoritism Charged

The term "Grecians" refers to the Jewish converts who had come from the Greek-speaking world. To those who had lost their jobs because of their conversion to Christ, it seemed that the Jews in Jerusalem who had accepted Christ were receiving larger and better portions of the food ration and so they felt neglected.

Acts 6:2-7

> Then the twelve called the multitude of the disciples unto them, and said, It is not reason that we should leave the word of God, and serve tables. Wherefore, brethren, look ye out among you seven men of honest report, full of the Holy Ghost and wisdom, whom we may appoint over this business. But we will give ourselves continually to prayer, and to the ministry of the word.
>
> And the saying pleased the whole multitude: and they chose Stephen, a man full of faith and of the Holy Ghost, and Philip, and Prochorus, and Nicanor, and Timon, and Parmenas, and Nicolas a proselyte of Antioch: Whom they set before the apostles: and when they had prayed, they laid their hands on them. And the word of God increased; and the number of the disciples multiplied in Jerusalem greatly; and a great company of the priests were obedient to the faith.

God's Multiplication Table

When this problem arose, it struck at the very heart of the preaching ministry of the 12 apostles. If they neglected the preaching of the Word of God to properly distribute the food, then the Word of God would not be preached. They were saying, when you enter the ministry of the gospel it is a full-time job. The ministry includes the time that you study the Word of God and preach it, the time you spend in meditation, prayer, and fasting, the time you devote your heart and mind to the needs of the people that will be met by the anointed preaching of the gospel. That took precedence over everything else then and it does today.

Without the lay people, the ministers would be so enmeshed in the practical affairs of the work of God that the preaching and the praying for the people would never get done. I praise God for obedient laymen and lay women who are willing and ready under the anointing of God, full of the same Holy Ghost and faith, to attend to the chores that are attendant upon the work of the Church any and everywhere. God bless you lay people. Notice that the apostles laid hands upon these lay people. This act shows that authority of God was being transmitted to these lay people to do a very special work. It was not the laying on of hands of ordination. It was not the laying on of hands for the healing of the sick. It was the setting aside of these people for a very special work. With this combination of the ministry, full-time, and God-anointed laity doing the practical matters of the work of the Church, God's Word increased and the number of converts multiplied in Jerusalem. God is a God of multiplication. He does not subtract. Good seed was being sown here and God was multiplying it.

Acts 6:8

> And Stephen, full of faith and power, did great wonders and miracles among the people.

God Anoints Laity

Two of these seven people, Stephen and Philip, made a mark upon the work of God. Stephen was a powerful preacher and became the first Christian martyr. Philip was an evangelist who opened up the Samaritans to the gospel. The miracle-working anointing of God is not limited to preachers. It is upon the laity, too, because every one of us is born again with the Spirit of God, we are filled with the Holy Spirit, and we have faith. When the faith of Stephen was released, the power of God was equally released in the form of great wonders and miracles among the people.

I know many lay people today whom God is using in prophecies, in dreams, in visions, in praying with tongues, and in interpretation. In fact, these lay people are ministering, not in the same sense that a minister of the gospel can — that is not possible — but they are ministering just the same. A minister's calling is the highest of all. He has equipment that no one else in the world has. But God uses lay people and I encourage every one of them to give God their best so God will give them His best.

41

Acts 6:9

> Then there arose certain of the synagogue, which is called the synagogue of the Libertines, and Cyrenians, and Alexandrians, and of them of Cilicia and of Asia, disputing with Stephen.

Saul's Region Represented

One of the regions represented by these disputers is Cilicia of which Tarsus, the hometown of Saul of Tarsus, was the capital. Evidently Saul of Tarsus was among this group that was disputing with Stephen. He may even have heard him preach and seen the wonders and miracles God did through him.

Acts 6:10

> And they were not able to resist the wisdom and the spirit by which he spake.

Allow Spirit to Emerge

These people with all their training and numbers could not handle one individual Christian. Not that Stephen was as well trained as some of them were in the wisdom of this world and theology, but he had the infilling of the Holy Spirit which gave him the word of wisdom and opened him to the nine gifts of the Spirit. They could not resist the Spirit by which he spake. People who argue mentally or intellectually are no match for the Spirit of God in the humblest of Christians, if that Christian will not argue back but just depend upon the Holy Spirit working through him or her.

Acts 6:11-14

> Then they suborned men, which said, We have heard him speak blasphemous words against Moses, and against God. And they stirred up the people, and the elders, and the scribes, and came upon him, and caught him, and brought him to the council. And set up false witnesses, which said, This man ceaseth not to speak blasphemous words against this holy place, and the law: For we have heard him say, that this Jesus of Nazareth shall destroy this place, and shall change the customs which Moses delivered us.

Some Hate Healing

The very same thing that they said and did to Jesus, they were now doing and saying to a Jesus-centered person. That Stephen was spoken against in the same way that our Master was should be very touching to you and me. In the beginning of my ministry the Lord told me to be like Jesus and heal the people as He did. Through all these years the healing ministry has been the one thing the opposers have come against. They have not come against my integrity or my honesty; it is the healing ministry that they hate. They despise the name of Jesus through which we pray for the healing of suffering humanity. Many times this is painful to me as it was to Stephen, but the glorious part of it is that it reveals we are trying to be like our Master and to heal the people as He did.

Acts 6:15

> And all that sat in the council, looking stedfastly on him, saw his face
> · as it had been the face of an angel.

Shining Faces

Remember that our Lord was transfigured in the mountain and His face shown. Again, Stephen was like his Master — his face shone.

Acts 7:1

> Then said the high priest, Are these things so?

A Reminder

Does that remind you of what they said to Jesus? Does that remind you of what they said to Peter and John and the apostles? Does that remind you of what people say to us today?

Acts 7:2

> And he said, Men, brethren, and fathers, hearken; The God of glory
> appeared unto our Father Abraham, when he was in Mesopotamia,
> before he dwelt in Charran . . .

A Powerful Sermon

Stephen begins his sermon by reviewing the history of the Jewish nation. The court of the Sanhedrin knew all the facts but they were shocked by the interpretation this young man Stephen was to give because it turned out to be revolutionary. It probably ranks as one of the most powerful sermons of all time. This is not a preacher, this is a lay person who is giving a review of the history of God's people and then bringing it to a climax, for the final sting is when he comes down to the end of it and lays the charge at their feet. It's a remarkable, remarkable message.

Acts 7:2-60

And he said, Men, brethren, and fathers, hearken; The God of glory appeared unto our father Abraham, when he was in Mesopotamia, before he dwelt in Charran, and said unto him, Get thee out of thy country, and from thy kindred, and come into the land which I shall shew thee. Then came he out of the land of the Chaldaeans, and dwelt in Charran: and from thence, when his father was dead, he removed him into this land, wherein ye now dwell. And he gave him none inheritance in it, no, not so much as to set his foot on: yet he promised that he would give it to him for a possession, and to his seed after him, when as yet he had no child.

And God spake on this wise, That his seed should sojourn in a strange land; and that they should bring them into bondage, and entreat them evil four hundred years. And the nation to whom they shall be in bondage will I judge, said God; and after that shall they come forth, and serve me in this place.

And he gave him the covenant of circumcision: and so Abraham begat Isaac, and circumcised him the eighth day; and Isaac begat Jacob; and Jacob begat the twelve patriarchs. And the patriarchs, moved with envy, sold Joseph into Egypt: but God was with him, and delivered him out of all his afflictions, and gave him favour and wisdom in the sight of Pharaoh king of Egypt; and he made him governor over Egypt and all his house.

Now there came a dearth over all the land of Egypt and Chanaan, and great affliction: and our fathers found no sustenance. But when Jacob heard that there was corn in Egypt, he sent out our fathers first. And at the second time Joseph was made known to his brethren; and Joseph's kindred was made known unto Pharaoh. Then sent Joseph, and called his father Jacob to him, and all his kindred, threescore and fifteen souls. So Jacob went down into Egypt, and died, he, and our fathers, and were carried over into Sychem, and laid in the sepulchre that Abraham bought for a sum of money of the sons of Emmor the father of Sychem.

But when the time of the promise drew nigh, which God had sworn to Abraham, the people grew and multiplied in Egypt. Till another king arose, who knew not Joseph. The same dealt subtilly with our kindred, and evil entreated our fathers, so that they cast out their young children, to the end they might not live. In which time Moses was born, and was exceeding fair, and nourished up in his father's house three months: And when he was cast out, Pharaoh's daughter took him up, and nourished him for her own son. And Moses was learned in all the wisdom of the Egyptians, and was mighty in words and in deeds.

And when he was full forty years old, it came into his heart to visit his brethren the children of Israel. And seeing one of them suffer wrong, he defended him, and avenged him that was oppressed, and smote the Egyptian: for he supposed his brethren would have understood how that God by his hand would deliver them: but they understood not.

And the next day he shewed himself unto them as they strove, and would have set them at one again, saying, Sirs, ye are brethren; why do ye wrong one to another? But he that did his neighbour wrong thrust him away, saying, Who made thee a ruler and a judge over us? Wilt thou kill me as thou diddest the Egyptian yesterday? Then fled Moses at this saying, and was a stranger in the land of Madian, where he begat two sons.

And when forty years were expired, there appeared to him in the wilderness of Mount Sina an angel of the Lord in a flame of fire in a bush. When Moses saw it, he wondered at the sight: and as he drew near to behold it, the voice of the Lord came unto him, saying, I am the God of thy fathers, the God of Abraham, and the God of Isaac, and the God of Jacob. Then Moses trembled, and durst not behold.

Then said the Lord to him, Put off thy shoes from thy feet: for the place where thou standest is holy ground. I have seen, I have seen the affliction of my people which is in Egypt, and I have heard their groaning, and am come down to deliver them. And now come, I will send thee into Egypt. This Moses whom they refused, saying, Who made thee a ruler and a judge? the same did God send to be a ruler and a deliverer by the hand of the angel which appeared to him in the bush. He brought them out, after that he had shewed wonders and signs in the land of Egypt, and in the Red Sea, and in the wilderness forty years.

This is that Moses, which said unto the children of Israel, A prophet shall the Lord your God raise up unto you of your brethren, like unto me; him shall ye hear. This is he, that was in the church in the wilderness with the angel which spake to him in the Mount Sina, and with our fathers: who received the lively oracles to give unto us: to whom our fathers would not obey, but thrust him from them, and in their hearts turned back again into Egypt, saying unto Aaron, Make us Gods to go before us: for as for this Moses, which brought us out of the land of Egypt, we wot not what is become of him.

And they made a calf in those days, and offered sacrifice unto the idol, and rejoiced in the works of their own hands. Then God turned, and gave them up to worship the hosts of heaven; as it is written in the book of the prophets, O ye house of Israel, have ye offered to me slain beasts and sacrifices by the space of forty years in the wilderness? Yea, ye took up the tabernacle of Moloch, and the star of your god Remphan, figures which ye made to worship them: and I will carry you away beyond Babylon. Our fathers had the tabernacle of witness in the wilderness, as he had appointed, speaking unto Moses, that he should make it according to the fashion that he had seen. Which also our fathers that came after brought in with Jesus into the possession of the Gentiles, whom God drave out before the face of our fathers, unto the days of David; who found favor before God, and desired to find a tabernacle for the God of Jacob.

But Solomon built him an house. Howbeit the most High dwelleth not in temples made with hands; as saith the prophet, Heaven is my throne, and earth is my footstool: what house will ye build me? saith the Lord: or what is the place of my rest? Hath not my hand made all these things? Ye stiffnecked and uncircumcised in heart and ears, ye do always resist the Holy Ghost: as your fathers did, so do ye. Which of the prophets have not your fathers persecuted? and they have slain them which shewed before of the coming of the Just One; of whom ye have been now the betrayers and murderers: who have received the law by the disposition of angels, and have not kept it. When they heard these things, they were cut to the heart, and they gnashed on him with their teeth. But he, being full of the Holy Ghost, looked up stedfastly into heaven, and saw the glory of God, and Jesus standing on the right hand of God. And said, Behold, I see the heavens opened, and the Son of man standing on the right hand of God. Then they cried out with a loud voice, and stopped their ears, and ran upon him with one accord, And cast him out of the city, and stoned him: and the witnesses laid down their clothes at a young man's feet, whose name was Saul. And they stoned Stephen, calling upon God, and saying, Lord Jesus, receive my spirit. And he kneeled down, and cried with a loud voice, Lord, lay not this sin to their charge. And when he had said this, he fell asleep.

Stephen's Death Christlike

Stephen traced the work of God from Abraham all the way to that present moment. He revealed how God came to Moses while he was in the wilderness and desert, in the burning bush, and told him how He had seen the afflictions of the descendants of Abraham in Egypt, how He had heard their cries and now He was sending Moses down to deliver them. Then Stephen showed how Moses had led them across the wilderness for 40 years. Moses transferred the mantle of leadership to Joshua. Then Stephen told how the descendants of Abraham had driven out the enemies until under David, the land was completely cleared of enemies and there was peace.

David had desired to build God a house but he let Solomon, his son, do this. But he was not completely pleased for it was only a half measure. God was saying, "Heaven is my throne and earth is my footstool, what house will ye build me?" Stephen was referring to their charge of blasphemy. When he referred to the temple, comparing it with the death and the burial and the resurrection of Jesus, he was saying, "You put so much store upon this temple. I remind you that God let you build it knowing that it could not contain Him." At that point it seemed that everything Stephen had related about the history of the Jewish nation came to a climax and he cried, "Which of the prophets have your fathers not killed? Do you know what you have done? You have killed the Messiah, the Holy One, yourself." Then his soul seemed to burst within him. He said, "Oh, you claim to be circumcised but you have no circumcision of your hearts and your ears. You are resisters of the Holy Spirit just as your fathers have been all through the ages. You received all this through the instrumentality of angels but you have not kept the law of God."

Stephen had delivered his soul but something catastrophic was going on in the hearts of those Jewish leaders. Their hearts were cut in two. They were so furious they gnashed on him with their teeth — gritting their teeth. As they yelled at him, he looked up and he saw the glory of God. Jesus, who had been sitting at the Father's right hand, stood up. Stephen said, "I see Him, I see Him, He is standing at the Father's right hand, and I see Him."

They could not stand it. They yelled at the top of their voices, put their hands on their ears, and picked him up, carried him outside the city, grabbed stones that were near, and began to stone him to death. Meanwhile, they took his clothes off his body and walked over to Saul of Tarsus, who was in charge of the whole sordid affair, and laid them at his feet. While they were stoning Stephen and the life was leaving his body, he was talking to the Lord. Just as his Savior had done on the cross, he said, "Father, here is my spirit," and kneeling down his last words were, "Lord, do not lay this sin to their charge," and he fell over and his soul went to God, the first Christian martyr.

Acts 8:1

And Saul was consenting unto his death.

This burned a hole in Saul's soul. He never got away from it. Saul kept on seeing the light on Stephen's face. He realized that death is the moment of truth. While Stephen was dying, he was able to look clear into heaven and see Jesus stand up and look down at him and nod His head as if to say, "Come on home, Son, welcome home, you have done a good job." It got hold of Saul. Ever afterward he told how he persecuted the Church. It was a burden to him; he never seemed to get over it. In fact, he always felt he could not do enough for the Lord to atone for his past.

Acts 8:1

> And Saul was consenting unto his death. And at that time there was a great persecution against the church which was at Jerusalem; and they were all scattered abroad throughout the regions of Judaea and Samaria, except the apostles.

Result of Persecution

The death of Stephen signaled the beginning of the first great persecution against the new Church. What followed was the first broadening of the Church's outreach. Except for the apostles, many of the others were driven out of Jerusalem. They began to go to the towns and cities round about Jerusalem. That is what persecution does. It does not put the light out, it just causes the inner light to shine that much more.

Acts 8:2-4

> And devout men carried Stephen to his burial, and made great lamentation over him. As for Saul, he made havock of the church, entering into every house, and haling men and women committed them to prison. Therefore they that were scattered abroad went every where preaching the word.

Saul's Futility

What a contrast. A bloodthirsty young man who presided over the martyrdom of Stephen was now trying to destroy the Church, and the only thing he accomplished was, first of all, to burn a hole in his own soul, and second, to cause the scattering of the Christians. They wound up preaching the Word of God wherever they went. He meant it for harm, but God meant it for good.

Acts 8:5

> Then Philip went down to the city of Samaria, and preached Christ unto them.

Because of the persecution, Philip went to the most despised area, the city of Samaria. They were sort of half cousins to the Jews. They also kept the law of Moses. However, there was a vast gulf between them and the Jews. The Jews looked down upon them but Philip, full of the Holy Ghost and faith, just did not have any prejudice. He went down to Samaria to preach Christ unto them. Jesus had done this in Samaria, and Philip was following in the steps of Jesus. You can see as you read the four gospels and the book of Acts that Jesus, the person, is the central figure. The Holy Spirit is causing the disciples to witness unto Him, to testify of Him, to speak His name, to preach His Word, but Jesus was first and foremost.

Can we say that is true of us today? Is it Jesus who is being preached? Is it Jesus who is being sung about? Is it Jesus whose name is being lifted up? In the youth services of the Church is it Jesus being lifted up? In evangelism is it Jesus being lifted up? In missions is it Jesus being lifted up? The question is, in the gospel is there any other name to be preached?

Acts 8:6-8

> And the people with one accord gave heed unto those things which Philip spake, hearing and seeing the miracles which he did. For unclean spirits, crying with loud voice, came out of many that were possessed with them: and many taken with palsies, and that were lame, were healed. And there was great joy in that city.

Importance of Leadership

It never changes wherever Christ is preached and people give heed to the miracles of our Lord — many people who were filled with unclean spirits are delivered. Sicknesses and diseases are often healed and always there is great joy among the people. Several times I have noted that the surest sign of Jesus' presence is joy. I have written that the joy of the Lord is your strength. There was great joy in that city, which means great strength, great power came among the people.

In Peter's Pentecost sermon, he said that God approved of Jesus with miracles, wonders, and signs. What was the approval that God gave Philip? It was the miracles that followed the preaching of the gospel which they heard and which they saw. As Philip preached

Christ — the unadulterated Christ who is the same yesterday, today, and forever — he had the same results that Jesus had. He also had the same divine approval upon his ministry and life that Jesus did. Isn't it time that you and I as individuals did what we can about this? We cannot make anybody else do anything but we can start with ourselves by saying Christ is going to be real in my life. I am going to release my faith that God will work, through me, His wonders. And then I will know that I have done what God called me to do.

One thing that we have to demand is that there is leadership — leadership of the ministers and leadership of lay leaders who are responsible for what goes on. That can be done; God expects it. No minister who is Spirit-filled and believes in the whole council of God need fear manifestations of the Spirit of God in his church service or her church service, providing he or she is a leader — where they know they have been placed there as overseers by the Holy Spirit and they are in charge of the service so that they can direct it if something gets out of hand. They can stand up and with loving authority correct it. There should be strong lay leaders to see to it that Satan does not cause a lot of wildfire to be created, a bad spirit to be developed, and a bad influence to take place. God has a way to work this out, if we follow Him — standing up for His Word and above all manifesting the love of Jesus so that the mighty miracle working of God would continue but not be distorted by those who wanted influence for personal reasons.

Acts 8:9,10

> But there was a certain man, called Simon, which beforetime in the same city used sorcery, and bewitched the people of Samaria, giving out that himself was some great one: to whom they all gave heed, from the least to the greatest, saying, This man is the great power of God.

Deceit a Snare

While the Samaritans observed the law of Moses and declared themselves equal or superior to the Jewish people who worshiped in the temple in Jerusalem, they allowed a man, who declared himself to be the sole agent of God, to deceive them. One of the most serious things we face is making decisions about WHAT we believe rather than in WHOM we believe. I have noticed throughout all the years of my ministry that people who really and truly believe in Jesus and put Jesus first are the hardest to deceive. They are the most apt to be balanced. When people do not believe Jesus strongly enough, but develop a doctrine they believe is above the Lord, they are more easily deceived.

Acts 8:11
> And to him they had regard, because that of long time he had bewitched them with sorceries.

Beware Deceivers

In the absence of the miracle-working power of God, the devil enters the vacuum with sorceries or with his idea of what miracles are. He appeals to the spiritual instincts in all of us. Right now, the same things are happening throughout the United States and the world. People who have rejected Jesus Christ as their personal Savior, as the Son of God, have turned to "things." Therefore they are open prey to the devil's agents, who come with witchcraft and the occult, and they open themselves up by believing that it is something miraculous. These things look miraculous and some people think they are, but they have no redeeming power. The devil's work does not change lives to the glory of God. It does not produce a personal relationship with the Lord. It does not uplift Jesus. It causes people to go off into a fantasy world which becomes too often a drug-related world, ultimately bringing about their destruction.

You and I are not to be carried away with the occult, witchcraft, and these people claiming to be something great, but denying Jesus Christ is the Son of God, denying His sacrificial death on the cross, rejecting His bodily resurrection from the dead, and rejecting the written Word of God as God's eternal plan for us. These people are not the people of God. They are not leaders of the Lord. They are deceivers. Just as the American dollar is counterfeited, so is the genuine work of God counterfeited. The one able to counterfeit the American dollar the closest is the most effective, and those things outside Christ most closely resembling genuine born-again Christianity are the most effective in being accepted as genuine by people today. Just as the counterfeit dollar is not really worth anything but will eventually cause the counterfeiter to be caught, prosecuted, and put away, so is this counterfeit of our Lord Jesus Christ's work worthless and will eventually bring about the deceiver's destruction.

At the same time, we must not shy away from the gifts of the Spirit, of following Christ and His miracles, wonders, and signs just

51

because we are concerned about that fringe element out there trying to duplicate or counterfeit the real thing.

Acts 8:12,13

> But when they believed Philip preaching the things concerning the kingdom of God, and the name of Jesus Christ, they were baptized, both men and women. Then Simon himself believed also; and when he was baptized, he continued with Philip, and wondered, beholding the miracles and signs which were done.

The Sorcerer Amazed

When Simon the sorcerer saw that his former followers had genuinely received Christ, then he said he believed in Jesus Christ and was even baptized, and he continued along with Philip, wondering about the miracles which he saw with his own eyes.

Acts 8:14-17

> Now when the apostles which were at Jerusalem heard that Samaria had received the word of God, they sent unto them Peter and John: who, when they were come down, prayed for them, that they might receive the Holy Ghost:(For as yet he was fallen upon none of them: only they were baptized in the name of the Lord Jesus.) Then laid they their hands on them, and they received the Holy Ghost.

This is the first correction from the ministers of the gospel to help the laymen keep everything in balance with the Lord. On the day of Pentecost, when Peter was preaching and the people heard him and were convicted and wanted to know what they must do, he said, in Acts 2:38, "Repent, and be baptized every one of you in the name of Jesus Christ for the remission of your sins, and ye shall receive the gift of the Holy Ghost." That was the pattern and there were 3,000 people who responded, repented, and were baptized in His name, receiving the Father, Son, and Holy Spirit. That was the pattern. But this lay person, apparently, was not quite prepared to take them all the way. Peter and John soon remedied that because it was part and parcel of the same thing, and immediately the Holy Spirit came upon these people and they received the gift of the Holy Spirit.

Acts 8:18-25

> And when Simon saw that through laying on of the apostles' hands

the Holy Ghost was given, he offered them money, saying, Give me also this power, that on whomsoever I lay hands, he may receive the Holy Ghost. But Peter said unto him, Thy money perish with thee, because thou hast thought that the gift of God may be purchased with money. Thou hast neither part nor lot in this matter: for thy heart is not right in the sight of God. Repent therefore of this thy wickedness, and pray God, if perhaps the thought of thine heart may be forgiven thee. For I perceive that thou art in the gall of bitterness, and in the bond of iniquity.

Then answered Simon, and said, Pray ye to the Lord for me, that none of these things which ye have spoken come upon me. And they, when they had testified and preached the word of the Lord, returned to Jerusalem, and preached the gospel in many villages of the Samaritans.

Laity Shortcomings, Potential

The discernment that Peter and John had through the Holy Spirit enabled them to see right through this charlatan, this sorcerer, Simon. Peter read Simon's pedigree and told Simon where he came from. Peter told Simon he was of the devil, that he did not know God, and that he was in the bond of iniquity. When Simon heard the results of this discerning of spirits, he said, "Pray to God for me that none of these things you have spoken of will come upon me." Notice, he did not repent. He did not pray and ask God to help him. Simon said, "You pray for me." He was not entering into the heart of the gospel. Jesus Christ was not being made number one in his life and we are not told what happened after that. It is very evident, however, that he did not go any further with the Lord.

But John and Peter had the authority of true leaders. On one hand, they did not quiet down the revival of miracles, signs, and wonders; on the other, they did not allow, first, the people not to know the Holy Spirit and to receive Him and, second, a counterfeiter to come in and take over the work of Philip.

Now I thank God for laity but in no way can they take the place of the ministers of the gospel. The ministers of the gospel are the ones to lead the way. The only exception I know of is when preachers do not preach, when they do not lift up Jesus, and when they do not believe He is the Son of God. When they reject Christ's bodily resurrection and deny the shed blood, then to me they are not preachers, they are just counterfeiters. Sometimes the laity are more spiritual than some pastors. It would be something if the laity would rise up and say, "You preachers are not standing upon the Word of

God, are not uplifting the name of Jesus. You are starving us to death spiritually and we are not going to put up with you." The Church would right itself again and be the force in our world that the early Church was in its world in the first century — God speed the day.

Acts 8:26-28

> And the angel of the Lord spake unto Philip, saying, Arise, and go toward the south unto the way that goeth down from Jerusalem unto Gaza, which is desert. And he arose and went: and, behold, a man of Ethiopia, an eunuch of great authority under Candace queen of the Ethiopians, who had the charge of all her treasure, and had come to Jerusalem for a worship, was returning, and sitting in his chariot read Esaias the prophet.

Right at the height of the great revival that Philip the evangelist was conducting in Samaria, the Lord came to him and told him to leave that flourishing spiritual crusade and go down to Gaza. Immediately, when the Lord told Philip to go, he went. This is what obedience to God is all about.

There was a man from Ethiopia, a Jewish convert, a high official who had been to Jerusalem to worship, returning to his own country, and he was reading from the prophecy of Isaiah, Chapter 53, Verses 7 and 8.

Acts 8:29-31

> Then the Spirit said unto Philip, Go near, and join thyself to this chariot. And Philip ran thither to him, and heard him read the prophet Esaias, and said, Understandest thou what thou readest? And he said, How can I, except some man should guide me? And he desired Philip that he would come up and sit with him.

Paul is to say in Romans 10:13,14, "For whosoever shall call upon the name of the Lord shall be saved. How then shall they call on him in whom they have not believed? and how shall they believe in him of whom they have not heard? and how shall they hear without a preacher?"

Word Produces Faith

Here we see in action what Paul was to tell us about the value of someone hearing the Word of God, which would produce faith in him to call the Lord to be saved.

Acts 8:31-35

And he said, How can I, except some man should guide me? And he desired Philip that he would come up and sit with him. The place of the scripture which he read was this, He was led as a sheep to the slaughter; and like a lamb dumb before his shearer, so opened he not his mouth: In his humiliation his judgment was taken away: and who shall declare his generation? for his life is taken from the earth.

And the eunuch answered Philip, and said, I pray thee, of whom speaketh the prophet this? of himself, or of some other man?

The Philip opened his mouth, and began at the same scripture, and preached unto him Jesus.

Preach Jesus

There is a world of difference between preaching Jesus and preaching some doctrine about Jesus. Christianity is not a doctrine about Jesus, Christianity is Jesus producing His way of life and His life itself, in us. When you preach Christ to people and they receive Christ, they have the Spirit of Christ — His love, His compassion, His faith, His truth. But when you try to preach only a doctrine about Jesus, you can get mad about it and never get into the love of Jesus or experience His compassion for lost and suffering humanity.

Acts 8:36,37

And as they went on their way, they came unto a certain water: and the eunuch said, See, here is water; what doth hinder me to be baptized? And Philip said, If thou believest with all thine heart, thou mayest. And he answered and said, I believe that Jesus Christ is the Son of God.

The Eunuch Believed

Philip was saying, "You want to be baptized in water? You can if you believe with your whole heart that Jesus Christ is the Son of God." The Ethiopian wanted to go down in that water which represented the death, the burial, and the resurrection of our Lord Jesus Christ, and he was saying, "I believe that Jesus Christ is the Son of God and He rose for me; He is my Christ, my Messiah."

Acts 8:38,39

And he commanded the chariot to stand still: and they went down both into the water, both Philip and the eunuch; and he baptized him.

And when they were come up out of the water, the Spirit of the Lord caught away Philip, that the eunuch saw him no more: and he went on his way rejoicing.

Joy in Jesus

The word "rejoicing" here is joy ... "and he went on his way with joy." How often we encounter the word "joy" when we are dealing with our Lord Jesus Christ. How often I have said the surest sign of God's presence in us is His joy.

It is about time that people realize that in coming to Christ they have a change of their inner nature. The outward nature that observes this wicked, lost, hell-bent world, is often so confused and filled with desolation, depression, and frustration, that when it turns around and receives Christ and lives in Christ, it comes to know true joy. People live the joy of the Lord. That does not mean they do not have burdens to carry, assignments to carry out, sufferings to endure, work to be done, but the layer underneath it all is the layer of joy, the joy of the Lord. Jesus said, "My joy will be full in you."

Acts 8:40

But Philip was found at Azotus: and passing through he preached in all the cities, till he came to Caesarea.

An Unexplained Miracle

How in the world did the Lord catch Philip away? How did He just reach down and bodily take him through space? We are told that it was the Spirit of the Lord. There are some mighty things in the gospel that many of us have not yet experienced. I am certain, however, just as this tremendous thing happened right after our Lord sent the Holy Spirit, so will many of them happen to us just before the Lord comes the second time. In Chapter 9, we will see a turning point for the early Church. It is one of the most important chapters in the Bible.

Acts 9:1,2

And Saul, yet breathing out threatenings and slaughter against the disciples of the Lord, went unto the high priest, and desired of him letters to Damascus to the synagogues, that if he found any of this way, whether they were men or women, he might bring them bound unto Jerusalem.

56

Frenzy Can Blind

The question arises, "How can a religious person want to kill other people? How can he just breathe out murder and death?" It is because he does not have God. God is love. Such a person does not have Jesus. He can work himself up into a frenzied belief that what he is doing is actually pleasing to God, but you can be sure, if there is a murderous intent in his heart, it is not of God.

Acts 9:3,4

> And as he journeyed, he came near Damascus: and suddenly there shined round about him a light from heaven: and he fell to the earth, and heard a voice saying unto him, Saul, Saul, why persecutest thou me?

When anyone persecutes a Christian, he is persecuting Jesus.

Acts 9:5

> And he said, Who art thou, Lord? And the Lord said, I am Jesus whom thou persecutest: it is hard for thee to kick against the pricks.

Self-Destructive Behavior

The Lord is referring to oxen, which, when hooked up to a carriage or a wagon, would kick, and the driver had a long goad with a sharp end and he would jab them. The more the oxen kicked, the more they wounded and bloodied themselves. Thus, Jesus is saying when we persecute Him and His work, we are kicking at God and in return we are wounding and bloodying and destroying ourselves.

Acts 9:6

> And he trembling and astonished said, Lord, what wilt thou have me to do? And the Lord said unto him, Arise, and go into the city, and it shall be told thee what thou must do.

When we come to Christ, it is always with the attitude, "Lord, what do You want me to do?" The Lord told Saul what he must do.

Acts 9:7-9

> And the men which journeyed with him stood speechless, hearing a voice, but seeing no man. And Saul arose from the earth; and when his eyes were opened, he saw no man: but they led him by the hand, and brought him into Damascus. And he was three days without sight,

and neither did eat nor drink.

The Hidden Meaning

The meaning hidden here is that Saul was identifying with Jesus Christ. The experience was so unsettling that he did not eat nor drink for three days.

Acts 9:10-12

And there was a certain disciple at Damascus, named Ananias; and to him said the Lord in a vision, Ananias. And he said, Behold, I am here, Lord. And the Lord said unto him, Arise, and go into the street which is called Straight, and enquire in the house of Judas for one called Saul of Tarsus: for, behold, he prayeth, and hath seen in a vision a man named Ananias coming in, and putting his hand on him, that he might receive his sight.

God in Visions

This is a clear explanation of how God works through visions. In an explicit way, God sometimes speaks to people and tells them precisely what to do. Now, the way we know this is of God is that it happens exactly as God says.

Acts 9:13-16

Then Ananias answered, Lord, I have heard by many of this man, how much evil he hath done to thy saints at Jerusalem: and here he hath authority from the chief priests to bind all that call on thy name.

But the Lord said unto him, Go thy way: for he is a chosen vessel unto me, to bear my name before the Gentiles, and kings, and the children of Israel: for I will shew him how great things he must suffer for my name's sake.

Selection Meant Suffering

This is a very special moment — a moment when a layman, Ananias, was spoken to by the Lord and obeyed Him in one of the most traumatic experiences of a Christian's life on this earth. Ananias would carry to a murderer a message from Jesus that this man was chosen of the Lord, even when he was not aware of it.

This Saul of Tarsus was the one who had consented to Stephen's death. No doubt when Stephen saw the light from heaven, Saul saw a little of it too. God had been dealing with Saul of Tarsus because he had never forgotten the experience of Stephen who, in his witness, cried unto the Lord, "Do not hold this sin to your charge." You never know when your Christian witness is going to touch people. It is very important to understand that Paul is going to have his ministry primarily with the Gentiles. The first Christians were Jews, and in their minds, Christianity was founded by Jews for Jews. Now the Lord is getting ready to enlarge their vision and let them see all of us in that vast Gentile world. Paul is going to get the gospel into the kings of the earth, and into the children of Israel. But in doing so, he is going to suffer many things for the name of Jesus. Had you lived when Christianity first began, you would have understood that standing up for Jesus was standing against the power of the devil, that the devil would come against you with his darkness because he does not love light. You and I are chosen of God to suffer for Jesus' name. We are not talking about sickness, we are talking about opposition, misunderstanding, persecution, people at times trying to put us to death. This is part and parcel of our witness for Christ. This was something Ananias was to tell Saul of Tarsus in his conversion experience.

Acts 9:17-22

And Ananias went his way, and entered into the house; and putting his hands on him said, Brother Saul, the Lord, even Jesus, that appeared unto thee in the way as thou camest, hath sent me, that thou mightest receive thy sight, and be filled with the Holy Ghost. And immediately there fell from his eyes as it had been scales: and he received sight forthwith, and arose, and was baptized. And when he had received meat, he was strengthened. Then was Saul certain days with the disciples which were at Damascus.

And straightway he preached Christ in the synagogues, that he is the Son of God. But all that heard him were amazed, and said; Is not this he that destroyed them which called on this name in Jerusalem, and came hither for that intent, that he might bring them bound unto the chief priest? But Saul increased the more in strength, and confounded the Jews which dwelt at Damascus, proving that this is very Christ.

A Great Combination

Ananias was so obedient to the Lord and able to discern what Christ was doing to such a great extent that when he reached Saul, his love was overflowing his heart and he said, "Brother Saul." That takes a lot of Jesus to go to your enemy and say, "Brother." "Brother Saul, the Lord, even Jesus, that you met in the way has sent me. He sent me that you might get your sight back and be filled with the Holy Spirit."

Oh, the preciousness of knowing that God sends you and that you are a witness! Saul got it all and was baptized. In a matter of days, he was able to find the Scriptures come rising up into his understanding so that he began to preach Christ — that He is the Son of God. A great combination is to know the Scriptures and then to know Jesus. But to know either one without the other makes you incomplete. Notice also that Saul lost his sight because of the blinding light of God from heaven during his conversion experience, and that he received his sight through the laying on of the hands and the faith of the layman Ananias in Damascus.

Acts 9:23-25

> And after that many days were fulfilled, the Jews took counsel to kill him: but their laying await was known of Saul. And they watched the gates day and night to kill him. Then the disciples took him by night, and let him down by the wall in a basket.

Hold the Rope

The persecutor became the persecuted, the hunter became the hunted. There he was converted by Christ, called to preach. Paul was so successful with the gospel that the ones with whom he was in league to kill, the Christians, now turned against him and hatched a plot to kill him. They watched the gates of the city of Damascus day and night so he would not escape. The disciples of Jesus, whom he once hunted and now with whom he was perfectly and personally identified, took him by night. They carried a basket and ropes to a certain place on the wall of Damascus, and there they put Saul in the basket. As they let him down to the ground, they whispered to him, "God bless you, Saul," as they held the rope for him. His feet touched the ground and he slipped away in the gathering night. They had no way of knowing that Saul of Tarsus would become Paul, the great apostle. All these Christians knew was that this was a child of God whose life was in danger, and they were filled with love and wanted to hold the rope for him. You never know how great a person you have on the end of your rope when you hold the rope for somebody in Jesus' name.

Acts 9:26-29

> And when Saul was come to Jerusalem, he assayed to join himself to the disciples: but they were all afraid of him, and believed not that he was a disciple. But Barnabas took him, and brought him to the apostles, and declared unto them how he had seen the Lord in the way, and that he had spoken to him, and how he had preached boldly at Damascus in the name of Jesus. And he was with them coming in and going out at Jerusalem. And he spake boldly in the name of the Lord Jesus . . .

It was a shock to the system of Saul upon his conversion and return to Jerusalem that the Christians there, among them the leaders, were frightened of him and did not believe that he was a disciple of Jesus Christ. But Barnabas, bless Barnabas, a good man full of the Holy Ghost and faith, took Saul by the hand and led him in to the apostles. The apostles could not refuse Barnabas because Barnabas had been such a great giver, and he said, "I want to tell you this man knows Jesus. This man is preaching Jesus. He has got a boldness about him that every one of us needs." Soon Barnabas prevailed. There is a need for many Barnabases today. It would not hurt us to have a little more of the spirit of Barnabas to stand up for somebody who loves Jesus but who is being persecuted — even by fellow Christians.

Acts 9:29

> And he spake boldly in the name of the Lord Jesus, and disputed against the Grecians: but they went about to slay him.

These are the Grecian Jews, or Greek-speaking Jews. These were the ones responsible for the killing of the first Christian martyr, Stephen. Now Saul, who had been in league with them concerning Stephen's death, was attacked by them, and he begins to dispute with them concerning the Lord Jesus Christ.

Acts 9:30

> Which when the brethren knew, they brought him down to Caesarea, and sent him forth to Tarsus.

Saul's Background

Saul's birthplace, Tarsus, was a great Roman Empire. It was there that Saul, as a young man, had gotten his university education. From there he had gone to Jerusalem to sit at the feet of Gamaliel at the theological seminary in Jerusalem. The word "Tarsus," in a sense, meant "great learning."

Acts 9:31

> Then had the churches rest throughout all Judaea and Galilee and Samaria, and were edified; and walking in the fear of the Lord, and in the comfort of the Holy Ghost, were multiplied.

Rome Distracted Jews

A period of peace came, but it was not necessarily because Paul was no longer a persecutor of the new Christians. History has it that the Romans, the overlords of Palestine, had decided to take statues of the Caesars and place them in the Jewish temple in Jerusalem. To do that, they had to send their armies because the Jews would not allow it without resisting. In other words, at this time, the Jews were so concerned about being persecuted themselves by the Romans that they had no time to persecute the Christians. Therefore, there was a period of peace for the Christian — that is, freedom to go here and there — and so the gospel went throughout Judea, Galilee, and Samaria. Christians multiplied, they were edified and instructed in the Lord and in the comfort of the Holy Ghost, and they really grew.

Acts 9:32-35

> And it came to pass, as Peter passed throughout all quarters, he came down also to the saints which dwelt at Lydda. And there he found a certain man named Aeneas, which had kept his bed eight years, and was sick of the palsy. And Peter said unto him, Aeneas, Jesus Christ maketh thee whole: arise, and make thy bed. And he arose immediately. And all that dwelt at Lydda and Saron saw him, and turned to the Lord.

Have Healing Attitude

It is said that this man kept his bed eight years and was sick of the palsy. There was the physical illness and there was the psychological attachment he had for his bed. There was no faith in him or expectation for a miracle. There is a great truth here for healing today. So many of us embrace our sicknesses. We really do not do anything about them. Even if we go to our doctors, we do not always cooperate. We must remember, if we go to a doctor, that doctor is trained to be against disease. He is trained for life to exist and for sickness to be defeated. We must go to a doctor with that same adamant desire to live, to be in health, and not simply to take our bed, or to accept our sickness as part of our natural being. Peter is here telling him to be whole and to get up and make up his bed. Make it up! Get out of it! Get back into health! God heals through doctors, through the power of prayer, and through the word of faith, such as Peter used here with Aeneas. But He heals also when you and I, in our sicknesses, strike a blow at our own wrong attitudes, when we stand up on the inside of our bodies where our spirit lives and we, in effect, say, "I will not have this thing, I will change my way of thinking and believing. I am going to be healed, I will make up my bed, and I will return to life."

I remember when I had been healed of tuberculosis at age 17 that my strength did not return to me immediately. Several days later I became discouraged and Mamma said, "Oral, you are discouraged." I said, "Yes." She said, "Don't think you were not healed. You were healed. Remember the man of God who prayed for you. Remember how you felt the healing power of the Lord. Son, it is okay to come in and rest in the afternoon, even to lie down. But Oral, don't take off your clothes, put on your pajamas, and get under the covers of the bed. Keep your clothes on. Lie across the bed. Don't get the feeling that you are going back to bed. It took a long time for you to lose your strength, and it is going to take some time for you to get your strength back."

My mother helped save my healing. It took about a year for my full strength to come back. When I lay down sometime during the day to rest, I always kept my clothes on. I did not develop the feeling that I had gotten back in bed, that I was going to take tuberculosis again. This is what Peter is saying. Make up your bed even though you have to lie in it some. Do not do it with the attitude, "I'm sick again." If you are suffering in your body with some kind of affliction or disease, I want to speak the word of faith to you in the same spirit that Peter said to Aeneas, "Rise and take up your bed." I speak to you in print today — not in my name or strength, but in the mighty, incomparable name of Jesus Christ of Nazareth whose I am and whom I serve. In His name receive your healing. Be healed from the crown of your head to the soles of your feet. Be set free and delivered from the power of sickness. Come into your health and be whole, whole in spirit, mind, and body. Be whole in your finances. Be whole in your family relationships. Be healed and set free by the power of the living God and give Him all the glory. Through Jesus Christ I pray and believe and I receive it with you.

Acts 9:36-42

Now there was at Joppa a certain disciple named Tabitha, which by interpretation is called Dorcas: this woman was full of good works and almsdeeds which she did. And it came to pass in those days, that she was sick, and died: whom when they had washed, they laid her in an upper chamber.

And forasmuch as Lydda was nigh to Joppa, and the disciples had heard that Peter was there, they sent unto him two men, desiring him that he would not delay to come to them. Then Peter arose and went with them. When he was come, they brought him into the upper chamber: and all the widows stood by him weeping, and shewing the coats and garments which Dorcas made, while she was with them.

But Peter put them all forth, and kneeled down and prayed; and turning him to the body said, Tabitha, arise. And she opened her eyes: and when she saw Peter, she sat up.

And he gave her his hand, and lifted her up, and when he had called the saints and widows, presented her alive. And it was known throughout all Joppa and many believed in the Lord.

Heal in the Spirit

This woman, who had done so many good seed-faith deeds, became ill. This is a world of sickness. We live in a physical body and sometimes we get sick in spite of our best Christian living; however, sometimes the Lord decides to do something very special about it as He did here. When they learned that Peter was nearby they sent for him and he came. When he arrived, they were all crying and carrying on, and he could not stand that, so he put them all out and knelt down and prayed.

There is a lesson. When we kneel down to pray or lay hands upon somebody, we must get out of sympathy into compassion. Compassion is not sympathy. Sympathy is "I am so sorry," but compassion is the almost irresistible urge to rid the person of what is wrong. It is really the love of God in action and devoid of human sympathy, but filled with the compassion with which Christ was moved. The raising of Dorcas was a tremendous testimony. Her being alive again was known and many believed on the Lord.

The great signs and wonders of God are still in effect today. When you want people to really believe, let miracles start happening as an accompaniment to the preaching of the gospel. When miracles happen, there will be many people who will believe the Lord. I know in my own ministry, directly after I began praying for the sick and seeing miracles of deliverance, hundreds of people would come to

Christ. When people could experience a healing, they could see with their eyes and feel with their spirit, and somehow the Word of God got hold of them.

Just a few short years after Jesus' ascension and sending the Holy Spirit, Peter was seeing fulfilled what Christ had said — that when He went away, His disciples would do greater things than He had done because He would go to His Father and send the Holy Spirit. Peter was there when the Lord had healed paralytics. He had heard Jesus say to a paralyzed man, "Rise, take up your bed and walk." He had been there and was one of the chosen to be with Christ when He raised the little girl, the daughter of Jairus, from the dead. Peter had no trouble believing that he could do greater works because, even though Jesus was bodily or physically absent, the Holy Spirit had come as the Divine Comforter and it was no problem at all for Peter to believe that the name of Jesus had the same power and that he could go and do the same things Christ did and even greater.

We have the same thing. We do not have the physical body of Jesus with us, but we have its replacement — the unlimited and invisible presence of Jesus in the power of the Holy Spirit, who indwells our bodies, our spirits, our minds, and who indwells our whole being. This is the way we ought to think all the time — that we are in the midst of doing greater things because Jesus said we would.

Acts 9:43

> And it came to pass, that he tarried many days in Joppa with one Simon a tanner.

Changes in Store

In Chapter 10, everything begins to change. It has been about eight years since the day of Pentecost when the Lord had poured out the gift of the Holy Spirit upon all flesh and had declared, in fulfillment of the prophecy of Joel, that whosoever would call upon the name of the Lord should be saved. Peter and the others who had been there at Pentecost and had been filled with the Holy Spirit, had not yet opened their minds that it was not a Jewish Christianity, but was a Christianity for all flesh.

Why are people prejudiced, and yet they know Jesus and they are Spirit-filled? Their little minds do not get opened. It does not mean they do not know the Lord or they are not filled with the Spirit. It means humans get little-minded and that is one reason Paul later said, "We must have our minds renewed by the Holy Spirit." The Holy Spirit not only will fill you and me, He also will do some opening up of our minds.

Acts 10:1-4

There was a certain man in Caesarea called Cornelius, a centurion of the band called the Italian band. A devout man, and one that feared God with all his house, which gave much alms to the people, and prayed to God alway. He saw in a vision evidently about the ninth hour of the day an angel of God coming in to him, and saying unto him, Cornelius. And when he looked on him, he was afraid, and said, What is it, Lord? And he said unto him, Thy prayers and thine alms are come up for a memorial before God.

Prayer Giving Memorials

Here was a man not a Jew. He was a man sent from Rome to Caesarea, there to maintain Roman rule and order. But in some way he had come to fear God, to have some measure of relationship with God. He became a great giver and he prayed to God all the time. Now he sees a vision and the Lord visits him. The Lord says something very special: "Your prayers and your giving are come up for a memorial before God."

When we truly pray and truly give to God, these become a memorial to us before God.

Acts 10:5-11

And now send men to Joppa, and call for one Simon, whose surname is Peter: he lodgeth with one Simon a tanner, whose house is by the sea side: he shall tell thee what thou oughtest to do. And when the angel which spake unto Cornelius was departed, he called two of his household servants, and a devout soldier of them that waited on him continually; And when he had declared all these things unto them, he sent them to Joppa.

On the morrow, as they went on their journey, and drew nigh unto the city, Peter went up on the housetop to pray about the sixth hour: and he became very hungry, and would have eaten: but while they made ready, he fell into a trance, and saw heaven opened . . .

As these messengers are coming from the Gentile, Cornelius, God is beginning His preparation of Simon Peter. Do not forget that Peter is baptized in the Holy Spirit and is the one who preached the great sermon at Pentecost. Do not forget he may be the leading Christian up to this time, but his mind still is closed to the Gentiles.

When Peter fell into this vision he saw heaven opened. Jesus saw heaven opened at His baptism by John the Baptist. Stephen saw heaven opened when he was being martyred. God has to open the windows of heaven to us or we will never get our minds open.

Acts 10:11-14

... and a certain vessel descending unto him, as it had been a great sheet knit at the four corners, and let down to the earth: wherein were all manner of fourfooted beasts of the earth, and wild beasts, and creeping things, and fowls of the air.

And there came a voice to him, Rise, Peter; kill, and eat. But Peter said, Not so, Lord; for I have never eaten any thing that is common or unclean.

Resisting God

In the midst of the Lord's dealings with him, Peter's theological mind is working overtime. The Lord was saying, "Do it," and Peter was saying, "No, I am not going to do it." Does that sound like you and me?

Acts 10:15

And the voice spake unto him again the second time, What God hath cleansed, that call not thou common.

A Stream of Stubbornness

Peter was saying that he had never eaten food that was not kosher. The Lord was saying, "This is kosher." The Lord was saying that He was abolishing all the dietary regulations of the law of Moses and He was saying it three different times to this hardheaded apostle called Peter. Peter had denied the Lord three times, and then at the seaside he affirmed Jesus three times. Now it takes the Lord three times to tell him that things are kosher that he thought were not kosher.

Acts 10:16-26

This was done thrice: and the vessel was received up again into heaven. Now while Peter doubted in himself what this vision which he had seen should mean, behold, the men which were sent from Cornelius had made inquiry for Simon's house, and stood before the gate, and called, and asked whether Simon, which was surnamed Peter, were lodged there.

While Peter thought on the vision, the Spirit said unto him, Behold, three men seek thee. Arise therefore, and get thee down, and go with them, doubting nothing: for I have sent them.

Then Peter went down to the men which were sent unto him from Cornelius; and said, Behold, I am he whom ye seek: what is the cause wherefore ye are come? And they said, Cornelius the centurion, a just man, and one that feareth God, and of good report among all the nation of the Jews, was warned from God by an holy angel to send for thee into his house, and to hear words of thee.

Then called he them in, and lodged them. And on the morrow Peter went away with them, and certain brethren from Joppa accompanied him. And the morrow after they entered into Caesarea, and Cornelius waited for them, and had called together his kinsmen and near friends. And as Peter was coming in, Cornelius met him, and fell down at his feet, and worshiped him. But Peter took him up, saying, Stand up; I myself also am a man.

A Bad Start

Cornelius was a man who had come to know something about the Lord. The Lord was really dealing with his heart. Yet, Cornelius violated the one thing that God forbade — "You are not to worship an idol or anything except God." Here, Cornelius falls down and worships Peter and Peter says, "No! No! No!" Peter might have been mixed up in his mind about whether God was going to include all the human race, but he was not mixed up about worshiping someone other than God.

Acts 10:27,28

And as he talked with him, he went in, and found many that were come together. And he said unto them, Ye know how that it is an unlawful thing for a man that is a Jew to keep company, or come unto one of another nation; but God hath shewed me that I should not call any man common or unclean.

No Inferiors

He is saying, "God has shown me I should not call any human being inferior."

Acts 10:29-33

Therefore came I unto you without gainsaying, as soon as I was sent for: I ask therefore for what intent ye have sent for me? And Cornelius said, Four days ago I was fasting until this hour; and at the ninth hour I prayed in my house, and, behold, a man stood before me in bright clothing, and said, Cornelius, thy prayer is heard, and thine alms are had in remembrance in the sight of God. Send therefore to Joppa, and call hither Simon, whose surname is Peter; he is lodged in the house of one Simon a tanner by the sea side: who, when he cometh, shall speak unto thee. Immediately therefore I sent to thee; and thou hast well done that thou art come. Now therefore are we all here present before God, to hear all things that are commanded thee of God.

Listen for God

This is the perfect way for any human being to listen to the preaching of the gospel. Be there listening for what God is going to say. Do not get upset by some peculiar mannerism of preachers or evangelists. All have different personalities — sometimes they clash. Listen to what we are saying of the gospel.

Acts 10:34-48

Then Peter opened his mouth, and said, Of a truth I perceive that God is no respecter of persons: But in every nation he that feareth him, and worketh righteousness, is accepted with him. The word which God sent unto the children of Israel, preaching peace by Jesus Christ: (he is Lord of all:) That word, I say, ye know, which was published throughout all Judaea, and began from Galilee, after the baptism which John preached; how God anointed Jesus of Nazareth with the Holy Ghost and with power: who went about doing good, and healing all that were oppressed of the devil; for God was with him.

And we are witnesses of all things which he did both in the land of the Jews, and in Jerusalem; whom they slew and hanged on a tree: him God raised up the third day, and shewed him openly; not to all the people, but unto witnesses chosen before of God, even to us, who did eat and drink with him after he rose from the dead.

And he commanded us to preach unto the people, and to testify that it is he which was ordained of God to be the Judge of quick and dead. To him give all the prophets witness, that through his name whosoever believeth in him shall receive remission of sins.

While Peter yet spake these words, the Holy Ghost fell on all them which heard the word. And they of the circumcision which believed were astonished, as many as came with Peter, because that on the

Gentiles also was poured out the gift of the Holy Ghost.

For they heard them speak with tongues, and magnify God. They answered Peter, Can any man forbid water, that these should not be baptized, which have received the Holy Ghost as well as we? And he commanded them to be baptized in the name of the Lord. Then prayed they him to tarry certain days.

Spirit to Gentiles

When Peter began to preach to the house of Cornelius, he opened his mouth by saying that he finally understood God was no respecter of persons. The Word of God was sent through the children of Israel to preach peace by Jesus Christ because he is Lord of all. Peter had personally seen and heard how God had anointed Jesus of Nazareth with the Holy Ghost and with power, whose mission was to go about doing good, to heal all that were oppressed of the devil, because God was with Him. Peter pointed out that sickness is the devil's oppression and Christ was anointed of the Father to heal people of those oppressions.

He spoke of the crucifixion of Jesus, how the people had hung Him on a tree, and that was followed, Peter said, by God raising Christ from the dead and showing Him openly. Peter said, "I was one who ate and drank with Him after He rose from the dead, and He commanded us to preach and to testify." This is powerful.

Next Peter told how Jesus is judge of both the living and the dead. Finally, he came to the climax. He said, "Through His name, the name of Jesus, whoever believes in Him shall receive remission of sins." At that split second, the Holy Ghost fell on all who heard the Word.

It is important to you to understand the sequence of affairs on the day of Pentecost and also here. For while Peter yet said these words, "Whoever believes on Him shall receive remission of sins," at that moment the Holy Spirit fell on them. They received the gift of the Holy Spirit.

That is the new order. People get so confused today about being told they ought to be saved, then sanctified, then baptized with the Holy Spirit, and then speak by tongues, and there is a sequence, a chronological way of looking at things.

At Pentecost, Peter put it in one single act of believing on the Lord for the remission of your sins and then you would receive the gift of the Holy Spirit. All you had to do, then, was to release the prayer language, or the tongues of the Holy Spirit within you. When the Holy Spirit fell upon these Gentiles, as their sins were remitted, they began to speak with tongues. The other Jews who observed this were absolutely astonished. First, that the Gentiles would be treated by God the same way He had treated those present on the day of Pentecost, and second, that God would forgive their sins and give them the gift of the Holy Spirit and enable them to release their prayer language, or the language of the Spirit to the heavenly Father.

This is a tremendous thing. It changes everything. Right here is where so many denominations go off on a tangent and build a way of doctrine that is divisive and separates. Those who will not receive tongues are divisive against those who do receive tongues. Those who release tongues often become divisive against those who do not release tongues. I tell you, the devil could not be more pleased with the way we are rejecting the common denominator of Christ. Paul later is saying in the eighth chapter of Romans, that when you receive Christ, the Spirit comes, and at that time you are to release your prayer language. The tongues are inside you. That is why you feel the Spirit coming up in the pit of your stomach, as Jesus said in John 7:37-39: "Out of your belly shall flow rivers of living water which spake he of the Holy Ghost." The Holy Spirit comes right up out of the pit of your stomach, out of your belly area, and He is coming up because He is giving you a new language of the Spirit, a new way to communicate with the Father. That is what happened here.

Afterward, Peter baptizes them in water. Some are baptized in water right after they are converted, others are baptized after they are aware the Holy Spirit has filled them. There is no particular sequence held up in the Bible for these things to happen. The proper sequence is that they do happen and that they become the common denominator among us so that we love one another. Also, we learn how to pray in the Spirit and learn how to witness for Christ together in our world.

Acts 11:1-3

> And the apostles and brethren that were in Judaea heard that the Gentiles had also received the word of God. And when Peter was come up to Jerusalem, they that were of the circumcision contended with him, saying, Thou wentest in to men uncircumcised, and didst eat with them.

Leaders Unconvinced

Although these elders were the Christian leaders, they had not yet come to the place where they could believe that anybody could be saved unless he was circumcised and kept the law of Moses. This is hard for us to believe today, but do not forget there are many traditions among Christians that are just as harmful.

Acts 11:4-9
> But Peter rehearsed the matter from the beginning, and expounded it by order unto them, saying, I was in the city of Joppa praying: and in a trance I saw a vision. A certain vessel descend, as it had been a great sheet, let down from heaven by four corners; and it came even to me: upon the which when I had fastened mine eyes, I considered, and saw fourfooted beasts of the earth, and wild beasts, and creeping things, and fowls of the air.
>
> And I heard a voice saying unto me, Arise, Peter; slay and eat. But I said, Not so, Lord: for nothing common or unclean hath at any time entered into my mouth. But the voice answered me again from heaven, What God hath cleansed, that call not thou common.

Do not say it is not right when God has declared it right.

Acts 11:10-12
> And this was done three times: and all were drawn up again into heaven. And, behold, immediately there were three men already come unto the house where I was, sent from Caesarea unto me. And the spirit bade me go with them, nothing doubting . . .

God was saying not to worry about His Gentiles.

Acts 11:12-16
> . . . Moreover these six brethren accompanied me, and we entered into the man's house: and he shewed us how he had seen an angel in his house, which stood and said unto him, Send men to Joppa, and call for Simon, whose surname is Peter; who shall tell thee words, whereby thou and all thy house shall be saved. And as I began to speak, the Holy Ghost fell on them, as on us at the beginning. Then remembered I the word of the Lord, how that he said, John indeed baptized with water; but ye shall be baptized with the Holy Ghost.

Spiritual Baptizing, Filling

Peter's mind goes all the way back to John the Baptist who was the first to tell people that Jesus was going to baptize them with the Holy Spirit. The term "baptized with the Holy Spirit" is the same as being "filled with the Holy Ghost."

Acts 11:17
> Forasmuch then as God gave them the like gift as he did unto us, who believed on the Lord Jesus Christ; what was I, that I could withstand God?

The Common Bond

This sheds a lot of light on the day of Pentecost. When these disciples, along with Mary the mother of Jesus and Peter and the others of the 120, received the gift of the Holy Spirit on the day of Pentecost, they had believed on the Lord Jesus Christ. That is a terribly important point for us to understand, that believing on the Lord Jesus Christ comes first. Many people have tried to set the time when the disciples of Jesus had believed on Him as their personal Savior or when they were converted. Were they converted before the day of Pentecost? We do not know the exact point after the resurrection and before the day of Pentecost when these people were actually converted. From my standpoint, as I see the Word of God, their full conversion, based upon believing on the Lord Jesus Christ as the risen Son of God, came to full fruition at the day of Pentecost.

In that same second chapter, in Acts 2:38, Peter was to say that when people repented of their sins, their sins were remitted; upon believing in the risen Christ, they would receive the gift of the Holy Spirit. In Acts 11:17, Peter is standing before the apostles and elders in Jerusalem, giving his report of the outpouring of the Spirit upon the Gentiles. He was saying, "For as much then as God gave them the like gift as he did unto us who believed on the Lord Jesus Christ, what was I that I could withstand God?" In other words, he was saying this is what unites the Gentiles and the Christians in a common bond. This is the common denominator. Believing on the Lord Jesus Christ as the personal Savior brings the gift of the Holy Spirit. It is one simultaneous act. Verse 18 gives the response of the Christian leaders in Jerusalem to the story that Peter had related to them concerning the Gentiles' belief and receiving the gift of the Spirit the same as they had.

Acts 11:18
> When they heard these things, they held their peace, and glorified God, saying, Then hath God also to the Gentiles granted repentance unto life.

An Uncomplicated God

On this, the entire Christian Church can come into unity. Concerning all the dissension about when the Holy Spirit is given, or at what stage in the Christian's life he receives the gift of the Holy Spirit, or the belief of some that they never receive the Holy Spirit, Peter makes it very clear that believing on the Lord Jesus Christ brings the gift of the Holy Spirit, which it did to them on Pentecost Day. He says it also happened in the exact manner at the house of Cornelius, about 8 or 10 years later.

When the Christian leaders in Jerusalem heard these things, they made this fundamental statement: God has granted to the Gentiles repentance unto life. All the separation among the Christians through denominational emphases should come to a close right here in Acts 11:18. God is not a complicated God. He did not make a complicated Christian experience. If we believe on the Lord Jesus Christ through repenting of our sins, the gift of the Spirit will come in.

We in the Oral Roberts Ministries, which represents people from virtually all Christian denominations, have this as a common denominator among us. We are charismatic in that we believe that our confession of faith in Jesus Christ through repentance causes the gift of the Holy Spirit to come into our lives. From that point on it is up to us with our will to release our prayer language so that we will speak in tongues just exactly as they did back there and for the same purpose.

Acts 11:19
> Now they which were scattered abroad upon the persecution that arose about Stephen travelled as far as Phenice, . . .

(This is the present-day Lebanon)

> . . . and Cyprus, and Antioch, preaching the word to none but unto the Jews only.

Historical Review

Luke goes back, before Caesarea at this point, and tells how the Christians go up to Antioch and there they preach only to the Jews. Remember, now, that this is before Caesarea and the Church is still slow to open to the Gentiles. It became open after Peter's experience of the Holy Spirit coming upon Cornelius and his household at Caesarea.

Acts 11:20

> And some of them were men of Cyprus and Cyrene, which, when they were come to Antioch, spake unto the Grecians, preaching the Lord Jesus.

The Grecians here refer to the Grecian Jews — the same ones who led the persecution of Stephen.

Acts 11:21,22

> And the hand of the Lord was with them: and a great number believed, and turned unto the Lord. Then tidings of these things came unto the ears of the church which was in Jerusalem: and they sent forth Barnabas, that he should go as far as Antioch.

Barnabas Prominent

There is that man Barnabas again. He is the big-minded Christian who first befriended Saul of Tarsus and believed in him. Barnabas is the one who gave so much of his income to the new Christian Church. Barnabas stands out in the early Church.

Acts 11:23,24

> Who, when he came, and had seen the grace of God, was glad, and exhorted them all, that with purpose of heart they would cleave unto the Lord. For he was a good man, and full of the Holy Ghost and of faith: and much people was added unto the Lord.

The Spirit's Viewpoint

Barnabas was allowing the Holy Spirit, who had filled him, to guide his life. Being filled with the Holy Spirit, he could see through the Spirit's eyes. He saw the grace of God was working there in Antioch among the Jews and the Gentiles and that this church was surely of the Lord. He was glad. It shows that the Holy Spirit in us sees things differently than man does. We have the heavenly view of the earth. We see through God's eyes. And we come to believe in the work of God wherever it is and we know it is genuine.

Acts 11:25,26

> Then departed Barnabas to Tarsus, for to seek Saul: and when he had found him, he brought him unto Antioch. And it came to pass, that a

whole year they assembled themselves with the church, and taught much people. And the disciples were called Christians first in Antioch.

Christians Identified

When Barnabas had seen God's mighty work in Antioch and had ministered there, he felt the need of more help for them, so he went over to Tarsus where Saul was and brought him back with him to Antioch. They stayed in Antioch for quite some time and taught great multitudes of people.

Then Dr. Luke slips in a great and interesting statement: "And the disciples were called Christians first in Antioch." Before this, the Christian way was called "in the way." This is a milestone in the life of the early Church. They were not called Christians on the day of Pentecost or even shortly thereafter. They were called Christians first when Barnabas and Saul of Tarsus had gone to Antioch and spent a year.

Acts 11:27-30

And in these days came prophets from Jerusalem unto Antioch. And there stood up one of them named Agabus, and signified by the spirit that there should be great dearth throughout all the world: which came to pass in the days of Claudius Caesar. Then the disciples, every man according to his ability, determined to send relief unto the brethren which dwelt in Judaea: which also they did, and sent it to the elders by the hands of Barnabas and Saul.

Giving Like Breathing

When the prophet Agabus foretold the coming famine in the earth, they immediately thought about the poor saints in Jerusalem. Early in Acts we said how many of the early believers were disfranchised by the Jewish nation. Their property was confiscated and they were thrown upon the apostles. People began to give unto God, and at one time there was a common storehouse from which these people were fed. The prophet forecasts a famine and they knew it would have a particularly bad effect upon those Christians in Jerusalem whose property had been confiscated.

Giving was just as natural as breathing with the first Christians. Any Christian has the same spirit. Now there are some people who call themselves Christians who do not have the spirit of giving. They certainly have been badly taught. The first Christians were Jews and the Jews were taught to give their tithes and offerings to God. There were two schools of thought. One was represented by the Pharisees, who did not believe that tithing would open the windows of heaven but would become an end in itself. Jesus rebuked them for it. There was the other school of thought that really believed in tithing. Jesus was a tither. Saul of Tarsus was a tither. All these people were tithers. They believed that God would open the windows of heaven, God would rebuke the devourer for their sake, and when a need arose they began to give as naturally as they breathed.

I have had that experience. I became a tither the night that I gave my life to Christ. I have been a happy tither ever since, making it a seed of faith that I plant unto God. The happiest Christians I know are tithers who become seed-faithers through their tithe, planting of their seeds of faith. One of the greatest revival movements that could happen in our time is a revival of giving the tithe as seed-faith to God with the richness of joy accompanying it.

Acts 12:1-3

Now about that time Herod the king stretched forth his hands to vex certain of the church. And he killed James the brother of John with the sword. And because he saw it pleased the Jews, he proceeded further to take Peter also. (Then were the days of unleavened bread.)

Herod's Death Plot

This particular Herod is a grandson of the Herod who was ruling at the time Jesus was born and tried to kill Him. Now his grandson Herod has inherited the same unbelief and the murderous intent of the original Herod. He killed James the brother of John. James and John, the sons of Zebedee, along with Peter, were the three whom Jesus usually had to accompany Him at major events of His ministry, such as going up on the Mount of Transfiguration, or going to the home of Jairus for the raising of his little daughter who had died. Peter, James, and John were very close to Jesus. Now James is killed. But Herod, when he saw this pleased the Jews, also took Peter. He was going to destroy the leaders.

Acts 12:4

And when he had apprehended him, he put him in prison, and delivered him to four quaternions of soldiers to keep him; intending after Easter to bring him forth to the people.

This is the first time that Easter is mentioned.

Acts 12:5

> Peter therefore was kept in prison: but prayer was made without ceasing of the church unto God for him.

Response to Prayers

The question arises, Does God answer prayer? Can I, as a Christian, get my prayers answered? This is probably the most asked question, either consciously or unconsciously by Christians today. Can I get my prayers answered? It is stated that when Peter was put in prison, the people of the Christian Church prayed without ceasing unto God for him. The answer to the question is yes, providing that we have the spirit of unceasing prayer. That doesn't mean that we can pray 24 hours a day because that is impossible. But we can have the unceasing attitude of prayer. We can prayer-soak ourselves — soaking up our very being in the attitude of calling upon our living Redeemer. Yes, God answers prayer. Yes, prayer, when it is unceasing as an attitude, demands an answer. God responds to that. He responds to a positive, unceasing attitude of believing, earnest beseeching of Him.

When Peter was put in prison, the Church did not disintegrate. The Christians did not throw up their hands and say, "What terrible thing has Peter done?" That goes on all over the Christian Church today when one of us in the lead is persecuted. We get more criticism from the Christians sometimes than we do from the world. That was not then because something else took place. While there was a 24-hour watch put around Peter while he was in prison, the Church went on a 24-hour vigil of prayer. They did not organize a "peace march," they did not cause a riot. They just went off with their own group and began praying. They did not stop praying. That is what counts today. Get with it with God in your prayer life!

Acts 12:6-9

> And when Herod would have brought him forth, the same night Peter was sleeping between two soldiers, bound with two chains: and the keepers before the door kept the prison.
>
> And, behold, the angel of the Lord came upon him, and a light shined in the prison: and he smote Peter on the side, and raised him up, saying, Arise up quickly.
>
> And his chains fell off from his hands.
>
> And the angel said unto him, Gird thyself, and bind on thy sandals. And so he did. And he saith unto him, Cast thy garment about thee, and follow me. And he went out, and followed him; and wist not that

it was true which was done by the angel; but thought he saw a vision.

The angel did certain things. He awoke him, he smote him on the side, he told him to dress himself, and said, "Follow me." On the other hand, there were things that the angel could not and did not do for Peter which Peter had to do for himself. It was a divine-human reciprocity. It was what God does and what we do as we come together in cooperation. This sounds so miraculous, and so it was, but the miraculous is never separated from the human.

Many people get the idea that when God does something He does it all by himself. When Peter realized that he and God were doing business together, it was as natural as breathing. Have we lost that? Some people say we have. Can we recapture it? I, Oral Roberts, say we can. Every miraculous experience I have had has had to do with what I have done, and what I have done has had to do with a miracle that God has done. Doing it together is God's way.

Acts 12:10
> When they were past the first and the second ward, they came unto the iron gate that leadeth unto the city, which opened to them of its own accord: . . .

Reed to Rock

By this time, Peter "the reed," to whom Christ had said, "Follow Me and I will make you into a rock," had become Peter "the rock." That big iron gate which opened up in the city could not remain closed when this rock of a Christian man approached it. Without being touched by human hands it just swung open. Can we ever understand how powerful our Christian faith is, that it even activates inanimate objects when it is necessary for the progress of the kingdom of God?

Acts 12:10-15
> . . . And they went out, and passed on through one street; and forthwith the angel departed from him. And when Peter was come to himself, he said, Now I know of a surety, that the Lord hath sent his angel, and hath delivered me out of the hand of Herod, and from all the expectation of the people of the Jews.
>
> And when he had considered the thing, he came to the house of Mary the mother of John, whose surname was Mark; where many were gathered together praying. And as Peter knocked at the door of the gate, a damsel came to hearken, named Rhoda. And when she

knew Peter's voice, she opened not the gate for gladness, but ran in, and told how Peter stood before the gate.

And they said unto her, Thou art mad. But she constantly affirmed that it was even so. Then said they, It is his angel.

Angels at Work

Can you just see this scene? This girl, Rhoda, who hears the knocking at the gate, rushes out. As Peter talks, she recognizes his voice, turns, runs into the house, and says, "I think I hear Peter out there! I think God has answered our prayers!" They said, "You have got to be out of your mind."

Here are people who have been praying around the clock, believing God to answer their prayers, and God had. Now the answer to their prayers walks up and talks. The girl recognizes his voice, relates her testimony, and they say, "You have got to be mad." But she kept on saying, "I think it is so. I heard his voice." And they said, "It cannot be, it is an angel. It is his angel."

This is a very important thing because in Matthew 18:10, Jesus spoke of guardian angels, that they always behold the face of our Father which is in heaven. The Christians then believed in guardian angels. I think every one of us is surrounded by the angels of God.

Acts 12:16,17

But Peter continued knocking: and when they had opened the door, and saw him, they were astonished.

But he, beckoning unto them with the hand to hold their peace, declared unto them how the Lord had brought him out of the prison. And he said, Go shew these things unto James, and to the brethren. And he departed, and went into another place.

Peter a Fugitive

This James is a different James. James, the son of Zebedee, the brother of John, had been killed by Herod, but this is James, the brother of the Lord Jesus, who was the head of the Church in Jerusalem. Peter had said, "Go and tell James, and all the brethren," and then he went underground.

Acts 12:18,19

Now as soon as it was day, there was no small stir among the soldiers, what was become of Peter. And when Herod had sought for him, and found him not, he examined the keepers, and commanded that they should be put to death. And he went down from Judaea to Caesarea, and there abode.

Harsh Roman Law

That was the law, that if your prisoner escaped you got put to death. You were sentenced to the escapee's sentence. That was Roman law.

Acts 12:20-24

And Herod was highly displeased with them of Tyre and Sidon: but they came with one accord to him, and, having made Blastus the king's chamberlain their friend, desired peace; because their country was nourished by the king's country.

And upon a set day Herod, arrayed in royal apparel, sat upon his throne, and made an oration unto them. And the people gave a shout, saying, It is the voice of a god, and not of a man. And immediately the angel of the Lord smote him, because he gave not God the glory: and he was eaten of worms, and gave up the ghost. But the word of God grew and multiplied.

Be Cautious of Cults

The historian for that day, Josephus, describes Herod as being so vain and sold on himself that this particular royal array he had upon his body was made of silver and it glistened in the sun. When he spoke with such an orator's voice the people shouted he was a god and he did not dispel the idea from their minds.

Remember in the 10th chapter of Acts when Peter visited the house of Cornelius to preach the gospel first to the Gentiles? Cornelius was overwhelmed and grabbed him and wanted to worship him but Peter said, "No, I am just a man, the same as you are." Herod does exactly the opposite and accepts the worship of the people.

The angel came down and the word "smote" is used. That is the word that was used when the angel smote Peter on the side while he was in prison. But that smiting was to release him from the chains. When the angel of the Lord smote Herod he got sick. He was eaten of worms and died. There may come a time when some person crosses your path who, in effect, will want to be worshiped, but true Christians do not want that. They would like to be appreciated, but God is their source. Therefore, if someone comes around and wants you to go beyond the ordinary, you be careful.

This is important to remember because there are some people following cult leaders. They give up their own minds and, in effect, almost worship these people. That is of the devil. We who are Christians, even those of us who are set in the Church as apostles or prophets or evangelists or pastors or teachers, are just human beings whom God has called. We have chosen to obey. Our obedience is the key.

Acts 12:25

> And Barnabas and Saul returned from Jerusalem, when they had fulfilled their ministry, and took with them John, whose surname was Mark.

New Directions Emerge

Barnabas and Saul, when they returned from Jerusalem, had fulfilled all they had set out to do. They had not done it halfway. They had done it all the way. Here we are told that Barnabas and Saul, who now have formed a team, choose young John Mark to be part of it. At this point, the second half of Acts really begins. The first half of the book of Acts is mostly built around the Jerusalem Church. Paul would come back to it, Peter would come and go, orders would be sent out of Jerusalem, people would be dispatched for certain missions. The extension of the gospel began with Jerusalem and began to go throughout all of Palestine, but now the center seems to change. In a sense, Jerusalem was replaced by Antioch.

Paul and Barnabas were anointed and dedicated at Antioch to go into the world of Asia and Europe. They were sponsored by the church at Antioch. It appears from that time on as far as the Gentile world was concerned, Antioch becomes the center. At that time, it was the capital of Syria. It was a very important city — one of the three largest in the Roman Empire. There is going to be a dramatic change in direction in where the Christian leaders go, the missionary journeys they take, and the extension of the gospel to the Gentile world. You are going to read about the move of the Holy Spirit in ways you haven't even thought of as being possible.

Acts 13:1,2

> Now there were in the church that was at Antioch certain prophets and teachers; as Barnabas, and Simeon that was called Niger, and Lucius of Cyrene, and Manaen, which had been brought up with Herod

the tetrarch, and Saul. As they ministered to the Lord, and fasted, the Holy Ghost said, Separate me Barnabas and Saul for the work whereunto I have called them.

The Spirit Calls

The statement, "The Holy Ghost said, Separate me Barnabas and Saul" really means the Holy Ghost gave the call. They did not just decide within themselves to act. The Holy Spirit spoke, maybe through prophecy or through tongues and interpretation or through a word of knowledge or through a divine impression or all of these. At any rate, He spoke in a way that they could understand. When one is called of God it is usually a rather narrowly outlined call. It is a specific call. That person is not able to be all things to all people — to scatter his talents. He's to specifically move in a certain way with a particular calling of God because he's set in the body, as a member of the body, and the Body of Christ is greater than the sum of its parts.

Acts 13:3

And when they had fasted and prayed, and laid their hands on them, they sent them away.

Christ's Word Fulfilled

In the gospel Jesus said that after He had gone, the time would come when His disciples would fast. Now we have a practical example and fulfillment of Christ's word — when they laid their hands on Barnabas and Saul, then sent them away. This was a dedication of them to these particular missionaries and evangelistic journeys and it implies that they also made some provisions for them. The mother church to the Gentiles would have a very definite part in supporting these men, in praying for them, and helping to take care of their needs.

Acts 13:4-12

So they, being sent forth by the Holy Ghost, departed unto Seleucia; and from thence they sailed to Cyprus. And when they were at Salamis, they preached the word of God in the synagogues of the Jews: and they had also John to their minister.

And when they had gone through the isle unto Paphos, they found a certain sorcerer, a false prophet, a Jew, whose name was Bar-jesus:

83

which was the the deputy of the country, Sergius Paulus, a prudent man; who called for Barnabas and Saul, and desired to hear the word of God.

But Elymas the sorcerer (for so is his name by interpretation) withstood them, seeking to turn away the deputy from the faith. Then Saul, (who also is called Paul,) filled with the Holy Ghost, set his eyes on him, and said, Oh full of all subtilty and all mischief, thou child of the devil, thou enemy of all righteousness, wilt thou not cease to pervert the right ways of the Lord?

And now, behold, the hand of the Lord is upon thee, and thou shalt be blind, not seeing the sun for a season. And immediately there fell on him a mist and a darkness; and he went about seeking some to lead him by the hand. Then the deputy, when he saw what was done, believed, being astonished at the doctrine of the Lord.

Gifts Prove Jesus Lives

When this false prophet began to hinder the work of Paul and Barnabas, the gift of discerning of spirits began to work powerfully in Paul. When we get to I Corinthians 12 we will notice the gift that Paul is using here — the gift of discerning of spirits. He read the intent of the heart of this false prophet. He also called upon him the hand of the Lord that would not let His gospel be perverted. The man was suddenly made blind. When the deputy saw all the manifestations of the gifts of God, he believed and was astonished at the doctrine of the Lord, which means he was astonished at the Lord's presence, that Jesus was a person working through other persons — Paul and Barnabas — and that Jesus was alive.

That is what the gifts of the Spirit mean: Jesus is alive. The gifts of the Spirit are just that much of Jesus acting in you and me as Christians.

Acts 13:13

Now when Paul and his company loosed from Paphos, they came to Perga in Pamphylia: and John departing from them returned to Jerusalem.

Mark Turns Back

This is a turning point, for Mark gets tired of the work and he leaves them. Young John Mark just could not take the pressure of working with these two men on the evangelistic and missionary fields of the Gentile world.

Acts 13:14-20

> But when they departed from Perga, they came to Antioch in Pisidia, and went into the synagogue on the sabbath day, and sat down. And after the reading of the law and the prophets the rulers of the synagogue sent unto them, saying, Ye men and brethren, if ye have any word of exhortation for the people, say on.
>
> Then Paul stood up, and beckoning with his hand said, Men of Israel, and ye that fear God, give audience. The God of this people of Israel chose our fathers, and exalted the people when they dwelt as strangers in the land of Egypt, and with an high arm brought he them out of it. And about the time of forty years suffered he their manners in the wilderness. And when he had destroyed seven nations in the land of Chanaan, he divided their land to them by lot. And after that he gave unto them judges about the space of four hundred and fifty years, until Samuel the prophet.

Paul Knew Scripture

Notice the scriptural knowledge that Paul had. He knew the Word of God. Yes, he had a testimony. He had a personal experience with Christ to share, but he also knew the Word of God.

Acts 13:21-23

> And afterward they desired a king: and God gave unto them Saul the son of Cis, a man of the tribe of Benjamin, by the space of forty years. And when he had removed him, he raised up unto them David to be their king; to whom also he gave testimony, and said, I have found David the son of Jesse, a man after mine own heart, which shall fulfil all my will. Of this man's seed hath God according to his promise raised unto Israel a Saviour, Jesus . . .

Seed of David Declared

As Paul is giving his message to the Jews in this Gentile city, a message based upon the Old Testament scriptures and the historical account of God's dealing with His people, Israel, he comes to David and declares that God used his seed. That seed became a Savior — Jesus Christ.

Acts 13:24,25

> When John had first preached before his coming the baptism of repentance to all the people of Israel. And as John fulfilled his course,

he said, Whom think ye that I am? I am not he.

John Disclaimed Honor

He is referring to the prophet that Moses talked about when Moses said, "There will be a prophet arise who is like me." All the Israelites knew that Moses was talking about the Messiah. Therefore, when John the Baptist came, they all wanted to know who he was. John said, "I am not He. I am not the prophet — I am not the Messiah."

Acts 13:25-43

But, behold, there cometh one after me, whose shoes of his feet I am not worthy to loose. Men and brethren, children of the stock of Abraham, and whosoever among you feareth God, to you is the word of this salvation sent. For they that dwell at Jerusalem, and their rulers, because they knew him not, nor yet the voices of the prophets which are read every sabbath day, they have fulfilled them in condemning him.

And though they found no cause of death in him, yet desired they Pilate that he should be slain. And when they had fulfilled all that was written of him, they took him down from the tree, and laid him in a sepulchre.

But God raised him from the dead: And he was seen many days of them which came up with him from Galilee to Jerusalem, who are his witnesses unto the people. And we declare unto you glad tidings, how that the promise which was made unto the fathers, God hath fulfilled the same unto us their children, in that he hath raised up Jesus again; as it is also written in the second psalm, Thou art my Son, this day have I begotten thee.

And as concerning that he raised him up from the dead, now no more to return to corruption, he said on this wise, I will give you the sure mercies of David. Wherefore he saith also in another psalm, Thou shalt not suffer thine Holy One to see corruption. For David, after he had served his own generation by the will of God, fell on sleep, and was laid unto his fathers, and saw corruption; but he whom God raised again, saw no corruption.

Be it known unto you therefore, men and brethren, that through this man is preached unto you the forgiveness of sins: and by him all that believe are justified from all things, from which ye could not be justified by the law of Moses. Beware therefore, lest that come upon you, which is spoken of in the prophets; Behold, ye despisers, and wonder, and perish: for I work a work in your days, a work which ye shall in no wise believe, though a man declare it unto you. And when the Jews were gone out of the synagogue, the Gentiles besought that these words might be preached to them the next sabbath.

Now when the congregation was broken up, many of the Jews and religious proselytes followed Paul and Barnabas: who, speaking to them, persuaded them to continue in the grace of God.

Preach, Teach, Heal

There were three things that Jesus told His followers to do: to preach, teach, and heal. Here is Paul teaching. He is teaching these Jewish people the Word of God.

Wherever in the world there were 10 Jewish men they could have a Jewish synagogue. Paul's custom was, wherever he went, to find the Jewish synagogue and there, if invited, preach the gospel — when he was invited to do so. In this sermon, he traced the dealings of God with the people of Israel, going all the way back to the fathers which were Abraham, Isaac, and Jacob. He then traced twelve sons who became the twelve patriarchs of Israel or the fathers of the twelve tribes of Israel, that God had delivered them from Egypt and brought them into the land of Canaan, had given them judges, and then raised up prophets like Samuel, given them their first king, Saul, and replaced him with David. David, because of his obedience to God, would bring forth a seed who would be the Messiah. When the Messiah appeared in Jerusalem, their counterparts in the Jewish faith had rejected Him since they did not know Him, and they hung Him on a tree. Paul says God raised Him from the dead.

The cornerstone of the Christian faith was and is the resurrection of Jesus from the dead. This is the preaching we must be doing today. This is the teaching we must be teaching today. Following this type of preaching and teaching will bring forth the great thing Christ said, "Heal the sick," because people are sick in mind, body, spirit, soul.

When Paul finished preaching, he warned them to be careful. They had now heard the gospel. They would receive it with God's blessings or the judgment of the prophets would come upon them. When the service ended the Jews left the synagogues, but the Gentile proselytes who had been proselyted into the Jewish faith and who had not been able to follow the Scriptures like the Jews, requested that on the next sabbath, gospel would be preached to them.

Acts 13:44,45

> And the next sabbath day came almost the whole city together to hear the word of God.

87

But when the Jews saw the multitudes, they were filled with envy,
and spake against those things which were spoken by Paul,
contradicting and blaspheming.

Similar Reactions

The Bible says that for envy the Jews crucified Jesus. When Paul
was doing the works of Jesus he created the same envy that Jesus
did. When we are Jesus' people we create the same things, the same
reactions in people that Jesus did. People are no longer neutral.
They get off the fence. They take a stand.

Acts 13:46,47

Then Paul and Barnabas waxed bold, and said, It was necessary that
the word of God should first have been spoken to you: but seeing ye
put it from you, and judge yourselves unworthy of everlasting life, lo,
we turn to the Gentiles. For so hath the Lord commanded us, saying,
I have set thee to be a light of the Gentiles that thou shouldest be
for salvation unto the ends of the earth.

Get Spiritual

Paul is quoting Isaiah 49:6. He is also referring to their father,
Abraham, where God had said that He had sent him as a light to
the Gentiles — to the whole world. Isn't it odd that devout, religious
people can ignore the Word of God? They contradicted, blasphemed,
and yet they were the most religious people in the world. Beware
of religion and get hold of spirituality — of being spiritually minded
according to the Scriptures and the risen Christ Jesus.

Acts 13:48

And when the Gentiles heard this, they were glad, and glorified the
word of the Lord: and as many as were ordained to eternal life believed.

An Historical Ordainment

Ordained to eternal life refers to an historical account rather than
a theological one. Historically there would be a time when people
would believe. Many take this as a theological statement — they
were ordained to eternal life, which means some were not. But this
is an historical statement, that history now has come due and these

people have reached their divinely ordained time when they can choose to believe the Lord — and they did.

Acts 13:49
> And the word of the Lord was published throughout all the region.

Standing for Jesus

Do you get the sense here in Paul's ministry to these people that he is serious about the Lord, that Jesus is his Lord, that the resurrection of Jesus from the dead is the fundamental fact of all Christian experience, that he does not compromise, that you know where he stands?

Throughout organized Christianity there is not enough of the positive belief that Jesus is the Son of God, that He is the only Savior and there is no retraction from it. Now I, Oral Roberts, have many faults, make mistakes, and am far from perfect, but I want you to know that in the Oral Roberts Ministries, we proclaim Jesus Christ the Son of the living God. In the honor code that all the students, faculty, staff, and administration sign at the Oral Roberts University is a statement that Jesus Christ is the Son of God and our personal Savior. I make no apology for standing up for Jesus Christ as the Son of God.

Acts 13:50-52
> But the Jews stirred up the devout and honourable women, and the chief men of the city, and raised persecution against Paul and Barnabas, and expelled them out of their coasts.
>
> But they shook off the dust of their feet against them, and came unto Iconium. And the disciples were filled with joy, and with the Holy Ghost.

Work With Believers

After the ministry in this city where they were rejected and expelled, they were filled with joy and the Holy Spirit. The Scriptures say that the kingdom of God is righteousness, peace, and joy in the Holy Ghost. What we need to do is to stand up for the Lord Jesus Christ who lives in us. When we do, we will be filled again and again and again with the Holy Spirit and with joy. That is what the Church needs. That is what we have got to have.

This old world is not going to pay any attention to a weak Christian

Church, to one which is not Spirit-filled or full of the joy of the Holy Spirit. This old world is too busy minding its own affairs and going to hell to listen to a bunch of so-called Christian people who just sit like knots on a log in their church services or go about in their work presumably under the banner of being a Christian but exhibit no overflowing joy of the Holy Spirit. People will take notice of our joy if we really manifest the Holy Spirit in our lives.

These Jews stirred up the power structure against Paul and Barnabas and those who believed in the Lord Jesus Christ. That is often what happens today. When the charismatic power of the Holy Spirit begins to move and multitudes are stirred and led to Christ, the enemies go to the power structure and stir them up against this move of God.

But two things happened. First, one was to obey what Jesus said, to shake off the very dust of their feet and go on to the next place. Second, one was to be filled with joy and again a new filling of the Holy Spirit. This is exactly what you and I as Christians should do today: put the past behind us and go where those people are who will receive the gospel of Jesus Christ; work with believing believers rather than doubting doubters; work with the people who will ultimately receive the gospel of Jesus Christ.

Acts 14:1-3

> And it came to pass in Iconium, that they went both together into the synagogue of the Jews, and so spake, that a great multitude both of the Jews and also of the Greeks believed.
>
> But the unbelieving Jews stirred up the Gentiles, and made their minds evil affected against the brethren. Long time therefore abode they speaking boldly in the Lord, which gave testimony unto the word of his grace, and granted signs and wonders to be done by their hands.

Healing a Confirmation

I said earlier that Jesus taught we are to preach, teach, and heal. Here is a reproduction of what Christ said. Paul and Barnabas preached, taught, and now they healed. God confirmed His Word by signs and wonders by their hands. They either laid their hands upon the people or did similar things through which God wrought miracles of deliverance. It happened every time. There is no situation so desperate in our world today in which — if we Christians obey Christ and preach, teach, and heal — there will not be results.

In building the theological seminary in the Oral Roberts University, we have tried to get back to these three fundamentals of Christ —

preach, teach, and heal. You know you can learn to preach, you can learn to teach, but when it comes to the miraculous healing power of Christ through faith, you are not going to learn that. That is going to be a confirmation of anointed preaching and teaching.

When they "so spake," their speaking in preaching and teaching was of such direction by the Holy Spirit that God confirmed it with signs and wonders, with miracles of healing and deliverance among the people.

God's time has come that not only the Oral Roberts University School of Theology, but others throughout the earth, will center themselves upon the written Word of God, upon the Holy Spirit's active work of testifying of Christ in our lives today, and of helping us to be anointed. I believe every college or university that calls itself Christian should be Christian, should believe the Bible, should preach the gospel with signs following.

Acts 14:4-18

But the multitude of the city was divided: and part held with the Jews, and part with the apostles. And when there was an assault made both of the Gentiles, and also of the Jews with their rulers, to use them despitefully and to stone them, they were ware of it, and fled unto Lystra and Derbe, cities of Lycaonia, and into the region that lieth round about: and there they preached the gospel.

And there sat a certain man at Lystra, impotent in his feet, being a cripple from his mother's womb, who never had walked: The same heard Paul speak: who stedfastly beholding him, and perceiving that he had faith to be healed, said with a loud voice, Stand upright on thy feet. And he leaped and walked.

And when the people saw what Paul had done, they lifted up their voices, saying in the speech of Lycaonia, The gods are come down to us in the likeness of men. And they called Barnabas, Jupiter; and Paul, Mercurius, because he was the chief speaker. Then the priest of Jupiter, which was before their city, brought oxen and garlands unto the gates, and would have done sacrifice with the people.

Which when the apostles, Barnabas and Paul, heard of, they rent their clothes, and ran in among the people, crying out, and saying, Sirs, why do ye these things? We also are men of like passions with you, and preach unto you that ye should turn from these vanities unto the living God, which made heaven and earth, and the sea, and all things that are therein: who in times past suffer nations to walk in their own ways.

Nevertheless he left not himself without witness, in that he did good, and gave us rain from heaven, and fruitful seasons, filling our hearts with food and gladness. And with these sayings scarce restrained they the people, that they had not done sacrifice unto them.

The Purpose of Preaching

When Paul was preaching he observed a man in the audience who had been born a cripple. He saw something in his face that no one else saw: the look of faith that he could be healed. In the middle of his sermon he laid aside what he had prepared to say and, focusing his eyes upon this man, feeling his faith, said in a loud voice, "Stand on your feet." The man leaped and walked.

God is not pleased with the special ways we cut and dry our spiritual services, where every word has to be in place just like the hairs on our head. God wants Holy Spirit interruptions. He wants us to be prepared for the unscheduled acts of the Holy Spirit to break in upon our prescribed ceremonies at any time God chooses. That requires a listening heart, a sensitive spirit, and a sincere faith that God is in the "now," that He is more concerned about that crippled person out there or any person with a need than He is anything else. That is the purpose of the gospel being preached, for it is the power of God unto salvation.

That is what I believe is beginning to happen again in our time. That is the thrust of the whole charismatic movement of the Holy Spirit moving in tens of thousands of lives, invading nearly every church denomination in the world.

There is a new hope. People everywhere are feeling a fresh breeze of the Spirit of God blowing in the world today. And I, Oral Roberts, am proud to be a part of it.

When this healing miracle happened, the people thought Paul and Barnabas were almost divine beings. They rushed up to make sacrifice to them, which Paul said they must not do. Then he began to tell how God had always had a witness or remnant of His people in the world, that it was God who had given people life and the desire to seek Him. With this type of preaching he calmed them down and eventually turned their minds to God.

Acts 14:19
> And there came thither certain Jews from Antioch and Iconium, who persuaded the people, and, having stoned Paul, drew him out of the city, supposing he had been dead.

Miracles Stir Opposition

When the Holy Spirit does a mighty miracle through one of God's servants, there is a great stir about it. There is always somebody sent from the devil to try to stop it or even to take the person's life. Now they actually stoned Paul and dragged him outside the city to die.

Acts 14:20-22

Howbeit, as the disciples stood round about him, he rose up, and came into the city: and the next day he departed with Barnabas to Derbe. And when they had preached the gospel to that city, and had taught many, they returned again to Lystra, and to Iconium and Antioch, confirming the souls of the disciples, and exhorting them to continue in the faith, and that we must through much tribulation enter into the kingdom of God.

Opposition Forces Decision

The disciples gathered around him and began to unite in their faith in his behalf and, lo and behold, Paul got up off the ground as life came back into his being. He went on preaching as though nothing had ever happened. As they went to other towns preaching, Paul said, "Let us go back. Let us go back where they stoned me," and they returned again. At the end of the message he exhorted the new converts to be strong in the faith of God. He told them that all Christians go through much tribulation to enter into the fullness of the kingdom of God. We have got to understand this.

There are tribulations, persecutions, and sufferings for the name of Jesus. Some of us have already been through things that we do not even want to discuss because we have been so near death at times because of the preaching of the gospel and our prayers for the healing of the sick. The more we preach the gospel with faith, causing God to confirm His Word with signs and miracles following, the more the devil's crowd will be stirred up.

It is through the very opposition of the devil that we will come to a decision of whether we will serve God or not. If we really are sincere and mean our serving of God, those tribulations will only be stepping stones through which we derive a greater anointing of God upon us.

Acts 14:23-26

And when they had ordained them elders in every church, and had prayed with fasting, they commended them to the Lord, on whom they believed. And after they had passed throughout Pisidia, they came to Pamphylia.

> And when they had preached the word in Perga, they went down to Attalia: and thence sailed to Antioch, from whence they had been recommended to the grace of God for the work which they fulfilled.

Now Paul and Barnabas returned to home base.

Acts 14:27,28

> And when they were come, and had gathered the church together, they rehearsed all that God had done with them, and how he had opened the door of faith unto the Gentiles. And there they abode long time with the disciples.

We Gentiles here in America and other places have not often thought of what men like Paul and Barnabas went through. Such faith they released from their hearts in order to open the door of faith to us as well as to the Jews!

We must remember God's servants then and in every generation who risked their lives in order to open the kingdom of God to people like us who are just waiting for the opportunity to hear and receive the gospel.

Acts 15:1,2

> And certain men which came down from Judaea taught the brethren, and said, Except ye be circumcised after the manner of Moses, ye cannot be saved.
>
> When therefore Paul and Barnabas had no small dissension and disputation with them, they determined that Paul and Barnabas, and certain other of them, should go up to Jerusalem unto the apostles and elders about this question.

The Circumcision Issue

Certain Jewish believers taught that in order to be Christian you had to be circumcised according to the law of Moses. The Jewish Christians hung onto that year after year, but you have to understand their background. This had been passed on to them generation after generation, hundreds and hundreds of times it had been taught them. It was difficult for them to turn loose of the past traditions and enter into the new covenant brought by Jesus Christ. Paul and Barnabas, who had gone out among the Gentiles and had seen God save them without any observance of the law of Moses, began to dispute with these people. They began to tell them they had no right to introduce something which had already been fulfilled by Christ at Calvary, in

His resurrection, and through sending the Holy Spirit. They decided then to send Paul and Barnabas up to Jerusalem to deal directly with the apostles and elders about this serious question.

Acts 15:3
> And being brought on their way by the church, they passed through Phenice and Samaria, declaring the conversion of the Gentiles: and they caused great joy unto all the brethren.

All genuine Christians are deeply affected when they hear of another soul being saved. It brings a vicarious joy into their hearts that someone else too has received Christ as they have. When we hear of people finding Christ among those who are not members of our particular denomination, the devil will often try to make us say, "But they do not belong to our church." Therefore, we do not get excited about it.

The true Church rises above all human denominations. It is a universal Body of Christ. When we are born into the kingdom of God we are not to think of it as being born into my denomination or yours. We are born into the living organism of Christ himself.

Acts 15:4-7
> And when they were come to Jerusalem, they were received of the church, and of the apostles and elders, and they declared all things that God had done with them. But there rose up certain of the sect of the Pharisees which believed, saying, That it was needful to circumcise them, and to command them to keep the law of Moses.
>
> And the apostles and elders came together for to consider of this matter. And when there had been much disputing, Peter rose up, and said unto them, Men and brethren, ye know how that a good while ago God made choice among us, that the Gentiles by my mouth should hear the word of the gospel, and believe.

Controversy Over Gentiles

Peter is reminding them that God had chosen him to go to the house of Cornelius and be the first one to preach the gospel of Christ to the Gentiles. Let us not forget that we have just read in Acts 14:27 where God had caused Paul to open the door of faith unto the Gentiles. One is not contrary to the other. Peter had done it officially by going to this Gentile's house in Caesarea. But Paul had done it in an international way — going across national boundaries, going into different continents in his missionary journeys and opening the door of faith to the Gentiles as a whole group of people rather than just a beginning such as Peter had made at the house of Cornelius.

Paul, from the very acceptance of himself into the kingdom of God, had been told by the Lord that he had been called to suffer great things and to take the gospel to the Gentiles. Paul's whole mind opened up like a flower to the Gentile world. Peter had come out of a prescribed, narrow group of people, the Jewish people who followed the law of Moses. While he had the faith to obey God to go to a Gentile's house and open the kingdom to them, his mind was not a growing mind at that time like Paul's. In the Christian faith there is some mind-growing as well as soul-growing.

Acts 15:8-12

> And God, which knoweth the hearts, bare them witness, giving them the Holy Ghost, even as he did unto us; And put no difference between us and them, purifying their hearts by faith.
>
> Now therefore why tempt ye God, to put a yoke upon the neck of the disciples, which neither our fathers nor we were able to bear? But we believe that through the grace of the Lord Jesus Christ we shall be saved, even as they.
>
> Then all the multitude kept silence, and gave audience to Barnabas and Paul, declaring what miracles and wonders God had wrought among the Gentiles by them.

Miraculous Power

Here are apostles, evangelists, missionaries. Barnabas and Paul began their account of their ministry among the Gentiles by pointing up the miracles and the wonders that God had done through them. The Christian faith is a miraculous undertaking of God in the world. It is not just an organization or an institution, it is a living organism. It comes out of the very heart of God, from the supernatural invading the natural world. We are so supernaturally natural and naturally supernatural that it is hard to tell those two apart in us when we truly become Christian, Christlike, and follow in the footsteps of our Lord.

Let it be known that Oral Roberts expects miracles to happen to people. I am a living example of the miraculous healing power of God in my body and through me to hundreds of thousands of people throughout the earth. My ministry today is seeing more miracles and wonders than ever before and the sun seldom sets upon the graduates of Oral Roberts University and other people who have been touched by this ministry as they are laboring for Christ all over the earth — their teaching, their testifying, and their work being confirmed with miracles and wonders of our Lord Jesus Christ. I am grateful to say that I am thrilled to be a Christian. Before I am a minister, before I am an apostle, an evangelist of healing, before all that, I am a Christian and I believe in the miracle-working power of our Savior.

Acts 15:13-31

And after they had held their peace, James answered, saying, Men and brethren, hearken unto me: Simeon hath declared how God at the first did visit the Gentiles, to take out of them a people for his name. And to this agree the words of the prophets; as it is written, After this I will return, and will build again the tabernacle of David, which is fallen down; and I will build again the ruins thereof, and I will set it up: that the residue of men might seek after the Lord, and all the Gentiles, upon whom my name is called, saith the Lord, who doeth all these things.

Known unto God are all his works from the beginning of the world.

Wherefore my sentence is, that we trouble not them, which from among the Gentiles are turned to God: but that we write unto them, that they abstain from pollutions of idols, and from fornication, and from things strangled, and from blood. For Moses of old time hath in every city them that preach him, being read in the synagogues every sabbath day. Then pleased it the apostles and elders, with the whole church, to send chosen men of their own company to Antioch with Paul and Barnabas: namely, Judas surnamed Barsabas, and Silas, chief men among the brethren: and they wrote letters by them after this manner; The apostles and elders and brethren send greeting unto the brethren which are of the Gentiles in Antioch and Syria and Cilicia. Forasmuch as we have heard, that certain which went out from us have troubled you with words, subverting your souls, saying, Ye must be circumcised, and keep the law: to whom we gave no such commandment: it seemed good unto us, being assembled with one accord, to send chosen men unto you with our beloved Barnabas and Paul, men that have hazarded their lives for the name of our Lord Jesus Christ. We have sent therefore Judas and Silas, who shall also tell you the same things by mouth.

For it seemed good to the Holy Ghost, and to us, to lay upon you no greater burden than these necessary things; that ye abstain from meats offered to idols, and from blood, and from things strangled, and from fornication: from which if ye keep yourselves, ye shall do well. Fare ye well.

So when they were dismissed, they came to Antioch: and when they had gathered the multitude together, they delivered the epistle:

which when they had read, they rejoiced for the consolation.

James, the brother of our Lord, was an apostle and was the leader of the apostles and elders in the church in Jerusalem. He said, "We are going to write the Gentiles a letter for you to read to them." In that letter, it was stated that they were to abstain from pollution of idols. The world was a worshiper of idols in those days. Their lives were polluted because of it. One of the things the Jewish people were concerned about was that there should be no idols. God was a spirit and any worship of idols was a violation of the spirit of God. Another was immorality. The letter told the people to abstain from immorality, from things strangled, and from blood. These were not to be used as food, for life is in the blood. They referred to Leviticus 17:11. These were given, not as conditions for the salvation of the Gentiles, but as a matter of fellowship among them. It is very important that we Gentiles understand that, because our salvation is through the shed blood of Jesus Christ and His resurrection.

Acts 15:32-35

> And Judas and Silas, being prophets also themselves, exhorted the brethren with many words, and confirmed them. And after they had tarried there a space, they were let go in peace from the brethren unto the apostles. Notwithstanding it pleased Silas to abide there still. Paul also and Barnabas continued in Antioch, teaching and preaching the word of the Lord, with many others also.

Second Journey Begins

Now as we read Verse 36, I want you to notice the beginning of the second missionary journey of Paul to Europe and to other places.

Acts 15:36-41

> And some days after Paul said unto Barnabas, Let us go again and visit our brethren in every city where we have preached the word of the Lord, and see how they do. And Barnabas determined to take with them John, whose surname was Mark. But Paul thought not good to take him with them, who departed from them from Pamphylia, and went not with them to the work. And the contention was so sharp between them, that they departed asunder one from the other: and so Barnabas took Mark, and sailed unto Cyprus; and Paul chose Silas, and departed, being recommended by the brethren unto the grace of God. And he went through Syria and Cilicia, confirming the churches.

Seek Blessings in Differences

Here we have one of the most serious fallings-out between two believers in the Bible. It shows the humanness of people who believe on the Lord. Paul and Barnabas loved each other, had traveled with each other, had opened the gospel to the whole Gentile world in effect. And now, as they begin their second missionary journey, Paul does not want to take the kinsman of Barnabas, young John Mark, who back in the thirteenth chapter of Acts had left them. But Barnabas wants him to join the second missionary journey. No doubt Barnabas wanted to give him a second chance.

Things are not clear-cut in every issue. Not everything is black or white; there is usually a lot of gray in between. That is true today when people fall out as believers. Paul knew the rough road that lay ahead of them in this second missionary journey and he wanted someone he could depend on. So he chose Silas. But Barnabas' love held onto young John Mark. Barnabas was a good man, he loved the Lord, he loved people. Barnabas took Mark and went on by ship to Cyprus to carry on God's work. But Paul chose Silas and went overland, beginning his second missionary journey.

Let us not get overly upset because there are dissensions among us. Maybe God wanted Barnabas to take Mark, because later on, Paul was to say, "Bring Mark, for he is profitable to me for the gospel." Maybe they both were right. Barnabas held onto Mark and somehow got him straightened out with the help of the Lord. Paul's making a sharp distinction here may have contributed to waking up young John Mark so it turned out right in the end. If we have a falling-out, let us not fall out forever. Let us just have our falling-out and say, "God, we love each other and if we have to part for awhile, maybe it is for a reason greater than we understand now."

Act 16:1-3

> Then came he to Derbe and Lystra: and, behold, a certain disciple was there, named Timotheus, the son of a certain woman, which was a Jewess, and believed; but his father was a Greek: which was well reported of by the brethren that were at Lystra and Iconium. Him would Paul have to go forth with him; and took and circumcised him because of the Jews which were in those quarters: for they knew all that his father was a Greek.

Led of God

I think it is well to point out that as an act of expediency, Paul had Timothy circumcised — not for religious reasons but because of the Jews, who knew that Timothy's father was a Greek. Now, we will learn in 1 Corinthians 9:22 that Paul said, "I am made all things to all men, that I might by all means save some." There were certain things Paul felt led of God to do because it was expedient for him in order to get the gospel across to the people. When the motive is right and you are following a principle, it is proper to do exactly as Paul did.

Let me give you a personal example in my ministry. When the Lord led us to establish Oral Roberts University in 1965, we established an honor code that caused the students to dress in a special way. The young men were to wear shirts and ties in class, in the library, and at meals, and the young women were to wear skirts rather than slacks. There was nothing religious about this because there is nothing wrong in dressing casually, but we were led to do that as part of the seriousness of our intent. One thing it has done through all these years is to call to the attention of the Oral Roberts University student body that the way they dress is important. It speaks of the intent of their heart, of the seriousness of purpose, and they become quite well adjusted to it. As a result, the visitors to the campus are always impressed by the decorum, by the way the students dress, their friendly attitude, and the seriousness of their intentions as students. In other words, for expediency's sake, to get across our testimony, we have the dress code at Oral Roberts University.

Acts 16:4-7

> And as they went through the cities, they delivered them the decrees for to keep, that were ordained of the apostles and elders which were at Jerusalem. And so were the churches established in the faith, and increased in number daily.
>
> Now when they had gone throughout Phrygia and the region of Galatia, and were forbidden of the Holy Ghost to preach the word in Asia, after they were come to Mysia, they assayed to go into Bithynia: but the Spirit suffered them not.

Diverted From Asia

These were the northern and western parts of Asia. For reasons known to the Holy Spirit, He would not permit Paul and his evangelistic and missionary team to go into those parts of Asia. It is a fact today that Asia is still one of the most difficult fields on earth for the gospel.

Acts 16:8,9
> And they passing by Mysia came down to Troas. And a vision appeared to Paul in the night; there stood a man of Macedonia, and prayed him, saying, Come over into Macedonia, and help us.

Europe Opens

When God closes one door, look for Him to open another.

Acts 16:10
> And after he had seen the vision, immediately we endeavored to go into Macedonia, assuredly gathering that the Lord had called us for to preach the gospel unto them.

Luke Joins Paul

The little word "we" is Luke's modest way of indicating that he had joined Paul's group. He said immediately "we" endeavored to go into Macedonia. Luke is a man who kept in the background — very careful not to impose himself into the limelight.

Acts 16:11,12
> Therefore loosing from Troas, we came with a straight course to Samothracia, and the next day to Neapolis; and from thence to Philippi, which is the chief city of that part of Macedonia, and a colony: and we were in that city abiding certain days.

The ministry of Paul had to do mostly with the great cities of the Roman Empire, especially the great seaport cities. This is important to understand, for Paul wanted to go to the cities of chief influence in the Roman Empire so the Word of God he preached could be carried by word of mouth or by people traveling on the high seas or overland. Paul used a lot of common sense to get the gospel out.

Acts 16:13-21
> And on the sabbath we went out of the city by a river side, where prayer was wont to be made; and we sat down, and spake unto the women which resorted thither. And a certain woman named Lydia, a seller of purple, of the city of Thyatira, which worshipped God, heard us: whose heart the Lord opened, that she attended unto the things which were spoken of Paul. And when she was baptized, and her household, she besought us, saying, If ye have judged me to be faithful

to the Lord, come into my house, and abide there. And she constrained us. And it came to pass, as we went to prayer, a certain damsel possessed with a spirit of divination met us, which brought her masters much gain by soothsaying:

The same followed Paul and us, and cried, saying, These men are the servants of the most high God, which shew unto us the way of salvation. And this did she many days. But Paul, being grieved, turned and said to the spirit, I command thee in the name of Jesus Christ to come out of her. And he came out the same hour. And when her masters saw that the hope of their gains was gone, they caught Paul and Silas, and drew them into the marketplace unto the rulers. And brought them to the magistrates, saying, These men, being Jews, do exceedingly trouble our city, and teach customs, which are not lawful for us to receive, neither to observe, being Romans.

Now, what the demon was trying to do was to tell the people of Philippi that the work of Paul was of the devil, was of demon worship, that he was actually allied with him. Paul's team was trying to show that the demon's work was based on magic. Paul was grieved over it, and using the name of Jesus he cast that demon spirit out of the girl and through it said to the people that the gospel of Jesus Christ is not allied with demons or with magic. It is the supreme power of God to set men and women free.

When the girl was delivered from demons she could not tell any fortunes and her masters got angry because they lost their source of money. They brought Paul and Silas and the others into court and declared that, being Jews, they troubled the city by teaching customs which were not lawful in the eyes of Rome. That meant Romans were very jealous about their national worship of Caesar. They would even banish the Jews from Rome. They took great care that no one would introduce a new religion in the Roman Empire. This was the charge against Paul.

Acts 16:22-34

And the multitude rose up together against them: and the magistrates rent off their clothes, and commanded to beat them. And when they had laid many stripes upon them, they cast them into prison, charging the jailor to keep them safely: who, having received such a charge, thrust them into the inner prison, and made their feet fast in the stocks.

And at midnight Paul and Silas prayed, and sang praises unto God: and the prisoners heard them. And suddenly there was a great earthquake, so that the foundations of the prison were shaken: and immediately all the doors were opened, and every one's bands were loosed. And the keeper of the prison awaking out of his sleep, and seeing the prison doors open, drew out his sword, and would have killed himself, supposing that the prisoners had been fled. But Paul cried with a loud voice, saying, Do thyself no harm: for we are all here. Then he called for a light, and sprang in, and came trembling, and fell down before Paul and Silas, and brought them out, and said, Sirs, what must I do to be saved?

And they said, Believe on the Lord Jesus Christ, and thou shalt be saved, and thy house. And they spake unto him the word of the Lord, and to all that were in his house. And he took them the same hour of the night, and washed their stripes; and was baptized, he and all his, straightway. And when he had brought them into his house, he set meat before them, and rejoiced, believing in God with all his house.

It is something extraordinary to be treated as Paul and Silas were treated, and then right in the midst of it to pray and to sing unto God. That takes the power of the Holy Spirit. I am personally persuaded that they were praying in the Spirit and also singing in the Spirit as well as singing in their own language and praying in their own language. We do know that the prisoners heard them.

Whether the earthquake was sent of God or was a natural phenomenon we may not exactly know, but one thing we do know — it had a terrific impact upon everything in that prison. Suddenly the bonds were off the prisoners, including Paul and Silas. The jailer woke up and saw it. According to Roman law, if a warden lost his prisoners, he would be put to death. So he took out his sword, intending to ram it into his heart. Paul cried with a loud voice for him to do himself no harm because they were all still there. The gospel had a powerful effect upon the jailer. He began to tremble and said, "Sirs, what must I do to be saved?" They said, "Believe on the Lord Jesus Christ and thou shalt be saved and thy house."

There is a very important point to be made here. The point is that many believers use this scripture in a form too simplistic. Someone wants to be saved and they say, "Believe on the Lord Jesus Christ and thou shalt be saved." You cannot take just one scripture. The jailer was desperate, he was under heavy conviction, he was not ready to give mere mental assent; he knew his need. He was right on the verge of getting saved. He did not need a long sermon, so Paul quickly got to the point: "Brother, you are ready. Believe on the Lord Jesus Christ and you will be saved."

That does not always work with everybody because sometimes some have to be told to repent, some have to be told to confess their sins. It depends upon the situation. It is all right to use this phrase, "Believe on the Lord Jesus Christ and thou shalt be saved," providing that is precisely what the person needs to hear. But if the person is not that well prepared, he needs more.

Let's pray. I would like to pray with you about your family, your loved ones, and friends.

> *Heavenly Father, I pray for this friend who is praying with me now and for the members of the family — the dear loved ones. I pray for salvation of those who are lost, for healing of them who are sick, for the supplying of the needs of those who have financial needs and other types of needs. Dear friend, I pray for you and for your family, for all your house to be saved, to be healed, to be blessed and to serve the Lord with all your heart, knowing that God is going to give you victory through Jesus Christ. Amen and amen.*

Acts 16:35-39

> And when it was day, the magistrates sent the serjeants, saying, Let those men go. And the keeper of the prison told this saying to Paul, The magistrates have sent to let you go: now therefore depart, and go in peace. But Paul said unto them, They have beaten us openly uncondemned, being Romans, and have cast us into prison; and now do they thrust us out privily? nay verily; but let them come themselves and fetch us out.
>
> And the serjeants told these words unto the magistrates: and they feared, when they heard that they were Romans. And they came and besought them, and brought them out, and desired them to depart out of the city.

Two-World Christians

Paul was very wise here. For the sake of the gospel, he had permitted himself to be beaten. God used that and other parts of his witness to win the jailer to Christ and to open the way for a church to be established at Philippi. Paul was a Roman citizen. History has it that his father had done some extraordinary thing for the Roman Empire. The Romans had conferred Roman citizenship upon him and his descendants. The Romans were very careful with their laws. Their citizens were immune from being condemned without a trial and they had the right to appeal to Caesar. This was a very important part of Roman law. Paul and his team had been beaten by the Roman leaders and told to leave town. Paul refused. He wanted the big shots to come and face him, for he was a Roman citizen. That frightened them. When they visited Paul, they begged him to leave town.

Jesus said to make friends of the mammon of this world. I have served on the boards of great corporations and people have asked me why. Because I was invited and when I was, I was led of the Lord to do it, and it has been beneficial for the advancement of the cause of Christ. Sometimes it does not pay for Christians to withdraw into a little sect all by themselves and let the world go by. Sometimes they need to become a member of some part of the power structure. Not to be of it, but to be there as a witness for Christ. We Christians are somebody. We belong to Christ. We are citizens of heaven, but our feet are here on the earth, so we actually live in two worlds. There is a place in both of them for us for the glory of God.

Acts 16:40

And they went out of the prison, and entered into the house of Lydia: and when they had seen the brethren, they comforted them, and departed.

One of the most important things about this incident of Paul's experience in Philippi was that from the miraculous intervention of God, the church of Philippi was born. Many great things come out of our most desperate experiences for Christ.

Acts 17:1-6

Now when they had passed through Amphipolis and Apollonia, they came to Thessalonica, where was a synagogue of the Jews. And Paul, as his manner was, went in unto them, and three sabbath days reasoned with them out of the scriptures, opening and alleging, that Christ must needs have suffered, and risen again from the dead; and that this Jesus, whom I preach unto you, is Christ. And some of them believed, and consorted with Paul and Silas; and of the devout Greeks a great multitude, and of the chief women not a few.

But the Jews which believed not, moved with envy, took unto them certain lewd fellows of the baser sort, and gathered a company, and set all the city on an uproar, and assaulted the house of Jason, and sought to bring them out to the people. And when they found them not, they drew Jason and certain brethren unto the rulers of the city, crying, These that have turned the world upside down are come hither also; . . .

The World Turners

They got that wrong. What they should have said was, "These that have turned the world right-side up have come to town."

Acts 17:7-11

> Whom Jason hath received: and these all do contrary to the decrees of Caesar, saying that there is another king, one Jesus. And they troubled the people and the rulers of the city, when they heard these things. And when they had taken security of Jason, and of the other, they let them go.
>
> And the brethren immediately sent away Paul and Silas by night unto Berea: who coming thither went into the synagogue of the Jews. These were more noble than those in Thessalonica, in that they received the word with all readiness of mind, and searched the scriptures daily, whether these things were so.

The Berean Readers

When the people in Thessalonica turned against Paul, the brethren shipped him out at night to Berea. Those in Berea were more honorable because they opened their minds to Paul's preaching. They went right to the Word of God, the Old Testament Scriptures. Paul was the first to write any of the books of the New Testament. His preaching was based primarily upon the old covenant or Old Testament, those scriptures that prove that Jesus was Christ. While he was preaching, these people would turn to the scriptures that Paul was reciting. They kept their minds open.

Acts 17:12

> Therefore many of them believed; also of honourable women which were Greeks, and of men, not a few.

The Importance of Scripture

This is one of the great insights into the human mind. When the mind opens up so it can receive God's truth, the gospel gets in. Also, when people search the Scriptures, the Scriptures have a power of their own. When they do it like these Bereans did, daily, it is almost certain that they will believe on the Lord Jesus Christ. One of the reasons most people have not become Christians is because their minds are closed, they do not read the Bible, they do not read the Bible daily, and they do not search to see if the gospel is really true.

Acts 17:13-15

> But when the Jews of Thessalonica had knowledge that the word of God was preached of Paul at Berea, they came thither also, and stirred

up the people. And then immediately the brethren sent away Paul to go as it were to the sea: but Silas and Timotheus abode there still. And they that conducted Paul brought him unto Athens: and receiving a commandment unto Silas and Timotheus for to come to him with all speed, they departed.

The Influence of Athens

This is Paul's first visit to Athens. At that time Athens already had a history of at least 1,000 years. There democracy and modern medicine had been founded. This is where Socrates, Plato, and Aristotle became great leaders. Athens was the center of intellectual learning throughout the world. Although the Romans were then in power, the Greek language had become the language of commerce. The Greek culture had invaded the known world, and Athens was still a powerful intellectual city. It was a court city. It was a city where the great men of the world gathered to talk, to philosophize, to discuss the latest ideas, and to form opinions that would affect the whole world.

Acts 17:16-18

Now while Paul waited for them at Athens, his spirit was stirred in him, when he saw the city wholly given to idolatry. Therefore disputed he in the synagogue with the Jews, and with the devout persons, and in the market daily with them that met with him. Then certain philosophers of the Epicureans, and of the Stoicks, encountered him. And some said, What will this babbler say? other some, He seemeth to be a setter forth of strange gods: because he preached unto them Jesus, and the resurrection.

Athenian Leaders Curious

The Epicureans were materialists and their main pursuit in life was pleasure, while the Stoicks were philosophers of self-sufficiency. They were the people of the long face. They heard that Paul was in the city and they encountered him. Paul never watered down the gospel. Whether he was with the uneducated, the unlettered, the uncultured, or in the very center of world culture in Athens, his message was the same — Jesus and the resurrection.

Acts 17:19

And they took him, and brought him unto Areopagus, saying, May we know what this new doctrine, whereof thou speakest, is?

Athenian Belief

The Athenians believed in the immortality of the soul but not in the bodily resurrection or the judgment of God. They were inquiring about this new doctrine that Paul is advocating.

Acts 17:20-23

> For thou bringest certain strange things to our ears: we would know therefore what these things mean. (For all the Athenians and strangers which were there spent their time in nothing else, but either to tell, or to hear some new thing.)
>
> Then Paul stood in the midst of Mars' hill, and said, Ye men of Athens, I perceive that in all things ye are too superstitious. For as I passed by, and beheld your devotions . . .

(As he saw all the objects of idolatry which they worshiped)

Acts 17:23,24

> . . . I found an altar with this inscription, TO THE UNKNOWN GOD. Whom therefore ye ignorantly worship, him declare I unto you. God that made the world and all things therein, seeing that he is Lord of heaven and earth, dwelleth not in temples made with hands . . .

Scene On Mars Hill

As Paul stood there on Mars Hill, with the stunning Acropolis nearby supported by tremendous columns, really a wonder of the world, you can see him stretching out his arms and saying that God dwelleth not in temples made with hands.

Acts 17:25-31

> Neither is worshipped with men's hands, as though he needed any thing, seeing he giveth to all life, and breath, and all things; and hath made of one blood all nations of men for to dwell on all the face of the earth, and hath determined the times before appointed, and the bounds of their habitation; that they should seek the Lord, if haply they might feel after him, and find him, though he be not far from every one of us: for in him we live, and move, and have our being; as certain also of your own poets have said, For we are also his offspring.
>
> Forasmuch then as we are the offspring of God, we ought not to think that the Godhead is like unto gold, or silver, or stone, graven by art and man's device. And the times of this ignorance God winked

at; but now commandeth all men every where to repent: because he hath appointed a day, in the which he will judge the world in righteousness by that man whom he hath ordained; whereof he hath given assurance unto all men, in that he hath raised him from the dead.

Speak From Knowledge

If ever a man knew the Word of God, the philosophy of the world, and the history of man, it was Paul. If ever a man had studied and given himself to learn about God's world, the creatures whom He created, and the Scriptures which He gave for men to live by, it was Paul. It is absolutely imperative that we Christians study, that we know the Scriptures and know the history of the Scriptures. We also need to know something about the philosophies of today's world. We need to know the mores of the human race — particularly those different nations and peoples of the earth. We need to think as well as believe. Paul was able to take just four words, an inscription that said, "TO THE UNKNOWN GOD," and preach an entire sermon about Jesus and the resurrection. While he preached he connected that sermon with their background. Paul took these Athenians all the way back to Babel, where God appointed the places on earth for the different nations that came into being through the confusion of languages. He also said that God had determined the times that were appointed unto man as well as the bounds of their habitations. He made a very important statement that people should seek after God because God is not far from every one of us. It is in God that every human being lives and moves and has his or her being. Then Paul began to quote their poets who had said the same thing. He brought the message to a conclusion by saying because you are the offspring of God, you ought not to think the Godhead is like unto anything that human hands can make.

Talk about preaching the gospel and doing it upon the background of the understanding of the hearers — Paul did it! And I think we Christians ought to wake up and learn a little more, so when we declare Jesus, we can do it in terms people understand.

Acts 17:32-34

> And when they heard of the resurrection of the dead, some mocked: and others said, We will hear thee again of this matter. So Paul departed from among them. Howbeit certain men clave unto him, and believed: among the which was Dionysius the Areopagite, and a woman named Damaris, and others with them.

Athens, Corinth Contrast

As we go from Chapter 17 where Paul ministered last in Athens through Chapter 18 where Paul went to Corinth, it is like going from one end of the world to the other. Paul in Athens was dealing with the highest intellectual people on earth at that time. They were people with great needs and they were highly religious, but not with wisdom nor with recognition of their own personal need of God. It was a sort of fetish with them to be religious; they were not spiritual. They did not have God personally in their lives; rather, they depended upon their intellectual knowledge and pursuits of knowledge. Paul did not have great success there except to plant the seed of faith — the Word of God.

From Athens he went to the great seaport city of Corinth where the world's ships called. It was strategically located in the Roman Empire and people came to it from all over the world. There, Paul met a people completely unlike those in Athens. They were not intellectuals in any sense of the word. They were a rowdy, fighting bunch of people, sailors who knew nothing but the seaports of the world, clawing and fighting their way through the world. When their ships would dock in Corinth they would meet their match. Corinth was almost wholly given over to sexual immorality and other sins. For example, in their big temples it is said they had more than 1,000 priestesses who were literally prostitutes. The final act of worship was to commit sexual intercourse with these prostitutes. It was a city of the lowbrow, while Athens was filled with the highbrows of the world. It is interesting that some things never change. The intellectuals of the world today do not seem to feel their need of God, when their need of God is so great. The people who are really involved in sin and are not religious in any sense of the word are usually much more open to God. Perhaps this is because they recognize their very deep need of something they do not have.

Acts 18:1-10

> After these things Paul departed from Athens and came to Corinth; and found a certain Jew named Aquila, born in Pontus, lately come from Italy, with his wife Priscilla; (because that Claudius had commanded all Jews to depart from Rome:) and came unto them. And because he was of the same craft, he abode with them, and wrought: for by their occupation they were tentmakers.
>
> And he reasoned in the synagogue every sabbath, and persuaded the Jews and the Greeks. And when Silas and Timotheus were come from Macedonia, Paul was pressed in the spirit, and testified to the Jews that Jesus was Christ.

And when they opposed themselves, and blasphemed, he shook his raiment, and said unto them, Your blood be upon your own heads; I am clean: from henceforth I will go unto the Gentiles.

And he departed thence, and entered into a certain man's house, named Justus, one that worshipped God, whose house joined hard to the synagogue. And Crispus, the chief ruler of the synagogue, believed on the Lord with all his house; and many of the Corinthians hearing believed, and were baptized.

Then spake the Lord to Paul in the night by a vision, Be not afraid, but speak, and hold not thy peace: for I am with thee, and no man shall set on thee to hurt thee: for I have much people in this city.

This is a tremendous statement of our Lord on a personal basis to Paul. First He is saying that Corinth is a ripe field for the gospel of Jesus Christ. Next He is saying that Paul should not be afraid of this brawling seaport town. God was saying to Paul, "Do not be afraid. Go ahead and preach the gospel. Do not hold back. I am with you. No man is going to hurt you, for I have many people in this city for you to reach."

Acts 18:11-17

And he continued there a year and six months, teaching the word of God among them. And when Gallio was the deputy of Achaia, the Jews made insurrection with one accord against Paul, and brought him to the judgment seat, saying, This fellow persuadeth men to worship God contrary to the law. And when Paul was now about to open his mouth, Gallio said unto the Jews, If it were a matter of wrong or wicked lewdness, O ye Jews, reason would that I should bear with you: but if it be a question of words and names, and of your law, look ye to it; for I will be no judge of such matters.

And he drave them from the judgment seat. Then all the Greeks took Sosthenes, the chief ruler of the synagogue, and beat him before the judgment seat. And Gallio cared for none of those things.

Perverted Reasoning

The Jewish people who held to the law of Moses were now violating the very spirit of that law. It is an awful thing to have started right and end wrong, to have known God through His ways and then to have perverted those ways for one's own personal prejudice. Here we have a prime example of how our Savior came to fulfill the law and to put men back on the path of justice, mercy, truth, love, and caring for one another.

Acts 18:18

> And Paul after this tarried there yet a good while, and then took his leave of the brethren, and sailed thence into Syria, and with him Priscilla and Aquila; having shorn his head in Cenchrea: for he had a vow.

Paul's "Vow"

This may have been like the Nazarite vow that was mentioned in Numbers 6:1-21.

Acts 18:19-22

> And he came to Ephesus, and left them there: but he himself entered into the synagogue, and reasoned with the Jews. When they desired him to tarry longer time with them, he consented not; but bade them farewell, saying, I must by all means keep this feast that cometh in Jerusalem: but I will return again unto you, if God will.
>
> And he sailed from Ephesus. And when he had landed at Caesarea, and gone up, and saluted the church, he went down to Antioch.

Terminology Explained

The statement "He went down to Antioch" was a symbolic one because Jerusalem, the spiritual center of God's work in the world, was looked upon as the high city. Although it is only about 3,000 or so feet above sea level, it was spiritually high, so that the old saying was when one left Jerusalem he "went down." When he came to Jerusalem he came up. So Paul is said here to have gone down to Antioch.

Acts 18:23-28

> And after he had spent some time there, he departed, and went over all the country of Galatia and Phrygia in order, strengthening all the disciples. And a certain Jew named Apollos, born at Alexandria, an eloquent man, and mighty in the scriptures, came to Ephesus. This man was instructed in the way of the Lord; and being fervent in the spirit, he spake and taught diligently the things of the Lord, knowing only the baptism of John.
>
> And he began to speak boldly in the synagogue: whom when Aquila and Priscilla had heard, they took him unto them, and expounded unto him the way of God more perfectly.
>
> And when he was disposed to pass into Achaia, the brethren wrote,

exhorting the disciples to receive him: who, when he was come, helped them much which had believed through grace: for he mightily convinced the Jews, and that publickly, shewing by the scriptures that Jesus was Christ.

Apollos' Error Corrected

Apollos was a Jewish pilgrim who came to Jerusalem while John the Baptist was preaching. He heard John the Baptist say that the long-awaited Messiah whose coming was predicted by the Scriptures had arrived. Well, it struck a responsive chord in Apollos. Apollos had been born in Alexandria, Egypt, a great university city, one of the three largest cities in the Roman Empire. He was evidently a highly educated man, but also very learned in the Old Testament scriptures. When he had gone to Jerusalem and heard John the Baptist, he had openly received a new faith — that is, a faith that the Messiah was at last here and was about to be revealed. It set his soul on fire. It brought forth all of the knowledge he had of the Scriptures. Wherever he went he boldly spoke of the coming Messiah. But his own personal experience with God was through the baptism of John only.

When Aquila and Priscilla, now very experienced in the ways of the Lord Jesus Christ, heard Apollos speak, they were very moved. But they were led of God to take him aside and to explain to him more perfectly the way of God. Apollos apparently had not even known that Jesus had been crucified, buried, risen from the dead, ascended to the Father, had sent the Holy Spirit, and was now evangelizing the world through people like themselves, Paul, and others. Even if he may have heard about it, he had not personally entered into the conversion experience of the Lord Jesus Christ. So Aquila and Priscilla took him deeper into the Lord.

Acts 19:1,2

> And it came to pass, that, while Apollos was at Corinth, Paul having passed through the upper coasts came to Ephesus: and finding certain disciples, he said unto them, Have ye received the Holy Ghost since ye believed? . . .

Original Cited

The original is this: "He said unto them, 'Did you receive the Holy Spirit when you believed?'"

Acts 19:2-4

...And they said unto him, We have not so much as heard whether there be any Holy Ghost. And he said unto them, Unto what then were ye baptized? And they said, Unto John's baptism. Then said Paul, John verily baptized with a baptism of repentance, saying unto the people, that they should believe on him which should come after him, that is, on Christ Jesus.

Paul Explains Baptism

John the Baptist said there is coming one after him who shall baptize with the Holy Ghost and with fire. Doubtless Paul was explaining that to these people.

Acts 19:5

When they heard this, they were baptized in the name of the Lord Jesus.

Baptism Understood

This baptism was in order with Peter's statement in Acts 2:38, where he told the people to repent for the remission of sins by being baptized in the name of Jesus, who carried the fullness of the Godhead bodily within Him. Being baptized in the name of Jesus, they would receive the gift of the Holy Spirit. That was the general understanding of the people in the book of Acts who composed the early Church.

Acts 19:6,7

And when Paul had laid his hands upon them, the Holy Ghost came on them; and they spake with tongues, and prophesied. And all the men were about twelve.

Early Church Unity

The laying on of Paul's hands was necessary only because these people had to have some help. It is like priming the pump with old pump handles; you had to pour water into the pump in order to bring up more water. Paul was laying his hands upon them — in a sense, priming their pump — so they could release their faith and their prayer language — speak in tongues and prophesy, which would include interpreting their own tongue. There were about twelve of these men who were once followers of John the Baptist, who now were led by Paul into Jesus Christ.

There was no divisiveness about being baptized in Jesus' name, nor was there any in receiving the Holy Spirit at the same time and releasing their prayer language. We are used to divisiveness — some people are for a particular thing in Christ, another group is violently opposed to it, and the result is disunity among God's dear Christian people. I long for the unity of us in the faith, that whatever differences we have, we rise above them and get back to the order that is in the New Testament, particularly here in the book of Acts.

Acts 19:8-12

> And he went into the synagogue, and spake boldly for the space of three months, disputing and persuading the things concerning the kingdom of God. But when divers were hardened, and believed not, but spake evil of that way before the multitude, he departed from them, and separated the disciples, disputing daily in the school of one Tyrannus.
>
> And this continued by the space of two years; so that all they which dwelt in Asia heard the word of the Lord Jesus, both Jews and Greeks.
>
> And God wrought special miracles by the hands of Paul: so that from his body were brought unto the sick handkerchiefs or aprons, and the diseases departed from them, and the evil spirits went out of them.

Paul's Healing Cloths

In this verse one can see the dogged determination of the apostle Paul as he remembers the words of the Lord through Ananias who had led him to Christ. Apparently Paul had been prepared for what he was going through. Everywhere he went it seemed that people rose up to dispute with him, to slam him into jail, to deliberately misunderstand him, to criticize him, or to make life uncomfortable and dangerous for him. But he went right on because Jesus was real in his life.

Through his obedience, which like his Master Jesus he had learned from the things he suffered, he reached the place in the Lord where God did special miracles by his hands. Some of those special miracles were that his body was so filled with the Holy Spirit and anointed by Jesus that pieces of cloth such as handkerchiefs and aprons were brought from his body. His physical body was indwelt by the Holy Spirit to the point where people who were diseased and even those who were demon possessed, who touched these cloths, were healed.

There have been more people healed through this one particular instrument — prayer handkerchiefs that I use from time to time every several months — than through almost anything that God has ever used in my ministry. The misunderstanding has been exceptionally bad, but the glory of it is that people get deliverance. Remember, it is not we who are instruments who are so important, it is the Lord Jesus Christ who does the special miracles through us.

Acts 19:13-20

Then certain of the vagabond Jews, exorcists, took upon them to call over them which had evil spirits the name of the Lord Jesus, saying, We adjure you by Jesus whom Paul preacheth. And there were seven sons of one Sceva, a Jew, and chief of the priests, which did so. And the evil spirit answered and said, Jesus I know, and Paul I know; but who are ye? And the man in whom the evil spirit was leaped on them, and overcame them, and prevailed against them, so that they fled out of that house naked and wounded.

And this was known to all the Jews and Greeks also dwelling at Ephesus; and fear fell on them all, and the name of the Lord Jesus was magnified. And many that believed came, and confessed, and shewed their deeds. Many of them also which used curious arts brought their books together, and burned them before all men; and they counted the price of them, and found it fifty thousand pieces of silver. So mightily grew the word of God and prevailed.

Jesus Prevails

When these particular Jews, who did not know Jesus but who wanted the power of Jesus that was in Paul's life, saw that through Paul, Jesus was casting out demons, seven sons of Sceva decided they would adjure by Jesus whom Paul preached that the demons would leave people. When they did this they were in for a shock. The evil spirit talked to them!

You may recall that a demon, an evil spirit, is the disembodiment of a former angel — one of those who fell with Lucifer the great archangel.

This demon is a personality, a living being. He said, "Jesus I know, and Paul I know, but who in the world are you?" This man who had the evil spirit attacked these seven sons of the chief priest. He fought them until he tore their clothes off. They ran out of the house naked and bruised. When this was spread abroad it really confirmed the gospel that Paul was preaching. A great fear fell upon the people

116

and a large number began to confess their sins, show their deeds, turn away from their so-called magic, and believe on Jesus Christ as their personal Savior.

When the gospel of Jesus Christ prevails upon a people, it is through a supernatural intervention of the Holy Spirit. It is the name of Jesus being lifted up, the name that is above everything that is named in this world and the world to come. The name of Jesus was against that demon. He is against demons today. His name is above these demons' names. This is what God is calling His people, His believers, His Church, the Body of Christ, back to, so that once again the Word of God will mightily grow and prevail.

Acts 19:21
> After these things were ended, Paul purposed in the spirit, . . .

"In the Spirit"

When you come across that phrase, "in the Spirit," it usually refers to praying in the Spirit, or praying in tongues.

Acts 19:21
> . . . when he had passed through Macedonia and Achaia, to go to Jerusalem, saying, After I have been there, I must also see Rome.

Rome was always on Paul's mind. It was the capital city of the Roman Empire. It was where the world came from north, south, east, and west. Caesar lived there. Paul's heart now is aching and he has determined by the Spirit of God, by praying in the Spirit, that once he had gone to Jerusalem, he intended also to see Rome.

Acts 19:22-41
> So he sent into Macedonia two of them that ministered unto him, Timotheus and Erastus; but he himself stayed in Asia for a season. And the same time there arose no small stir about that way. For a certain man named Demetrius, a silversmith, which made silver shrines for Diana, brought no small gain unto the craftsmen; whom he called together with the workmen of like occupation, and said, Sirs, ye know that by this craft we have our wealth. Moreover ye see and hear, that not alone at Ephesus, but almost throughout all Asia, this Paul hath persuaded and turned away much people, saying that they be no gods, which are made with hands: so that not only this our craft is in danger to be set at nought; but also that the temple of the great goddess Diana should be despised, and her magnificence

117

should be destroyed, whom all Asia and the world worshippeth.

And when they heard these sayings, they were full of wrath, and cried out, saying, Great is Diana of the Ephesians. And the whole city was filled with confusion: and having caught Gaius and Aristarchus, men of Macedonia, Paul's companions in travel, they rushed with one accord into the theatre. And when Paul would have entered in unto the people, the disciples suffered him not. And certain of the chief of Asia, which were his friends, sent unto him, desiring him that he would not adventure himself into the theatre. Some therefore cried one thing, and some another: for the assembly was confused; and the more part knew not wherefore they were come together. And they drew Alexander out of the multitude, the Jews putting him forward. And Alexander beckoned with the hand, and would have made his defence unto the people. But when they knew that he was a Jew, all with one voice about the space of two hours cried out, Great is Diana of the Ephesians.

And when the townclerk had appeased the people, he said, Ye men of Ephesus, what man is there that knoweth not how that the city of the Ephesians is a worshipper of the great goddess Diana, and of the image which fell down from Jupiter? Seeing then that these things cannot be spoken against, ye ought to be quiet, and to do nothing rashly. For ye have brought hither these men, which are neither robbers of churches, nor yet blasphemers of your goddess. Wherefore if Demetrius, and the craftsmen which are with him, have a matter against any man, the law is open, and there are deputies: let them implead one another. But if ye enquire any thing concerning other matters, it shall be determined in a lawful assembly. For we are in danger to be called in question for this day's uproar, there being no cause whereby we may give an account of this concourse. And when he had thus spoken, he dismissed the assembly.

Persecution Continues Today

Paul was not preaching against Diana of the Ephesians. He was preaching Jesus Christ. He was expanding the Word of God.

Paul was not singling out certain sins or certain things of practice that the Ephesians were doing or even their great goddess Diana. He was simply giving the positive message of Jesus Christ. That is what upset the whole city, causing the leader of the silversmiths, Demetrius, to call his fellow craftsmen together and to point out to them that their occupation was in danger. The gospel was changing the thinking of the people toward these dead gods. They were turning toward the living God. When the silversmiths found they could not get their hands on the leader, the Apostle Paul, they seized other followers of Jesus Christ who were members of Paul's team.

If we in the Church of our Lord Jesus today would preach the Word of God, lifting up Jesus of Nazareth as the Son of God, we would not have to specify certain sins. God's power would sweep through the hearts of men and change their lives and they would begin to close down the pornographic houses, the houses of prostitution, the dens of merchandise that Jesus talked about when He cleansed the temple in Jerusalem. The real way to go is to preach Christ, and Christ then convicts people of sin, specific sins, and causes them to lay them aside.

The silversmiths incited a great riot in the city. The people thronged the squares of the city and eventually entered the theater, which was a public meeting place. When Paul saw the theater, he wanted to enter but wiser heads prevailed and urged him to stay out. Meanwhile, Demetrius and the others were stirring up the people and they were going wild. The town clerk, an agent of Rome, heard about it. He rushed in, demanded silence, and said, "Ye men of Ephesus, what in the world are you doing? If you have an issue of law, bring it to the court. We will see that the issue is resolved according to the laws of Rome. Meanwhile, you leave these men alone. They are not robbers of your goddess. They are merely lifting up the one they believe in. Therefore, I am going to dissolve this assembly, for we are in danger of being called into question by Rome itself." Then he dismissed the crowd.

This reminds me of when I was in Australia in the late 1950's. We had 10,000 people the first night. Hundreds of people were converted, and the next night the crowd was even larger. But the third night there was an uproar of the people and they infiltrated the tent, running up and down the aisles, shouting obscenities, coming up and shaking their fists in my face as I preached and spitting on me. They were stopping the people as they came forward to accept Christ, and suddenly, we almost had a riot on our hands. So we closed the service early to prevent bloodshed.

The following night one of the leaders of the city, an elected official, was called upon to appear. He stood on the platform with me and asked me all about myself: what universities I had attended; was I ordained to preach the gospel; why was I in Australia? I answered his questions in a positive manner and when he finished he said, "There is nothing wrong here. Australia is a law-abiding country. These people have the right to preach the gospel." We thought everything would be settled. But after the service was over, there was a death threat upon my life, and we were fortunate to get safely out of the place.

119

I went ahead to my room and went to sleep. The next morning we discovered that our people had received news that the tent was going to be destroyed. When I awakened, they had the big tent dismantled and on a ship headed for America.

I am only sharing this to indicate that things we are reading about in Acts, Chapter 19, did not stop there. The main thing we have to do is to lift up Jesus. If they do not receive us in one place, we go to another place, exactly as Paul did here. When they no longer received him in Ephesus, then he went to the next place and continued his ministry. We do not stop just because we are persecuted. We continue lifting up our Savior, the Lord Jesus Christ.

Acts 20:1-7

And after the uproar was ceased, Paul called unto him the disciples, and embraced them, and departed for to go into Macedonia. And when he had gone over those parts, and had given them much exhortation, he came into Greece, and there abode three months.

And when the Jews laid wait for him, as he was about to sail into Syria, he purposed to return through Macedonia. And there accompanied him into Asia Sopater of Berea; and of the Thessalonians, Aristarchus and Secundus; and Gaius of Derbe, and Timotheus; and of Asia, Tychicus and Trophimus. These going before tarried for us at Troas.

And we sailed away from Philippi after the days of unleavened bread, and came unto them to Troas in five days; where we abode seven days. And upon the first day of the week, when the disciples came together to break bread, Paul preached unto them, ready to depart on the morrow; and continued his speech until midnight.

Preaching, Communion Combined

Here we have the best combination that is in the gospel. We have the breaking of bread of the Holy Communion and we have the man of God preaching the gospel in conjunction with it. Now, that is a very important point. Some in the Church make preaching central. Some in the Christian Church make the Holy Communion, or mass, central. But neither is true in the early Church. Both have their part and place.

Acts 20:8-12

And there were many lights in the upper chamber, where they were gathered together. And there sat in a window a certain young man named Eutychus, being fallen into a deep sleep: and as Paul was long

120

preaching, he sunk down with sleep, and fell down from the third loft, and was taken up dead.

And Paul went down, and fell on him, and embracing him said, Trouble not yourselves; for his life is in him. When he therefore was come up again, and had broken bread, and eaten, and talked a long while, even till break of day, so he departed. And they brought the young man alive, and were not a little comforted.

Miracles in Order

Miracles were a common occurrence in Paul's day. I think that miracles should be the order of the day in our time because we, too, are lifting up the name of Jesus.

After the experience of the young man being restored to life, the service resumed. Again they had Holy Communion; again Paul preached, only this time until the sun came up. Then he went on his way. And the young man being restored was brought back to them, and everybody was comforted.

Acts 20:13-16

And we went before to ship, and sailed unto Assos, there intending to take in Paul: for so had he appointed, minding himself to go afoot. And when he met with us at Assos, we took him in, and came to Mitylene. And we sailed thence, and came the next day over against Chios; and the next day we arrived at Samos, and tarried at Trogyllium; and the next day we came to Miletus. For Paul had determined to sail by Ephesus, because he would not spend the time in Asia: for he hasted, if it were possible for him, to be at Jerusalem the day of Pentecost.

Holy Spirit Day Named

This is the first time since the day of Pentecost that the day of Pentecost is mentioned. Apparently, it was a day now connected with the Holy Spirit as well as the longtime feast known by that name.

Acts 20:17-21

And from Miletus he sent to Ephesus, and called the elders of the church. And when they were come to him, he said unto them, Ye know, from the first day that I came into Asia, after what manner I have been with you at all seasons, serving the Lord with all humility of mind, and with many tears, and temptations, which befell me by the lying in wait of the Jews: and how I kept back nothing that was profitable unto you, but have shewed you, and have taught you publickly, and from house to house, testifying both to the Jews, and also to the Greeks, repentance toward God, and faith toward our Lord Jesus Christ.

Paul Multitalented

Paul not only preached publicly but also from house to house. It means a lot to me as I hear Paul talking about going from house to house. He was an evangelist, apostle, a prophet, a teacher. There are some places he even pastored. He carried on with the five major callings of the ministry that God has set in the Church.

Acts 20:22-34

And now, behold, I go bound in the spirit unto Jerusalem, not knowing the things that shall befall me there: save that the Holy Ghost witnesseth in every city, saying that bonds and afflictions abide me. But none of these things move me, neither count I my life dear unto myself, so that I might finish my course with joy, and the ministry, which I have received of the Lord Jesus, to testify the gospel of the grace of God. And now, behold, I know that ye all, among whom I have gone preaching the kingdom of God, shall see my face no more. Wherefore I take you to record this day, that I am pure from the blood of all men. For I have not shunned to declare unto you all the counsel of God.

Take heed therefore unto yourselves, and to all the flock, over the which the Holy Ghost hath made you overseers, to feed the church of God, which he hath purchased with his own blood. For I know this, that after my departing shall grievous wolves enter in among you, not sparing the flock. Also of your own selves shall men arise, speaking perverse things, to draw away disciples after them. Therefore watch, and remember, that by the space of three years I ceased not to warn every one night and day with tears. And now, brethren, I commend you to God, and to the word of his grace, which is able to build you up, and to give you an inheritance among all them which are sanctified.

I have coveted no man's silver, or gold, or apparel. Yea, ye yourselves know, that these hands have ministered unto my necessities, and to them that were with me.

This is one of the most touching scenes of a man of God in the entire New Testament. Ephesus had been a city of great importance in the life of the gospel. It was one of the great Roman cities that

Paul went to with his message. There he had had tremendous success in turning men and women to Christ, but because of it, great riots ripped the town apart. Now Paul is on his way to Jerusalem to keep the day of Pentecost, and he calls the people of Ephesus down to a little seaport town called Miletus. He did not want to go back into Ephesus for fear of another riot.

The elders came down to him, to Miletus, and he embraced them and began to tell them (much as Jesus Christ had done when He had come to the end of His earthly life) he must go away. He told them that they would not see him again in the form of flesh, but would see him again in the resurrection.

At this point he begins to pour out his heart to them. He tells them how he served the Lord despite all persecutions, how he kept nothing back and worked for the Lord, even going from house to house. He said, "I told them all to repent toward God and to have faith in our Lord Jesus Christ. Now I am feeling heavy in my spirit as I am on my way to Jerusalem, knowing the things that will happen to me there, for the Spirit tells me that there are many difficulties." He was even feeling his imprisonment, but he said none of these things influence him because he does not count his life so dear, that he might finish his course and his ministry with joy.

No doubt Paul was referring to the priests in Jerusalem who served in the temple for certain periods of time and then returned to their homes. But Paul emphasized that his service was for a lifetime. He had received his ministry from the Lord Jesus Christ. His one desire was to finish his ministry with joy. Without joy it might have been in vain. He wanted the last of his Christian life and ministry to culminate in the highest joy of all. But the thing that really moved Paul was that these dear people would see his face no more. He took that occasion to say, "Look, brethren, I want you to notice that I am pure from the blood of all men. I have not shunned preaching the whole gospel. Therefore, take heed to yourselves because God, the Holy Spirit, has made you overseers of His flock. You are to feed the people of God whom He purchased with His own blood."

Paul reminded them that people like grievous wolves would come in among them after he had left. They would rend the flock and they would draw people after them, not caring about the Lord but only about themselves. Then he said something very important: "Cease not to warn you every one both day and night with tears." When you feel deeply enough, you are going to cry. Our Lord cried. You and I are not beyond crying. Let us pray, you and I. And let's pray in the spirit of Paul that our lives will not be moved away from Christ.

Dear Father, I pray in the name of Your Son Jesus Christ of

Nazareth, my Lord and Savior, that You will strengthen us in our inner man and that we will exercise our will, release our faith, and stand in agreement now that we will stand true to God. We will not count our lives or our property dear when it comes to serving God but will be givers whenever opportunity arises, and we will finish what You called us to do. We will fulfill our lives in Christ and we will leave something behind as a witness unto Your name. And now, dear friend, I agree with you and receive this with you through Jesus Christ our Lord. Amen and amen.

Acts 20:35

I have shewed you all things, how that so labouring ye ought to support the weak, and to remember the words of the Lord Jesus, how he said, It is more blessed to give than to receive.

Giving is Productive

I want you to notice also that Paul made a statement that is not mentioned anywhere else in the Bible. Jesus Christ's words were recalled: "It is more blessed to give than to receive." The literal rendering is: "It is more productive to give than to receive because it is not what you receive that is multiplied but what you plant, what you give. It is more productive to plant, for without planting, God has nothing to use to multiply or to increase."

For hundreds of years ministers have taught the people of Christ that the whole emphasis is to be upon giving and virtually none upon receiving. It is against the teaching of the whole Word of God. In God's teaching to us to tithe, He said He would open the windows of heaven and pour out upon us a blessing so great we would not even have the capacity to receive it. He said, "I will rebuke the devourer for your sake." Even God, when He gave His Son Jesus Christ, gave to receive our souls to be saved. He is the highest gift of God. The gift itself was to restore us to our heavenly Father so that we would receive eternal salvation. Every time you read this verse, read it like this: "It is more productive to give than to receive, because it is what you give that God multiplies."

Acts 20:36-38

And when he had thus spoken, he kneeled down, and prayed with them all. And they all wept sore, and fell on Paul's neck, and kissed him, sorrowing most of all for the words which he spake, that they should see his face no more. And they accompanied him unto the ship.

This is the only address that Paul gave to believers in the book of Acts. He said many things in the book of Acts. He spoke to cities and other groups, but here he was talking directly to believers — men and women who were precious to him in the Lord.

Now when Paul finished reciting the words of the Lord Jesus — "It is more productive to give than to receive" — he knelt down, hugged these brethren, and prayed with them. They fell on his neck and kissed him. They sorrowed most of all because they would see his face no more.

This kind of emotion comes to all of us. We ought to bear one thing in mind and that is to finish our course with joy, to come to the end of life's work on earth with the Lord's joy.

Throughout Chapter 21 we will see again and again how the people of God would go down to the seashore when Paul's ship docked. One or more of them would give a word of knowledge under the inspiration of the Holy Spirit to tell him what persecutions lay ahead of him. They even told how the Jews would bind him in Jerusalem, and that he might be put to death. Paul appreciated the words from those anointed people. He was steadfast in his determination to go to Jerusalem because Pentecost Day was coming up and God was leading him there, although it may have been the last time he would ever see Jerusalem. He knew he had to go on his way to Rome. When these people would bring the message, he would tell them. No matter how much it broke his heart, he had set his mind steadfastly to obeying God.

More and more men and women of God are led by the Holy Spirit in our time to undertake certain things or make missionary or evangelistic journeys. In my own life I have been forbidden to enter certain cities to hold crusades, but we went anyway because the laws of the land opened the way. Many of our friends come to us with a message of inspiration of the Holy Spirit telling us what the problems are going to be, how persecution will come against us. Others prophesy that God is going to anoint us and help us to find some significant breakthrough. We have to weigh each of these, but the bottom line is, are we going to obey God? In your own life you have undertaken certain missions. For example, seeing your children through Sunday school and church. You have determined to let nothing stand in the way of your faith in your church. Each of us goes through certain things that seem to be against the grain of this world. But the will of God is involved and our choice must be to obey God.

Acts 21:1-13

And it came to pass, that after we were gotten from them, and had launched, we came with a straight course unto Coos, and the day following unto Rhodes, and from thence unto Patara: and finding a ship sailing over unto Phenicia, we went aboard, and set forth. Now when we had discovered Cyprus, we left it on the left hand, and sailed into Syria, and landed at Tyre: for there the ship was to unlade her burden. And finding disciples, we tarried there seven days: who said to Paul through the Spirit, that he should not go up to Jerusalem. And when we had accomplished those days, we departed and went our way; and they all brought us on our way, with wives and children, till we were out of the city: and we kneeled down on the shore, and prayed. And when we had taken our leave one of another, we took ship; and they returned home again.

And when we had finished our course from Tyre, we came to Ptolemais, and saluted the brethren, and abode with them one day. And the next day we that were of Paul's company departed, and came unto Caesarea: and we entered into the house of Philip the evangelist, which was one of the seven; and abode with him. And the same man had four daughters, virgins, which did prophesy.

And as we tarried there many days, there came down from Judaea a certain prophet, named Agabus. And when he was come unto us, he took Paul's girdle, and bound his own hands and feet, and said, Thus saith the Holy Ghost, So shall the Jews at Jerusalem bind the man that owneth this girdle, and shall deliver him into the hands of the Gentiles. And when we heard these things, both we, and they of that place, besought him not to go up to Jerusalem.

Then Paul answered, What mean ye to weep and to break mine heart? for I am ready not to be bound only, but also to die at Jerusalem for the name of the Lord Jesus.

When Paul's ship docked at certain places, Christians came with their families and fell upon his neck. They rejoiced and wept when they learned that he was on his way to Jerusalem. They felt the Holy Spirit giving them knowledge about the sufferings and dangers which awaited him. Because they were concerned about him, their prophecy was that he should not go. They even felt that the Holy Spirit had told them to tell him not to go.

When they reached Caesarea they stayed in the house of Philip the evangelist. This is the first time we discover Philip after his great revival as an evangelist in the city of Samaria, when he led the Ethiopian ruler to Christ out on the desert and was then caught away by the Spirit to another place. Here Paul learns Philip has four daughters, all virgins, all of whom prophesied. Whether these young women prophesied to Paul or not, is not reported. But others prophesied and each time it was a warning that he would be delivered into the hands of the enemy.

Paul's reply was, "I am ready for anything, even to die at Jerusalem for the name of the Lord Jesus Christ." No prophecy could persuade him. He kept saying, "The will of the Lord be done," and he went on up to Jerusalem.

In charismatic groups, words of prophecy are frequently given to individuals or to the group or to the church. Those prophecies have to be tested by the Word of God and by the witness in our own spirit. We cannot accept every prophecy that comes along. At the same time, we are not saying that the prophecy is not genuine. There are many tests of a prophecy but the final test is what you and the Lord feel together about what you are to do, and that is exactly how Paul tested the prophecies. He did not despise them nor set them aside. He listened to them.

I listen to many prophecies about my ministry. I am also interested in a prophecy of the Lord concerning Oral Roberts. And I have been moved by them. But the main thing is that I have to make the final decision between me and the Lord Jesus Christ about how I am to conduct my life or what I am to attempt to do in His name. I personally think that is true of every other believer.

Acts 21:14-24

And when he would not be persuaded, we ceased, saying, The will of the Lord be done. And after those days we took up our carriages, and went up to Jerusalem. There went with us also certain of the disciples of Caesarea, and brought with them one Mnason of Cyprus, an old disciple, with whom we should lodge.

And when we were come to Jerusalem, the brethren received us gladly. And the day following Paul went in with us unto James; and all the elders were present. And when he had saluted them, he declared particularly what things God had wrought among the Gentiles by his ministry. And when they heard it, they glorified the Lord, and said unto him, Thou seest, brother, how many thousands of Jews there are which believe; and they are all zealous of the law: and they are informed of thee, that thou teachest all the Jews which are among the Gentiles to forsake Moses, saying that they ought not to circumcise their children, neither to walk after the customs. What is it therefore? the multitude must needs come together: for they will hear that thou art come.

Do therefore this that we say to thee: We have four men which have a vow on them; them take, and purify thyself with them, and be at charges with them, that they may shave their heads: and all may know that those things, whereof they were informed concerning thee, are nothing; but that thou thyself also walkest orderly, and keepest the law.

This is Paul's last visit to Jerusalem. One of his reasons was to reveal the movement of the gospel from the Jews to the Gentiles. This is a major changing point in the thrust of the gospel for all time.

He visits James and all the others who are heads of the church. They sort of relived the experiences they had with Paul and faced results of his ministry which he had built solely on the life of Jesus as the Redeemer.

Acts 21:25-30

As touching the Gentiles which believe, we have written and concluded that they observe no such thing, save only that they keep themselves from things offered to idols, and from blood, and from strangled, and from fornication.

Then Paul took the men, and the next day purifying himself with them entered into the temple, to signify the accomplishment of the days of purification, until that an offering should be offered for every one of them. And when the seven days were almost ended, the Jews which were of Asia, when they saw him in the temple, stirred up all the people, and laid hands on him, crying out, Men of Israel, help: This is the man, that teacheth all men every where against the people, and the law, and this place: and further brought Greeks also into the temple, and hath polluted this holy place. (For they had seen before with him in the city Trophimus an Ephesian, whom they supposed that Paul had brought into the temple.) And all the city was moved, and the people ran together: and they took Paul, and drew him out of the temple: and forthwith the doors were shut.

Paul Confounds Mosaic Law

Paul has returned from the Gentile world to Jerusalem for his final visit to the beloved city in which he grew up as a student. James and the elders had been very concerned about the reports they continued to hear about Paul's ministry amongst the Gentiles. They had heard that he did not give a whit anymore about the circumcision and all the law of Moses, because he was preaching the grace of God and that unto Christ you come by faith alone. Paul had made a great point in going beyond the law of Moses back to the fathers who were Abraham, Isaac, and Jacob, back to where Abraham, by faith, had come to God some 13 or 14 years before he was circumcised. Some 400 years before the law of Moses was ever given,

Abraham was a man of faith. Abraham believed in taking God at His word. Abraham did not depend on anything other than sincere belief that God is God and that he would do whatever God said. God wanted to establish a nation. Circumcision was in a sense a seal of Abraham as the father of a new type of people, a new nation.

The law was given primarily for two purposes: one, to show the people a sense of their sinfulness, and two, to show them their need of a Redeemer. So many of the Jewish people followed the law for the law's sake. They even tithed for tithing's sake — not for the purposes for which the law, or tithe, was given. So Paul had blazed a new path showing that Jesus Christ had fulfilled all of that because the law in itself could not bring redemption to fallen man. They had to go back to faith, which was begun in Abraham.

Paul, by the keen insight of the Spirit, had seen this eternal truth. The Jews rejected it wherever he preached it. So God led him to the Gentiles, where he had great success. Now Paul is standing before James and the others, giving a great report of his ministry that cheers their hearts.

In return James tells him of the thousands of Jews who also had believed, yet were zealous of the law. Then James said that they had four men in the city who had taken the vow of a Nazarite and urged Paul to take them into the temple so that the Jews, upon seeing them with Paul, would relax and not take violent action against him. Paul did exactly what was suggested. When he got into the temple there were people present from Asia who were Jews, who had known Paul out there in the field. They thought these four men, whom James had suggested Paul take with him into the temple, were Gentiles. They thought these four men were out of place in the temple of God and were actually polluting it by their presence. They were not Gentiles, they were Jews. But they were mistaken for Gentiles. The Jews used that as an excuse to point out Paul to the multitude as the one who had set the world on fire with Jesus Christ and the gospel. It was he who was telling the people to turn from the law of Moses, that there was no need to circumcise their children and no further need for the temple. They touched the wrong nerve in the Jewish people who had rejected Christ and held onto the old customs which Jesus had fulfilled.

Acts 21:31-40

> And as they went about to kill him, tidings came unto the chief captain of the band, that all Jerusalem was in an uproar. Who immediately took soldiers and centurions, and ran down unto them: and when they saw the chief captain and the soldiers, they left beating of Paul.
>
> Then the chief captain came near, and took him, and commanded

him to be bound with two chains; and demanded who he was, and what he had done. And some cried one thing, some another, among the multitude: and when he could not know the certainty for the tumult, he commanded him to be carried into the castle. And when he came upon the stairs, so it was, that he was borne of the soldiers for the violence of the people. For the multitude of the people followed after, crying, Away with him.

And as Paul was to be led into the castle, he said unto the chief captain, May I speak unto thee? Who said, Canst thou speak Greek? Art not thou that Egyptian, which before these days madest an uproar, and leddest out into the wilderness four thousand men that were murderers?

But Paul said, I am a man which am a Jew of Tarsus, a city in Cilicia, a citizen of no mean city: and, I beseech thee, suffer me to speak unto the people. And when he had given him licence, Paul stood on the stairs, and beckoned with the hand unto the people. And when there was made a great silence, he spake unto them in the Hebrew tongue ...

They ran and grabbed Paul. They began to beat him and were killing him until the chief captain of the Romans heard about it and rushed to find out what was going on. He rescued Paul, thinking that he was an Egyptian murderer. When he spoke to Paul and learned that Paul spoke Greek, he was surprised because he learned that Paul was not whom he suspected.

Then Paul said, "I am a Jew of the city of Tarsus, a great Roman city and province. Let me speak to the people." There was not much this Roman officer could do because he realized he was dealing with a very important person. While the mob was gathered around, Paul put forth his hand, got their attention, and began to speak in the Hebrew language.

Acts 22:1-24

... saying, Men, brethren, and fathers, hear ye my defence which I make now unto you. (And when they heard that he spake in the Hebrew tongue to them, they kept the more silence; and he saith,) I am verily a man which am a Jew, born in Tarsus, a city in Cilicia, yet brought up in this city at the feet of Gamaliel, and taught according to the perfect manner of the law of the fathers, and was zealous toward God, as ye all are this day. And I persecuted this way unto the death, binding and delivering into prisons both men and women. As also the high priest doth bear me witness, and all the estate of the elders: from whom also I received letters unto the brethren, and went to Damascus, to bring them which were there bound unto Jerusalem, for to be punished.

And it came to pass, that, as I made my journey, and was come nigh unto Damascus about noon, suddenly there shone from heaven a great light round about me. And I fell unto the ground, and heard a voice saying unto me, Saul, Saul, why persecutest thou me? And I answered, Who art thou, Lord? And he said unto me, I am Jesus of Nazareth, whom thou persecutest. And they that were with me saw indeed the light, and were afraid; but they heard not the voice of him that spake to me.

And I said, What shall I do, Lord? And the Lord said unto me, Arise, and go into Damascus; and there it shall be told thee of all things which are appointed for thee to do. And when I could not see for the glory of that light, being led by the hand of them that were with me, I came into Damascus. And one Ananias, a devout man according to the law, having a good report of all the Jews which dwelt there, came unto me, and stood, and said unto me, Brother Saul, receive thy sight. And the same hour I looked up upon him.

And he said, The God of our fathers hath chosen thee, that thou shouldest know his will, and see that Just One, and shouldest hear the voice of his mouth. For thou shalt be his witness unto all men of what thou hast seen and heard. And now why tarriest thou? arise, and be baptised, and wash away thy sins, calling on the name of the Lord.

And it came to pass, that, when I was come again to Jerusalem, even while I prayed in the temple, I was in a trance; and saw him saying unto me, Make haste, and get thee quickly out of Jerusalem: for they will not receive thy testimony concerning me. And I said, Lord, they know that I imprisoned and beat in every synagogue them that believed on thee: and when the blood of thy martyr Stephen was shed, I also was standing by, and consenting unto his death, and kept the raiment of them that slew him.

And he said unto me, Depart: for I will send thee far hence unto the Gentiles.

And they gave him audience unto this word, and then lifted up their voices, and said, Away with such a fellow from the earth: for it is not fit that he should live. And as they cried out, and cast off their clothes, and threw dust into the air, the chief captain commanded him to be brought into the castle, and bade that he should be examined by scourging; that he might know wherefore they cried so against him.

Paul's Temple Ignored

Now, when they heard Paul speak in Hebrew they really got quiet. Paul relates his testimony of meeting Christ on the Damascus road.

The Lord had become real to him, giving him his purpose for life and the calling into the ministry of the gospel. When he got to the part where God said to him, "I will send thee far hence unto the Gentiles," that is as far as the mob would let him go and they went wild. When they would have torn him apart, the chief captain got him and said, "Let us take him in here and scourge him so he will open his mouth and he will really tell us the truth."

Acts 22:25-30

> And as they bound him with thongs, Paul said unto the centurion that stood by, Is it lawful for you to scourge a man that is a Roman, and uncondemned? When the centurion heard that, he went and told the chief captain, saying, Take heed what thou doest: for this man is a Roman. Then the chief captain came, and said unto him, Tell me, art thou a Roman? He said, Yea. And the chief captain answered, With a great sum obtained I this freedom. And Paul said, But I was free born.
>
> Then straightway they departed from him which should have examined him: and the chief captain also was afraid, after he knew that he was a Roman, and because he had bound him. On the morrow, because he would have known the certainty wherefore he was accused of the Jews, he loosed him from his bands, and commanded the chief priests and all their council to appear, and brought Paul down, and set him before them.

God's Hand Moves

Paul had asked, "Would you scourge a Roman when he has not even been condemned?" The man said, "You mean to say you are a Roman?" He said, "I am." He said, "I had to buy my Roman freedom. Where did you get yours?" Paul said, "I was born a Roman. I was born without having to pay for it." That meant that Paul's father had been a Roman citizen and tradition has it that he had performed a great service for Caesar and Roman citizenship had been conferred upon him. Because Paul was a Roman, under Roman law he was allowed to be charged and the charges written before he was condemned, and he even had a right to appeal to Caesar. The Roman captain got scared. He decided to call the Jewish council together and have Paul tell them whatever he wanted to say in reply to their charges. It was really a momentous event. You can see that the hand of God would have to be involved to get all these major scenes into action.

Acts 23:1-5

> And Paul, earnestly beholding the council, said, Men and brethren, I have lived in all good conscience before God unto this day. And the high priest Ananias commanded them that stood by him to smite him on the mouth. Then said Paul unto him, God shall smite thee, thou whited wall: for sittest thou to judge me after the law, and commandest me to be smitten contrary to the law? And they that stood by said, Revilest thou God's high priest? Then said Paul, I wist not, brethren, that he was the high priest: for it is written, Thou shalt not speak evil of the ruler of thy people.

Paul Reveals Irony

Again he began to tell his testimony of how he had lived in good conscience until that very hour. The high priest ordered him slapped, and Paul knew that was wrong — that was not according to the law. He said, "You hypocrite, why do you have me slapped when you know it is against the law?" And someone else said, "Do you revile the high priest?" He said, "I really did not know a man like this was the high priest. Had I known by looking at him and by his actions that he was a high priest, I would have obeyed the scripture (Exodus 22:28) that says, 'Thou shalt not speak evil of the ruler of thy people.'" There is a little irony there because Paul knew the man carried the name of high priest, but that his life was that of a hypocrite.

Acts 23:6-10

> But when Paul perceived that the one part were Sadducees, and the other Pharisees, he cried out in the council, Men and brethren, I am a Pharisee, the son of a Pharisee: of the hope and resurrection of the dead I am called in question.
>
> And when he had so said, there arose a dissension between the Pharisees and the Sadducees: and the multitude was divided. For the Sadducees say that there is no resurrection, neither angel, nor spirit: but the Pharisees confess both.
>
> And there arose a great cry: and the scribes that were of the Pharisees' part arose, and strove, saying, We find no evil in this man: but if a spirit or an angel hath spoken to him, let us not fight against God. And when there arose a great dissension, the chief captain, fearing lest Paul should have been pulled in pieces of them, commanded the soldiers to go down, and to take him by force from among them, and to bring him into the castle.

Paul Divides the Mob

Paul looked over that crowd of Pharisees and Sadducees and knew the Sadducees did not believe in the resurrection or angels or anything miraculous, but that the Pharisees did. So he reminded them of the truth. "I am a Pharisee," he said. "I was born one. I am the son of one." Then he got right down to the nitty gritty, saying, "Really, what I am here for, and why I am being charged, is for the hope of the resurrection of the dead. That is what this thing is all about. It is not about me. It is about the resurrection of the dead."

The Pharisees and Sadducees got into a big scrap amongst themselves, and finally the Pharisees said, "Let him go because maybe the Spirit of God has come and revealed these things unto him." But the Sadducees would not accept that. They began to grab at him and pull him apart. The chief captain realized that everything he could have done would be in vain, so he sent his soldiers down to rescue Paul.

Acts 23:11-24

And the night following the Lord stood by him, and said, Be of good cheer, Paul: for as thou hast testified of me in Jerusalem, so must thou bear witness also at Rome.

And when it was day, certain of the Jews banded together, and bound themselves under a curse, saying that they would neither eat nor drink till they had killed Paul. And they were more than forty which had made this conspiracy. And they came to the chief priests and elders, and said, We have bound ourselves under a great curse, that we will eat nothing until we have slain Paul. Now therefore ye with the council signify to the chief captain that he bring him down unto you to morrow, as though ye would enquire something more perfectly concerning him: and we, or ever he come near, are ready to kill him.

And when Paul's sister's son heard of their lying in wait, he went and entered into the castle, and told Paul. Then Paul called one of the centurions unto him, and said, Bring this young man unto the chief captain: for he hath a certain thing to tell him. So he took him, and brought him to the chief captain, and said, Paul the prisoner called me unto him, and prayed me to bring this young man unto thee, who hath something to say unto thee.

Then the chief captain took him by the hand, and went with him aside privately, and asked him, What is that thou hast to tell me? And he said, The Jews have agreed to desire thee that thou wouldest bring down Paul to morrow into the council, as though they would enquire somewhat of him more perfectly. But do not thou yield unto them:

for there lie in wait for him of them more than forty men, which have bound themselves with an oath, that they will neither eat nor drink till they have killed him: and now are they ready, looking for a promise from thee. So the chief captain then let the young man depart, and charged him, See thou tell no man that thou hast shewed these things to me.

And he called unto him two centurions, saying, Make ready two hundred soldiers to go to Caesarea, and horsemen threescore and ten, and spearmen two hundred, at the third hour of the night; and provide them beasts, that they may set Paul on, and bring him safe unto Felix the governor.

Conspiracy Thwarted

And that night, the Lord stood by him and said to Paul, "Do not be discouraged, be of good cheer, for you have been testifying for Me here in Jerusalem. I want you to give the same testimony in Rome." Meanwhile Paul's nephew discovered that a band of about 40 Jews had made a conspiracy that while Paul was being taken to Caesarea to a higher Roman court, they would waylay him and kill him. The nephew told the chief captain, who surrounded Paul with several hundred Roman soldiers so he would have protection. He arrived safely. Meanwhile the chief captain had sent a letter ahead to the scribe, to the court, about what Paul had done.

Acts 23:25-24:3

And he wrote a letter after this manner: Claudius Lysias unto the most excellent governor Felix sendeth greeting. This man was taken of the Jews, and should have been killed of them: then came I with an army, and rescued him, having understood that he was a Roman. And when I would have known the cause wherefore they accused him, I brought him forth into their council: whom I perceived to be accused of questions of their law, but to have nothing laid to his charge worthy of death or of bonds. And when it was told me how that the Jews laid wait for the man, I sent straightway to thee, and gave commandment to his accusers also to say before thee what they had against him. Farewell.

Then the soldiers, as it was commanded them, took Paul, and brought him by night to Antipatris. On the morrow they left the horsemen to go with him, and returned to the castle: who, when they came to Caesarea, and delivered the epistle to the governor, presented Paul also before him.

And when the governor had read the letter, he asked of what

province he was. And when he understood that he was of Cilicia;
I will hear thee, said he, when thine accusers are also come. And he commanded him to be kept in Herod's judgment hall.

And after five days Ananias the high priest descended with the elders, and with a certain orator named Tertullus, who informed the governor against Paul. And when he was called forth, Tertullus began to accuse him, saying, Seeing that by thee we enjoy great quietness, and that very worthy deeds are done unto this nation by thy providence, we accept it always, and in all places, most noble Felix, with all thankfulness.

(Felix was Pilate's successor.)

Acts 24:4,5

Notwithstanding, that I be not further tedious unto thee, I pray thee that thou wouldest hear us of thy clemency a few words. For we have found this man a pestilent fellow, and a mover of sedition among all the Jews throughout the world, and a ringleader of the sect of the Nazarenes: . . .

Nazarenes Invoked

This is the only statement in the New Testament about the sect of the Nazarenes being used in connection with the Christians.

Acts 24:6-9

. . . who also hath gone about to profane the temple: whom we took, and would have judged according to our law. But the chief captain Lysias came upon us, and with great violence took him away out of our hands, Commanding his accusers to come unto thee: by examining of whom thyself mayest take knowledge of all these things, whereof we accuse him. And the Jews also assented, saying that these things were so.

Lawyer Meets Match

The attorney of the Jews, Tertullus, who was well versed in Roman law and had great experience in the court, had used the most carefully chosen words in his approach to the governor. But he is no match for Paul.

Acts 24:10-21

Then Paul, after that the governor had beckoned unto him to speak, answered, Forasmuch as I know that thou hast been of many years a judge unto this nation, I do the more cheerfully answer for myself: because that thou mayest understand, that there are yet but twelve days since I went up to Jerusalem for to worship. And they neither found me in the temple disputing with any man, neither raising up the people, neither in the synagogues, nor in the city: neither can they prove the things whereof they now accuse me. But this I confess unto thee, that after the way which they call heresy, so worship I the God of my fathers, believing all things which are written in the law and in the prophets: and have hope toward God, which they themselves also allow, that there shall be a resurrection of the dead, both of the just and unjust.

And herein do I exercise myself, to have always a conscience void of offence toward God, and toward men. Now after many years I came to bring alms to my nation, and offerings. Whereupon certain Jews from Asia found me purified in the temple, neither with multitude, nor with tumult. Who ought to have been here before thee, and object, if they had ought against me. Or else let these same here say, if they have found any evil doing in me, while I stood before the council, Except it be for this one voice, that I cried standing among them, Touching the resurrection of the dead I am called in question by you this day.

Paul's Brilliant Defense

The governor turned to Paul and said, "Speak for yourself." Paul put his best foot forward, for he, too, was well versed in the law. He knew the truth, the facts. He began, "I very cheerfully and gladly answer for myself because, Judge, I know that you have been our leader. Judge, I know how carefully you have tried to observe Roman law." Soon he had the judge listening as well as everybody else. Again he went into the reason why he was in court and it was not the reason that this attorney had said. Paul said, "All these people the attorney refers to, who have accused me, where are these people? Why are they not here? These are trumped-up charges, Governor. If you really want to know why I am here, it has nothing to do with the charges. I am here because they say that I worship the God of my fathers and believe all the things which are written in the law and in the prophets. I have hope in God. These people say that is heresy and that I am a heretic, but I want you to know, there is a resurrection from the dead, both of the just and the unjust, and I have declared this according to the Scriptures. I have done it with good conscience and I am void of offense toward God and toward men.

"After many years of being in a Gentile world, I came back to my own nation, to my people, to bring an offering, a gift. Certain Asian Jews saw me in the temple and they did not see me stirring up the people or causing tumult. If they did see it, why are they not here to testify against me? These people here of the council, they did not witness my presence in the temple. They are here because they heard me cry out to the multitude as touching the resurrection of the dead. That is what the question is all about today."

Acts 24:22-27

And when Felix heard these things, having more perfect knowledge of that way, he deferred them, and said, When Lysias the chief captain shall come down, I will know the uttermost of your matter.

And he commanded a centurion to keep Paul, and to let him have liberty, and that he should forbid none of his acquaintance to minister or come unto him. And after certain days, when Felix came with his wife Drusilla, which was a Jewess, he sent for Paul, and heard him concerning the faith in Christ. And as he reasoned of righteousness, temperance, and judgment to come, Felix trembled, and answered, Go thy way for this time; when I have a convenient season, I will call for thee. He hoped also that money should have been given him of Paul, that he might loose him: wherefore he sent for him the oftener, and communed with him. But after two years Porcius Festus came into Felix' room: and Felix, willing to shew the Jews a pleasure, left Paul bound.

Felix Convicted

When the governor, Felix, heard Paul's defense, he straddled the fence. He said when Lysias, the chief captain, came down from Jerusalem, he would ask him what happened. Meanwhile he gave Paul his freedom and a company of soldiers. Felix allowed any of Paul's friends to visit him. After several days had passed, Felix brought his wife, Drusilla, who was a Jewess. He sent for Paul and heard him concerning the faith in Christ.

How amazing are the ways of God and how true are His ways! He made it possible for Felix to want to hear about the faith in Christ. He had His man there, Paul, who could do the best job. Paul began to reason with him. In effect, he is saying, "Governor, listen to me. I want to tell you about something you already know —

righteousness, temperance, and the judgment. You know there is going to be a judgment. You know there is going to be a resurrection from the dead of the just and the unjust. Felix, you know this."

While Paul talked, Felix trembled. He shook like a leaf in a March wind. He got convicted of his sins, but he shook it off and told Paul, "I will tell you what. You go on away and when I have got time I will call for you." Then the Scriptures say he also hoped for a big bribe because that was the custom. Had Paul given him a bribe, Felix would have freed him. So Paul was kept in Caesarea for two whole years.

While Paul was held in Caesarea for two years, Luke had his liberty. That was probably the time that Luke did much of his investigative work concerning Jesus' birth and His life. It was during this time that he talked with Mary, Jesus' mother, and many other eyewitnesses. Luke's gospel is about the human side of Jesus more than the others were.

Do you see the hand of God in all of this? Nothing is allowed to drift along. God's purpose is carried out.

Acts 25:1

Now when Festus was come into the province, after three days he ascended from Caesarea to Jerusalem.

Festus New Governor

Festus replaced Felix. He became the Roman governor who would preside in Caesarea and would have charge of Paul's trial.

Acts 25:2-13

Then the high priest and the chief of the Jews informed him against Paul, and besought him, And desired favour against him, that he would send for him to Jerusalem, laying wait in the way to kill him. But Festus answered, that Paul should be kept at Caesarea, and that he himself would depart shortly thither. Let them therefore, said he, which among you are able, go down with me, and accuse this man, if there be any wickedness in him.

And when he had tarried among them more than ten days, he went down unto Caesarea; and the next day sitting on the judgment seat commanded Paul to be brought. And when he was come, the Jews which came down from Jerusalem stood round about, and laid many and grievous complaints against Paul, which they could not prove. While he answered for himself, Neither against the law of the Jews, neither against the temple, nor yet against Caesar, have I offended any thing at all. But Festus, willing to do the Jews a pleasure, answered Paul, and said, Wilt thou go up to Jerusalem, and there be judged of these things before me?

Then said Paul, I stand at Caesar's judgment seat, where I ought to be judged: to the Jews have I done no wrong, as thou very well knowest. For if I be an offender, or have committed any thing worthy of death, I refuse not to die: but if there be none of these things whereof these accuse me, no man may deliver me unto them. I appeal unto Caesar.

Then Festus, when he had conferred with the council, answered, Hast thou appealed unto Caesar? unto Caesar shalt thou go. And after certain days king Agrippa and Bernice came unto Caesarea to salute Festus.

Agrippa Comes Visiting

King Agrippa was known as Herod Agrippa. He was the son of the Herod who had James killed and was later eaten by worms.

Acts 25:14-22

And when they had been there many days, Festus declared Paul's cause unto the king, saying, There is a certain man left in bonds by Felix: about whom, when I was at Jerusalem, the chief priests and the elders of the Jews informed me, desiring to have judgment against him. To whom I answered, It is not the manner of the Romans to deliver any man to die, before that he which is accused have the accusers face to face, and have licence to answer for himself concerning the crime laid against him.

Therefore, when they were come hither, without any delay on the morrow I sat on the judgment seat, and commanded the man to be brought forth. Against whom when the accusers stood up, they brought none accusation of such things as I supposed: but had certain questions against him of their own superstition, and of one Jesus, which was dead, whom Paul affirmed to be alive.

And because I doubted of such manner of questions, I asked him whether he would go to Jerusalem, and there be judged of these matters. But when Paul had appealed to be reserved unto the hearing of Augustus, I commanded him to be kept till I might send him to Caesar. Then Agrippa said unto Festus, I would also hear the man myself. To morrow, said he, thou shalt hear him.

Festus, the Roman governor, now has a serious problem, at least serious to him because he has inherited Paul. He does not know what to do with this Christian, this apostle.

When he gets a chance to talk to Agrippa, he says Paul has appealed to Caesar Augustus. "I have told him he can go, but, really, I do not have any reason to send him there since his accusers have not faced him in the manner that our government requires. Agrippa, I have this problem. Will you help me with it?" So Agrippa says, "Yes, I will. I would like to hear him for myself."

There are many governments in the world today that do not know what to do with the Christians in their midsts. For example, Russia and other communist countries do not know what to do with people who believe that Jesus Christ is the Son of God and are willing to give their lives for their testimony. So Paul's experience with Festus and Agrippa is not an isolated instance 'way back there 2,000 years ago. It is being lived again and again in our time.

Acts 25:23-26:14

> And on the morrow, when Agrippa was come, and Bernice, with great pomp, and was entered into the place of hearing, with the chief captains, and principal men of the city, at Festus' commandment Paul was brought forth. And Festus said, King Agrippa, and all men which are here present with us, ye see this man, about whom all the multitude of the Jews have dealt with me, both at Jerusalem, and also here, crying that he ought not to live any longer. But when I found that he had committed nothing worthy of death, and that he himself hath appealed to Augustus, I have determined to send him. Of whom I have no certain thing to write unto my Lord.

> Wherefore I have brought him forth before you, and specially before thee, O king Agrippa, that, after examination had, I might have somewhat to write. For it seemeth to me unreasonable to send a prisoner, and not withal to signify the crimes laid against him.

> Then Agrippa said unto Paul, Thou art permitted to speak for thyself. Then Paul stretched forth the hand, and answered for himself:

> I think myself happy, king Agrippa, because I shall answer for myself this day before thee touching all the things whereof I am accused of the Jews: especially because I know thee to be expert in all customs and questions which are among the Jews: wherefore I beseech thee to hear me patiently.

> My manner of life from my youth, which was at the first among mine own nation at Jerusalem, know all the Jews; which knew me from the beginning, if they would testify, that after the most straitest sect of our religion I lived a Pharisee. And now I stand and am judged for the hope of the promise made of God unto our fathers: unto which promise our twelve tribes, instantly serving God day and night, hope to come. For which hope's sake, king Agrippa, I am accused of the Jews.

Why should it be thought a thing incredible with you, that God should raise the dead? I verily thought with myself, that I ought to do many things contrary to the name of Jesus of Nazareth. Which thing I also did in Jerusalem: and many of the saints did I shut up in prison, having received authority from the chief priests; and when they were put to death, I gave my voice against them. And I punished them oft in every synagogue, and compelled them to blaspheme; and being exceedingly mad against them, I persecuted them even unto strange cities.

Whereupon as I went to Damascus with authority and commission from the chief priests, at midday, O king, I saw in the way a light from heaven, above the brightness of the sun, shining round about me and them which journeyed with me. And when we were all fallen to the earth, I heard a voice speaking unto me, and saying in the Hebrew tongue, Saul, Saul, why persecutest thou me? it is hard for thee to kick against the pricks.

Testimony Vital to Gospel

Paul is now giving his testimony for the third time. For some reason, God wanted this testimony given to different groups of people, including kings, who were going to send him to Rome.

The gospel is not all in preaching nor in teaching nor even in healing. It is also in one's personal testimony. Throughout Acts, as Paul has testified about meeting Christ, he relates it the same every time with one exception. From time to time, he adds other things that Jesus said to him or that Ananias said. These things were added so that the story is more complete.

Acts 26:15-19

And I said, Who art thou, Lord? And he said, I am Jesus whom thou persecutest. But rise, and stand upon thy feet: for I have appeared unto thee for this purpose, to make thee a minister and a witness both of these things which thou hast seen, and of those things in the which I will appear unto thee; delivering thee from the people, and from the Gentiles, unto whom now I send thee, to open their eyes, and to turn them from darkness to light, and from the power of Satan unto God, that they may receive forgiveness of sins, and inheritance among them which are sanctified by faith that is in me. Whereupon, O king Agrippa, I was not disobedient unto the heavenly vision: . . .

Vision, Obedience Linked

Jesus is saying to Paul and to all of us that He has a purpose for our lives. Not only is He going to reveal himself to us in our conversion experience, but also in days and years to come. He spells out that purpose for each of us if we listen. That purpose is a dream, a vision, that God puts in our hearts.

Paul made the statement of statements: "I was not disobedient unto the heavenly vision," a vision ordained of God, a vision to which he could be obedient or disobedient. Obedience is something we must do. God does not do it for us. God gives us the dream, the vision, but the disobedience or the obedience is ours. Obedience is something we have to learn. We learn it through struggle, through the things we suffer as we are put to the test time and time again. The devil will not leave us alone with such a dream or vision from God. I thank God that if Saul of Tarsus could be obedient to his heavenly vision, you and I can be obedient to ours.

Acts 26:19,20

Whereupon, O king Agrippa, I was not disobedient unto the heavenly vision: but shewed first unto them of Damascus, and at Jerusalem, and throughout all the coasts of Judaea, and then to the Gentiles, that they should repent and turn to God, and do works meet for repentance.

Paul's Vision Explained

Paul is now describing his heavenly vision. He was to carry the message of the gospel that people should repent and turn to God and that the things they did for repentance should be worthy of God's deliverance power in their lives.

Acts 26:21-27

For these causes the Jews caught me in the temple, and went about to kill me. Having therefore obtained help of God, I continue unto this day, witnessing both to small and great, saying none other things than those which the prophets and Moses did say should come:

That Christ should suffer, and that he should be the first that should rise from the dead, and should shew light unto the people, and to the Gentiles.

And as he thus spake for himself, Festus said with a loud voice, Paul, thou art beside thyself; much learning doth make thee mad. But he said, I am not mad, most noble Festus; but I speak forth the words of truth and soberness. For the king knoweth of these things, before whom also I speak freely: for I am persuaded that none of these things are hidden from him; for this thing was not done in a corner.

King Agrippa, believest thou the prophets? I know that thou believest.

Paul Corners Agrippa

Paul quickly puts Agrippa in a corner, a corner with Rome on the one side and Jesus on the other. He told him he knew the prophets. He knew everything Paul was talking about. He is a Roman governor, but now he is face to face with gospels of Jesus. God will never allow anybody to continue straddling the fence.

Acts 26:28

Then Agrippa said unto Paul, Almost thou persuadest me to be a Christian.

Some say that what Agrippa meant was, "Almost thou persuadest me to play the role of a Christian." Others say that Herod Agrippa meant, "In so short a time you think you can make me to become a Christian?" Others of us believe that he said it just like he meant it and meant it the way he said it: "Paul, almost thou persuadest me to be a Christian."

Acts 26:29-32

And Paul said, I would to God, that not only thou, but also all that hear me this day, were both almost, and altogether such as I am, except these bonds.

And when he had thus spoken, the king rose up, and the governor, and Bernice, and they that sat with them: and when they were gone aside, they talked between themselves, saying, This man doeth nothing worthy of death or of bonds. Then said Agrippa unto Festus, This man might have been set at liberty, if he had not appealed unto Caesar.

"Almost" Not Enough

When Paul for the third time was testifying before the authorities, people sitting in judgment on his life were deeply moved.

The gospel is the power of God, and it is the power of God unto salvation. This was a stunning testimony on a magnificent occasion.

King Agrippa is there. He knew all about the prophets. The woman he was with, Bernice, was not his wife — she was his sister. They had been brought up in Rome under pomp and circumstance, and they were there in Caesarea with Festus nearby listening to this man, Paul, a Christian, relate the story of the light of Christ, the voice of the Lord Jesus speaking to Paul, calling him by name, giving him a purpose for his life, and how that he was not disobedient unto that heavenly vision. He said, "King Agrippa, you know all about this. This was not done in a corner. This was not done in some far-fetched place on the earth where no one would know about it or hear about it. You know about it; everybody knows about it. And you believe it. You know it is true."

Then Agrippa cried out, "You know, Paul, you have almost persuaded me." But almost is not enough.

The gospel of Jesus Christ is not hidden. Many of us are on nationwide, worldwide television and radio. Not long ago, in a national poll, Oral Roberts' name was known to 87 percent of the population of the United States. That is, they have seen me on television or heard me on radio or come across my name. But not only me, but also other men and women of God. This is not only true in America; people all over the earth know about us and they know about others.

Above all, they know that their conscience is dealing with them, because everybody, sooner or later, comes into contact with the gospel of Christ. They meet or hear or read somebody's testimony. God has His witnesses. Kings are being confronted with Christ — presidents, other leaders, heads of armies, heads of state, heads of businesses, big people, little people, old people, middle-aged people, young people, and children. This is not done in a corner.

The 26th chapter ends with the inference that Paul could have avoided going to Rome. They had given him an alternative to go back to Jerusalem and there testify again, or as a Roman citizen, claim his prerogative to appear before Rome. God told him that he was to appear in Rome, and he knew they could not kill him until he had done his work for God in Rome.

They could not kill Paul until God was through with him. There is a protection around us, a divine providence that we can depend on. We are going to live until the time God is through with us, particularly when we know we are obeying God. Paul knew he was putting Christ first in his life.

Acts 27:1-9

> And when it was determined that we should sail into Italy, they
> delivered Paul and certain other prisoners unto one named Julius a

centurion of Augustus' band. And entering into a ship of Adramyttium, we launched, meaning to sail by the coasts of Asia; one Aristarchus, a Macedonian of Thessalonica, being with us. And the next day we touched at Sidon. And Julius courteously entreated Paul, and gave him liberty to go unto his friends to refresh himself.

And when we had launched from thence, we sailed under Cyprus, because the winds were contrary. And when we had sailed over the sea of Cilicia and Pamphylia, we came to Myra, a city of Lycia. And there the centurion found a ship of Alexandria sailing into Italy; and he put us therein. And when we had sailed slowly many days, and scarce were come over against Cnidus, the wind not suffering us, we sailed under Crete, over against Salmone; and, hardly passing it, came unto a place which is called The fair havens; nigh whereunto was the city of Lasea. Now when much time was spent, and when sailing was now dangerous, because the fast was now already past, Paul admonished them, . . .

Paul's Sailing Advice

When Luke talked about the fast being already over, he was referring to the Day of Atonement. As far as we can tell, this happened about October 5, A.D. 59. This was a very dangerous time of the year to sail. The danger began in October and went on through November. Then for three months after that they did not sail. In December, January, and February, it was death to almost any ship. Luke is indicating here that they have run into dangerous waters and uncertain winds already, as early as October, and Paul admonishes them. He is giving them a word of knowledge. Later we will see in I Corinthians 12 that Paul talks of nine gifts of the Spirit, one of them being the word of knowledge.

Acts 27:10,11

. . . and said unto them, Sirs, I perceive that this voyage will be with hurt and much damage, not only of the lading and ship, but also of our lives. Nevertheless the centurion believed the master and the owner of the ship, more than those things which were spoken by Paul.

Heed God's Words

That is when the centurion made a fatal mistake. He believed the man who owned the ship, who was in a hurry to get there, more than he did the word of God through Paul, which was given to save

146

lives. Paul will say in I Thessalonians 5:20: "Despise not prophesyings." In the Corinthian letter, he talks about the validity of the gifts of the Spirit, including the word of knowledge.

We need to give heed to these things of God when they are spoken because God knows the end from the beginning. God knows what is going to happen. We ought not to get caught up in our money-making ways so much that we put that above our lives or above the call of God upon our lives. As long as we have our lives and God's call is upon us in a particular purpose to be carried out, then our lives are not only precious because they are our lives, but they are even more precious because God's purpose is riding on our lives.

Acts 27:12-20

And because the haven was not commodious to winter in, the more part advised to depart thence also, if by any means they might attain to Phenice, and there to winter; which is an haven of Crete, and lieth toward the south west and north west. And when the south wind blew softly, supposing that they had obtained their purpose, loosing thence, they sailed close by Crete.

But not long after there arose against it a tempestuous wind, called Euroclydon. And when the ship was caught, and could not bear up into the wind, we let her drive. And running under a certain island which is called Clauda, we had much work to come by the boat: which when they had taken up, they used helps, undergirding the ship; and, fearing lest they should fall into the quicksands, strake sail, and so were driven.

And we being exceedingly tossed with a tempest, the next day they lightened the ship; and the third day we cast out with our own hands the tackling of the ship. And when neither sun nor stars in many days appeared, and no small tempest lay on us, all hope that we should be saved was then taken away.

Weather Storms With God

Luke had knowledge of the sea. In these few words, he has told the story of life and death. The storm is roaring in upon them until all hope of being saved is gone. This is a perfect picture of what you and I go through, although not necessarily in a boat or on a sea or in a physical storm. We start off on a trip and the first thing we know, everything in the world has gone wrong. Almost within minutes our backs are to the wall. It looks like we are going to be out of it or we will be knocked flat on our backs. That comes sometimes through disease or a tragedy in the family. There are times when hope seems to be gone. But remember, there is a God. As long as there is God, there is hope.

Acts 27:21-25

But after long abstinence Paul stood forth in the midst of them, and said, Sirs, ye should have hearkened unto me, and not have loosed from Crete, and to have gained this harm and loss. And now I exhort you to be of good cheer; for there shall be no loss of any man's life among you, but of the ship.

For there stood by me this night the angel of God, whose I am, and whom I serve, saying, Fear not, Paul; thou must be brought before Caesar: and, lo, God hath given thee all them that sail with thee.

Wherefore, sirs, be of good cheer: for I believe God, that it shall be even as it was told me.

Honor God's People

More lives are saved than people realize because of the will of God that His ministers are to be at certain places at certain times. It is for their sake that God often saves many other human lives. Value the people of God. Although I am an evangelist, I certainly am not tooting my own horn. We ought to honor the witness of any children of God, for in their goings to and fro on this earth, God is at work. God has intended for us to be at certain places at particular times, to accomplish His eternal mission for us and for other people.

Paul is telling these people that no matter how foolish they were in not listening to the previous word of knowledge that God had given them, go ahead and be of good cheer, because God intends for him to appear before Caesar with the gospel, and not one of their lives would be lost, but the ship. Notice in Verse 26 and thereon how Paul gets them ready for what is going to happen.

Acts 27:26-44

Howbeit we must be cast upon a certain island. But when the fourteenth night was come, as we were driven up and down in Adria, about midnight the shipmen deemed that they drew near to some country; and sounded, and found it twenty fathoms: and when they had gone a little further, they sounded again, and found it fifteen fathoms. Then fearing lest we should have fallen upon rocks, they cast four anchors out of the stern, and wished for the day.

And as the shipmen were about to flee out of the ship, when they had let down the boat into the sea, under colour as though they would have cast anchors out of the foreship, Paul said to the centurion and to the soldiers, Except these abide in the ship, ye cannot be saved.

Then the soldiers cut off the ropes of the boat, and let her fall off. And while the day was coming on, Paul besought them all to take meat, saying, This day is the fourteenth day that ye have tarried and continued fasting, having taken nothing. Wherefore I pray you to take some meat: for this is for your health: for there shall not an hair fall from the head of any of you.

And when he had thus spoken, he took bread, and gave thanks to God in presence of them all: and when he had broken it, he began to eat. Then were they all of good cheer, and they also took some meat. And we were in all in the ship two hundred threescore and sixteen souls. And when they had eaten enough, they lightened the ship, and cast out the wheat into the sea.

And when it was day, they knew not the land: but they discovered a certain creek with a shore, into the which they were minded, if it were possible, to thrust in the ship. And when they had taken up the anchors, they committed themselves unto the sea, and loosed the rudder bands, and hoisted up the mainsail to the wind, and made toward shore. And falling into a place where two seas met, they ran the ship aground; and the forepart stuck fast, and remained unmoveable, but the hinder part was broken with the violence of the waves.

And the soldiers' counsel was to kill the prisoners, lest any of them should swim out, and escape. But the centurion, willing to save Paul, kept them from their purpose; and commanded that they which could swim should cast themselves first into the sea, and get to land: and the rest, some on boards, and some on broken pieces of the ship. And so it came to pass, that they escaped all safe to land.

It is fascinating, first of all, to see that Luke knew so much about the sea and was able to describe every detail of what the ship went through and what the sea did to the ship. Even more fascinating is his account of Paul. This man knew Jesus, and Jesus knew where Paul was at all times. Jesus knew where Paul was on the Damascus road, in Damascus, in Arabia, and when Barnabas took Paul by the hand and brought him to the apostles and said, "He is real, brethren." Jesus knew where Paul was when he was in Antioch. There the Holy Spirit called him and Barnabas to be missionaries and evangelists to the Gentiles. Jesus even knew where Paul was when he was in that wild, Gentile world. Paul also knew where Jesus was, and they went arm in arm.

Finally, when the ship was being smashed to pieces and the criminals were about to escape and the others cried out about it,

Jesus knew where Paul was because He impressed the centurion even to save the criminals because of Paul. Finally, they landed on shore, and Jesus knew where Paul was then.

Jesus knows where you are. He knows where you are at all times, and He is never a half inch away from you. He is closer to you than your breath. Jesus knows all about you, cares about you, and is with you right now. Let us pray. And let us remember that God can keep us.

> *I pray for your safety. I pray for traveling mercies and care. I pray that God will help you take the broken pieces of your life — wherever your life has been broken — and put them together again. I pray that you will escape out of the hands of evil people and from the power of the devil, that you will be kept by the power of God, and I am in agreement with you now. I stand in faith that God hears our prayer and so shall it be done through Jesus Christ our Lord. Amen and amen.*

Chapter 28 is the last chapter in this tremendous book of the Acts of the Holy Spirit. In this chapter we are really going to find out what Jesus does with a person who obeys Him.

Acts 28:1-4
> And when they were escaped, then they knew that the island was called Melita. And the barbarous people shewed us no little kindness: for they kindled a fire, and received us every one, because of the present rain, and because of the cold. And when Paul had gathered a bundle of sticks, and laid them on the fire, there came a viper out of the heat, and fastened on his hand.
>
> And when the barbarians saw the venomous beast hang on his hand, they said among themselves, No doubt this man is a murderer, whom, though he hath escaped the sea, yet vengeance suffereth not to live.

God is Everywhere

These barbarous people, heathens, had an inner understanding that there is a God. You cannot go anywhere on this earth, among any group of people, and not find signs of God's existence. God has placed himself within people, within their knowledge, within their conscience.

I have traveled six continents. Everywhere I have gone, I have encountered God, even though the people were called heathen. I remember in the deepest jungles of Africa, 11,000 natives had come to hear me preach. I had three interpreters, so when I would give a sentence, the first interpreter said it in his language to that group present and stopped. The second interpreter spoke it, followed by the third interpreter, and by the time it got back to me, I had forgotten what I had said. This went on for 10 or 15 minutes. Finally, I was led of God to tell the interpreters to stop and let me speak in my own tongue. I spoke for an hour to 11,000 natives, most of whom did not know the name of Jesus as I knew it. In the midst of it, a little rain began to fall upon us. I kept on preaching. People did not move. They had their eyes fastened on me, and it was not long until, as I preached and looked into their faces, I realized they were understanding me. I do not mean my words, my English words, but they were understanding that God was speaking to them through me. It was the day of Pentecost in reverse. They were understanding me. I was not speaking in tongues, I was using my own tongue. In reverse, God was using my language. They understood what I was saying.

I made the invitation to come to Christ, which most of them did. I began praying for the healing of the sick, and the first miracle was the healing of a broken neck. This woman who was healed of a broken neck began to testify to those 11,000 natives and in seconds, we were in the midst of one of the greatest healing revivals my ministry had ever known.

When this poisonous snake fastened on Paul's hand and just hung there biting him, those people spoke up from their inner being that there was a justice, there was a judgment. Not knowing Paul, they thought he was a murderer, and though he had escaped the storm of the sea, yet a divine vengeance would not let him live. It is important to know that God is everywhere.

Acts 28:5-10

> And he shook off the beast into the fire, and felt no harm. Howbeit, they looked when he should have swollen, or fallen down dead suddenly: but after they had looked a great while, and saw no harm come to him, they changed their minds, and said that he was a god.
>
> In the same quarters were possessions of the chief man of the island, whose name was Publius; who received us, and lodged us three days courteously. And it came to pass, that the father of Publius lay sick of a fever and of a bloody flux: to whom Paul entered in, and prayed, and laid his hands on him, and healed him.
>
> So when this was done, others also, which had diseases in the island, came, and were healed: who also honoured us with many

honours; and when we departed, they laded us with such things as were necessary.

"Signs" Follow Belief

When that poisonous snake bit Paul's hand, the Bible says he shook off the beast into the fire and felt no harm. He did not handle the snake. He did not pick up the snake and handle it to show how religious he was or how much faith he had. There is no such teaching in the Bible. Paul did not handle the serpent. It had jumped on him. The first thing he did was to shake it off. Everybody knew for certain that the poison entering his body would cause him to swell and fall dead, but he was not harmed. It changed their minds.

When Mark finished his gospel and came down to the last statement, he said, "These signs shall follow them that believe." The signs followed people who would believe. Believers did not follow the signs; signs followed the faith. "They shall take up serpents" means their enemies, and in this particular instance it was a serpent that was an enemy. "They shall take them up" means they shall not suffer harm by them. "If they drink any deadly thing, it shall not hurt them, means while we are ministering in the work of God, there is a divine protection around us until we finish the purpose of the Lord. Without that, none of us would be missionaries or evangelists or even pastors. We would not blaze new trails for the gospel because there are too many enemies out there. However, by believing, these signs follow us, that there will not be hurt or harm enough to stop us. When Paul had this great miracle, he was talked about among all the people of the island, including the head man, the chief, whose father was dying with a heavy fever and a bloody flux. Paul visited him and prayed for him. God healed him, and people all over the island who were diseased came and were healed. Then they honored them with many honors and gave them the necessary things they needed for the rest of their journey.

There is a great lesson here. Those who preach the gospel shall live of the gospel. Paul was called a prisoner in this journey. Yet he wound up being in charge. He who was a captive became a deliverer of the captives. Isn't that just like God, to use us, who are spit on and cast aside and victims of all the things the devil can do? But when the going gets rough, they know where to turn. To those who know Jesus, Jesus is the answer.

Acts 28:11-13

And after three months we departed in a ship of Alexandria, which had wintered in the isle, whose sign was Castor and Pollux. And landing at Syracuse, we tarried there three days. And from thence we fetched a compass, and came to Rhegium: and after one day the south wind blew, and we came the next day to Puteoli: . . .

This is the modern bay of Naples in Italy.

Acts 28:14,15

Where we found brethren, and were desired to tarry with them seven days: and so we went toward Rome. And from thence, when the brethren heard of us, they came to meet us as far as Appii forum, and The three taverns: whom when Paul saw, he thanked God, and took courage.

The brethren mentioned here are Christians from Rome who had heard of Paul's coming and came to meet him after the ship docked where the Appian Way begins. It had been a long, dangerous journey from Caesarea to Rome. He had many fascinating experiences, many dangerous hours. God had revealed himself to Paul in the midst of the storm. He had been bitten by a poisonous snake, shaken it off, and suffered no harm. As a result of that, God used him to bring healing and salvation to the people of that island. Now he had landed on the shores of Italy. Some of the saints of Rome came down to meet him and when Paul saw them, he said, "Thank You, God," and new courage came into his breast.

The appearance of the Christians meant much to Paul after having been alone so long and having been in charge of that ship's journey. Paul got the travelers through because God was in Paul and Paul was being obedient to the heavenly vision. When he reached shore, it meant a lot to him for other Christians to recognize him and to accept him.

It is amazing how we Christians can encourage each other. When we overcome the spirit of criticism and misunderstanding and just love each other, value each other, and come to say an encouraging word, it changes everything. Sometimes, the more a Christian is used, the more the devil tries to keep other Christians away from him or from her. But Paul saw them and thanked God and took courage.

Acts 28:16

And when we came to Rome, the centurion delivered the prisoners to the captain of the guard: but Paul was suffered to dwell by himself with a soldier that kept him.

That means he was chained to a soldier, but at least he was not in with the other prisoners. Verse 17 leads into one of the most significant times in Christian history.

Acts 28:17-28

And it came to pass, that after three days Paul called the chief of the Jews together: and when they were come together, he said unto them, Men and brethren, though I have committed nothing against the people, or customs of our fathers, yet was I delivered prisoner from Jerusalem into the hands of the Romans, who, when they had examined me, would have let me go, because there was no cause of death in me. But when the Jews spake against it, I was constrained to appeal unto Caesar; not that I had ought to accuse my nation of. For this cause therefore have I called for you, to see you, and to speak with you: because that for the hope of Israel I am bound with this chain.

And they said unto him, We neither received letters out of Judaea concerning thee, neither any of the brethren that came shewed or spake any harm of thee. But we desire to hear of thee what thou thinkest: for as concerning this sect, we know that everywhere it is spoken against.

And when they had appointed him a day, there came many to him into his lodging; to whom he expounded and testified the kingdom of God, persuading them concerning Jesus, both out of the law of Moses, and out of the prophets, from morning till evening. And some believed the things which were spoken, and some believed not.

And when they agreed not among themselves they departed, after that Paul had spoken one word, Well spake the Holy Ghost by Esaias the prophet unto our fathers, saying, Go unto this people, and say, Hearing ye shall hear, and shall not understand; and seeing ye shall see, and not perceive: for the heart of this people is waxed gross, and their ears are dull of hearing, and their eyes have they closed; lest they should see with their eyes, and hear with their ears, and understand with their heart, and should be converted, and I should heal them.

Be it known therefore unto you, that the salvation of God is sent unto the Gentiles, and that they will hear it.

Gentiles Would Listen

The Gentiles would hear and receive the Word of God, and that upset the Jews. Not the remnant, not those who really believed Moses and the prophets, but those who believed the traditions or the oral things added to the written things of the Word of God, those who had made a religion out of being religious, those who had a form of godliness, but denied the power of God thereof. Those people got so religious, their religion got in their way. That was the glorious moment of the Gentiles, because the Gentiles were sinners and knew it. When they would hear the Word of God, many of them, millions of them would have a heart ready to receive and believe. Thank God, we Gentiles got in.

Acts 28:29-31

And when he had said these words, the Jews departed, and had great reasoning among themselves. And Paul dwelt two whole years in his own hired house, and received all that came in unto him, preaching the kingdom of God, and teaching those things which concern the Lord Jesus Christ, with all confidence, no man forbidding him.

Thus ends the book of Acts. Israel's rebellion is now complete. A new era begins as the Gentile world begins to open ears, eyes, and hearts to the gospel. There is no logical ending to the book of Acts. Its main hero, Paul, is left in jail.

Although given the right to rent his own hall and to continue preaching about the Lord Jesus Christ, he is still a prisoner. The book of Acts ends like that with no logical reason. Why? Perhaps it is because the book of Acts is not over. It is still being written in the faith of the saints, the people of God. It is still being written because of the fires of persecution and opposition. It is still being written, because the acts of the Holy Spirit continue in the servants of God.

The Epistle of Paul the Apostle to the
Romans

The Epistle of Paul
the Apostle to the
Romans

Romans is the first of the letters that Paul wrote. We have been reading objective reports about the life of our Lord Jesus Christ and reports of the activity of the gospel in the first century, but a letter is different from a report. A letter is a very intimate and warm expression from one heart to another.

This letter was written to some new Christians who lived in Rome, the capital of the Roman Empire. If you think of yourself as living under a world dictatorship, you can identify with this letter and with the Christians of the kingdom of God who established the Christian church right in the presence of Caesar, the Roman emperor. The Caesars were the chosen leaders politically, economically, and spiritually. Understand that any Caesar was like any ruler who carried a particular name when he ascended to power. Augustus Caesar, Claudius Caesar, Caesar Nero — all were Caesars. Imagine that you live in this great city, had been present at the day of Pentecost in Jerusalem, had returned to Rome, and with others had formed the first Christian church there and were living in the presence of the emperor himself who is declared to be a god.

The Romans had a great system of law. They were eminently fair in the way they treated people, with a few exceptions. If you invaded their religion and tried to bring your faith to replace theirs, they would get vile. They eventually beheaded Paul because of this. Suppose you had heard of the greatest man in the Christian Church whose name is Paul. You have not seen him because he has not been to Rome yet. His practice is to go to the great cities of the world, principally the seaport cities of that particular time, for they were centers of greatest influence. Now you hear he is on his way to Rome. He wants to make it a center of evangelism and missionary work throughout all Europe and other areas. Paul has been so successful in spreading the gospel to the Gentiles that he has been persecuted beyond belief. It was Peter who opened the door of the gospel to the Gentiles; it was Paul who was led to take the gospel to the Gentile world, and Paul's greater ministry has been spent among the Gentiles. You have heard of him, you have wanted to see him, you care about him. He has a very deep feeling about you. He has not arrived yet, but he sends a letter.

In those days, letters were written on thick paper made in Egypt. Paul's letters were dictated to secretaries. Imagine him as he strides up and down the room, talking, and the secretaries writing his words down. He is pouring out his heart. With his great training in philosophy, in religion, with his trained intellect, and now with his reborn heart, he is trying to put together the new Christian faith so that you, a new Christian, can understand.

Every letter Paul wrote, including the letter to Rome, was written to a particular group of people or to an individual who faced a situation or problem. And that problem was not unique — it was a problem that Christians in every generation would face. You and I, living today, face the same things Paul was covering in his letter to the Romans.

Romans is a powerful letter and full of great things for us. Let us pray before we begin the book of Romans.

> *Heavenly Father, we know that Romans is one of the great books of the New Testament. It rises to such heights until we feel our souls will take flight into ecstasies in our Lord. On the other hand, there are many things in it very difficult to understand, hard to apply to our lives in the now. But we believe that as we read the book of Romans, You are going to be with us, You are going to open our spiritual eyes and enable us to comprehend what You are saying to us. We stand in agreement that the book of Romans will become the great book You planned it to be in our lives, now and forever, through Jesus Christ. Amen and amen.*

Romans 1:1-7

Paul, a servant of Jesus Christ, called to be an apostle, separated unto the gospel of God, (Which he had promised afore by his prophets in the holy scriptures,) concerning his Son Jesus Christ our Lord, which was made of the seed of David according to the flesh; and declared to be the Son of God with power, according to the spirit of holiness, by the resurrection from the dead: by whom we have received grace and apostleship, for obedience to the faith among all nations, for his name; among whom are ye also the called of Jesus Christ: to all that

be in Rome, beloved of God, called to be saints: Grace to you and
peace from God our Father, and the Lord Jesus Christ.

A Great Greeting

You can feel the throbbing heart of Paul as he greets you, and
your heart is probably beating wildly as you hear these words from
him. (About half of the Roman Church is made up of Jews who have
become Christians, and the other half is made up of Christians who
are Gentiles.) You begin to think: Here is Paul, a servant of Jesus
Christ, a bond slave. He is saying, "I am Christ's property and He
has called me and separated me from all others to bring the gospel
of God. Jesus is the Christ, the Son of God, and the proof of it is
that He was raised from the dead." The moment you hear "raised
from the dead," you would instantly think about Caesar, because
this is striking at the heart of the Roman religion, which is based
upon idols and has never known about the resurrection. Now Paul
is saying, "This Jesus that I am preaching was raised from the dead,
and it is by Him that ye and we have received grace and faith. And
it is through Him that you are the called ones." It is a beautiful and
tender greeting.

Romans 1:8-15

First, I thank my God through Jesus Christ for you all, that your faith
is spoken of throughout the whole world. For God is my witness,
whom I serve with my spirit in the gospel of his Son, that without
ceasing I make mention of you always in my prayers; making request,
if by any means now at length I might have a prosperous journey by
the will of God to come unto you. For I long to see you, that I may
impart unto you some spiritual gift, to the end ye may be established;
that is, that I may be comforted together with you by the mutual faith
both of you and me.

Now I would not have you ignorant, brethren, that oftentimes I
purposed to come unto you, (but was let hitherto,) that I might have
some fruit among you also, even as among other Gentiles. I am debtor
both to the Greeks, and to the Barbarians; both to the wise, and to
the unwise. So, as much as in me is, I am ready to preach the gospel
to you that are at Rome also.

Paul's Teaching Pattern

As you listen to Paul's letter being read to you, you hear him say,

"I thank my God that your faith is so strong. I have heard of it wherever I have gone in the world. God is my witness that I have prayed for you every day." Paul said, "I long to impart unto you some spiritual gift." Paul's teaching on the gifts of the Spirit is that they were not the possession of the man or woman through whom they worked but were delivered to the need of a person. For example, the gift of healing worked through Paul to be given to a person who was sick. Paul is not saying he wanted to impart the gift of healing, the gift of miracles, the gift of faith, and so on. He wanted to impart the power of God working through that gift that they might be established in the faith and that he would also receive fruit from them. Paul's pattern, as we will study in Philippians, was giving and receiving. The result of the love of God is to give and to receive.

Then you hear Paul say this in his letter: "With all that I have in me from God, I am ready to preach the gospel to you that are at Rome also." Visiting Rome meant he would invade the very citadels of the ruling powers of the world dictatorship of Caesar. It meant he would be in the city that was the melting pot of the world. It meant he would visit a small group of people, new Christians, whose lives were endangered every day, and he said, "I am ready, I am ready to come into Rome."

Romans 1:16,17

> For I am not ashamed of the gospel of Christ: for it is the power of God unto salvation to every one that believeth; to the Jew first, and also to the Greek. For therein is the righteousness of God revealed from faith to faith: as it is written, The just shall live by faith.

The Key to Romans

Listening to Paul's letter you hear him say, "I am not ashamed of the gospel, the good news of this man, for the gospel is the power of God unto salvation." The word "salvation," which he wrote in the Greek — "Soteria" — means both deliverance of soul and body. It means spiritual salvation or healing and it means physical healing. It carries the same meaning that Jesus gave it when He said, "To everyone that believes — to the Jew first and also to the Greek" (or the Gentile). He does not mean we have to preach to the Jew first. He is simply saying that chronologically, the Jew had it first. The Jew believed it first. It happened in Jerusalem first. The Jews were the first to be saved and accept Christ, but it also includes the Gentiles.

Then Paul adds, "Everything about the gospel comes out in one word, faith." This is the key issue of the book of Romans: faith. You have the evidence and the proof that you can trust God with your whole life and you will do whatever God says. You will believe the whole gospel, you will rest your whole life now and forever upon God.

Romans 1:18-23

For the wrath of God is revealed from heaven against all ungodliness and unrighteousness of men, who hold the truth in unrighteousness; because that which may be known of God is manifest in them; for God hath shewed it unto them.

For the invisible things of him from the creation of the world are clearly seen, being understood by the things that are made, even his eternal power and Godhead; so that they are without excuse: because that, when they knew God, they glorified him not as God, neither were thankful; but became vain in their imaginations, and their foolish heart was darkened.

Professing themselves to be wise, they became fools, and changed the glory of the uncorruptible God into an image made like to corruptible man, and to birds, and to fourfooted beasts, and creeping things.

God's Work His Witness

Think again of being in that little Christian church in Rome, listening to Paul's letter. Suddenly his voice rises as he says, "Even though they knew in their heart that there is a God, they did not turn to Him. They were not thankful for His presence, but professing themselves to be wise, they became fools and changed the invisible presence and the glory of the incorruptible God into something they could see, feel, and touch — a physical image like man or like birds or four-footed beasts. Therefore, Roman Christians, understand that the wrath of God, or the moral order of God, is at work in this universe." Paul was saying you can see that God exists by the things He has created.

Romans 1:24-27

Wherefore God also gave them up to uncleanness through the lusts of their own hearts, to dishonour their own bodies between themselves: who changed the truth of God into a lie, and worshipped and served the creature more than the Creator, who is blessed for ever. Amen.

For this cause God gave them up unto vile affections: for even their women did change the natural use into that which is against nature:

163

and likewise also the men, leaving the natural use of the woman, burned in their lust one to another; men with men working that which is unseemly, and receiving in themselves that recompence of their error which was meet.

The Homosexual Condemnation

Paul brings this to a quick climax and says, concerning the people who doubt the existence of God right in the presence of the things they can see, feel, and touch, that God gave them up through the desires of their own hearts to dishonor their bodies between themselves. They have tried to rearrange the moral order of the universe.

This term "wrath of God" has really turned a lot of people off. They say, "How could a God of love have wrath?" This will help you. The wrath of God means that God's moral order of things has been rearranged by man; man has attacked it, misjudged it, misused it, and turned loose another power in the universe he cannot handle. For example, if an architect breaks the rules of architecture in a house, the house will collapse. If a person building a bridge violates the laws of construction, the bridge will collapse and great suffering will result. When the moral order of God is reversed by man and disregarded, then that disarranged moral order releases its own destruction. Because of this, God has given them up to vile affections.

As you are there in that Christian church in Rome, you know that Caesar is a homosexual. You know that Rome is the most homosexual city the world ever knew. You realize that Paul is beginning to confront the Roman religion which allows homosexuality in its leaders.

In my evangelistic ministry, I come in contact with virtually all types of people. Many times people who are homosexuals say, "God made me this way, I was born this way." That is a lie of the devil. Everybody is born with sin in the heart and everybody has a besetting sin that he has to fight. It may be that one is born with a propensity to love money or to commit adultery or to steal. A tendency toward homosexuality may be there the same as any other tendency, but God delivers from those tendencies and destroys the power of sin in our lives, as Paul brings out so clearly in his letter to the Romans.

In Verse 27, these people receive in themselves the rewards of their error. The full force of the misuse of human nature strikes them and makes them unnatural in their relationships, unnatural in their thinking, unnatural in their thoughts toward one another or toward God. They do not feel at home with the rest of the world.

They feel alienated by society, as if God has made them that way, and they hate God because of it. And yet, it is of their own desires, Paul says.

New medical evidence today supports Paul's statement that these people receive the recompense of their error. One report has to do with herpes, for which there is no cure. The medical reports are pointing out that certain types of cancer are more often found in the male homosexual. Paul is saying that you cannot misuse the normal functions of the body. It is the temple of God.

Many tell me that homosexuality is an alternate life-style, but so could murderers say that murder is an alternate life-style. Thieves could say stealing is an alternate life-style. People who love money could say that is an alternate life-style. We would have a thousand alternate life-styles if we just accepted homosexuality as an alternate life-style. And we would also be wrong in overemphasizing the error of homosexuality without pointing out other sins as well. Other sins have their recompense of error, and people feel the brunt of them and people secretly would like deliverance.

Many homosexuals I have talked with have been open to salvation because they want to be free from that filthy satanic thing that is against the moral order of God who created us. Paul is saying there is hope. He is saying to the Christians in Rome, "Do not be entangled with it, but also be encouraged to share the good news of the gospel, for it is the power of God unto salvation. You can be free, free, free."

Romans 1:28-32

> And even as they did not like to retain God in their knowledge, God gave them over to a reprobate mind, to do those things which are not convenient; being filled with all unrighteousness, fornication, wickedness, covetousness, maliciousness; full of envy, murder, debate, deceit, malignity; whisperers, backbiters, haters of God, despiteful, proud, boasters, inventors of evil things, disobedient to parents, without understanding, covenant breakers, without natural affection, implacable, unmerciful: who knowing the judgment of God, that they which commit such things are worthy of death, not only do the same, but have pleasure in them that do them.

An Uncontrolled Age

Understand that people who are devoid of God go into a life-style which separates them into various camps. Some are murderers, some are covetous, some are deceitful, some are gossipers, some hate God, some are proud and vain. Others invent evil things that no one has ever thought of before; others practice disobedience to parents. In other words, it was an age out of control, just as our age is out of control today.

Romans 2:1-11

> Therefore thou art inexcusable, O man, whosoever thou art that judgest; for wherein thou judgest another, thou condemnest thyself; for thou that judgest doest the same things. But we are sure that the judgment of God is according to truth against them which commit such things. And thinkest thou this, O man, that judgest them which do such things, and doest the same, that thou shalt escape the judgment of God? Or despisest thou the riches of his goodness and forbearance and longsuffering; not knowing that the goodness of God leadeth thee to repentance?
>
> But after thy hardness and impenitent heart treasurest up unto thyself wrath against the day of wrath and revelation of the righteous judgment of God; who will render to every man according to his deeds: to them who by patient continuance in well doing seek for glory and honour and immortality, eternal life: but unto them that are contentious, and do not obey the truth, but obey unrighteousness, indignation and wrath, tribulation and anguish, upon every soul of man that doeth evil, of the Jew first, and also of the Gentile; but glory, honour, and peace, to every man that worketh good, to the Jew first, and also to the Gentile: for there is no respect of persons with God.

The Oneness of God

Paul says, "Now, you are viewing Rome and seeing the terrible things I am talking about. Do not judge them unless you are judging yourself. Be sure you are not doing the same things." Then he adds the most shattering line of all: "For there is no respect of persons with God."

In one statement he wipes out centuries of division between the Jews and the Gentiles. He is saying that there is one God, there is one faith, there is one law, there is one way to live for everybody. He is saying there is one reward and there is one punishment. Paul did not want the Christians at Rome to feel superior to others while in their own hearts they were lusting after the same things.

That is what God is saying to you and me today as we recoil from what is happening in this wicked generation. Let us look into our hearts. Are we doing the things we say we are against or that we condemn? Do we understand there is one reward for righteousness and one punishment for sin? Do we understand it does not make any difference what our name is, what our race is, what our different churches are, what denomination we belong to or do not belong to? There is no respect of persons with God and we are to live for Christ regardless of what happens in the world.

Romans 2:12-16

For as many as have sinned without law shall also perish without law: and as many as have sinned in the law shall be judged by the law; (For not the hearers of the law are just before God, but the doers of the law shall be justified. For when the Gentiles, which have not the law, do by nature the things contained in the law, these, having not the law, are a law unto themselves: which shew the work of the law written in their hearts, their conscience also bearing witness, and their thoughts the mean while accusing or else excusing one another;) in the day when God shall judge the secrets of men by Jesus Christ according to my gospel.

Origin of God's Law

The Jewish law, going back to the law of Moses, was the law by which the Jews had lived. It was the Jew first who received God. But Paul is pointing out that Gentiles, if their hearts were open to God and they were ready to obey God, were in the same position as those who followed the law and did it correctly. They stood without offense toward God and their consciences were clear. In effect, God is saying that their consciences actually became their law.

God's law is not only written in the Bible. His law for us to live by — His moral order in this universe — was set forth long before men wrote the Bible. It began with God himself. When He created man He put himself in man, and when man stops to examine his heart, to be open to his Creator, he finds his conscience still works just as it did when God put it there.

Romans 2:17-29

Behold, thou art called a Jew, and restest in the law, and makest thy boast of God, and knowest his will, and approvest the things that are more excellent, being instructed out of the law; and art confident that thou thyself art a guide of the blind, a light of them which are in darkness, an instructor of the foolish, a teacher of babes, which hast the form of knowledge and of the truth in the law.

Thou therefore which teachest another, teachest thou not thyself? thou that preachest a man should not steal, dost thou steal? thou that sayest a man should not commit adultery, dost thou commit adultery? thou that abhorrest idols, dost thou commit sacrilege? thou that makest thy boast of the law, through breaking the law dishonourest thou God?

For the name of God is blasphemed among the Gentiles through you, as it is written. For circumcision verily profiteth, if thou keep the law: but if thou be a breaker of the law, thy circumcision is made uncircumcision. Therefore if the uncircumcision keep the righteousness of the law, shall not his uncircumcision be counted for circumcision? And shall not uncircumcision which is by nature, if it fulfil the law, judge thee, who by the letter and circumcision dost transgress the law?

For he is not a Jew, which is one outwardly, neither is that circumcision, which is outward in the flesh: but he is a Jew, which is one inwardly; and circumcision is that of the heart, in the spirit, and not in the letter; whose praise is not of men, but of God.

Truth is in Spirit

Jewishness is not a matter of race. Jewishness is not a matter of circumcision. Jewishness is a matter of faith in God. Paul is saying that it is what is inside our hearts that counts. Our faith in God rises above the fleshly circumcision and, in effect, becomes a circumcision of the spirit, of the heart, rather than of the flesh. Paul is continuing to emphasize that it is the invisible that is the true reality, for the visible things were made from those that are invisible. It is not the outward trappings of religion but the invisible part, your soul, your spirit, which are in obedience to God and which trust in Him as the God of your life and upon whom you rely.

Romans 3:1-8

What advantage then hath the Jew? or what profit is there of circumcision? Much every way: chiefly, because that unto them were committed the oracles of God. For what if some did not believe? shall their unbelief make the faith of God without effect? God forbid: yea, let God be true, but every man a liar; as it is written, That thou mightest be justified in thy sayings, and mightest overcome when thou art judged.

But if our unrighteousness commend the righteousness of God, what shall we say? Is God unrighteous who taketh vengeance? (I speak as a man.) God forbid: for then how shall God judge the world? For if the truth of God hath more abounded through my lie unto his glory; why yet am I also judged as a sinner? And not rather, (as we be slanderously reported, and as some affirm that we say,) Let us do evil, that good may come? whose damnation is just.

Minority Not Cancelled

Paul is rhetorically asking the question, "What is the advantage of being Jewish?" And then he says, "There are many advantages. Chiefly, God gave the Jews the Ten Commandments." The fact is that the majority of the Jewish people never did follow the Lord. It was the remnant who kept the law, who kept the Ten Commandments, who followed God. Paul is saying that the unbelief of the majority of the Jewish people does not cancel out the belief in God of the remnant. All those so-called religious people who do not follow God do not cancel out the faith of that minority in every generation that does follow God. Faith is still faith. As Paul says, God is revealed from faith to faith, from generation to generation.

Romans 3:9-18

What then? are we better than they? No, in no wise: for we have before proved both Jews and Gentiles, that they are all under sin; as it is written, There is none righteous, no, not one: there is none that understandeth, there is none that seeketh after God.

They are all gone out of the way, they are together become unprofitable; there is none that doeth good, no, not one. Their throat is an open sepulchre; with their tongues they have used deceit; the poison of asps is under their lips: whose mouth is full of cursing and bitterness:

Their feet are swift to shed blood: destruction and misery are in their ways: and the way of peace have they not known: there is no fear of God before their eyes.

The Gospel or Nothing

Paul is quoting from Psalms. Verse 12 is the key to what Paul is saying: "They are all gone out of the way. They are together become unprofitable, there is none that doeth good, no, not one."

Paul is saying that if you do not get into the purity of the gospel, into the purity of your faith in God, you do not have anything. You are unprofitable, you are breaking the moral order of God in His universe, and you are becoming a law unto yourself. There is no fear of God in your heart.

Romans 3:19-26

> Now we know that what things soever the law saith, it saith to them who are under the law: that every mouth may be stopped, and all the world may become guilty before God. Therefore by the deeds of the law there shall no flesh be justified in his sight: for by the law is the knowledge of sin.
>
> But now the righteousness of God without the law is manifested, being witnessed by the law and the prophets; even the righteousness of God which is by faith of Jesus Christ unto all and upon all them that believe: for there is no difference:
>
> For all have sinned, and come short of the glory of God; being justified freely by his grace through the redemption that is in Christ Jesus: whom God hath set forth to be a propitiation through faith in his blood, to declare his righteousness for the remission of sins that are past, through the forbearance of God; to declare, I say, at this time his righteousness: that he might be just, and the justifier of him which believeth in Jesus.

The Cults' Mistake

Paul is pointing out that God gave the law as a spotlight upon people so they would have a sense of sin. Having a sense of sin, they would feel their need of a Redeemer. It was the Jews, then, who began to believe God's promise of a Redeemer. But now God has sent that Messiah, and for one to be righteous before God through his faith, that faith must be in Jesus Christ, whom God gave as the sacrifice for the remission of our sins that are past.

This applies to cults. So many times they lay down restrictions wherein members have to work out their salvation. That is saying, in effect, as the Jews said, that it is by the deeds of the law that they are justified. Paul says, "Not so. It is by the shed blood of Jesus Christ."

Romans 3:27-31

> Where is boasting then? It is excluded. By what law? of works? Nay: but by the law of faith. Therefore we conclude that a man is justified by faith without the deeds of the law. Is he the God of the Jews only? is he not also of the Gentiles? Yes, of the Gentiles also: seeing it is one God, which shall justify the circumcision by faith, and uncircumcision through faith. Do we then make void the law through faith? God forbid: yea, we establish the law.

Law, Gospel Contrasted

Paul is pointing out the reason for the law, and saying that just keeping it is not what God had in mind. It is what the law is leading to that God had in mind. Through your sense of sin you feel the need of a Redeemer. That Redeemer has come now and has established a new law: the law of faith. That is the law we live by, the law of faith in God.

That does not mean that when we enter into the faith of Jesus Christ, we do away with the Ten Commandments and the various laws of God. It means that we now can keep them in spirit. We can do what God had in mind all the time. All the things that Paul spoke against, such as murder and adultery, we reject. We now can keep that moral order of God in the universe because we have faith in God.

Imagine again for a moment that you are in the church in Rome. You are a Christian, and the tendency you have is to be jealous. You are saying, "I am not going to be jealous, I am not going to be jealous." You can say that for the rest of your life. What you need is to turn yourself fully by faith to Jesus Christ. When Jesus takes over your life, jealousy just falls away. This is the difference between the laws that were put upon God's people through those years, and the gospel of the sacrifice of Christ which removes the things the law was against so that in Christ, we have a new desire. We are new creatures and we want to do something. That "want to" is based upon our Savior Jesus Christ living in our hearts. We are His property and He is our Lord.

Romans 4:1-8

What shall we say then that Abraham our father, as pertaining to the flesh, hath found? For if Abraham were justified by works, he hath whereof to glory; but not before God.

For what saith the scripture? Abraham believed God, and it was counted unto him for righteousness. Now to him that worketh is the reward not reckoned of grace, but of debt. But to him that worketh not, but believeth on him that justifieth the ungodly, his faith is counted for righteousness.

Even as David also describeth the blessedness of the man, unto whom God imputeth righteousness without works, saying, Blessed are they whose iniquities are forgiven, and whose sins are covered. Blessed is the man to whom the Lord will not impute sin.

Faith Produces Works

Paul takes this opportunity to point out that Abraham was not justified before God by his works, but by his simple faith of believing that God is God, that he could trust his life in His hands, and that through faith he would do whatever God told him. Then Paul refers to David, who says of the man who is blessed that that man has been blessed because of his faith, and his faith, of course, is what produces the works. Paul is saying that your works do not create faith, your faith produces your works.

Romans 4:9-12

> Cometh this blessedness then upon the circumcision only, or upon the uncircumcision also? for we say that faith was reckoned to Abraham for righteousness. How was it then reckoned? when he was in circumcision, or in uncircumcision? Not in circumcision, but in uncircumcision.
>
> And he received the sign of circumcision, a seal of the righteousness of the faith which he had yet being uncircumcised: that he might be the father of all them that believe, though they be not circumcised; that righteousness might be imputed unto them also: and the father of circumcision to them who are not of the circumcision only, but who also walk in the steps of that faith of our father Abraham, which he had being yet uncircumcised.

Get Right With God

Paul is asking here, "Where did all this faith and blessedness in Abraham come from?" It certainly didn't come from his circumcision, for the fact is that Abraham received God's covenant some 13 or 14 years before he was circumcised. He believed God and his faith was counted for righteousness years before he was physically circumcised. So, Paul is saying, the gateway is not circumcision or uncircumcision. It is our belief in God, our faith.

The Jews thought that because they physically descended from Abraham, that made them sons of Abraham. But Paul is saying that the sons of Abraham are those who walk in the steps of the faith of our father Abraham — that kind of faith which enabled him to follow God without question. That is what Paul is talking about.

We have come to a place in our denominational lives where some of us can trace back through many generations our membership in a certain denomination. But remember, before any denomination was founded, Jesus Christ died on the cross and rose from the dead. While we are to love and appreciate and support the denominations to which we belong, they are not our ticket to heaven. They are not our way. Jesus said, "I am the way, the truth, and the life." You might be Pentecostal, Catholic, Methodist, Presbyterian, or of some other denomination, but that does not necessarily make you a follower of Christ. If you do not put Jesus first in your life, you are on the wrong road. It is a very personal matter between you and God, whether you have faith in Christ or not. Getting right with God through your faith is your way to salvation.

Romans 4:13-17

> For the promise, that he should be the heir of the world, was not to Abraham, or to his seed, through the law, but through the righteousness of faith. For if they which are of the law be heirs, faith is made void, and the promise made of none effect: because the law worketh wrath: for where no law is, there is no transgression.
>
> Therefore it is of faith, that it might be by grace; to the end the promise might be sure to all the seed; not to that only which is of the law, but to that also which is of the faith of Abraham; who is the father of us all, (As it is written, I have made thee a father of many nations,) before him whom he believed, even God, who quickeneth the dead, and calleth those things which be not as though they were.

Impossible Becomes Possible

Once again I want you to imagine that you are a Christian in that new Christian church in Rome while Paul's letter is being read aloud. You are starting to understand that it was not Abraham or the descendants of Abraham, but the faith that Abraham had (and the faith that the descendants of Abraham had) that was so important. Abraham believed God, "going out where he knew not" because God told him to start, obeying from his heart. So it is when you obey God. You do whatever the Word of God tells you to do and do it with faith although you do not understand it. Then, you are walking in the steps of the faith of Abraham. And that is by grace — a free gift of God. It is not through some work that you do, something that you earn, some mark that you get, or attending Sunday school, or how often you fall on your knees to pray. It is that simple faith in your heart.

Because of Abraham's faith, God quickened the dead and called those things which were not as though they were. He is referring to Sarah, Abraham's wife, who at age 90 was still barren, and to Abraham, at 100, whose body was the same as dead. God called forth a son to this elderly couple who could not have children. He called that which was not as though it were. He said, "You are going to have a son. I promise you a son." That which was impossible

173

became possible. Faith is believing that the impossible is possible. He is saying here that our faith can call into being things which are not.

Romans 4:18-25

Who against hope believed in hope, that he might become the father of many nations, according to that which was spoken, So shall thy seed be. And being not weak in faith, he considered not his own body now dead, when he was about an hundred years old, neither yet the deadness of Sarah's womb:

He staggered not at the promise of God through unbelief; but was strong in faith, giving glory to God; and being fully persuaded that, what he had promised, he was able also to perform. And therefore it was imputed to him for righteousness. Now it was not written for his sake alone, that it was imputed to him; but for us also, to whom it shall be imputed, if we believe on him that raised up Jesus our Lord from the dead; who was delivered for our offences, and was raised again for our justification.

Belief Eradicates Sin

Abraham was able to use his faith in an impossible situation. That's the way God will work with you if you believe in God who raised Jesus from the dead. Paul was telling the Roman Christians that their hope in Christ was not without foundation. The foundation was based on the fact that God had lived through the ages, blessing men like Abraham for their faith, and had completed the foundation with His Son Jesus Christ whom He raised from the dead. If you believe on Jesus, who is alive, who is alive right now as you are reading this — if you believe on the Lord Jesus Christ, you are justified by faith, you are raised in the newness of life, and you are a Christian.

Romans 5:1-5

Therefore being justified by faith, we have peace with God through our Lord Jesus Christ: by whom also we have access by faith into this grace wherein we stand, and rejoice in hope of the glory of God. And not only so, but we glory in tribulations also: knowing that tribulation worketh patience; and patience, experience; and experience, hope: and hope maketh not ashamed; because the love of God is shed abroad in our hearts by the Holy Ghost which is given unto us.

Hope Through Experience

Paul is saying to the Roman Christians, as he says to us today, that as we have been justified by faith, we have gone into the peace of God. We continue to move forward through the grace which gives us standing grace, and we are able then to have hope. This hope is not a blind hope, but one that through tribulation and patience and experience comes alive in us. When we really experience the hope of God in our hearts, we are not intimidated by anything in this world that comes against us, because we have experienced the love of God, given to us by the Holy Spirit who indwells our lives.

Romans 5:6-11

For when we were yet without strength, in due time Christ died for the ungodly. For scarcely for a righteous man will one die: yet peradventure for a good man some would even dare to die. But God commendeth his love toward us, in that, while we were yet sinners, Christ died for us. Much more then, being now justified by his blood, we shall be saved from wrath through him.

For if, when we were enemies, we were reconciled to God by the death of his Son, much more, being reconciled, we shall be saved by his life. And not only so, but we also joy in God through our Lord Jesus Christ, by whom we have now received the atonement.

Living Through His Love

When you and I were helpless, when we did not have any way out, Christ came and died. His death is the final proof that God truly loves you, because nobody is going to die for a bad person. Maybe once in a while someone will die for a very fine human being, but Jesus died for us when we were helpless, worthless.

Think of His resurrection. Think of the life that He imparts unto us. Because He lives, we live. We are truly enjoying the atonement which covers our sins forever. It is easy for people to say to us, "I love you," or for us to say to others, "I love you," but the love that God had for us through Christ is the most concrete love that anyone ever had for anyone else.

Romans 5:12-21

Wherefore, as by one man sin entered into the world, and death by sin; and so death passed upon all men, for that all have sinned: (For until the law sin was in the world: but sin is not imputed when there is no law. Nevertheless death reigned from Adam to Moses, even over

175

them that had not sinned after the similitude of Adam's transgression, who is the figure of him that was to come. But not as the offence, so also is the free gift. For if through the offence of one many be dead, much more the grace of God, and the gift by grace, which is by one man, Jesus Christ, hath abounded unto many. And not as it was by one that sinned, so is the gift: for the judgment was by one to condemnation, but the free gift is of many offences unto justification.

For if by one man's offence death reigned by one; much more they which receive abundance of grace and of the gift of righteousness shall reign in life by one, Jesus Christ.) Therefore as by the offence of one judgment came upon all men to condemnation; even so by the righteousness of one the free gift came upon all men unto justification of life. For as by one man's disobedience many were made sinners, so by the obedience of one shall many be made righteous. Moreover the law entered, that the offence might abound. But where sin abounded, grace did much more abound: that as sin hath reigned unto death, even so might grace reign through righteousness unto eternal life by Jesus Christ our Lord.

Singularity of Sin, Salvation

This may be difficult for us to understand today unless we go back to the Jewish thinking Paul was replying to when he wrote this fifth chapter of Romans. The Jewish people did not consider themselves as single individuals, but as a people. Therefore, everything happened to and through them as a people, and the whole was the power by which they lived.

Paul is saying that in Jewish thought, sin entered the world by one man. Because that one man was part of the whole, sin was passed onto all of us. On the other hand, when Jesus came to die on the cross, He too was part of the whole. Through one man sin came into the world, but also through one man salvation came into the world for us to accept. It is a free gift. It is the gift of God that we receive by faith, faith in Him as Lord. By the obedience of that one man, Jesus Christ, the whole human race can now be saved.

Romans 6:1-11

What shall we say then? Shall we continue in sin, that grace may abound? God forbid. How shall we, that are dead to sin, live any longer therein? Know ye not, that so many of us as were baptized into Jesus Christ were baptized into his death? Therefore we are buried with him by baptism into death: that like as Christ was raised up from the dead by the glory of the Father, even so we also should walk in newness of life.

For if we have been planted together in the likeness of his death, we shall be also in the likeness of his resurrection: knowing this, that our old man is crucified with him, that the body of sin might be destroyed, that henceforth we should not serve sin. For he that is dead is freed from sin.

Now if we be dead with Christ, we believe that we shall also live with him: knowing that Christ being raised from the dead dieth no more; death hath no more dominion over him. For in that he died, he died unto sin once: but in that he liveth, he liveth unto God. Likewise reckon ye also yourselves to be dead indeed unto sin, but alive unto God through Jesus Christ our Lord.

Christianity is Life

There is a change in your life when Christ comes into your heart. Paul talks in language and symbolism that the people then understood. For example, all the Jewish people believed strongly in baptism, which symbolized that their old lives had ended and their new lives had begun. The Christians in Rome who were Gentiles also understood it, because many of them (who were part of Greek culture and thought) had a form they followed: They were buried in the ground up to their necks, showing that they had reached a certain mark in life which was now to be put in the past. As they came up out of the ground, they were entering into a new life.

Likewise, just as Christ was buried and was raised from the dead, our old lives are buried through baptism, and we rise through the resurrection power into newness of life. We, like Christ, are now alive. We are no longer dead in sin, that is, without spiritual life. Paul wanted them to know that Christianity is life. It goes all the way back to Jesus our Lord who said, "I am come that ye might have life and have it more abundantly." He also said, "I am the way, the truth, and the life." He is telling us that in our Christian lives, there is a before and an after. There was before, when we did not know Christ, and there is the after, or the now, when we know Jesus and things are changed. We are living a different kind of life. We are living Christ's life. We are following in His steps rather than following our own wild human nature. We have accepted the nature of God and we are walking in His love.

Romans 6:12-14

Let not sin therefore reign in your mortal body, that ye should obey it in the lusts thereof. Neither yield ye your members as instruments of unrighteousness unto sin: but yield yourselves unto God, as those that are alive from the dead, and your members as instruments of righteousness unto God. For sin shall not have dominion over you: for ye are not under the law, but under grace.

Putting Down Sin

Paul is saying, "Therefore, quit sinning. Quit using your power of choice to obey those lusts or desires which are trying to pull you away from God." Paul had given up sinning. He had once been a murderer and had indulged in other ungodly behavior, but he now had a new life in Christ. He was yielding himself — spirit, mind, and body — to God.

This statement of Paul to the Christians in Rome must have been a powerful encouragement to them, because Rome was such a center of sin. Everything that could lead them into sin was readily available. Paul was saying, "Do not pay attention to that filthy thing called sin. You have life in Jesus Christ. You have something infinitely better than anything Rome or this world has to offer."

That is true today. Everything around us is designed to appeal to our senses so that we will give ourselves up in some way to sin. But do not forget that greater is He who is in you than he that is in the world. The Christ who is in you is greater than this whole world of sin. If we simply keep our minds on Christ, knowing He is the source of everything that is good, God is going to show us that sin can be put down.

Romans 6:15-23

What then? shall we sin, because we are not under the law, but under grace? God forbid. Know ye not, that to whom ye yield yourselves servants to obey, his servants ye are to whom ye obey; whether of sin unto death, or of obedience unto righteousness? But God be thanked, that ye were the servants of sin, but ye have obeyed from the heart that form of doctrine which was delivered you.

Being then made free from sin, ye became the servants of righteousness. I speak after the manner of men because of the infirmity of your flesh: for as ye have yielded your members servants to uncleanness and to iniquity unto iniquity; even so now yield your members servants to righteousness unto holiness. For when ye were the servants of sin, ye were free from righteousness.

What fruit had ye then in those things whereof ye are now ashamed? for the end of those things is death. But now being made free from sin, and become servants to God, ye have your fruit unto holiness, and the end everlasting life. For the wages of sin is death; but the gift of God is eternal life through Jesus Christ our Lord.

Slaves to Sin

During the days of the Roman Empire, there were many slaves. Slaves never were their own in any moment of their existence. They tried to please their masters, and if they did not please them they were coerced, intimidated, and beaten. Paul compares that to being a slave to sin. When you yield your life, your body, your senses to doing those things which are in disobedience to God, you become a slave to sin. And just as a slave got some form of wages — that is, his keep, shelter, and a few other things — so does sin have wages: death. But Christians are no longer slaves to sin. They have become, like Paul, a bond slave to Jesus Christ. In that very slavery, you are free. You have a freedom that you never had before and you are producing the fruits of that freedom. What you have is the gift of God, and that gift of God is eternal life. Not only are you going to live in this world free from sin — you are going into a world beyond death that is forever free from sin.

What he is saying to us is that our being in Christ is not just one hour a week in church on Sunday morning where we go and say, "Well, I am a Christian and through this I am serving God." It is a total commitment. Paul said, "You were servants of sin; now you are servants of God." By this you have eternal life through Jesus Christ. It is a 100-percent commitment, seven days a week. We live our lives in Christ. Let's pray.

Father, as we have read the words of Paul, "For the wages of sin is death, but the gift of God is eternal life through Jesus Christ our Lord," I pray that not a man who has been reading this will go to hell, not a woman who has been reading this today will go to hell, not a young person who has been reading this will go to hell, but each and all will be saved and will know the gift of God which is eternal life through Jesus Christ our Lord.

Father, I stand in agreement now with these friends that salvation is sure and eternal and that they are coming to Christ and knowing that they know Christ and that they have a sense of eternal life in their beings with a certainty beyond anything else in this world. Thank You, Father, for hearing

*me pray through Jesus Christ our Lord. Amen and
amen.*

Romans 7:1-6

Know ye not, brethren, (for I speak to them that know the law,) how
that the law hath dominion over a man as long as he liveth? For the
woman which hath an husband is bound by the law to her husband
so long as he liveth; but if the husband be dead, she is loosed from
the law of her husband. So then if, while her husband liveth, she be
married to another man, she shall be called an adulteress: but if her
husband be dead, she is free from that law; so that she is no adulteress,
though she be married to another man.

Wherefore, my brethren, ye also are become dead to the law by
the body of Christ; that ye should be married to another, even to him
who is raised from the dead, that we should bring forth fruit unto
God. For when we were in the flesh, the motions of sins, which were
by the law, did work in our members to bring forth fruit unto death.
But now we are delivered from the law, that being dead wherein we
were held; that we should serve in newness of spirit, and not in the
oldness of the letter.

Christ Changed Things

The Jewish people believed that they were married to the law.
Paul is talking to them in terms that they understand by saying that,
although they were married to the law just as a husband is married
to his wife, since Jesus came and died for our sins we are free from
the law to become married to Christ and married to Him forever.
We are delivered from the letter of the law into the Spirit of God
himself, into a new marriage — a new love. When we get to the
book of Revelation, we will read about the marriage supper of the
Lamb, for truly we are married to Christ who is alive forevermore.

Romans 7:7-14

What shall we say then? Is the law sin? God forbid. Nay, I had not
known sin, but by the law: for I had not known lust, except the law
had said, Thou shalt not covet. But sin, taking occasion by the
commandment, wrought in me all manner of concupiscence. For
without the law sin was dead. For I was alive without the law once:
but when the commandment came, sin revived, and I died. And the
commandment, which was ordained to life, I found to be unto death.
For sin, taking occasion by the commandment, deceived me, and by
it slew me.

Wherefore the law is holy, and the commandment holy, and just, and good. Was then that which is good made death unto me? God forbid. But sin, that it might appear sin, working death in me by that which is good; that sin by the commandment might become exceeding sinful. For we know that the law is spiritual: but I am carnal, sold under sin.

Mistakes Not Sin

Paul is telling the Christians at Rome that the law of Moses is a good thing. It came to reveal to each of them their sense of sinfulness and their need of a Redeemer. As long as the law was not there, they could do certain things without feeling that it was a sin. They could even covet or lust. But the commandment which said, "Thou shalt not covet," showed them that when they coveted, they sinned.

In other words, he is saying that when you make a mistake you make a mistake because you do not know better. But when you sin, you sin when you know better than to sin. Sin is something you do when you know it is wrong. A mistake is something you do when you do not know it is wrong. But the law itself is not a bad thing. It is spiritual. Without it, without a proper relationship toward it, we become sinful and that sin is held against us. At the same time, the law in itself cannot deliver us from that sin. It is as though we are sold to sin.

Notice that in the rest of this chapter, Paul is speaking personally. He is showing his own inward struggles because he knew that those who read his letter would identify with his troubles because they had the same struggles. Paul was not able to control himself when he was in sin, but through God, he was able to bring sin under control.

Romans 7:15-25

For that which I do I allow not: for what I would, that do I not; but what I hate, that do I. If then I do that which I would not, I consent unto the law that it is good. Now then it is no more I that do it, but sin that dwelleth in me. For I know that in me (that is, in my flesh,) dwelleth no good thing: for to will is present with me; but how to perform that which is good I find not.

For the good that I would I do not: but the evil which I would not, that I do. Now if I do that I would not, it is no more I that do it, but sin that dwelleth in me. I find then a law, that, when I would do good, evil is present with me. For I delight in the law of God after the inward man: but I see another law in my members, warring against the law of my mind, and bringing me into captivity to the law of sin which is

181

in my members.

O wretched man that I am! who shall deliver me from the body of this death? I thank God through Jesus Christ our Lord. So then with the mind I myself serve the law of God; but with the flesh the law of sin.

God Delivers!

Paul is saying that knowing what is right and doing it are two different things. He is saying that if he still lives under the law, he wants to do right but he finds that there is a law of sin in his members. As he yields to that law of sin, he ends up being a wretched man, crying, "Who shall deliver me from this kind of death-life?" Then he answers his own question: "I thank God, through Jesus Christ our Lord." Then he begins the eighth chapter with triumph over the old kind of life in sin.

As you read Chapter 8, I want you to bear in mind that it could be called the chapter of the Holy Spirit. Pay particular attention to the triumph that Paul says comes through the Holy Spirit.

Romans 8:1-4

There is therefore now no condemnation to them which are in Christ Jesus, who walk not after the flesh, but after the Spirit. For the law of the Spirit of life in Christ Jesus hath made me free from the law of sin and death. For what the law could not do, in that it was weak through the flesh, God sending his own Son in the likeness of sinful flesh, and for sin, condemned sin in the flesh: that the righteousness of the law might be fulfilled in us, who walk not after the flesh, but after the Spirit.

You can just see those Christians in Rome listening to the letter being read, experiencing the analogy that Paul was making: by living under the law, they really could not overcome sin in their lives. They did not have the power of God to do it.

Then Paul abruptly shifts and tells them that there is victory, and that victory comes through the Holy Spirit who gives them the power (as He indwells them) to overcome the law of sin and death. And he speaks personally, saying that he had been delivered from it. He mentions that the law was weak through the flesh, but that God sent His own Son in the likeness of sinful flesh in order to condemn sin in the flesh. He said that God sent His Son in the likeness of sinful flesh — not in sinful flesh per se but in the likeness of it. The difference in Jesus' life is that He was conceived by the Holy Spirit and lived His life in the power of the Holy Spirit. Paul is telling us that if we live in the Spirit, we can live in the likeness of Jesus Christ, that we too can overcome sin in the same way He did.

Romans 8:5-11

For they that are after the flesh do mind the things of the flesh; but they that are after the Spirit the things of the Spirit. For to be carnally minded is death; but to be spiritually minded is life and peace. Because the carnal mind is enmity against God: for it is not subject to the law of God, neither indeed can be. So then they that are in the flesh cannot please God.

But ye are not in the flesh, but in the Spirit, if so be that the Spirit of God dwell in you. Now if any man have not the Spirit of Christ, he is none of his. And if Christ be in you, the body is dead because of sin; but the Spirit is life because of righteousness. But if the Spirit of him that raised up Jesus from the dead dwell in you, he that raised up Christ from the dead shall also quicken your mortal bodies by his Spirit that dwelleth in you.

Holy Spirit Chapter

Paul mentions the Spirit some 20 times in this eighth chapter of Romans. Paul is emphasizing, such as in Verse 9, that if you have not the Spirit, you do not have Christ and do not belong to Christ. However, if you have the Spirit, you dwell in Jesus Christ and He dwells in you. That is, it is through the Spirit of God living in you that you are able to overcome sin in this world and able to live a life different from this world system, different from unredeemed human nature. When unredeemed human nature has its own way, the end is death — spiritual death, everlasting death. But by the Spirit of God there is incomparable power.

The moment Paul speaks of the Holy Spirit, he is thinking of that divine or that supernatural power that comes into your life and enables you to do the impossible. For example, he says, "If the Spirit that raised Christ from the dead lives in you, He will also resurrect your mortal body when you die." Not only is there life in Christ here on this earth while you are living in the flesh (your human flesh), but after your human flesh dies, the Holy Spirit will be the agent to raise your body from the dead. He is pointing you and me to the greater one: the Holy Spirit through whom we shall do greater things because the Spirit lives in us.

Romans 8:12-15

Therefore, brethren, we are debtors, not to the flesh, to live after the flesh. For if ye live after the flesh, ye shall die: but if ye through the Spirit do mortify the deeds of the body, ye shall live. For as many as are led by the Spirit of God, they are the sons of God. For ye have not received the spirit of bondage again to fear; but ye have received the Spirit of adoption, whereby we cry, Abba, Father.

"Adoption" Reference Clarified

Paul now uses the word "adoption," which he knew those in Rome would readily understand. In referring to one coming into Christ, he is saying that is an adoption. He refers to a practice in Rome where the father in a Roman household was almost an absolute ruler. He was in charge until he died. No matter how many sons or daughters he had, he really ruled. That gave him tremendous power. Therefore, if he adopted a son or a daughter, he made that son or daughter equal with his other children. If he didn't have a child and he adopted a child, he gave that child all legal rights. Now, the father, having such ruling power over his family, could give all that legal power. And that son had all the power of the father.

In the adoption process there were seven witnesses, seven powerful people who stood by during the actual adoption process. They were there to witness the scene, the transfer of the child to the father, the signing of the documents, and all the details. Later, if someone tried to say that the child was not adopted or this was not legal, the father would call on one or more of those seven witnesses who would come forward and say, "I was there. I witnessed it."

Romans 8:16,17

The Spirit itself beareth witness with our spirit, that we are the children of God: and if children, then heirs; heirs of God, and joint-heirs with Christ; if so be that we suffer with him, that we may be also glorified together.

Spirit of Witness

When we are adopted into the kingdom of God by our heavenly Father, who has absolute power, He makes us a complete child — son or daughter — or heir to all that He has. If we are one of several children, we are joint-heirs with the other children.

When the devil tries to make you and me doubt that we are God's children, the Holy Spirit himself says, "I saw it, I witnessed it, I know it. It is everlastingly true." The Spirit's witness is going on all the time in our hearts against the opposing powers of our lives. Through the Spirit and adoption, we become God's heirs and joint-heirs with His Son Jesus Christ.

Romans 8:18-25

> For I reckon that the sufferings of this present time are not worthy to be compared with the glory which shall be revealed in us. For the earnest expectation of the creature waiteth for the manifestation of the sons of God. For the creature was made subject to vanity, not willingly, but by reason of him who hath subjected the same in hope, Because the creature itself also shall be delivered from the bondage of corruption into the glorious liberty of the children of God.
>
> For we know that the whole creation groaneth and travaileth in pain together until now. And not only they, but ourselves also, which have the firstfruits of the Spirit, even we ourselves groan within ourselves, waiting for the adoption, to wit, the redemption of our body.
>
> For we are saved by hope: but hope that is seen is not hope: for what a man seeth, why doth he yet hope for? But if we hope for that we see not, then do we with patience wait for it.

Death Due to Lose

Paul understood that as he talked, the Christians in Rome, the same way we do today, were thinking, "Well, now that I'm born of God and I'm living in the Spirit, I want the rest of it. I want my body to be redeemed the same way my spirit is. I want the earth restored to its original glory. I want things complete as they once were." And Paul is saying that is going to happen.

The things that you are suffering now really cannot be compared with the glory of restoration that God is going to perform. He is even going to give you an adoption, which means the redemption of your body, and which also means the redemption of this earth.

Everything in the resurrection is going to be changed in the same way that your spirit is reborn. In the resurrection your body will be reborn. The whole earth, the entire creation, every living thing will be reborn. We will come into this world that we hope for just as we, through the hope of God, have entered into the experience of the Holy Spirit and are new creatures.

By that same hope our bodies will be raised from the dead, and the earth will be restored. The relationship we have with God spiritually and which, through the Spirit, we have to some extent in our bodies, we are going to have 100 percent physically and creationally when our God redeems everything.

Paul says in Verse 23 that we "groan within ourselves waiting for the adoption, to wit, the redemption of our body." I am in the healing ministry. I believe in the healing or salvation of the soul. I believe God also heals the body, but there is a difference.

When God saves the soul, the Holy Spirit witnesses to that salvation. Therefore, through the Holy Spirit, we will live forever. But our souls live in a body — a physical body. That body, according to Paul, also needs to be renewed. It needs to be redeemed. But remember, the devil controls death and death is the last enemy. The only thing the devil still has after the death of Christ is his hold on death. But in the resurrection, death will be swallowed up in victory. In the resurrection the devil's hold upon our bodies will be forever loosed. The decay in our bodies, the weakness in our bodies, the ever-dying of our bodies, and even that moment of death itself is going to have a redemption. Therefore, I believe that every time one of us is healed, that is a touch of the resurrection. And I believe whatever is missed in our bodies in this life will be given to us, physically, in our resurrection from the dead. So the resurrection is our "ticket." We cannot lose as Christians, even physically, because the resurrection will not only restore the universe, the creation, but will redeem our bodies also.

I know there are very sincere, dedicated people who believe that what happens to the soul in salvation is going to happen to the body in the same way on this earth. The same thing that happened to our souls in salvation WILL happen to our bodies ultimately in the resurrection, but it will not happen altogether in this lifetime. That we can have better health, yea and amen! That is why God has given us doctors and medicine, the chemicals of this earth. That is why we built the City of Faith Health Care Center in Tulsa — to unite God's healing streams of medicine and prayer.

But beyond medical skill is the prayer of faith. God raises up the sick through the prayer of faith and we are healed of that particular sickness. But healing does not stop the flaw of death that is in this world. Death is the absolute proof that man sinned and fell in the Garden of Eden. It is the proof around us every day. It is the proof in our own mortal flesh. But it will not defeat us. There will be many healings for us in this life, healings that will enable us to live a victorious life. However, it is appointed unto man once to die, and we will die, every one of us. It will be a physical death. But thank God the resurrection is the absolute proof that Jesus came and died on Calvary for us.

While death is the absolute proof that Adam sinned and fell in the Garden of Eden and organically and spiritually brought all mankind down into sin and death, at the same time the resurrection of Jesus from the dead is absolute proof that we shall live spiritually, physically, and even the creation itself shall forevermore be restored to the original likeness of our God. Hallelujah!

Romans 8:26,27

> Likewise the Spirit also helpeth our infirmities: for we know not what we should pray for as we ought: but the Spirit itself maketh intercession for us with groanings which cannot be uttered. And he that searcheth the hearts knoweth what is the mind of the Spirit, because he maketh intercession for the saints according to the will of God.

Holy Spirit Prayer

Paul is saying to the Roman Christians and to us that in the same way that the Spirit of God is doing His mighty work to save us, to redeem our bodies, and even to redeem the creation, likewise the Spirit is working in us to help us with our weaknesses, because we do not even know what to pray for as we ought.

Paul knew by his own experience that the most precious thing is to know how to get your prayers answered. He states that in our human flesh we really do not know what to pray for. Why don't we? First, we do not know what to pray for because we do not know the future. We do not even know what will happen a year from now, or a month, a week, a day, an hour, even the next minute. We do not know what the future holds. Therefore, we do not know what to pray for.

Also, we do not know what is best for us. Many times we pray for something and it does not happen and as time passes, we look back and we say, "Oh, thank God that prayer was not answered," because we did not know what to pray for. We did not know what was best for us.

Paul flatly says we do not know what we should pray for as we ought. He was understanding the heart cry of those Christians and of us today who want so much to know how to pray as we ought. Then he gives the answer: The Holy Spirit knows how to pray, and He makes intercession for us with groanings which cannot be uttered or in ways that we humans are just incapable of doing; we cannot articulate what our hearts want to say, need to say, and should say. But the Holy Spirit is searching our hearts all the time to find out what is in them, to find the things that need to be brought into harmony with God so He can make intercession for us according to the will of God, who knows the future, and who knows what is best for us.

I will comment more about this in I Corinthians 14, but as for Verses 26 and 27, we can know how to pray because of the Holy Spirit who prays within us. When we understand that, we can join His prayer by our spirit.

Romans 8:28-30

> And we know that all things work together for good to them that love God, to them who are the called according to his purpose. For whom he did foreknow, he also did predestinate to be conformed to the image of his Son, that he might be the firstborn among many brethren. Moreover whom he did predestinate, them he also called: and whom he called, them he also justified: and whom he justified, them he also glorified.

"Good" is Conditional

The Christians in Rome were very aware of the Stoics, the leading philosophers in Rome at that time. They too believed that all things work together for a person's good. Paul referred to it from God's point of view. Paul said, "We know that all things work together for good." Then he added, "to them that love God, to them who are the called according to his purpose."

Paul is saying, "We know what the Stoics are saying, but they are wrong because all things working together for good is not for every person. It is for those who love God. It is for those who are the called according to His purpose, who have opened their hearts to the purpose of God for their lives, and have loved God for having this purpose for them which they pursue with all their hearts."

Then Paul adds a word about those who are called according to His purpose: Each one of you who knows God must know in your heart that God has known from the beginning that you would love Him. We who love God and are the called according to His purpose are the ones whom God knew, for He has known from the beginning who would choose Him.

Verse 28 is very rightfully a verse that most of us Christians love and say over and over: "And we know that all things work together for good to them that love God, to those who are the called according to his purpose." What we need to look at in a very important way is this statement, "to them who are the called according to his purpose." Paul explains who the called are. He is saying that, although God gave man the power of choice, He knew in advance who was going to exercise that power of choice and accept His purpose for their lives, and who would use their power of choice to reject God's purpose and therefore would not be called. The calling of God, therefore, is in our free choice of accepting His purpose for our lives. In our acceptance we become the called. Therefore, in being the called, God is intermingling everything that happens to us so that overall, everything, when it is intermingled with all other things, works together for our good. It works together for our good because we are among those who are called. We are in that body of believers. We are in the Body of Christ. We have all the power of the eternal God working in our behalf as different things come at us, both good and bad, to see to it that when it is over we will say, God did it just right.

That is very encouraging to me because I have gone through so much. So many good and bad things have come my way — terrible losses and persecutions of virtually every description until the devil would have me believe that all things are not going to work for my good. But I do not believe the devil. I believe that we Christians are among the called because we have obeyed the purpose of the Lord, and therefore He glorifies himself in us because we choose Him. In choosing Him, we are the called. His mighty power is constantly working in our behalf day and night, 24 hours a day. Therefore, we know that all things work together for our good because of our love for God and because we have chosen His purpose for our lives.

Romans 8:31-39

> What shall we then say to these things? If God be for us, who can be against us? He that spared not his own Son, but delivered him up for us all, how shall he not with him also freely give us all things?
>
> Who shall lay any thing to the charge of God's elect? It is God that justifieth. Who is he that condemneth? It is Christ that died, yea rather, that is risen again, who is even at the right hand of God, who also maketh intercession for us. Who shall separate us from the love of Christ? shall tribulation, or distress, or persecution, or famine, or nakedness, or peril, or sword? As it is written, For thy sake we are killed all the day long; we are accounted as sheep for the slaughter. Nay, in all these things we are more than conquerors through him that loved us.
>
> For I am persuaded, that neither death, nor life, nor angels, nor principalities, nor powers, nor things present, nor things to come, nor height, nor depth, nor any other creature, shall be able to separate us from the love of God, which is in Christ Jesus our Lord.

Christ's Unifying Power

Paul is saying, If God loves us so much and was on our side so much that He gave His Son to die for us, then surely He is for us. And if He who did not even spare His own Son is for us, who in the world can be against us? Through Him He acquitted us from the charges of sin. When we stand at the judgment there will be no charge laid at the feet of us, or God's elect, because it is God who does the justifying. Christ died, is now risen from the dead, and is at the right hand of God where He intercedes for us. Who then thinks he can separate us from the love of Christ? Shall tribulation? Shall distress or persecution or famine or nakedness or danger or even the sword? These things bring us closer to God. No, none of these things have the power to separate us, for in all these things we are more than conquerors because Jesus Christ loves us.

Then Paul speaks personally: "I am persuaded that death cannot separate us." Everyone has real concern about death. Many have fear. But Paul is saying that death cannot separate us from God because it is the gateway into the presence of God. Neither can life separate us — life itself, life that is so daily, life that we have all the time. That will not separate us.

Nor can angels separate us from God. They knew what he was talking about because, in Jewish thought, angels played a prominent part. They were in everything. The Jewish rabbis, of whom Paul had been one, believed that there were several orders of angels. They even believed that in the beginning when God created man, the angels were jealous. That is one reason why Lucifer (who became the devil), while he was an archangel, rebelled against God and tried to take God's place. He did not like it because God was making man. When he saw that God was making man, he saw that God was making a masterpiece — that man was God's masterpiece. So, he coveted man. He wanted to take charge of man.

Paul was saying that not even angels who may have had a grudge against man shall be able to separate us. Paul was speaking rhetorically there, according to Jewish thought, and was saying that even according to that belief, the angels shall not be able to separate us.

Nor can any principalities — earthly or satanic — separate us from the love of Christ. Nor can the powers that rule the world. Nor can things present on earth or things beyond this earth. Nor can height or depth. Here, he is speaking of astrology. In that time, the world was carried away with astrology, which had been made famous in ancient Babylon. Height and depth here refer to the zenith of a star, when the star reaches its zenith, or when it comes down to its lowest point. He is saying to the astrologers that people are not born under stars. Stars do not have anything to do with human beings and what happens to them or their eternal destiny, either when the stars are at their zenith or at their lowest points. It makes no difference. Neither height nor depth of the stars can separate us from the love of God.

People who read horoscopes in the newspaper or who have their "futures" read or told to them often live in fear of where the star will be at a certain time or where the star was in the heavens when they were born. Paul is saying that has nothing to do with it. In fact, he is saying, "There is nothing to it." In Christ there is no such height or depth that can separate us from the love of Christ.

"Or any other creature." Paul simply says that nothing else shall be able to separate us from the love of God which is in Jesus Christ our Lord. There in Rome where danger was on every hand, where the Caesars were absolute monarchs and called themselves gods, where people followed astrology, where Christians were killed in the coliseum, where the sword was ever present — there in rotten, polluted Rome, there was nothing that could separate any of those Christians from God's love.

Paul's words reigned through the centuries, and they speak to you and me today that nothing, absolutely nothing, will be able to separate you or me from the love of Christ as long as we choose to serve the Lord. If we put Him first in our lives, I tell you, nothing will be able to take us out of God's hands.

As you read Chapter 9, you are going to face the riddle of the Jews. A paradox existed in the heart of Paul. He felt called to the Gentiles and yet loved Israel, or the Jews, with a heart that is very difficult to describe today. As you read this, there will be times, it appears, that Paul is angry at his own people, but he is not. Remember, he is talking and writing not in anger but with the deepest sorrow, compassion, and even hope and faith. In Chapters 9-11, you will learn the way God looks at His ancient people and at the Gentiles. And finally, you will see how the Gentiles and the Jews come together in the Body of Christ.

When Frederick the Great was in power in Germany, he had a court preacher. One day they were discussing the role of the Jewish people in history. Then the conversation turned to the existence of God. Frederick the Great said to the court preacher, "Give me in one word the unanswerable proof that God exists." Quick as a flash the court preacher said, "The Jew, your majesty." The greatest proof of God in the world is the Jew. There are many other proofs, but the continuity of the Jewish people for over 3,500 years is seen here in Paul's writings. It is going to touch our hearts.

Romans 9:1-6

> I say the truth in Christ, I lie not, my conscience also bearing me witness in the Holy Ghost, that I have great heaviness and continual sorrow in my heart.
>
> For I could wish that myself were accursed from Christ for my brethren, my kinsmen according to the flesh: who are Israelites; to whom pertaineth the adoption, and the glory, and the covenants, and the giving of the law, and the service of God, and the promises; whose are the fathers, and of whom as concerning the flesh Christ came, who is over all, God blessed for ever. Amen.
>
> Not as though the word of God hath taken none effect. For they are not all Israel, which are of Israel: . . .

Paul's Jewish Feelings

I think that Paul is appealing to the Christians who were Jews in the Roman Church and also to the Gentiles concerning something that was on his heart day and night: his people, the Jews. He was a Jew in the flesh and he was a Jew in the faith. Now, he had just ended the eighth chapter of Romans by telling them and us that there is nothing that can separate us from the love of God. Yet he declares that his heart is so heavy and so full of love for his own Jewish people that he would be willing to be accursed, to be separated from the love of God, if that would bring his people, the Jews, to Christ. I do not know if Paul faced the same feelings that we do about Jewish people today. Someone has said we love the Jewish people but not the Jewish person. (In contrast is the black man; often people admire the individual black man but not the black "nation" or the black race.) It is a paradox, in a way, that so many of us care for Israel but on a one-to-one basis, there is not always that same feeling between a Christian and a Jewish person. But Paul is gathering it all up, both the nation and the individual Jew.

He said, "I could wish that myself were accursed from Christ for my brethren." Accursed means the spiritual ban from almighty God, that one is placed in the hands of God to be banished from the human race and also from the presence of God. The word is "anathema." "I could be anathema, accursed, cast out."

This is the same spirit that Moses had in Deuteronomy 32 when he came down from Mt. Sinai with the Ten Commandments and found that Aaron, his brother, and the Israelites had built a golden calf. They were worshiping the calf rather than the God who had given the divine ordinances and the law for them to come to a sense of their sinfulness and to recognize their need of a Redeemer. He threw the tablets down and broke them. Then he turned around and did something very strange — it was almost a love-hate relationship. On the one hand he was so upset that he threw down the Ten Commandments (which were inscribed by God's finger upon stone) and broke them. On the other hand he said, "Forgive their sin and if You do not, just blot me out of the book of remembrance which You keep in heaven." Moses loved them so much that in spite of what they had done, he was willing to be accursed.

That is the same spirit that Paul had and in Verse 4 he tells why. They are Israelites, to whom pertaineth the adoption, and the glory, and the covenants, and the giving of the law. These people were adopted into the kingdom of God and it is into the family of Israel that we are adopted by faith. Also, He gave them the glory, the shekinah glory that came down in the tabernacle and also in the temple, His presence that revealed to them that He was real, that He was God and they would be His people.

He mentioned the covenants. It was the covenant, or the pledge, that God used with His people — with this people. He pledged himself to these people and asked them to pledge themselves to Him in a covenant which He would never break. They might break it but He would not. Also, the giving of the law was to them as was the service of the temple, the worship of God that went on century after century in the temple in Jerusalem where the high day of atonement was held, the shedding of blood for remission of sin for one year at a time, looking forward to the shed blood of Christ, "and the promises" — the promises of the prophets that the Messiah would come.

Of the Jews are the fathers, the patriarchs, the founding fathers of the Jewish faith. He was saying that the present Jews had not created a relationship with God. It had been passed down through faith from generation to generation, and they were standing on the shoulders of those who had walked the path before them, the fathers. Finally, he said, "of whom is the Christ." It was from these people that Christ came in the flesh, over all, blessed by God forever.

Then he adds this: "For not all are Israel ... which are of Israel." Not all of those people were true Israelites. There was the remnant. But even the remnant was precious, and there is continual sorrow in the heart of Paul and in the heart of every genuine Christian.

Many of us have a very strong heritage in the Christian faith. Many of us, like Oral Roberts, were born into a Christian family and were raised on the Bible and the church. Yet many of us have gone away from it. We have never taken advantage of the glorious aspects of the gospel, even as the Jews had not when Paul's heart was so heavy over them that he was willing to leave Christ if that would bring them to Christ. Many of us have this hurt in our hearts for the souls of people who have been raised in the Christian faith, who know something of the Bible and go to church once in a while and are glad it is there but do nothing by faith of their own. I plead with you today, if in any way you have left Christ out of your life, to remember that He is real and that some of us might even be willing to do what Paul did — to give up our own rights in Christ to win our fellow man to Jesus Christ.

Romans 9:7-13

Neither, because they are the seed of Abraham, are they all children: but, In Isaac shall thy seed be called. That is, They which are the children of the flesh, these are not the children of God: but the children of the promise are counted for the seed. For this is the word of promise, At this time will I come, and Sarah shall have a son.

And not only this; but when Rebecca also had conceived by one, even by our father Isaac; (For the children being not yet born, neither having done any good or evil, that the purpose of God according to election might stand, not of works, but of him that calleth;) it was said unto her, The elder shall serve the younger. As it is written, Jacob have I loved, but Esau have I hated.

Abraham's Exceptions

Paul is pointing out to the Jewish people that although they are the physical descendants of Abraham, being his seed, they are not his only children, for he said, "In Isaac shall thy seed be called." What he was saying is that Abraham had more than one son. He had Ishmael, who became the father of the Arabs. But the real son of Abraham was the son of promise because he was born by a miracle.

When Abraham and Sarah were too old to have children, it was by their faith in God that God enabled them to have a promised child. Through him, because of faith, all who descended from him would have the privilege of being the sons and daughters of Abraham. That privilege would be connected to their faith and not just to their physical birth.

Then Paul pointed out that when Isaac married Rebecca, twins were born, Jacob and Esau. Before they were even born, God had said that Esau, "the elder," would serve Jacob, "the younger." The Jews thought that whatever happened to one of them happened to all. But God was pointing out that not everybody who descended from Abraham is of the promised seed. "Jacob have I loved, but Esau have I hated."

Someone might say, "That is a terrible thing." Oh, no! God knew in advance that Jacob, although he would be a treacherous boy in his youth, would come to the point when he would have his nature changed by God and would be just as close to God as his father Isaac and his grandfather Abraham. God knew that Jacob would be the father of the twelve tribes of Israel. He also knew that Esau would never care anything about the God of Abraham. God knew that before Esau was born, and God predicted in advance what was going to happen.

So Paul is saying that just because someone is of Jewish blood, that is, of the blood of Abraham, that does not make him a child of God any more than it made Ishmael or Esau one. Ishmael, Abraham's son, became the father of the Arabs, and Esau, Isaac's son, became the father of the Edomites. Paul knew that the Jews understood what he was saying. They did not think of Arabs as chosen of God or the Edomites as the chosen of God. He knew that they knew THEY were the chosen of God because of the faith of the fathers and the faith of those who had come from the fathers — those descendants who had counted themselves as Jews because of their faith and not because of their bloodline.

Then Paul asks the question, "Shall we say then that God is unrighteous?" (Verse 14). He answers, "No way." He then quotes a scripture in Exodus 33:19 where God said to Moses, "I will have mercy upon whom I will have mercy." One thing I run across all the time is that everybody says, "Well, I am a human being." No matter how they are living before God, against God, or for God, or in apathy — "Well, I am a human being." In effect they are saying, "I should have everything that God has no matter how I react or respond toward Him." But it is not so. Throughout history God has known the end from the beginning. He has known which hearts would be open to Him and which would not. He has known who would have faith and who would not, and who would claim, just because they are "human beings," that they are going to be saved regardless of their receiving or rejecting the Son of God. God knows that in advance. So just because you have a grandfather, grandmother, mother, or other loved one who has served Christ, that does not mean you are serving Christ. God has no grandchildren; He only has sons and daughters. That means you and I have to believe Christ for ourselves. Paul is coming down to where you and I live. Christianity is eminently a personal and intimate relationship with God. Do you have it?

Romans 9:14-18

What shall we say then? Is there unrighteousness with God? God forbid. For he saith to Moses, I will have mercy on whom I will have mercy, and I will have compassion on whom I will have compassion. So then it is not of him that willeth, nor of him that runneth, but of God that sheweth mercy.

For the scripture saith unto Pharaoh, Even for this same purpose have I raised thee up, that I might shew my power in thee, and that my name might be declared throughout all the earth. Therefore hath he mercy on whom he will have mercy, and whom he will he hardeneth.

A Choice of Heart

Paul is pointing out that God is God. He will do what He will do. He demonstrated that through the hardening of the heart of Pharaoh. When the Israelites were in Egyptian bondage and Moses came down to deliver them, Pharaoh would not let them go. His heart was hardened. Here Paul says that God raised up Pharaoh so that a man with a hard heart would stand against His people and so that those people would rise up in faith, overcome him, and come out of Egypt and enter the Promised Land.

God did not simply harden Pharaoh's heart. God put a situation in front of Pharaoh where he could cooperate with God and let His people go or he could dig his heels in the ground and say, "No, I will not believe in this God. I will not be influenced by the God of the Israelites. I will do what I want to do." By his own choice he hardened his heart.

Within God's purpose God knew there would be a Pharaoh, a man who would harden his heart and stand against the people of God. God knew they would see this and rise up against it through their faith. Through Moses performing tremendous miracles of deliverance, God would set His people free in spite of a man who hardened his heart. Understand that Paul is not saying that God hardens a person's heart without that person's choice. He is pointing out that we have the choice of hardening our hearts, or softening our hearts toward God and His will.

Romans 9:19-29

Thou wilt say then unto me, Why doth he yet find fault? For who hath resisted his will? Nay but, O man, who art thou that repliest against God? Shall the thing formed say to him that formed it, Why hast thou made me thus? Hath not the potter power over the clay, of the same lump to make one vessel unto honour, and another unto dishonour? What if God, willing to shew his wrath, and to make his power known, endured with much longsuffering the vessels of wrath fitted to destruction: and that he might make known the riches of his glory on the vessels of mercy, which he had afore prepared unto glory, even us, whom he hath called, not of the Jews only, but also of the Gentiles? As he saith also in Osee (Hosea), I will call them my people, which were not my people; and her beloved, which was not beloved. And it shall come to pass, that in the place where it was said unto them, Ye are not my people; there shall they be called the children of the living God.

Esaias also crieth concerning Israel, Though the number of the children of Israel be as the sand of the sea, a remnant shall be saved: for he will finish the work, and cut it short in righteousness: because a short work will the Lord make upon the earth. And as Esaias said before, Except the Lord of Sabaoth had left us a seed, we had been as Sodoma, and been made like unto Gomorrha.

God Counts Hearts

This is a rather difficult scripture and yet it has great meaning. Some people may think that God is unfair, but look at the example of the potter. Is it the potter who uses the clay to make a vessel, or is it the clay that uses the potter to make itself? Paul is saying that God is God and God has a will. God has a moral order for His universe. Notice Verse 22: "What if God, willing to shew his wrath?" In other words, what if God, determined to keep the moral order of the universe going, decided that He was going to do certain things and that through longsuffering He would work with these vessels, these human vessels who had chosen their own destruction, and that He would show the riches of His glory and mercy by dealing with these people so that they would turn to God, just like the potter would deal with the clay — working it, fashioning it with His hands? This is a reference to Jeremiah, who gave the parable of the potter and the clay and showed that when the clay did not respond and did not turn out right, the potter kept on working until he had finally made the vessel that he had intended.

God has continued to work through the centuries with a people, some of whom have turned away from God, but He has worked with the remnant. He said there is a remnant. God has never implied that all of Israel, one by one, served Him or had any right to be called a part of Israel. He depended on that remnant, those who would respond by faith. That is what God is saying to us. Not everybody who says, "Lord, Lord," shall enter into God's kingdom. Not everybody who says he is a Christian is a Christian. There is a remnant, there is a minority in practically every local church in the world. I suppose God will be happy if He can find a few who really and truly love and serve Him. God does not count all the numbers of people we have on our church books. God counts hearts.

God also is saying that that remnant is strong enough to keep His moral order of the universe intact. When someone tries to disrupt that moral order of God in the universe, God is not going to work with that person. That person is going to butt his brains out, in effect. He is going to seal his own destruction. In Verse 29, Paul says that the remnant responded. Had they not, then those of the Hebrew faith would have been like Sodom and Gomorrha. Because of the remnant keeping the moral order of God, following in the steps of faith, the remnant had preserved the whole. Otherwise, God's anger would have flared like it did against Sodom and Gomorrha when they were destroyed by fire and brimstone, which is described back in the book of Genesis.

Romans 9:30-33

> What shall we say then? That the Gentiles, which followed not after righteousness, have attained to righteousness, even the righteousness which is of faith. But Israel, which followed after the law of righteousness, hath not attained to the law of righteousness. Wherefore? Because they sought it not by faith, but as it were by the works of the law. For they stumbled at that stumblingstone; as it is written, Behold, I lay in Sion a stumblingstone and rock of offence: and whosoever believeth on him shall not be ashamed.

Paul knows that the Christians in Rome, who are both Jews and Gentiles, will understand what he is saying. The Gentiles have come in because they turned by faith to God while Israel has been left out because they tried to attain by their own righteousness their relationship with God. In effect, he is saying that the Jews sought to put God in their debt, but the Gentiles were content to be in God's debt.

The Jews were trying to build up a credit balance so that God would owe them something. Paul was saying that they were 180 degrees wrong. You do not have a corner on God. God has a corner on you.

Romans 10:1-13

> Brethren, my heart's desire and prayer to God for Israel is, that they might be saved. For I bear them record that they have a zeal of God, but not according to knowledge. For they being ignorant of God's righteousness, and going about to establish their own righteousness, have not submitted themselves unto the righteousness of God.

For Christ is the end of the law for righteousness to every one that believeth. For Moses describeth the righteousness which is of the law, That the man which doeth those things shall live by them. But the righteousness which is of faith speaketh on this wise, Say not in thine heart, Who shall ascend into heaven? (that is, to bring Christ down from above.) or, Who shall descend into the deep? (that is, to bring up Christ again from the dead.)

But what saith it? The word is nigh thee, even in thy mouth, and in thy heart: that is, the word of faith, which we preach; that if thou shalt confess with thy mouth the Lord Jesus, and shalt believe in thine heart that God hath raised him from the dead, thou shalt be saved.

For with the heart man believeth unto righteousness; and with the mouth confession is made unto salvation. For the scripture saith, Whosoever believeth on him shall not be ashamed. For there is no difference between the Jew and the Greek; for the same Lord over all is rich unto all that call upon him. For whosoever shall call upon the name of the Lord shall be saved.

How to Be Saved

Here, again, Paul tells the Christians in Rome and us also that the deep desire of his heart and his constant prayer was that Israel should be saved. They are not saved because they have rejected their Messiah, they have rejected the gospel. They have had a zeal for God but not according to knowledge. God has said that without knowledge His people perish. Without knowledge they were ignorant of God's righteousness. They went about to mouth the things of the law of Moses, instead of believing them with their heart. Yet, Paul says that through all the generations the words of God have been in their hearts and in their mouths. They had all the words of God and the proofs of God right in their hearts and mouths, which he said is the word of faith which he preached.

Then he gets right down to what it is to be saved, whether a person is a Jew or a Gentile: "If thou shalt confess with thy mouth the Lord Jesus and shalt believe in thine heart that God hath raised him from the dead, thou shalt be saved. For with your heart you believe and with your mouth you make your confessions. For the scripture says when you call on the Lord you will not be cast out or be ashamed." Then he says that there is no difference between Jew and Greek, for the Lord is rich in love toward all, and whosoever shall call upon the name of the Lord shall be saved.

It is important to point out that the word "lord" in the Greek is "kurios," or lord. The word was used in the Roman Empire, was used by Caesar himself — Lord Caesar. He was lord over all in the Roman Empire. But Paul is saying there is a greater Lord. There is the Lord of lords and He is the Lord Jesus.

Just mouthing words about Him is not going to get it done. One must begin in the heart and believe in the heart the word of faith which has been delivered and preached. You must believe that He is Lord, He is the Lord of your life. When you believe it in your heart, then you confess it with your lips. You confess before men and you say you are on the right side. You believe in your heart, you confess with your mouth.

Do you know what Paul is really saying to you and me? God has no hothouse Christians. God is saying this is not a private affair. So many people like to hide behind the refuge of, "Oh, this is so personal I cannot say anything about it. I do not really want anybody to know." That is a lie of the devil. The devil could not beat that if he wrote the script himself.

God is saying that Jesus is Lord and that whosoever calls upon Him can be saved. Calling upon the Lord means calling from deep within your heart. Your heart cries out, "God, I am a sinner. I am not saved, I am not born again. I want Jesus to be Lord of my life." When you do that, believe me, you will know that you know that you know that you believe. You will know it. The belief in Christ in your heart will become so strong that it will just erupt, coming up through your lips. You will discover yourself talking about Him, saying, "Jesus, Jesus, Jesus is my Savior, my personal Savior. He is my Lord." You will take your stand. Then Paul, in the thirteenth verse, just shouts it: "Whosoever shall call upon the name of the Lord shall be saved." But it is not just a mere call, words. It comes out of the heart, then through the mouth.

Romans 10:14-21

How then shall they call on him in whom they have not believed? and how shall they believe in him of whom they have not heard? and how shall they hear without a preacher? and how shall they preach, except they be sent? as it is written, How beautiful are the feet of them that preach the gospel of peace, and bring glad tidings of good things!

But they have not all obeyed the gospel. For Esaias saith, Lord, who hath believed our report? So then faith cometh by hearing, and hearing by the word of God. But I say, Have they not heard? Yes verily, their sound went into all the earth, and their words unto the ends of the world.

But I say, Did not Israel know? First Moses saith, I will provoke you to jealousy by them that are no people, and by a foolish nation I will anger you. But Esaias is very bold, and saith, I was found of them that sought me not; I was made manifest unto them that asked not after me. But to Israel he saith, All day long I have stretched forth my hands unto a disobedient and gainsaying people.

Preaching, Hearing the Word

Paul wrote this just after another of his missionary journeys on which he had been sent by the church of Antioch. He had gone over the Gentile world preaching. Upon hearing the Word preached, people had faith and believed. He declared that whoever would call on the Lord could be saved. But how could they be saved unless they heard, unless they had a preacher to deliver the Word? Then, when they heard the Word, they would have to believe it and act on it. Paul declares that even the feet of those who preach the gospel are beautiful. The Word of God had been preached through the generations to the people of Israel and now to the Gentiles. The climax has come.

Paul is saying that the Word of God, that was first delivered to Israel and was preached by the prophets and then culminated in Jesus and His calling of people to preach the gospel, has to be faced. When you hear it you cannot just dismiss it. You cannot say, "Oh, that is just another sermon," which is what so many people do. In fact, I am afraid some of us preachers do not always realize how important it is that we preach the Word of God.

Instead of giving personal opinions and the current events, our main thrust is to preach the gospel — the good news that Jesus brought in the new covenant, fulfilling the old by shedding His blood and becoming the eternal sacrifice. God confirmed it by raising Him from the dead, making Him unique forever, one of a kind, our Savior — the one who delivers us from the body of sin, from its guilt and terror and from the wages of sin that lead to death. It is all-important that the Word of God be preached.

God called me to be an evangelist, to preach the gospel. Like Paul said, I magnify my calling because Oral Roberts is not just saying words. I am preaching the Word of God and I know when you hear it. When you hear it you believe it or you turn away from it. Whenever you believe the Word of God, the good news of the gospel, you are going to be saved because you believe with your heart and you confess with your mouth that Jesus is Lord. The hearing of the gospel is absolutely important. If you escape or you diminish the Word of God, you have sealed your own doom.

Those who criticize those of us who preach on radio and television ought to be praising God because we are reaching millions of people who never darken the door of a church. We are getting the gospel out so people have a chance to hear, and all who hear feel faith rising in their hearts because that is how faith comes. The Word of God preached with the anointing of the Holy Spirit brings forth faith that people can release and through which they can be saved.

Paul said the Word of God has gone out, the sound of it has reached the ends of the earth. But Israel had not believed what was heard. Israel had squelched the faith that was rising in their hearts. They chose to be a disobedient and stiff-necked people. Also, he was saying, "Lest you think that it was only Israel, you Gentiles listen to what I am saying. You can be just like them or worse."

Everyone who hears the Word of God will find faith coming up. By that faith they will be saved or, if they reject that faith, they will be lost. So it is terribly important to hear the Word of God and to believe it. But it is not going to be heard without preachers.

I know some of us preachers miss the mark and people say, "Why, that is just another preacher." Or they hear about some preacher doing some terrible thing and then dismiss the whole gospel. But you do not throw out the baby with the bath water. You do not throw away a genuine dollar because there is a counterfeit somewhere. You stay with the genuine. We who are called of God will make mistakes and we are the first to tell you that. But in the main, we are preaching the gospel, we are giving God our best, we are giving you our best. When you hear the Word, the Word is going to create faith in your heart. You have the matchless opportunity of believing God and knowing that you are saved, knowing that you are His child, knowing that you are a Christian on earth, and that when you die you are going to heaven and someday your body will be resurrected from the dead. We call that eternal life.

Romans 11:1-12

I say then, Hath God cast away his people? God forbid. For I also am an Israelite, of the seed of Abraham, of the tribe of Benjamin. God hath not cast away his people which he foreknew. Wot ye not what the scripture saith of Elias? how he maketh intercession to God against Israel, saying, Lord, they have killed thy prophets, and digged down their altars; and I am left alone, and they seek my life. But what saith the answer of God unto him? I have reserved to myself seven thousand men, who have not bowed the knee to the image of Baal.

Even so then at this present time also there is a remnant according to the election of grace. And if by grace, then is it no more of works: otherwise grace is no more grace. But if it be of works, then is it no more grace: otherwise work is no more work. What then? Israel hath not obtained that which he seeketh for; but the election hath obtained it, and the rest were blinded. (According as it is written, God hath given them the spirit of slumber, eyes that they should not see, and ears that they should not hear;) unto this day.

And David saith, Let their table be made a snare, and a trap, and a stumblingblock, and recompence unto them: let their eyes be darkened, that they may not see, and bow down their back alway. I say then, Have they stumbled that they should fall? God forbid: but rather through their fall salvation is come unto the Gentiles, for to provoke them to jealousy. Now if the fall of them be the riches of the world, and the diminishing of them the riches of the Gentiles; how much more their fulness?

Jewish Comeback Foreseen

Paul is dealing with the Jewish issue, not only for those in Rome but for all the people of the world and in all succeeding generations, because the Jew will not go away. Paul remembers that the first believers in Jesus Christ were Jews, not Gentiles. It was the Romans who put Jesus to death. I know everybody says the Jews killed Christ. In one way they did, but they did not have the power of death. That was in the hands of the Romans. Although the Jews rejected Him, Rome actually put Jesus to death.

On the day of Pentecost it was Jewish people who had accepted Christ — Peter, James, John, and others, including Jesus' mother, who received the Holy Spirit. That day Jewish people from all over the world were present, including some from Rome. Some of these people in the Christian Church in Rome were doubtless present on the day of Pentecost. They had believed on the Lord Jesus Christ then.

Paul is tracing the history of the way these people, the Jews, have believed God or have rejected God. He goes back to their beginnings: how Pharaoh tried to keep them in Egypt; how Moses gave them the law; and how God selected these people because of their faith in following their fathers — Abraham, Isaac, Jacob, and the 12 sons of Jacob, who became the fathers of the 12 tribes. He shows how the fathers had lived by faith, doing the things that please God and giving their descendants that heritage. A remnant of them had accepted that faith and lived by it. The others mouthed the laws of God. They gave mouth evidence but not heart evidence. Ultimately, when the Messiah came, those who were mouthing it turned Him down, turned against Him, rejected Him, and brought Him to the point where the Romans crucified Him. It was the remnant who had stood by Him, and many of them immediately believed on the Lord Jesus Christ.

Paul asks concerning those who have not yet believed, "Is God going to cast them away as His people?" He answers, "God forbid. The evidence is right here in me — I am also an Israelite. I am of the seed of Abraham, of the tribe of Benjamin." God knew in the beginning what these people would do.

Then Paul tells how Elijah at one time was so persecuted by the Israelites that he thought he was the only one left. Elijah said, "Lord, take away my life because I am the only one left." And God said, "Oh no, you are not. There are 7,000 in Israel who have not bowed the knee to the idol gods." He was referring to that remnant who had been selected because of their faith. Their faith had worked upon grace, which is the free gift of God. They had not tried to earn it, but neither had they merely mouthed it and counted on that to get them through. They had believed and God had blessed their faith by the gift of grace, that is, His lovingkindness and forgiving spirit. Paul says that all of the gospel is based on grace, the free gift of God, which we enter by our faith.

Then Paul makes a tremendous point: The fall of the Jews was a point at which God acted toward the Gentiles. At the same time, God is making the Israelites jealous by allowing the Gentiles who have believed to come in. If the fall of the Jewish people as a nation was so complete, if they had been diminished to that point so that the Gentiles were able to come into the kingdom, then think what will happen when the Jewish people accept the Messiah and come back, when they become a full people again. What a glorious thing that is going to be!

When you look at the Jewish nation of Israel today, when you see Jewish individuals or groups today who have not accepted Christ, and most of them are more secular than they are spiritual — remember what Paul is saying: These people are not going away. These people know a lot that they are not carrying out. There seems to be an inborn ability in a Jew to know there is a God. He is far different from the typical Gentile who, when he gets so secular, indicates that he never heard of God. The Jews really do not ever get away from God.

Some people ask, "Why don't the Jews get saved? Look what the Christians have done for them." The Jews will reply that during World War II, when Germany put so many of them to death, Germany was a Christian nation. Outwardly, Germany was Christian. Therefore, the Jews put to death in the Holocaust became evidence to the Jews who escaped it that the Christians really are Jew-killers. Yet, right in the midst of that were Christian people who hid Jews from the Germans. Corrie ten Boom, one of the great Christians of all time, hid Jews in her native land, Holland. Corrie ten Boom is just one of thousands of Christians who did this.

All over the world today there are so-called Christians who hate the Jews and there are Christians who love the Jews. The Jews are caught in the middle. The Jew sometimes does not really know about Christians. But there is one thing he knows: In his heart something has been passed down to him from Abraham. He knows that there is God, and there is a tension in the Jews about it.

Christians should not be gloating over the Jewish fall. If their fall let Gentiles in, think of what is going to happen when the Jews believe on God again and the glory of the Lord comes upon them. We have just got to remember that we are equal partners when we have faith in God.

Romans 11:13-24

> For I speak to you Gentiles, inasmuch as I am the apostle of the Gentiles, I magnify mine office: if by any means I may provoke to emulation them which are my flesh, and might save some of them. For if the casting away of them be the reconciling of the world, what shall the receiving of them be, but life from the dead? For if the firstfruit be holy, the lump is also holy: and if the root be holy, so are the branches. And if some of the branches be broken off, and thou, being a wild olive tree, wert graffed in among them, and with them partakest of the root and fatness of the olive tree; boast not against the branches. But if thou boast, thou bearest not the root, but the root thee.
>
> Thou wilt say then, The branches were broken off, that I might be graffed in. Well; because of unbelief they were broken off, and thou standest by faith. Be not highminded, but fear: for if God spared not the natural branches, take heed lest he also spare not thee. Behold therefore the goodness and severity of God: on them which fell, severity; but toward thee, goodness, if thou continue in his goodness: otherwise thou also shalt be cut off. And they also, if they abide not still in unbelief, shall be graffed in: for God is able to graff them in again.
>
> For if thou wert cut out of the olive tree which is wild by nature, and wert graffed contrary to nature into a good olive tree: how much more shall these, which be the natural branches, be graffed into their own olive tree?

Old Testament Important

Paul is making an outstanding statement here which is even

against nature. First, he compares Israel with an olive tree. Then he compares the Gentiles with a wild olive tree. Compared with the olive tree called Israel, which was a garden variety, one that God had planted and nourished, the Gentiles were like a wild olive tree that just sprang up in the wilderness. They were a wild people. Paul pictures the Gentiles' salvation as God grafting them in as wild olive branches into the garden olive tree. That is contrary to nature because you usually do not graft like that. You graft the garden variety into that which is wild. But God reverses it.

Paul uses that to make his point to the Jews and Gentiles who were Christians in Rome, and to us today. It is evident that Paul is giving a severe warning to all of us who are Gentiles not to be high-minded or to boast or to put down the Jews. We are to be grateful that God grafted us into them. The Jews were the ones who, as the sons and daughters of Abraham, gave us the way of the Lord and from whom came our Savior Jesus Christ.

Remember that at this time most of the New Testament had not been written and that Paul is again and again referring them to the Old Testament Scriptures which they knew. Today most Christians do not know the Old Testament, the very roots of our Christian faith. They stay only with the New Testament, but that was never intended. Although it is the new covenant, it is based on the old. It did not destroy the old, it merely fulfilled it. Unless you also study the Old Testament and learn your spiritual roots, you will not ever understand the New Testament. You need to study the whole Bible. Paul is indicating that as he talks to the Christians in Rome.

Romans 11:25-32

> For I would not, brethren, that ye should be ignorant of this mystery, lest ye should be wise in your own conceits; that blindness in part is happened to Israel, until the fulness of the Gentiles be come in. And so all Israel shall be saved: as it is written, There shall come out of Sion the Deliverer, and shall turn away ungodliness from Jacob: For this is my covenant unto them, when I shall take away their sins.
>
> As concerning the gospel, they are enemies for your sakes: but as touching the election, they are beloved for the fathers' sakes. For the gifts and calling of God are without repentance. For as ye in times past have not believed God, yet have now obtained mercy through their unbelief, Even so have these also now not believed, that through your mercy they also may obtain mercy. For God hath concluded them all in unbelief, that he might have mercy upon all.

Love the Jews

Let me point out to you the importance of Paul's statement that all Israel shall be saved. He means enough of the remnant who will be representative of the nation of Israel so that God will have that nation again. God made His covenant with them and someday they will come back to that covenant, because God's gifts and God's callings are never recalled.

For example, say that a person believes God and then becomes an apostate, that is, he turns against the very thing he believed and calls it of the devil and believes it. He is not a mere backslider who can come back to God through repentance. He is an apostate and now rejects the very agency of his salvation. Say he dies and goes to hell. Or just say that once he was a preacher. He will still preach in hell; he just will not have any converts. Any gift of God that you have or I have will never be recalled. Any calling we have will never be taken from us. We will have it until the day we die. We may use it correctly or half-correctly or use it totally in a wrong way. We may even become apostates. (When we read Hebrews we will study what apostasy is, how a person who has believed in God can turn away from God forever and lose his soul in hell.)

Here Paul is saying with regard to Israel, "Do not think that God has turned these people loose forever and cast them away. God is still holding onto them." And then he says, "Because of your mercy toward them, they will obtain mercy." In reality he is saying to us Christians, "Love the Jews. Love them into coming back to God. Do not hate them. Do not fight them. Do not ridicule them. Do not mock them. Do not kill them. Love them . . . like you love anyone else. Let love rule in your heart. Do not forget, all of you were in unbelief, but God has had mercy upon all."

Romans 11:33-36

O the depth of the riches both of the wisdom and knowledge of God! how unsearchable are his judgments, and his ways past finding out! For who hath known the mind of the Lord? or who hath been his counsellor? Or who hath first given to him, and it shall be recompensed unto him again? For of him, and through him, and to him, are all things: to whom be glory for ever. Amen.

God is Great!

There are five doxologies in the book of Romans and this is one of them: "Oh, the depth of the riches of the wisdom and knowledge

of God!" Paul's heart just overflows when he states that the Jews
have gone away from God. They are in unbelief. Because of it, the
Gentiles have been let into the kingdom of God, but in the end God
will not have recalled His gifts or His callings, Israel will be saved,
and the Gentiles and the Jews shall come together in a new nation,
a new people. Oh, the riches and the glory of that, Paul is saying.
How great is God!

I can just see him walking up and down the floor, dictating these
words to his secretary, and suddenly throwing up his hands, saying,
"Oh, thank God! Praise God! God is great!" That is the way we feel
at times. I feel it now and I know you do too.

Romans 12:1-8

> I beseech you therefore, brethren, by the mercies of God, that ye
> present your bodies a living sacrifice, holy, acceptable unto God,
> which is your reasonable service. And be not conformed to this world:
> but be ye transformed by the renewing of your mind, that ye may
> prove what is that good, and acceptable, and perfect, will of God.
>
> For I say, through the grace given unto me, to every man that is
> among you, not to think of himself more highly than he ought to
> think; but to think soberly, according as God hath dealt to every man
> the measure of faith. For as we have many members in one body, and
> all members have not the same office: so we, being many, are one
> body in Christ, and every one members one of another. Having then
> gifts differing according to the grace that is given to us, whether
> prophecy, let us prophesy according to the proportion of faith; or
> ministry, let us wait on our ministering: or he that teacheth, on
> teaching; Or he that exhorteth, on exhortation: he that giveth, let him
> do it with simplicity; he that ruleth, with diligence; he that sheweth
> mercy, with cheerfulness.

Let God Use You

Paul knows that the Christians in Rome, from a Jewish background,
understand the sacrifice of the bodies of animals unto God. Just as
the ancient sacrifice had to be holy and without blemish, so in your
everyday life, live a holy and responsible life. Do it physically,
spiritually, and every other way so that you are not conforming your
life to the way this world operates. You are in the world but you
are not part of the world system. You are not part of the way they
think or live or do business, but you devote yourself to that which
is good, to the will of God.

God has given to every one of you some gift, some blessing, and

He has given it to you so that you may use it according to the measure of faith that God has given to every man. Here is a scripture I have used for 35 years: "God hath dealt to every man the measure of faith." I used to think that faith was something you get, until one day God revealed this scripture to me. He showed me that faith is not something we get, it is something He has already given us. Therefore, we have got to release it to God. Faith is not faith until you release it, until you act upon it.

Paul tells us that we are the family of Christ. We are His body. Though there are many of us and each of us has a different personality and gifts that differ, each of us fits into the body. If by prophecy, we ought to prophesy by faith; if by ministry, we ought to minister with our faith; if by teaching, then we should teach through our faith in God. If we do anything, such as in the business world or as a housewife or as a child growing up in the family, we should do it with faith in God. Do it with cheerfulness. Be joyous. Be thrilled in your heart that you are a part of the family of God.

Another thing Paul is saying to you and me today is to know our gifts. You and I can tell what our gifts are by the leading we have and by the natural talents with which we were born. How was I to know that God was going to manifest His gift of healing through me? I did not know, but all my life I have had a deep feeling for sick people. God was calling me into the healing ministry. I had those natural talents already, but it took more than my natural talent. The Holy Spirit began to move upon those natural talents with gifts from above and soon I realized what my calling is — that I am an evangelist of God's healing power.

I am also called to be an apostle in the healing ministry, to blaze new trails. I try to live my life so that I am in the Body of Christ. Everything I do is for the Body of Christ: to bring in people who need Christ, to pray for people who are sick so they may be healed, to bring them into the City of Faith so they may receive the best medical treatment along with the ministry of the prayer partners there, to give a Christian education to thousands upon thousands of young people today, to stand up on television and present the gospel with signs and wonders following. I am a part of the Body of Christ. I thank God for it, and I expect to be part of it until He calls me away.

You, too, have gifts and callings from God. You ought to look at yourself, studying your Bible, seeking the Lord, listening to the Holy Spirit speak in your heart so that you know what your talents are and how the Holy Spirit moves upon those talents with some particular gift of God or some particular calling of God. Do not be envious of others. Do not desire what they have. Just be yourself in the Lord, and let God use you.

Romans 12:9-13

> Let love be without dissimulation. Abhor that which is evil; cleave to that which is good. Be kindly affectioned one to another with brotherly love; in honour preferring one another; Not slothful in business; fervent in spirit; serving the Lord; rejoicing in hope; patient in tribulation; continuing instant in prayer; distributing to the necessity of saints; given to hospitality.

Get With It!

Do not get off in a corner with your Christian experience and sit there and say, "I am not supposed to do this, and I am not supposed to do that." Paul is saying, "Go to the extreme and abhor that which is evil. Cleave to that which is good. Be careful in business but fervent in spirit at the same time." He is saying, "Get with it." Be a good citizen. Become active in your church. Become active in your community. Stand up on the side of those things that are right. Raise your voice. Let yourself be known. Do something constructive. Do not be a nonentity. Do not be an echo, be a voice. Be someone who is living for Christ. You have got the power. Use your faith. Use your gift and your talent and do something good. Let good come out of your being to others.

Romans 12:14-21

> Bless them which persecute you: bless, and curse not. Rejoice with them that do rejoice, and weep with them that weep. Be of the same mind one toward another. Mind not high things, but condescend to men of low estate. Be not wise in your own conceits. Recompense to no man evil for evil. Provide things honest in the sight of all men. If it be possible, as much as lieth in you, live peaceably with all men.
> Dearly beloved, avenge not yourselves, but rather give place unto wrath: for it is written, Vengeance is mine; I will repay, saith the Lord. Therefore if thine enemy hunger, feed him; if he thirst, give him drink: for in so doing thou shalt heap coals of fire on his head. Be not overcome of evil, but overcome evil with good.

Vengeance is God's

Paul is reminding these Christians in the midst of Rome where the persecution is so great that they are not to retaliate but to bless those people. They are to do good, and not be high-minded because they are Christians and others are not. They are to provide honest things in the sight of all men.

Rome was so treacherous, so full of deadbeats, so full of people who claimed so much and would beat their bills and not pay them. Paul is saying to every Christian then and now — pay your debts. Meet your bills. Go out of your way to be of a peaceful nature and leave vengeance to God, for God says, "I will repay."

Only God can absorb the punishment that vengeance brings. When you take vengeance on somebody, you get hurt more than they get hurt. But when God takes vengeance, evil just flies off Him. He can absorb the punishing blows of it. You and I cannot. We simply have to put it in God's hands and say, "God, I trust You." That does not mean you just let people walk all over you like a doormat and you agree with them just to be agreeable. That does not mean you do not have convictions. It means that you stand up for what you believe is right, but you do it in a loving way. You do not strike at the people who strike at you. After you have done all you know to do, you trust that God will work it out. Ultimately, if it is not all worked out here, it will be worked out in the resurrection because the resurrection is our final and eternal hope.

We have come to the last verse of Chapter 12, "Be not overcome of evil but overcome evil with good." The whole chapter is practical advice for you and me to live a close Christian life for our Lord. Let us pray now that we will be able to implement these things in our lives today.

Father, we know that we have a will and that as we hear the Word of God, the faith in our heart comes forth. We know that Paul is teaching us the same as he taught the people in Rome, saying these words to us as individuals. Now help us to have an open heart to receive them and to ponder these words of Paul and to apply them to our daily lives. Father, we want to be ongoing Christians. We want to serve You seven days a week, 24 hours a day. We want to overcome evil and to do it with the good of our heavenly Father. We are in agreement now through Jesus Christ our Lord that we are doing this. We receive it in His name. Amen and amen.

Romans 13:1-7

Let every soul be subject unto the higher powers. For there is no power but of God: the powers that be are ordained of God. Whosoever

211

therefore resisteth the power, resisteth the ordinance of God: and they that resist shall receive to themselves damnation.

For rulers are not a terror to good works, but to the evil. Wilt thou then not be afraid of the power? do that which is good, and thou shalt have praise of the same: for he is the minister of God to thee for good. But if thou do that which is evil, be afraid; for he beareth not the sword in vain: for he is the minister of God, a revenger to execute wrath upon him that doeth evil.

Wherefore ye must needs be subject, not only for wrath, but also for conscience sake. For this cause pay ye tribute also: for they are God's ministers, attending continually upon this very thing. Render therefore to all their dues: tribute to whom tribute is due; custom to whom custom; fear to whom fear; honour to whom honour.

Christian Distinction Shown

Paul was writing to the Christian Jews and Gentiles in Rome against a background of terrorism in the Holy Land. There were Jewish zealots there whose aims were strictly political. They were not acting in the faith of God or because they loved people. They wanted to overthrow the Roman Empire, but the methods they were using were in violation of the love of God.

Paul lived by faith. He also lived in the Roman Empire, which was a dictatorship. He did not believe in all the things of Rome, but he knew that under Roman government the Savior had been born, and protection had been given this child. Paul knew also that under Roman government it was his privilege to change from a Jewish rabbi, a zealous Pharisee, one who hated Christ and the Christians, and to become a true Christian, an apostle, an evangelist. He had enjoyed the freedom, under the protection of the Roman Empire, to travel with the gospel in most of the great cities and seaport towns of the empire. He had seen himself and others protected by the Romans against the Jews. He had experienced great freedom.

Paul was not covering for the evils of the Roman Empire. Again and again he has pointed out those evils. Rather, Paul was setting up a contrast between the Christians and the Jews. The Jews did not want to pay taxes. They did not want to render unto Caesar that which was Caesar's as Christ himself had said. Paul wanted the Christians to pay their taxes, to render unto Caesar his just due, and to show that there is a distinction between Judaism and Christianity.

Romans 13:8-10
Owe no man any thing, but to love one another: for he that loveth

another hath fulfilled the law. For this, Thou shalt not commit adultery, Thou shalt not kill, Thou shalt not steal, Thou shalt not bear false witness, Thou shalt not covet; and if there be any other commandment, it is briefly comprehended in this saying, namely, Thou shalt love thy neighbour as thyself. Love worketh no ill to his neighbour: therefore love is the fulfilling of the law.

Christians Pay Debts

Paul has been talking about public debts of a Christian. Now he gets down to the nitty-gritty of the personal debts of the individual Christian. He begins in Verse 8 by saying, "Owe no man anything." There were some in those days who would use the Lord's Prayer, that part which says, "Forgive us our debts," as an excuse not to pay debts. This would give Christians a terrible name in the community. Paul was saying, "Pay your debts. Go out of your way to meet your obligations. Do everything in your power."

Then Paul says that, as a matter of fact, when it comes to the commandments there is really one way to keep them: Love your neighbour as you love yourself. Love is a debt we pay every day, every hour, every moment, every breath that we draw — the love of God.

In my own personal experience, when I became a Christian and entered the ministry I felt something rising in me that Oral Roberts must not owe any man anything. I must never leave an unpaid bill. When this ministry became large and we entered into 46 different nations personally, plus more than 80 nations with our literature and radio and TV, there were many financial obligations that had to be taken care of, and we never left an unpaid bill anywhere on this earth. While I have been criticized for many things, there is one thing they have not hung around my neck — that I have left any unpaid bill on this earth. I know without Christ coming into my heart and putting that in my spirit, I could not have done this. But I do praise God that it can be done and that it is being done. I can tell you right now that every bill is paid. We have bills tomorrow, we have bills next week and bills next month for the work of Christ, but as of this moment all bills are paid. Praise be unto God.

Romans 13:11-14

And that, knowing the time, that now it is high time to awake out of sleep: for now is our salvation nearer than when we believed. The night is far spent, the day is at hand: let us therefore cast off the works of darkness, and let us put on the armour of light. Let us walk honestly, as in the day; not in rioting and drunkenness, not in chambering and wantonness, not in strife and envying. But put ye on the Lord Jesus Christ, and make not provision for the flesh, to fulfil the lusts thereof.

Time is Short

Paul is now concerned with the shortness of time. He knows it will not be long until he will go to be with God. He, also, with the other early-church Christians, believed in the imminent second coming of the Savior, the Lord Jesus Christ. He knew that his salvation and their salvation and our salvation is nearer than when we all first believed. That belief must take hold of us. The time is growing short. We ought to live honestly and be delivered from drunkenness and carrying on with illegal sex and illicit things of this world, not fighting with one another or being envious of the achievements of a fellow Christian. We must put on the Lord Jesus Christ.

Romans 14:1-6

Him that is weak in the faith receive ye, but not to doubtful disputations. For one believeth that he may eat all things: another, who is weak, eateth herbs. Let not him that eateth despise him that eateth not; and let not him which eateth not judge him that eateth: for God hath received him. Who art thou that judgest another man's servant? To his own master he standeth or falleth. Yea, he shall be holden up: for God is able to make him stand.

One man esteemeth one day above another: another esteemeth every day alike. Let every man be fully persuaded in his own mind. He that regardeth the day, regardeth it unto the Lord; and he that regardeth not the day, to the Lord he doth not regard it. He that eateth, eateth to the Lord, for he giveth God thanks; and he that eateth not, to the Lord he eateth not, and giveth God thanks.

Unite in Christ

Paul is speaking against the background of some very strict food laws. The Jewish people were to eat kosher food. But they had even gone beyond what was taught in Leviticus. When they became Christians they divided into two groups. One group wanted to hold to the old dietary laws, and the others wanted their freedom in Christ.

Paul is saying, "Do not fall out over things like this. You that want your freedom in Christ, do not criticize the others who feel conviction in their hearts to hold to their dietary laws. And you with dietary laws, do not criticize those who are free from legalism. Christ is the one who is to be worshiped. He is the one to keep foremost in your mind. Whatever you do, do it unto God."

Today there are those who hold to the old belief that the gifts of the Spirit ended in the early church and that there are no gifts of the Spirit now. They believe, for example, that God does not heal the sick now. Then there are others who are so charismatically filled with the Holy Spirit that they do not want any regulations at all. They just want to be completely free to speak in tongues anytime they want, publicly, without interpretation or without their interpretation being judged by those who are spiritual in the faith. They want to cast out God's other healing streams where God heals through medicine. Some have a very deep conviction that they should just trust God and not do anything other than pray. Paul is simply saying, "Both of you come together in the Holy Spirit and put Christ first in your life."

Do not fall out over the fact that some of you take medicine and pray while others pray and do not take medicine, while some exercise the gifts of the Spirit and others are frightened of them. Keep your mind on Jesus. Have your heart full of love and whatever you do, do it unto Jesus.

Romans 14:7-9
> For none of us liveth to himself, and no man dieth to himself. For whether we live, we live unto the Lord; and whether we die, we die unto the Lord: whether we live therefore, or die, we are the Lord's. For to this end Christ both died, and rose, and revived, that he might be Lord both of the dead and living.

Forsake Isolation

Paul is saying that there is no way you can isolate yourself from your past. You cannot isolate yourself from your present. You cannot isolate yourself from your future. You cannot isolate yourself from Jesus Christ. You cannot isolate yourself from people around you or your brothers and sisters in Christ. You certainly cannot isolate yourself either from living life or from death itself. There is no way you are going to live to yourself or when you come down to die that you will die in total isolation. So whether you live or whether you die, in your living and in your dying, love God, love other people, and make use of the time that God has given you on earth. These moments of life are very precious. It was to this end that Jesus himself was born, lived, and died, rose and was resurrected, that He might be the Lord both of those who are living and the Lord of those who have died.

Today there are some dear people who want to separate themselves from others, to go off to their own little group, to do their little thing, and just let the world go by, as well as the Body of Christ or the Church universal. Paul says that we do not live or die unto ourselves. As for Oral Roberts, I believe in getting in the middle of the big ring, getting out there where the dust and the grime and the blood are, touching people and being touched by people, being in the midst of an unredeemed, sick, and lost world, pouring out my life that someone might be saved, someone might be healed, someone I may never know about. We are involved with Christ in this present world and that is the way we live it.

Romans 14:10-17

But why dost thou judge thy brother? or why dost thou set at nought thy brother? for we shall all stand before the judgment seat of Christ. For it is written, As I live, saith the Lord, every knee shall bow to me, and every tongue shall confess to God. So then every one of us shall give account of himself to God. Let us not therefore judge one another any more: but judge this rather, that no man put a stumblingblock or an occasion to fall in his brother's way.

I know, and am persuaded by the Lord Jesus, that there is nothing unclean of itself: but to him that esteemeth any thing to be unclean, to him it is unclean. But if thy brother be grieved with thy meat, now walkest thou not charitably. Destroy not him with thy meat, for whom Christ died. Let not then your good be evil spoken of: for the kingdom of God is not meat and drink; but righteousness, and peace, and joy in the Holy Ghost.

Focus on Important Things

Paul is continuing what he was saying concerning the fact that none of us lives to ourselves or dies to ourselves. He tells us that he is persuaded that these things are to be judged in the light of whether what we do brings people together in Christ or divides them. He says the kingdom of God is not meat and drink. It is not rules and regulations or the lack of rules and regulations. What it is, is the kingdom of God. The kingdom of God is a right relationship with the Lord, God's peace in our hearts, living peacefully with all people, having the joy of the Holy Spirit in our hearts.

We should examine the motivating factor in our lives. Is our attitude lifting up Jesus? Is our feeling toward other Christians one of Christian love? Or is it spitefulness? Is it jealousy? Is it bickering? We are never going to agree on every little thing.

For example, one of the dearest friends I ever had, who is now in heaven, would not eat pork. He and I often had dinner together, and if I wanted to order pork he did not get mad. When he said, "Brother Oral, I have the conviction that I should not eat pork," I did not say, "Ah, come off it." I said, "Fine. Order beef, order fish, order vegetables." I have eaten with many people who are vegetarians. Others I have lived with loved beef so much, they wished they had it for every meal, and some who loved pork so much, they wished they had it for every meal. So what? I am not going to get upset over things like that!

There are more important things to be doing and thinking about in the kingdom of God such as a right relationship with our Father, having the peace of God in our hearts, and being filled with the joy of the Holy Spirit. To me the Holy Spirit in the charismatic dimension is the common denominator because the Holy Spirit witnesses of Jesus, and He puts Jesus foremost in our lives.

Romans 14:18-23

For he that in these things serveth Christ is acceptable to God, and approved of men. Let us therefore follow after the things which make for peace, and things wherewith one may edify another.

For meat destroy not the work of God. All things indeed are pure; but it is evil for that man who eateth with offence. It is good neither to eat flesh, nor to drink wine, nor any thing whereby thy brother stumbleth, or is offended, or is made weak.

Hast thou faith? have it to thyself before God. Happy is he that condemneth not himself in that thing which he alloweth. And he that doubteth is damned if he eat, because he eateth not of faith: for whatsoever is not of faith is sin.

Christ Before "Legalism"

When a person's conviction is that he should do something or not do something, that conviction must be born of faith in God, not just to be odd or eccentric or different from somebody else or different for difference's sake, because faith is the heart of Christianity. Faith is believing God, believing that He will do whatever He says. You know what I think Paul was trying to do with the Roman

Christians and with us today? He was trying to lift us up above what is called legalism.

For example, the Jewish people had a tyranny of the sabbath. They not only put the sabbath up as high as God originally intended, but they went far beyond that and put people in bondage to it so they could only take so many steps on the sabbath day. You had to number your steps, and if you made one step too many you were condemned. Paul is saying to be careful about these things. Even if people are like that, do not get overly upset. Practice your faith in God. Some people think that one day is more special than another, but in Christ that is not so — every day is God's day. Christ is what it is all about — lifting Him up, not exalting a day or exalting the kind of meat we eat or what we drink or do not drink. It is exalting Christ because it is faith that counts.

Romans 15:1-6

We then that are strong ought to bear the infirmities of the weak, and not to please ourselves. Let every one of us please his neighbour for his good to edification. For even Christ pleased not himself: but, as it is written, The reproaches of them that reproached thee fell on me.

For whatsoever things were written aforetime were written for our learning, that we through patience and comfort of the scriptures might have hope. Now the God of patience and consolation grant you to be likeminded one toward another according to Christ Jesus: that ye may with one mind and one mouth glorify God, even the Father of our Lord Jesus Christ.

Follow, Praise Christ

It is proper to point out that those people who are still tied to legalism are the weak ones. The ones who have freedom in Christ are the strong ones who should be kind and patient with people who are still tied to some kind of legalism as many of the Jews were who had accepted Christ.

Paul said we should not please ourselves but follow the steps of Christ who did not even please himself. Paul wanted to live a life that would influence others for Christ, bring them to God. Therefore, he took many things including the reproaches of the enemies upon himself. He depended upon the comfort of the Scriptures that brought him hope. So we also should depend upon the Scriptures that bring us hope.

Paul brings this line of thought to a close by another of the five doxologies found in the book of Romans. He says, "Now the God of patience and consolation grant you to be likeminded one toward another according to Jesus Christ, that ye may with one mind and one mouth glorify God, even the Father of our Lord Jesus Christ." What a beautiful doxology! Some Christians might ask, "What is a doxology?" It is a praise song, like the doxology "Praise God from whom all blessings flow. Praise Him all creatures here below. Praise Him above ye heavenly hosts. Praise Father, Son, and Holy Ghost." It is a praise song to God. You can just see Paul as he walked the floor, dictating this letter to the Roman Christians, as he had come to the point where praise just burst forth from his soul, and he began to glorify God in a praise song.

Romans 15:7-13

Wherefore receive ye one another, as Christ also received us to the glory of God. Now I say that Jesus Christ was a minister of the circumcision for the truth of God, to confirm the promises made unto the fathers: and that the Gentiles might glorify God for his mercy; as it is written, For this cause I will confess to thee among the Gentiles, and sing unto thy name.

And again he saith, Rejoice, ye Gentiles, with his people. And again, Praise the Lord, all ye Gentiles; and laud him, all ye people. And again, Esaias saith, There shall be a root of Jesse, and he that shall rise to reign over the Gentiles; in him shall the Gentiles trust. Now the God of hope fill you with all joy and peace in believing, that ye may abound in hope, through the power of the Holy Ghost.

Jesus Fulfilled the Law

Here Paul is saying that Jesus Christ was born a Jew, lived a Jew, lived according to the law, and was actually a minister of the law of Moses. He did it in order to fulfill the law. He did it also to confirm the promises that were made to the fathers, to Abraham, Isaac, Jacob, Moses, and David. Then Paul quotes several scriptures which pointed up that what Jesus did was for the salvation of all people, not just the Jews. Then, again, he breaks into a doxology. The Spirit of God is erupting in Paul's heart. He knows that he has written God's letter to His people for all ages, and he just cannot help praising God.

Back in Chapter 11 of Romans, Paul concluded his remarks about the Jews. Now at Verse 13 of this chapter, he concludes most of his remarks about the Gentiles. He begins to close the letter and to talk of personal things.

Romans 15:14-16

And I myself also am persuaded of you, my brethren, that ye also are full of goodness, filled with all knowledge, able also to admonish one another. Nevertheless, brethren, I have written the more boldly unto you in some sort, as putting you in mind, because of the grace that is given to me of God, that I should be the minister of Jesus Christ to the Gentiles, ministering the gospel of God, that the offering up of the Gentiles might be acceptable, being sanctified by the Holy Ghost.

Paul Helped Free Gentiles

Paul is now bringing to a head his own ministry of being called to the Gentiles. His deep desire was to preach the gospel to them in such a way and win so many to Christ that he could make them an offering up to God, an acceptable sacrifice to God of that vast, wild, uncontrollable Gentile world where Paul had gone. Others had not cared. Even the Jewish nation had not cared. Oh, the prophets had cared. Abraham had cared. But the Jews had come to a point where they had not cared for anybody. In many respects, they hated the Gentiles.

But Paul, having received his salvation and call to go to the Gentiles with the gospel, now saw that great shapeless mass of humanity and he saw inside them saints. Through his gospel he wanted to deliver them and present them to God as an offering that was sanctified by the Holy Spirit. That was his great desire. He felt like he was releasing those Gentiles, chipping away at all the legalism that had prevented them from being released, telling them the good news. When they heard it, many could not wait to get into the kingdom of God and praise the Lord.

Romans 15:17-21

I have therefore whereof I may glory through Jesus Christ in those things which pertain to God. For I will not dare to speak of any of those things which Christ hath not wrought by me, to make the Gentiles obedient, by word and deed, through mighty signs and wonders, by the power of the Spirit of God; so that from Jerusalem, and round about unto Illyricum, I have fully preached the gospel of Christ.

Yea, so have I strived to preach the gospel, not where Christ was named, lest I should build upon another man's foundation: but as it is written, To whom he was not spoken of, they shall see: and they that have not heard shall understand.

Four Steps to Obedience

Now Paul speaks very intimately and personally with the Christians at Rome about his own work for Christ. He said that he had refused to go where others had been. He wanted to go where the name of Jesus had not been known, to be a true apostle, which was to pioneer new paths. He said he went into the hardest field of all — that of the Gentiles — to make them obedient to God.

He did it by using four things: first, the Word of God; second, the deeds of the gospel as lived through his own faith; third, mighty signs and wonders; and, fourth, the power of the Holy Spirit. By those four methods, he said, "I have fully preached the gospel of Christ."

This is very heart-touching to me, Oral Roberts, for this has been my method to pioneer new paths in the healing gospel of Jesus Christ. God has given me so many things that other people have not said and has sent me with His healing message to my generation where His light is dim, His voice is not known or heard, and His power has not yet been revealed. It has been some experience through these 35 years to stand before multitudes, to preach the words of God that have not been heard before, and to pray for the healing of people who had never known that God could or would heal.

I have done it first by the Word of God which I place first, for it is by the Word of God that people have faith and it comes forth in them. And I have done it by the deeds of my own faith, through the signs and wonders which follow my believing — the miracles of God, miracles that have saved and healed people and delivered them and supplied their needs. And always it has been by the power of the Holy Spirit. I know a little of what Paul feels here, for he tells how he was striving to do this. It was no easy task; it never is. But he was determined that they who had not seen would see and those who had not heard would hear. In that way they would come into the newness of life of the gospel and know what it is to be free human beings.

Romans 15:22-29

> For which cause also I have been much hindered from coming to you. But now having no more place in these parts, and having a great desire these many years to come unto you; whensoever I take my journey into Spain, I will come to you: for I trust to see you in my journey, and to be brought on my way thitherward by you, if first I be somewhat filled with your company.
>
> But now I go unto Jerusalem to minister unto the saints. For it hath pleased them of Macedonia and Achaia to make a certain contribution

for the poor saints which are at Jerusalem. It hath pleased them verily; and their debtors they are. For if the Gentiles have been made partakers of their spiritual things, their duty is also to minister unto them in carnal things.

When therefore I have performed this, and have sealed to them this fruit, I will come by you into Spain. And I am sure that, when I come unto you, I shall come in the fulness of the blessing of the gospel of Christ.

Israel Merits Consideration

Paul admits here that he has wanted to visit Rome on many other occasions but had been hindered. Now things are clearing up. He is finishing his ministry at this time in Corinth and he is planning a trip to Spain. Spain at that time was a rising star. It was at the outer limits of the Roman Empire, but many great things were taking place in Spain. Paul wanted to go there to make it a jumping-off place for the gospel into regions beyond, and to get to Spain he had to go through Rome. So it was expeditious for him to go to Spain through Rome and stop there with the Roman Christians.

But first, he said, "I am on my way to Jerusalem. I have to go there. This time I am taking an offering for those Jews who, in accepting Christ, have lost everything." Many of them worked in the temple. In fact, thousands upon thousands in those times had their employment in Jerusalem in connection with the great temple, but when they received Christ they were cut off. An offering had been taken in several areas and brought to Paul who was entrusted to take it back to the brethren in Jerusalem to distribute among those poor Jewish Christians.

Then Paul made a powerful statement: "You Gentiles have partaken of spiritual things because of the Jews; now you owe them something." I tell you today, I feel that very keenly. I feel very keenly about Israel and about the Jewish people. I hear people criticizing Israel, and certainly Israel is not above criticism. But you are not going to hear Oral Roberts criticizing Israel. I know that whoever blesses Israel will be blessed and whoever curses it will be cursed. I feel very, very deeply about this. I know our Lord is coming back to the Mount of Olives. His feet will land there. He will walk down through a new valley into Jerusalem, and I intend to be with Him.

All of us who really believe the Bible have a special feeling in our hearts about the Jewish people, including those who do not believe in our Lord. We are praying for them, but not because we feel superior — not at all. We feel what Paul said he felt when he opened the book of Romans: "I am in debt, to the Jew first and then to the Gentile." Yes, I feel that indebtedness to the Gentiles, but I feel it in a very peculiar way toward the Jews. I pray for them. I honor them. I respect them. And I want good to come to them.

Notice in Verse 28 that he counted this offering that he was taking to Jerusalem as seed which would produce fruit. There is a beautiful illustration of seed-faith. When we plant our seed we are going to have produce, a crop, fruit that will be put down to our account.

Romans 15:30-33

> Now I beseech you, brethren, for the Lord Jesus Christ's sake, and for the love of the Spirit, that ye strive together with me in your prayers to God for me; that I may be delivered from them that do not believe in Judaea; and that my service which I have for Jerusalem may be accepted of the saints; that I may come unto you with joy by the will of God, and may with you be refreshed. Now the God of peace be with you all. Amen.

Prayer Defined

He was urging the Roman Christians to pray for him. He said, "Hold together with me in your prayers to God for me, that I may be delivered from them in Judaea and Jerusalem when I bring this offering to those saints." What did he mean? He knew Jerusalem. He had been there several times before and each time it was a very hurtful experience. He nearly lost his life there. They had tried to kill him there. Even the leaders of the Christian church had not always understood Paul. You can imagine the humanness of the man. He believed in prayer and he wanted them to pray that he would be delivered so he could come to them with joy.

Prayer is so vital. It is the sincere desire of the heart expressed to God in behalf of ourselves, in behalf of others, and especially in behalf of those who are preaching the gospel. I guess if I had to choose one thing I wanted above all others, I would want you to pray for Oral Roberts. There is something about it that I feel. I feel the waves of it as it passes by me on the way to the Father. God answers those prayers. Paul knew that, and he was saying to you and me to pray for one another. I believe God hears prayer today.

God, we thank You as we pray together that You hear and answer prayer.

Notice another doxology: "Now the God of peace be with you all." Paul just cannot contain himself. He is coming to the close of this letter. His heart is full. He breaks out in his praise songs.

Chapter 16 is almost like a "P.S.," and that can be extremely important in a letter, as you know. Paul is going to mention a number of different people here by name. About some of them he just says one sentence, which sums up their whole life.

Romans 16:1,2

> I commend unto you Phebe our sister, which is a servant of the church which is at Cenchrea, that ye receive her in the Lord, as becometh saints, and that ye assist her in whatsoever business she hath need of you: for she hath been a succourer of many, and of myself also.

Paul Praised Women

It is believed that Phebe, this devout Christian woman, was the one who delivered the actual letter Paul had written to the Romans, and that when she delivered it there would be other business that she would take care of for the apostle. He was asking that they cooperate with her because she was a true servant or bond slave of Jesus Christ in the same spirit as Paul.

I am grateful he began naming these people by starting with a woman, because women played such a large role in Bible times, and they play a major role today. It was the women who really carried some of the heavier parts of the load that the Church was under. I think it is a good time in history to uphold our women, the women who are women of faith and carry on God's work.

Romans 16:3-4

> Greet Priscilla and Aquila my helpers in Christ Jesus: Who have for my life laid down their own necks: unto whom not only I give thanks, but also all the churches of the Gentiles.

Being There When Needed

When we read Acts, we came across this man and his wife several times. They were with Paul in Ephesus and Corinth and other places, and many times they risked their very lives. They were involved in the spread of the gospel among all the churches of the Gentiles — either directly or indirectly. They were there when Paul needed them. They carried on for God when Paul sent them. They would pastor or evangelize or work with their hands or comfort the saints or stick out their necks for the apostle. They would stand up for Christ under all circumstances. Paul said, "Greet them because they are my helpers in Christ Jesus. Also, they are a great part of all the churches among the Gentiles."

Romans 16:5
    Likewise greet the church that is in their house . . .

Pray for One Another

It is evident that during this time the early church had no church buildings. Even in Rome, the heart of the Roman Empire, they met in a house, and Priscilla and Aquila had opened their house for the church. In that first century the church was not in buildings like we have now but in homes, and the church was a living organism.

It is time that we thought of ourselves as a living organism in Jesus Christ. No matter what denomination we belong to or do not belong to, do we belong to Christ? If we belong to Christ, are we aware we belong to one another? If we are aware we belong to one another, are we praying for one another? Are we uplifting one another? Now, the rest of Verse 5 . . .

Romans 16:5
    . . . salute my well beloved Epaenetus, who is the firstfruits of Achaia unto Christ.

Paul remembers his first convert to Christ in that whole region of Achaia.

Romans 16:6
    Greet Mary, who bestowed much labour on us.

Any servant of God remembers the good things done to help speed his way or her way on to preaching the gospel, and Paul remembered Mary.

Romans 16:7
    Salute Andronicus and Junia, my kinsmen, and my fellow- prisoners, who are of note among the apostles, who also were in Christ before me.

Reasons for Salute

He wanted them to salute Adronicus and Junia: first, because they were his kinsmen; second, because they had been in prison with him; third, because they had been Christians before he was; and fourth, they were among the apostles.

Romans 16:8-12
> Greet Amplias my beloved in the Lord. Salute Urbane, our helper in Christ, and Stachys my beloved. Salute Apelles approved in Christ. Salute them which are of Aristobulus' household. Salute Herodion my kinsman. Greet them that be of the household of Narcissus, which are in the Lord. Salute Tryphena and Tryphosa, who labour in the Lord . . .

Twins Greeted

I was really inspired in my study of these two women, who apparently were twins. They were dainty but laboured in the Lord to the extent of utter exhaustion for the gospel. Paul really wanted them greeted.

Romans 16:12-13
> . . . Salute the beloved Persis, which laboured much in the Lord. Salute Rufus chosen in the Lord, and his mother and mine.

Son of Cross-Bearer

In Mark 15:21, Mark tells us that when Jesus was on His way to the cross, a man named Simon from Cyrene, in North Africa, was tapped on the shoulder by the Romans and told to help carry the cross. Simon had no idea that was what he would get into. Doubtless he was resentful. But something happened to him as he helped carry that cross on the way to Golgotha. Later his two sons, Alexander and Rufus, found Christ. Doubtless Rufus had done a great work for God with Paul, and his mother had been like a mother to Paul.

Romans 16:14-16
> Salute Asyncritus, Phlegon, Hermas, Patrobas, Hermes, and the brethren which are with them. Salute Philologus, and Julia, Nereus, and his sister, and Olympas, and all the saints which are with them. Salute one another with an holy kiss. The churches of Christ salute you.

Friends, Helpers Remembered

Many of these people were servants to Caesar. The gospel had even invaded the palace of Caesar. It is amazing where the gospel goes. Paul remembered these people. Doubtless they had come to him on various occasions. Many of them he had led to Christ himself, but all of them had a part in the gospel with him and he remembered it.

I know when I get to heaven and the Lord gives me the reward which He is preparing, only a part of it will touch me, for there are thousands of men and women and young people who have stood by me through thick and thin. Many of them I know by name. Many of them I know by name as I write and answer their letters, although I have never seen them face to face. Besides these beloved friends and partners will be my direct co-laborers. The partners are co-laborers, too, but I speak now of those who work with me day by day. I think of those who began with me in the gospel 35 years ago.

To try to name the names would take hours, but I remember them: those who have gone on and those who are still here, all those who are helping me on television and radio, those who help me carry on Oral Roberts University and raise up these young people to go to the ends of the earth with the gospel. I remember those who help me carry on the City of Faith Health Care Center, combining medicine and prayer as God has commanded for the healing of millions; those who are helping me build and finish the Research Center — that part of the City of Faith that is now beginning a direct attack upon the diseases like cancer; and those who with me are determined to find God's cure for suffering people. I remember pastors everywhere who have been sponsors, co-evangelists, and men and women in the field today who are not a direct part of my work but whom I love and respect and who are my dear friends. There are many I have never known face to face but whom I know in spirit, and they know me.

Romans 16:17-20

Now I beseech you, brethren, mark them which cause divisions and offences contrary to the doctrine which ye have learned; and avoid them. For they that are such serve not our Lord Jesus Christ, but their own belly; and by good words and fair speeches deceive the hearts of the simple.

For your obedience is come abroad unto all men. I am glad therefore on your behalf: but yet I would have you wise unto that which is good, and simple concerning evil. And the God of peace shall bruise Satan under your feet shortly. The grace of our Lord Jesus Christ be with you. Amen.

Optimism for Christianity

Here is another doxology of Paul as his heart erupts again in praise to God. His doxology follows his very important advice to them and to us to watch for those people who are dividers of the people of God, for they do not serve our Lord Jesus Christ but have some private dream that is contrary to God. Watch for those people. Have nothing to do with them. Then Paul says, "The God of peace shall bruise Satan under your feet shortly." What a powerful and glorious statement! It is an optimistic statement that Christianity is advancing, that it is hitting the devil where it hurts. It is getting him down, getting him under our feet. We are winning this battle.

Romans 16:21

> Timotheus my workfellow, and Lucius, and Jason, and Sosipater, my kinsmen, salute you.

Co-Laborers Honored

Paul now changes from mentioning dear people there in Rome to those direct co-laborers of his, beginning with his right-hand man, young Timothy. Then he mentions Lucius, who apparently was one of those at Antioch who helped send Paul out on his first missionary journey. Concerning Jason, who at Corinth stood up for Paul, and Sosipater, who was kin to him, he said, "They are with me and they salute you."

Romans 16:22

> I Tertius, who wrote this epistle, salute you in the Lord.

Secretary Joins Greetings

This is the first time in Paul's letters that one of his secretaries identifies himself. Remember, Tertius was the secretary. He simply wrote down what Paul said. The Holy Spirit was the author and gave it to Paul who dictated it to this person Tertius who wanted to get in on Paul's salutations.

Romans 16:23

> Gaius mine host, and of the whole church, saluteth you. Erastus the chamberlain of the city saluteth you, and Quartus a brother.

Gaius Hosted Church

Remember that Paul is writing this letter to the Roman church from Corinth. Gaius had been Paul's host, but there was also a church in Gaius' house. He opened his house unto the Lord's work. Paul also gave them greetings from the treasurer of the entire city, Erastus, and from Quartus, a brother in the Lord.

Romans 16:24
> The grace of our Lord Jesus Christ be with you all. Amen.

The Bible Simplified

There goes that doxology again! As we come to the last four verses of Paul's letter to the Romans, I want to point out to you that the Bible is about people. It is written to people, people like you and me, people that we are going to live with forever, brothers and sisters in Christ of different ages but still in the Body of Christ. Notice, as we are reading the Bible and I am teaching it to you, that it is losing a lot of its complexity and so-called bigness. We are getting down to the simplicity of what it really is: God reaching out to our hearts, touching our heartstrings, appealing to what He put within us with which we respond to Him: our faith.

Romans 16:25-27
> Now to him that is of power to stablish you according to my gospel, and the preaching of Jesus Christ, according to the revelation of the mystery, which was kept secret since the world began, but now is made manifest, and by the scriptures of the prophets, according to the commandment of the everlasting God, made known to all nations for the obedience of faith: to God only wise, be glory through Jesus Christ for ever. Amen.

High Road of Christ

Now, can you see that group in Rome? The letter has finally been read. They are folding the parchment and carefully putting it away. It will be copied many times and taken by hand to many other churches. From it will come our translations of the Bible. The Christians in Rome sigh and feel lifted up and know that they are on the right road — the high road of Jesus Christ. Don't you feel that way?

229

I heard a story once. It was when Jesus returned to heaven with all the marks of His sufferings, the nail prints in His hands, and the angels came around to talk with Him. They had been involved with Him on earth, and now they were looking upon Him as He had completed the Father's mission. They said to Him, "Do You think those people down there understood what You did for them?"

The Lord answered, "No, not completely. Some of them, but not many."

"Well, do You think they will tell the good news? Will they share what You have done for people in the world?"

"Some will. Not all."

"Well, what plans have You made?"

"I told Peter, James, and John and others to be witnesses of Me, and those they reach to be witnesses."

"Did You have an alternate plan in case they failed or they forgot? What about when the 20th century arrives, and somehow they have forgotten and the message has died out? What alternate plans did You make?"

Jesus said, "I have no other plans. I counted on them."

I think that story illustrates that Jesus Christ is counting on you and me, and by His grace we are not going to let Him down. This ends the reading of Paul's letter to the Romans.

The First
Epistle of Paul
the Apostle to the
Corinthians

The First
Epistle of Paul
the Apostle to the
Corinthians

The book of I Corinthians is a personal letter from the heart of
the great Apostle Paul to a new church of people who have recently
received Christ and who live in one of the greatest cities of the
Roman Empire. Paul was deeply moved by the trouble in Corinth
and stirred by the Spirit to share with them not only how to receive
Christ, but how to walk in the steps of the Lord Jesus Christ.

Corinth was located in Greece, on a strip of land that connected
Greece's northern and southern parts. It became one of the great
seaport cities of the Roman Empire. The city was a center of
commercial activity, a heathen city with a huge population. Corinth
was also shot through with drunkenness and debauchery. Ship
owners, sailors, and travelers gathered there not only to sell their
goods and to do business, but also to engage in every kind of
immorality possible. On the Acropolis was the temple of Aphrodite,
the goddess of love, which had a thousand priestesses, or what they
called "sacred prostitutes." When people went there to worship, the
act of worship was consummated by intercourse with one of these
religious prostitutes. Corinth was also a Roman colony. Rebuilt by
Julius Caesar in 46 B.C., it became the capital of Achaea and nearly
all of Greece. Many Jews had come to Corinth and established several
synagogues.

It was to this most unlikely city that Paul came as an evangelist,
as he did to the other great seaport cities of the Roman Empire. The
world of the Romans was squeezed together around the
Mediterranean Sea. Corinth was more representative of the spiritual
state of the world than any of the other cities. Nevertheless, Corinth
was a place where Christ did one of the greatest works through Paul
that had ever been done. And the Christian church there was, in
some respects, the greatest church of all. Some say the church at

Philippi was the greatest. Others say the one at Ephesus was the greatest. But the Christian church at Corinth came up out of the worst sin, faced the worst problems, and came to know the grace of God in the most difficult of circumstances. And Paul, time after time, spoke to the Corinthians as frankly as he possibly could under the inspiration of the Holy Spirit, spending as much as 18 months at a time in Corinth.

When Paul wrote the epistle to the Romans, he had not been to Rome and he did not know most of those people there. But when he wrote to the Christians in Corinth, he knew them. He had led them to Christ. He had established them in the faith. He loved them and cared for them. So, it is a warm letter. It fits more churches, more cities, more Christian people, is more down to earth, and gets down to the nitty-gritty of the things Christians today have to face almost every day than nearly anything Paul wrote.

There was trouble then in the church at Corinth, and Paul wrote to them out of his heart. You can almost hear the throbbing heart of the great apostle as he pours his love into his letter to the Christians at Corinth.

I Corinthians 1:1-9

Paul, called to be an apostle of Jesus Christ through the will of God, and Sosthenes our brother, unto the church of God which is at Corinth, to them that are sanctified in Christ Jesus, called to be saints, with all that in every place call upon the name of Jesus Christ our Lord, both theirs and ours: Grace be unto you, and peace, from God our Father, and from the Lord Jesus Christ.

I thank my God always on your behalf, for the grace of God which is given you by Jesus Christ; that in every thing ye are enriched by him, in all utterance, and in all knowledge; even as the testimony of Christ was confirmed in you: so that ye come behind in no gift; waiting for the coming of our Lord Jesus Christ: who shall also confirm you unto the end, that ye may be blameless in the day of our Lord Jesus Christ. God is faithful, by whom ye were called unto the fellowship of his Son Jesus Christ our Lord.

Corinth Church Spiritual

As Paul dictates this letter, he reminds them of who he is. He is an apostle. He is saying, "My dear Christian brothers at Corinth, I want to remind you that I am an apostle and an evangelist of the Lord Jesus Christ. I am writing to all of you at the church of God at Corinth who are consecrated in Jesus Christ."

He is saying, "You are called ones. You are called to be saints." They had the call of God upon them to become saints. They had not reached sainthood. Most of us probably don't in this life, but we have the calling to become saints — to be so much like Christ that in God's eyes we are saints. He is saying that Christ is not the single possession of anybody, that He is the Lord of those who believe in Him. Then he says, "I thank God for you, for the grace of God that is given to you, that in all things you are enriched, in utterance and knowledge and the testimony of Christ in the gifts of God." Later, in I Corinthians 12, he will talk to them about the nine gifts of the Spirit, saying, "You Christians at Corinth are not behind in any way in the gifts of the Holy Spirit. You are waiting for the coming of our Lord Jesus Christ. He is going to confirm you to the end."

This encouragement that Paul gives the Corinthians is gratifying, especially in light of the fact that a great many people today knock the Christians at Corinth and do not like the speaking in tongues or other gifts of the Spirit that Paul talks about, along with certain divisions that exist there. They just snap their fingers and say the Corinthian church was nothing. But these people at Corinth had some redeeming qualities along with their problems, qualities we can identify with.

I Corinthians 1:10-17

Now I beseech you, brethren, by the name of our Lord Jesus Christ, that ye all speak the same thing, and that there be no divisions among you; but that ye be perfectly joined together in the same mind and in the same judgment. For it hath been declared unto me of you, my brethren, by them which are of the house of Chloe, that there are contentions among you. Now this I say, that every one of you saith, I am of Paul; and I of Apollos; and I of Cephas; and I of Christ.

Is Christ divided? was Paul crucified for you? or were ye baptized in the name of Paul? I thank God that I baptized none of you, but Crispus and Gaius; lest any should say that I had baptized in mine own name. And I baptized also the household of Stephanas: besides, I know not whether I baptized any other. For Christ sent me not to baptize, but to preach the gospel: not with wisdom of words, lest the cross of Christ should be made of none effect.

Disturbing News

Immediately after Paul told them how much he loved them and acknowledged their state in Christ and the gifts of God working among them, he got right down to business. He said that some church members from the house of Chloe had brought him disturbing news. Despite the fact they have received Christ, he says, "There are divisions among you. You are not perfectly joined together in the same mind and the same judgment. Some of you are saying, 'I am of Paul,' others are saying, 'I am of Apollos,' and others say, 'I am of Cephus or of Peter,' and others say, 'But I am of Christ.' Let me tell you," he said, "you four parties need to reform into one party, the party of Jesus Christ. Do you think that Jesus Christ is divided? Do you think that you were baptized into Paul's name so that I can say you are my absolute possession? Not on your life," he is saying, "because I did not baptize many of you to begin with. Anyway, Jesus Christ did not send me out to do the baptizing. He sent me to preach the gospel. Others could baptize you, but I want to preach the gospel of Jesus Christ to you. Not with the wisdom of words lest the cross of Christ should be made of none effect."

Paul was saying something very important here. Just to have a gospel of words is to have a gospel that has no power. He is going to get down to brass tacks on this. He is going to tell us that Christianity is not a bunch of words, not preachers getting up and preaching nice sermons. He is going to describe the results of being a Christian.

I Corinthians 1:18-25

For the preaching of the cross is to them that perish foolishness; but unto us which are saved it is the power of God. For it is written, I will destroy the wisdom of the wise, and will bring to nothing the understanding of the prudent. Where is the wise? where is the scribe? where is the disputer of this world? hath not God made foolish the wisdom of this world?

For after that in the wisdom of God the world by wisdom knew not God, it pleased God by the foolishness of preaching to save them that believe. For the Jews require a sign, and the Greeks seek after wisdom: but we preach Christ crucified, unto the Jews a stumblingblock, and unto the Greeks foolishness; but unto them which are called, both Jews and Greeks, Christ the power of God, and the wisdom of God. Because the foolishness of God is wiser than men; and the weakness of God is stronger than men.

Glory in the Heart

Paul gets down to the real issue, that the preaching of the cross has serious implications. He said, "It pleased God, right in the midst of a world that called itself wise, by the foolishness of preaching to save them that believed." Notice he did not say, "foolish preaching" but "by the foolishness of" it. It seemed so foolish to people then, as it does to many today, for Paul and others to preach the simplicity of the gospel of Jesus Christ and that it would save people who respond to it by faith. Then he said, "The Jews require a sign of the restoration of Israel. The Greeks were seeking after wisdom — some intellectual attainment that would swell their heads. But we preach Christ crucified, and that crucifixion is a stumblingblock to the Jews because they believe 'cursed is every man that hangs on a tree.' And unto the Greeks it was foolishness because they believed that God was detached and that in no way could a God suffer." Therefore, when he preached Christ crucified, they sneered at such a preaching. "But," he says, "unto them who are called — the Jews, the Greeks, the Gentiles, the whole world — Christ the incarnation of God is His power, is His wisdom, and that wisdom is greater than all the wisdom of men. Even the foolishness of God is wiser than men and the weakness of God is stronger than men." Then Paul makes a very unusual statement to the effect that God has not called many of the so-called great people of the world, but the humble, or just ordinary folks.

At that time there were about 60 million slaves in the Roman Empire, many of them Greeks, many of them what would today be called "street people." The church of God at Corinth was made up primarily of these ordinary people who were sneered at by the Jews and the Greeks. But Paul was praising God because He would accept anybody great or small who would have faith in Him and through that faith would establish the right relationship with the Lord. He was indicating this was true so that no human flesh, that is, no order of people, could glory in themselves but would be able to glory only in the fact that God was in their hearts.

I Corinthians 1:26-31

> For ye see your calling, brethren, how that not many wise men after the flesh, not many mighty, not many noble, are called; but God hath chosen the foolish things of the world to confound the wise; and God hath chosen the weak things of the world to confound the things which are mighty; and base things of the world, and things which are despised, hath God chosen, yea, and things which are not, to bring to nought things that are: that no flesh should glory in his presence. But of him are ye in Christ Jesus, who of God is made unto us wisdom, and righteousness, and sanctification and redemption: that, according as it is written, He that glorieth, let him glory in the Lord.

Seek Christ, Not Glory

Paul is telling these Corinthians, who for the most part are not the wisest folks in the city of Corinth from the standpoint of philosophy, that they are not the wealthiest and not the most famous. He is telling them that because they are in Christ, they have it all. For Christ is made unto us wisdom. He is our wisdom. He is our righteousness. He is our ability to be consecrated to God. And He is our redemption. Paul is telling the Corinthians not to be embarrassed or intimidated by the so-called big shots of the world, but to know their heritage in Christ and to know that Christ is everything.

Some are worried about the fact that not many great and talented people are being called into the preaching of the gospel (or at least, if they are called, most of them do not obey but go the way of the world and use their talents in the secular world rather than in the ministry of our Lord Jesus Christ). There are people in the world who have so much on the ball but do not let Jesus have it. Just think what we could do. But on the other hand, maybe it is all right, because Paul points out that "no flesh shall glory in God's presence" but will be used of God — and God will get the glory.

I Corinthians 2:1-5

And I, brethren, when I came to you, came not with excellency of speech or of wisdom, declaring unto you the testimony of God. For I determined not to know any thing among you, save Jesus Christ, and him crucified. And I was with you in weakness, and in fear, and in much trembling. And my speech and my preaching was not with enticing words of man's wisdom, but in demonstration of the Spirit and of power: that your faith should not stand in the wisdom of men, but in the power of God.

Trust Christ First

Paul was one of the most learned and capable men in the world of that time. Yet, when he came to Corinth, he did not come in the way that the philosophers came. He did not come to establish what a great orator he was or how much of this world's knowledge he had; he came preaching Jesus Christ and Him crucified. It was not that he was not a wise man in the philosophies of the world. It was not that he couldn't use all those big words and string those great sentences together. He wanted to express the simplicity of Jesus

Christ because salvation is not in big words or the wisdom of men but in Christ and Him crucified. Paul said, "I came in the demonstration of the Spirit and of power."

In Romans 15, Paul said that he preached in both word and deed and with signs and wonders, fully preaching the gospel of Jesus Christ. Why? So that their faith should not stand in the philosophies, the wisdom, and knowledge of men, but in the power of God, which is the gospel of Jesus Christ.

Where does that put us today? Here we have Oral Roberts University, a place of learning. The tremendous library has in it the knowledge of thousands upon thousands of great scholars through the centuries. We are adding to that knowledge and passing it on. We have some of the most learned men in the world, tremendous scholars of the knowledge of the things of man and of the earth and of the philosophies of mankind. But right in the middle of it we have the Prayer Tower where prayer is sent up to God 24 hours a day, 7 days a week. In the midst of Oral Roberts University is the number-one book, the Bible, and we meet in a required worship service twice a week to hear the Word of God. Our faith will not stand in the things that we are learning about our world, but upon the Rock of Ages, the Word of God, upon Christ crucified, risen from the dead, and the Holy Spirit indwelling our lives.

When Paul says he didn't come with enticing words or the wisdom of men, he is not fighting education. He is not telling us we should be ignoramuses or that we should not be well informed. We are to be educated people insofar as we are able. But right in the middle of it, we do not trust our lives to education. We trust our lives to Jesus Christ.

I Corinthians 2:6-8

> Howbeit we speak wisdom among them that are perfect: yet not the wisdom of this world, nor of the princes of this world, that come to nought: but we speak the wisdom of God in a mystery, even the hidden wisdom, which God ordained before the world unto our glory: which none of the princes of this world knew: for had they known it, they would not have crucified the Lord of glory.

God's Hidden Wisdom

Paul is saying there is wisdom in this world that is of God, wisdom far above what any human being has ever acquired. He is saying that if men had known about this hidden wisdom of God, they would not have been so ignorant as to have crucified Jesus Christ.

239

I Corinthians 2:9-14

> But as it is written, Eye hath not seen, nor ear heard, neither have entered into the heart of man, the things which God hath prepared for them that love him. But God hath revealed them unto us by his Spirit: for the Spirit searcheth all things, yea, the deep things of God. For what man knoweth the things of a man, save the spirit of man which is in him? even so the things of God knoweth no man, but the Spirit of God.
>
> Now we have received, not the spirit of the world, but the spirit which is of God; that we might know the things that are freely given to us of God. Which things also we speak, not in the words which man's wisdom teacheth, but which the Holy Ghost teacheth; comparing spiritual things with spiritual. But the natural man receiveth not the things of the Spirit of God: for they are foolishness unto him: neither can he know them, because they are spiritually discerned.

Spiritual Revelation

In Verse 9, Paul makes the statement that everybody who loves Christ should know. He says, "Eye hath not seen, nor ear heard, neither hath entered the heart of man, the things which God hath prepared for them that love him," while people today say, "Oh, yeah, when I get to heaven God's going to reveal everything to me." Verse 10 says, "But God hath revealed them unto us by his Spirit." He is saying that right now all the things that "eye hath not seen nor ear heard, neither have entered into the heart of man" to believe that it was possible, God, by His Spirit, has revealed unto us. "You Corinthians," he is saying, "have this revelation from God because the Holy Spirit indwells you."

Those of us who are in Christ by the Holy Spirit are in a state of revelation at all times. The Spirit is revealing to us the hidden things, the spiritual things, the eternal things. This world has a mind that is incapable of understanding that because its mind is on a different wavelength, the wavelength of the value judgments of this secular world. The spiritual mind is on the wavelength of the Holy Spirit.

This can be illustrated by the story of a man who had a dream in which he went to heaven, and the Lord Jesus showed him all the glorious things of that celestial city. On his way back to the gate, they passed one magnificent building they had not visited, and the man said, "Lord Jesus, what is in that building?" He said, "All the things that you have ever wanted but that you have never asked Me for."

The truth is that God wants to heal you now. God wants to prosper you now. Jesus is saying that by the Spirit of God these things are being revealed to us. God is offering us His healing power. God is offering us His power to prosper us and to supply all our needs according to His riches by Christ Jesus in glory. And these things are NOW.

I Corinthians 2:15,16

> But he that is spiritual judgeth all things, yet he himself is judged of no man. For who hath known the mind of the Lord, that he may instruct him? But we have the mind of Christ.

The Mind of Christ

Paul is telling us that we have Christ's mind in our minds. His mind waters and blossoms our minds. We are not down here on the earth by ourselves just trying to find our way in the world through our minds alone; we have our minds and Christ's mind. This is great news. This is the gospel.

I Corinthians 3:1-9

> And I, brethren, could not speak unto you as unto spiritual, but as unto carnal, even as unto babes in Christ. I have fed you with milk, and not with meat: for hitherto ye were not able to bear it, neither yet now are ye able. For ye are yet carnal: for whereas there is among you envying, and strife, and divisions, are ye not carnal, and walk as men? For while one saith, I am of Paul; and another, I am of Apollos; are ye not carnal?
>
> Who then is Paul, and who is Apollos, but ministers by whom ye believed, even as the Lord gave to every man? I have planted, Apollos watered; but God gave the increase. So then neither is he that planteth any thing, neither he that watereth; but God that giveth the increase. Now he that planteth and he that watereth are one: and every man shall receive his own reward according to his own labour. For we are labourers together with God: ye are God's husbandry, ye are God's building.

On the one hand he goes into the hearts and minds of the Christians of the church of God in Corinth by telling them who they are in the Lord, what magnificent gifts they have. And then he suddenly shifts gears and tells them there is another side of them that has to be corrected. How could there be such a polarization in the same Christian body, the same Christian individual? You must understand even more of their background, that the city of Corinth was a hotbed of sin. They had been addicted to the things of Corinth. Those who were Greeks and had accepted Christ had come out of the Greek culture. Those who were Jews and had accepted Christ had come out of both Judaism and Greek culture. And all of them had been terribly and heavily influenced by the immorality and the lack of God-consciousness in the city of Corinth. So, on the one hand, they were spiritual, they were moving with God. On the other, they were like little babies, just newborn babies in Jesus who could take only milk and not the deeper things of the gospel. Paul pointed as evidence to their divisions — their fallings out — saying, in effect:

"Now, in this problem of division, you are bogged down. Quit saying, 'I am of Paul.' You other people quit saying, 'I am of Apollos.' Quit saying all that. Quit saying, 'I am a Baptist,' 'I am a Methodist,' 'I am a Catholic,' 'I am a Lutheran,' 'I am a Pentecostal.' Why don't you just say, 'I'm a Christian. I am in Christ'?"

It is not your denomination or Oral Roberts or some other evangelist or pastor or teacher or prophet that counts. That is not the issue. We are ministers of the Lord. But it is the Lord that does the work. One of us plants, another waters, but God gives the increase. When we work for the Lord as His ministers, His servants, and the Lord is our source, then we are laborers together.

I Corinthians 3:10-17

> According to the grace of God which is given unto me, as a wise masterbuilder, I have laid the foundation, and another buildeth thereon. But let every man take heed how he buildeth thereupon. For other foundation can no man lay than that is laid, which is Jesus Christ. Now if any man build upon this foundation gold, silver, precious stones, wood, hay, stubble; every man's work shall be made manifest: for the day shall declare it, because it shall be revealed by fire; and the fire shall try every man's work of what sort it is.
>
> If any man's work abide which he hath built thereupon, he shall receive a reward. If any man's work shall be burned, he shall suffer loss: but he himself shall be saved; yet so as by fire. Know ye not that ye are the temple of God, and that the Spirit of God dwelleth in you? If any man defile the temple of God, him shall God destroy; for the temple of God is holy, which temple ye are.

Consider Your "Temple"

Paul is reminding the Christians at Corinth and us today that our individual lives must be built upon Christ. If we use any material other than Christ to build our lives, that work will be burned up. It will not survive time or eternity. He says, "Don't you understand that you are the temple of God?" Paul is, in effect, pointing out to them the great temple of Aphrodite, the goddess of love, there on the Acropolis, and saying, "You think the temple is the greatest thing in the world. Let me tell you, your body is greater than that temple. Your body is a temple itself. It is a temple of Almighty God and His Spirit who dwells in you. You get upset when you think about somebody destroying that magnificent temple of Aphrodite, but do you see how God gets upset when you do anything to your body? God will destroy those who destroy the temple of God, because it is holy."

Today we cannot listen to everything that comes along, or read every book or believe everything on television, or listen to the kind of music that is contrary to the gospel of Jesus Christ. Some of it is attuned to Satan. We cannot put that material into the making of our lives with Christ, because we are a divine temple, and God indwells us.

I Corinthians 3:18-23

> Let no man deceive himself. If any man among you seemeth to be wise in this world, let him become a fool, that he may be wise. For the wisdom of this world is foolishness with God. For it is written, He taketh the wise in their own craftiness. And again, The Lord knoweth the thoughts of the wise, that they are vain. Therefore let no man glory in men. For all things are yours; whether Paul, or Apollos, or Cephas, or the world, or life, or death, or things present, or things to come; all are yours; and ye are Christ's; and Christ is God's.

Christ is Leader

Paul is saying, "It does not matter whether I or Apollos or Cephas brought you the gospel. You really belong to Christ and Christ is God's. The source is God, so you look to God as your source." And you take people like Oral Roberts and all the rest and say, They are instruments of God to help me. None of them have the full understanding. Only God has the full understanding. Therefore, while we hear these men and women and value them, yet we listen primarily and in finality to God himself through His Holy Word and by His Spirit. Having this kind of knowledge and reminding ourselves of these heavenly gifts and privileges, we can pray this prayer:

Heavenly Father, we are reminded again that it is not the one who leads us to Christ but it is the Christ who has come into our lives, and through Him we can survive life, death, things present, and things to come. And in Him all things are ours. And, Father, we determine today to believe God and that we receive all things that are ours. We thank You for it, and we receive it through Jesus Christ our Lord. Amen and amen.

I Corinthians 4:1-5

Let a man so account of us, as of the ministers of Christ, and stewards of the mysteries of God. Moreover it is required in stewards, that a man be found faithful. But with me it is a very small thing that I should be judged of you, or of man's judgment: yea, I judge not mine own self.

For I know nothing by myself; yet am I not hereby justified: but he that judgeth me is the Lord. Therefore judge nothing before the time, until the Lord come, who both will bring to light the hidden things of darkness, and will make manifest the counsels of the hearts: and then shall every man have praise of God.

Let God Judge

He said, "Consider we who came as ministers of Christ and stewards of the mysteries of God." The term "minister" as he uses it here was a term for a slave who toiled in a boat, in the back of the boat, rowing and doing the hardest work. He is saying, "We who came to minister to you are really bond slaves of Jesus Christ. We are doing the hardest work of all." The word "steward" was a term used for one who ruled over an estate that was not his. He was merely keeping that estate. Paul is saying, "It is not the minister, not the steward that you should get your minds on, and neither should you try to judge which one is greater or which one is the least. All that judgment will not take place in this present time, but in the Lord's time it will come."

He adds in Verse 5 that only God knows the hidden things or the deep secret desires and counsels of the heart, and He is the one who is going to judge it. We should not judge anybody because we never know their motives or all there is to know. Only God knows.

I Corinthians 4:6-13

And these things, brethren, I have in a figure transferred to myself and to Apollos for your sakes; that ye might learn in us not to think of men above that which is written, that no one of you be puffed up for one against another. For who maketh thee to differ from another? and what hast thou that thou didst not receive? now if thou didst receive it, why dost thou glory, as if thou hadst not received it? Now ye are full, now ye are rich, ye have reigned as kings without us: and I would to God ye did reign, that we also might reign with you. For I think that God hath set forth us the apostles last, as it were appointed to death: for we are made a spectacle unto the world, and to angels, and to men.

We are fools for Christ's sake, but ye are wise in Christ; we are weak, but ye are strong; ye are honourable, but we are despised. Even unto this present hour we both hunger, and thirst, and are naked, and are buffeted, and have no certain dwellingplace; and labour, working with our own hands: being reviled, we bless; being persecuted, we suffer it: being defamed, we intreat: we are made as the filth of the world, and are the offscouring of all things unto this day.

Choose Jesus Over Praise

In effect, Paul is chiding these new Christians at Corinth who, on the one hand, have done so well and, on the other, have been caught up in division, thinking that they are so important. He calls their attention to something they understand. He refers to a Roman general who, after winning a great victory, has come to Corinth to parade down the main street with his troops in triumph, while behind is a little group of captives who will be thrown to the lions. He is saying, "While you Corinthians are flaunting yourselves, I, Paul, the apostle, and others like us are like that little group of captives. We are thrown to the lions, and we are looked upon as the offscouring of the world. We are put down by everybody. While all of you are so great and outstanding and are praised, we are not praised, we are buffeted, we are kicked around. We do not always know where we are going to spend the night; we do not know where our next meal is coming from all the time. We even labor with our own hands that we might minister to you, and we suffer whatever the world throws at us."

Today, the situation is no different. Some of us have been out there in the heat, in the tents, on street corners, in the jungles. We went out there preaching the gospel and praying for the sick, and while so many of the other ministers are called the great people in the world, we were called every name under the sun. That is what Paul is saying, and that is what Oral Roberts is saying.

I build a university and get kicked. I build a medical center where prayer and medicine are joined, and I get put down. Jesus told me not to be like other men. He told me to be like Jesus and to heal the people as He did. While I have not been thrown to the lions, I have been thrown to the media. Yes, I understand to a great extent what Paul is saying here. But, along with him, I would rather have Jesus than anything else in the world.

I Corinthians 4:14-21

I write not these things to shame you, but as my beloved sons I warn you. For though ye have ten thousand instructors in Christ, yet have ye not many fathers: for in Christ Jesus I have begotten you through the gospel. Wherefore I beseech you, be ye followers of me. For this cause have I sent unto you Timotheus, who is my beloved son, and faithful in the Lord, who shall bring you into remembrance of my ways which be in Christ, as I teach every where in every church.

Now some are puffed up, as though I would not come to you. But I will come to you shortly, if the Lord will, and will know, not the speech of them which are puffed up, but the power. For the kingdom of God is not in word, but in power. What will ye? shall I come unto you with a rod, or in love, and in the spirit of meekness?

Reminded of God's Power

When Paul mentions the term "instructor" here, he is referring to the Greek term for "tutor," one who was usually an old Greek slave who took the children to and from school and molded their moral characters. He is saying, "You may have many instructors like that, but not many fathers. For I am the one who led you to Christ; therefore, I beseech you to be followers of me even as I follow after God. And that is the reason I have sent Timothy to you with this letter. He is going to show you this letter and you will learn from it what I am saying, but he will also tell you other things which I teach everywhere in every church." He adds, "Some of you are so puffed up, you are saying, 'Paul won't come,' but I tell you I will come. When I come, it will not just be with speech but with power, for the kingdom of God is not in mere word; it is in the power of God."

As we begin to read Chapters 5 and 6, bear in mind that Paul has stopped discussing the divisions in the church and gone to specific sins, such as sexual immorality. Here, we are going to discover the original teachings of Christ concerning our personal, private lives as we live as Christians in the world today.

I Corinthians 5:1-8

It is reported commonly that there is fornication among you, and such fornication as is not so much as named among the Gentiles, that one should have his father's wife. And ye are puffed up, and have not rather mourned, that he that hath done this deed might be taken away from among you.

For I verily, as absent in body, but present in spirit, have judged already, as though I were present, concerning him that hath so done this deed. In the name of our Lord Jesus Christ, when ye are gathered together, and my spirit, with the power of our Lord Jesus Christ, to deliver such an one unto Satan for the destruction of the flesh, that the spirit may be saved in the day of the Lord Jesus.

Your glorying is not good. Know ye not that a little leaven leaveneth the whole lump? Purge out therefore the old leaven, that ye may be a new lump, as ye are unleavened. For even Christ our passover is sacrificed for us: therefore let us keep the feast, not with old leaven, neither with the leaven of malice and wickedness; but with the unleavened bread of sincerity and truth.

Hate Sin, Love People

Paul had heard that there was something practiced among the Corinthian Christians that was unheard of even in the Gentile world, and that was incest. Here is a Christian living with his stepmother, and the Christians at Corinth were puffed up about it. They were not mourning and praying and helping that young man. They had not done anything to help the young person overcome his sin or, when he refused to change, to take him away from their congregation. But Paul said, "Listen, God has already judged this, and so have I. And I tell you in the name of Jesus Christ our Lord to deliver this person back into the world of the devil, but do not give up on him. Do it in the spirit and the power of our Lord Jesus Christ. Do not simply excommunicate him without love or without hope that he can be delivered and restored to the Church. If the person cannot be delivered from that thing in his flesh, then deliver him to Satan who has the power of death. So while the devil may kill his body, he will not be able to destroy his soul."

He reminds them when Israel was being delivered from Egyptian bondage, that on the night before the Passover they took unleavened bread, that is, bread without yeast, and they went through the house looking for little pieces of bread that might be leavened bread, so that the house would be clean. Christ became our "passover" through His sacrifice on Calvary for us, that in Him we might be saved and that in our body there might not be sin and that in the body of the Church there would not be sin, because sin has a tendency to grow and multiply and engulf the people of God. Paul not only was dealing with an actual case of sin which was permeating the church at Corinth, he was preparing people to face up to the consequences of such behavior and deliver themselves from it.

Paul is to be admired for taking this stand — not against the person, but against the sin in the person. He hated the sin, but he loved the person who was engaging in the sin, and hoping and trusting that through this merciful judgment that person might be restored to God and to his church.

I Corinthians 5:9-13
> I wrote unto you in an epistle not to company with fornicators: yet not altogether with the fornicators of this world, or with the covetous, or extortioners, or with idolaters; for then must ye needs go out of the world. But now I have written unto you not to keep company, if any man that is called a brother be a fornicator, or covetous, or an idolater, or a railer, or a drunkard, or an extortioner; with such an one no not to eat. For what have I to do to judge them also that are without? do not ye judge them that are within? But them that are without God judgeth. Therefore put away from among yourselves that wicked person.

Purity of Christian Example

He said, "Do not be so carried away that you become like hermits and live off to yourselves, because you have to live in this world. However," he said, "you are keeping company with people who call themselves Christian brothers, and yet they are fornicators; they are full of covetousness; they are idolaters, full of superstition; they are drunkards; they are extortioners and thieves; and I am telling you that this is the type of the person who lives in Corinth in the Gentile world of wickedness, and such must not be in the Church. The Christian Church is an island of purity in that vast ocean of sin, and you must shine in the light of God and be a pure Church."

The Gentile world did not know Christian purity. They thought the practice of sin was the normal way to live. But the Christians were cleaned up from that through the sacrifice of Christ on the cross. Paul is saying, "Eliminate such people, but do it in Christian love so that they might be saved and restored to the Church."

The kind of world you and I live in today, in a way, is so bad that it makes the world back there look good. We have the same sins that those people had, only in greater numbers, because the human population is hundreds of times larger than it was then. Men and women have become far more practiced and sophisticated in the committing of various kinds of sins, and this world today is shot through with every kind of sin you can imagine. Like a pure island in the midst of that ocean of garbage are the children of God, you and I who serve our Lord Jesus Christ. But there were also Christians in Corinth who were living in that kind of world, who overcame the sins of that day; however, there were some who did not. The situation is similar today. There are people who will do almost anything in the world that is of the devil, that is sinful. Yet they claim to be the children of God and pretend to be Christians. But Paul is saying we are to walk in the purity of the gospel, and while we cannot escape this world, we have to associate with all kinds of people, including the most sinful ones; but we are to be an island of purity in the midst of spiritual garbage.

I Corinthians 6:1-8

Dare any of you, having a matter against another, go to law before the unjust, and not before the saints? Do ye not know that the saints shall judge the world? and if the world shall be judged by you, are ye unworthy to judge the smallest matters? Know ye not that we shall judge angels? how much more things that pertain to this life? If then ye have judgments of things pertaining to this life, set them to judge who are least esteemed in the church.

I speak to your shame. Is it so, that there is not a wise man among you? no, not one that shall be able to judge between his brethren? But brother goeth to law with brother, and that before the unbelievers. Now therefore there is utterly a fault among you, because ye go to law one with another. Why do ye not rather take wrong? why do ye not rather suffer yourselves to be defrauded? Nay, ye do wrong, and defraud, and that your brethren.

Christian Legal Viewpoint

Paul is dealing in the midst of a Gentile world with Greek culture, and the Greeks were litigious by nature. They wanted to go to court for any and everything, and now these Corinthians who were saved out of that kind of people were drifting back into the old habits. When they had trouble one with another, they began to take each other into court. Paul said, "Isn't there at least one wise person among you who as a Christian can stand up and arbitrate the matters

249

between you as brothers and sisters in Christ?"

When there's any problem among those of us who are Christians, we are to act as believers in Christ because we have the ability in Christ to know what is right and wrong. If we come to where we cannot solve a problem, there is a point where a Christian suffers certain things rather than make a public spectacle of our faith in Christ.

At Oral Roberts University, we have the O.W. Coburn School of Law. And we have a different kind of law school in that we not only teach law as most other law schools teach it, but we teach it by going a step further. That is, we teach Christian mediation so that Christians will not sue one another. We graduate lawyers who are healers. Not that our law graduates will not practice law in the various fields of the world, but they are being carefully trained to mediate things between brothers and sisters in Christ. I am not saying we should never go to court, but it should certainly be the last resort. Some people, including Christians, are entirely too quick to sue. It seems that everybody wants to sue everybody these days, and Paul is simply telling us Christians that this is not God's way.

I Corinthians 6:9-11

> Know ye not that the unrighteous shall not inherit the kingdom of God? Be not deceived: neither fornicators, nor idolaters, nor adulterers, nor effeminate, nor abusers of themselves with mankind, nor thieves, nor covetous, nor drunkards, nor revilers, nor extortioners, shall inherit the kingdom of God. And such were some of you: but ye are washed, but ye are sanctified, but ye are justified in the name of the Lord Jesus, and by the Spirit of our God.

The Solution to Sin

Paul tells the Christians not to be deceived. He lists a group of people and their sins who shall not inherit the kingdom of God. He calls them "fornicators," which, at that time, referred to a male homosexual; "nor idolaters," such as those who worshiped in the temple of Aphrodite, and those who were "effeminate," that is, they were trying to be as sensual and sexual as possible; "nor abusers of themselves with mankind." Again, he was speaking of homosexuality. "Nor thieves," and in that time thievery was everywhere. "Nor greedy," grasping people, people who would extort. He said, "These people shall not inherit the kingdom of God."

Then he just shouts out, "But such were some of you. Some of you Christians here in Corinth were just like that, even though by the blood of Jesus you were washed and consecrated and set free by the Spirit of God." Paul praised God because of the life-changing power of the blood of Jesus Christ.

If someone today is like this or if a family has a member who has gone away into these sins, I encourage you to keep on believing God, because through the shed blood of Christ and repentance and faith, there is deliverance from any and all of these sins and from every other kind of sin in the world. Through Christ, we are made free from these sins by the Spirit of God.

I Corinthians 6:12-20

> All things are lawful unto me, but all things are not expedient: all things are lawful for me, but I will not be brought under the power of any. Meats for the belly, and the belly for meats: but God shall destroy both it and them. Now the body is not for fornication, but for the Lord; and the Lord for the body. And God hath both raised up the Lord, and will also raise up us by his own power. Know ye not that your bodies are the members of Christ? shall I then take the members of Christ, and make them the members of a harlot? God forbid.
>
> What? know ye not that he which is joined to an harlot is one body? for two, saith he, shall be one flesh. But he that is joined unto the Lord is one spirit. Flee fornication. Every sin that a man doeth is without the body; but he that committeth fornication sinneth against his own body. What? know ye not that your body is the temple of the Holy Ghost which is in you, which ye have of God, and ye are not your own? For ye are bought with a price: therefore glorify God in your body, and in your spirit, which are God's.

The Body as Temple

The Greeks treated their bodies as something quite worthless in regard to the value of their soul. It was lawful for them to gratify their bodies in any way they desired, whenever they desired. Paul is saying, "It is lawful, yes, in this wicked Gentile world. It is lawful, but not expedient; it is not in harmony with the Spirit of God. And although it is lawful for me to do that, I will not. I will not allow my body to be brought under their rules. I will keep it in the will of God, in the control of the Holy Spirit."

All through the years, we have been hearing, "Do your own thing. If it feels good it's okay." But Paul is saying, not so. That is not the Spirit of God. He refers to Genesis 2:24, where God spoke of marriage, how man shall "leave his father and mother and cleave only unto his wife, and they shall be one flesh." Paul says, "When you commit adultery or fornication, you are joining your body to the body of another person. And outside of marriage, as you join yourself, you violate the marriage covenant of God; you violate the way God created you." Then he says, "Don't you understand that your body is different from the way the Greeks say it is? It is a temple of the Holy Spirit, who indwells you."

He was referring to the time when God had the great temple built in Jerusalem to be a dwelling place where He in His presence would dwell and bless His people. Therefore, that temple was a sacred place. Paul is saying that your body is like that temple, the dwelling place of God, and that body is not your own; it belongs to God. It was bought with a great price. When Christ died He redeemed not only the soul but the mind and the body. He redeemed the whole person, and the price He paid was His own shed blood. Therefore, glorify God with your body. Treat your body as a sacred, holy temple because your body belongs to God just as much as your spirit belongs to God. They are both God's property.

He never told us to do something we cannot do, and I know in my own life that when I met Christ at age 17 all those old sins fell off me like water off a duck's back, and I became a new creature. However, all through these years, as the temptations have come from the devil, by exercising my will and trusting in Christ, I can testify that a man or a woman can live a consecrated, sanctified life. Now I would like to pray with you.

> *Heavenly Father, we are taught here in the Word that we are to clean up our lives, to exercise our will and turn away from the things of this world — from sin that destroys us. And You remind us that our bodies are indwelt by the Holy Spirit. We are not our own. We belong to God because He bought us with the price of His own Son on the cross. And I thank You today that we are rededicating ourselves, including our bodies, so that we are clean before God. And we are His property. We thank You for it through Jesus Christ. Amen and amen.*

I Corinthians 7:1-9

> Now concerning the things whereof ye wrote unto me: It is good for a man not to touch a woman. Nevertheless, to avoid fornication, let every man have his own wife, and let every woman have her own husband. Let the husband render unto the wife due benevolence: and likewise also the wife unto the husband. The wife hath not power of her own body, but the husband: and likewise also the husband hath not power of his own body, but the wife.

Defraud ye not one the other, except it be with consent for a time, that ye may give yourselves to fasting and prayer; and come together again, that Satan tempt you not for your incontinency. But I speak this by permission, and not of commandment. For I would that all men were even as I myself. But every man hath his proper gift of God, one after this manner, and another after that. I say therefore to the unmarried and widows, It is good for them if they abide even as I. But if they cannot contain, let them marry: for it is better to marry than to burn.

Passion, Marriage Discussed

There were two teachings going around at this time. First, that since these Christians in the church of God at Corinth had been saved out of that world of impurity, they should not get married at all. The second teaching was that if they got married, they should not have sexual intercourse. So Paul says, "Yes, it is fine if you do not get married, but to avoid fornication, every one of you should have his own wife or her own husband, and when you get married, carry out the marriage contract. Let the husband give unto the wife sexually and her to him in a normal way, because neither of you can function in marriage without the other. So do not refrain from sexual intercourse in a normal way, except for special seasons like the several days you may want to give to fasting and prayer. But immediately come together again sexually, so that Satan will not tempt you to be unfaithful to one another in your marriage vows."

Then he said, "Let me tell you something from my own experience. In some ways, it would be better for you to be like me, because I do not carry around a wife." He was saying that at some time in his life he had been married. I say this for two reasons. Paul had been a rabbi, and rabbis were supposed to marry. There was an old saying about the Jewish rabbis: If they did not marry, they had slain their posterity, that is, they would never have children. The second reason is that when Stephen was martyred, Paul had cast his vote for it, meaning he was a member of the Sanhedrin Court in Jerusalem composed of 70 men. And it was a regulation that a member of the Sanhedrin should be married. We do not know why Paul did not have a wife. It is only important that we understand what Paul is saying here.

Then Paul recognizes human passion. In the ninth verse, he says that if they cannot contain themselves, let them marry, for it is better to "marry than to burn," that is, to burn with sexual passion. He recognizes the way that God has made us, both men and women.

He is saying it is perfectly normal and natural for people to have
passion, that God has given a way for it to be consummated, and
that is in marriage.

I Corinthians 7:10-20

> And unto the married I command, yet not I, but the Lord, Let not the
> wife depart from her husband: but and if she depart, let her remain
> unmarried, or be reconciled to her husband: and let not the husband
> put away his wife. But to the rest speak I, not the Lord, If any brother
> hath a wife that believeth not, and she be pleased to dwell with him,
> let him not put her away. And the woman which hath an husband
> that believeth not, and if he be pleased to dwell with her, let her not
> leave him.

> For the unbelieving husband is sanctified by the wife, and the
> unbelieving wife is sanctified by the husband: else were your children
> unclean; but now are they holy. But if the unbelieving depart, let him
> depart. A brother or a sister is not under bondage in such cases: but
> God hath called us to peace. For what knowest thou, O wife, whether
> thou shalt save thy husband? or how knowest thou, O man, whether
> thou shalt save thy wife?

> But as God hath distributed to every man, as the Lord hath called
> every one, so let him walk. And so ordain I in all churches. Is any
> man called being circumcised? let him not become uncircumcised.
> Is any called in uncircumcision? let him not be circumcised.
> Circumcision is nothing, and uncircumcision is nothing, but the
> keeping of the commandments of God. Let every man abide in the
> same calling wherein he was called.

Paul Sought Purity

There was a teaching going around in Corinth, after the
establishment of the Christian Church, that if you became a Christian
and your husband or wife did not, you ought to leave them. Paul is
saying, "That is not the case at all. You can stay with them and win
them to the Lord, and also your children will have the blessing of
the Lord upon them."

There are so many people who take this chapter and try to
interpret it to say that Paul was against marriage or that he wanted
people to be strong so they would not have to marry. That is not
what Paul is saying. Paul is 100 percent for marriage, but he wanted
marriage to constitute one flesh, where you have unity and
partnership in marriage. He did not want people to play at marriage.
Paul was strong on marriage, but he wanted purity, whether you

were married or whether you were not married. He was seeking for your right relationship with God.

I Corinthians 7:21-40

Art thou called being a servant? care not for it: but if thou mayest be made free, use it rather. For he that is called in the Lord, being a servant, is the Lord's freeman: likewise also he that is called, being free, is Christ's servant. Ye are bought with a price; be not ye the servants of men. Brethren, let every man, wherein he is called, therein abide with God.

Now concerning virgins I have no commandment of the Lord: yet I give my judgment, as one that hath obtained mercy of the Lord to be faithful. I suppose therefore that this is good for the present distress, I say, that it is good for a man so to be. Art thou bound unto a wife? seek not to be loosed. Art thou loosed from a wife? seek not a wife. But and if thou marry, thou hast not sinned; and if a virgin marry, she hath not sinned. Nevertheless such shall have trouble in the flesh: but I spare you. But this I say, brethren, the time is short: it remaineth, that both they that have wives be as though they had none; and they that weep, as though they wept not; and they that rejoice, as though they rejoiced not; and they that buy, as though they possessed not; and they that use this world, as not abusing it: for the fashion of this world passeth away. But I would have you without carefulness. He that is unmarried careth for the things that belong to the Lord, how he may please the Lord: But he that is married careth for the things that are of the world, how he may please his wife.

There is difference also between a wife and a virgin. The unmarried woman careth for the things of the Lord, that she may be holy both in body and in spirit: but she that is married careth for the things of the world, how she may please her husband. And this I speak for your own profit; not that I may cast a snare upon you, but for that which is comely, and that ye may attend upon the Lord without distraction. But if any man think that he behaveth himself uncomely toward his virgin, if she pass the flower of her age, and need so require, let him do what he will, he sinneth not: let them marry.

Nevertheless he that standeth stedfast in his heart, having no necessity, but hath power over his own will, and hath so decreed in his heart that he will keep his virgin, doeth well. So then he that giveth her in marriage doeth well; but he that giveth her not in marriage doeth better. The wife is bound by the law as long as her husband liveth; but if her husband be dead, she is at liberty to be married to whom she will; only in the Lord. But she is happier if she so abide, after my judgment: and I think also that I have the Spirit of God.

Living for Christ First

Paul is dealing with several errors in the Christian Church. One concerned living within your circumstances. For example, there were many Greek slaves at that time, but there were certain instances in which they could do a special deed or pay a certain price to obtain Roman citizenship and be free. There were others who already were Roman citizens. Paul was saying, "Do not fret over either condition, because whatever that condition is you are a free person in Jesus Christ. The power of Christ rests upon you, and do not forget it."

Another thing he was saying was that these Christians, having come out of such a sordid background in Corinth, were confused about marriage. Should they get married or should they not? Paul is saying, "You live for Christ whatever the circumstances. You put Christ first. You keep Him uppermost in your mind. That is the key issue."

The final thing in the chapter is that many of them thought that they were married for eternity. Paul is saying, "Not so, because if one of you dies, then you can remarry. When you become a Christian, do not make your Christian experience something abnormal. Bloom where you are planted. Serve God where you are. Let your light shine in whatever area of darkness of the world you live in." Paul is saying, "Since time is short, since the Lord is coming soon, do not add any extra stress to your life, to your marriage, to your Christian witness. The main thing is to realize that you are put in the world for a purpose as a child of God. So don't mess it up."

I Corinthians 8:1-13

Now as touching things offered unto idols, we know that we all have knowledge. Knowledge puffeth up, but charity edifieth. And if any man think that he knoweth any thing, he knoweth nothing yet as he ought to know. But if any man love God, the same is known of him. As concerning therefore the eating of those things that are offered in sacrifice unto idols, we know that an idol is nothing in the world, and that there is none other God but one.

For though there be that are called gods, whether in heaven or in earth, (as there be gods many, and lords many,) but to us there is but one God, the Father, of whom are all things, and we in him; and one Lord Jesus Christ, by whom are all things, and we by him. Howbeit there is not in every man that knowledge: for some with conscience of the idol unto this hour eat it as a thing offered unto an idol; and their conscience being weak is defiled. But meat commendeth us not to God: for neither, if we eat, are we the better; neither, if we eat not, are we the worse. But take heed lest by any means this liberty of yours become a stumblingblock to them that are weak.

For if any man see thee which hast knowledge sit at meat in the idol's temple, shall not the conscience of him which is weak be emboldened to eat those things which are offered to idols; and through thy knowledge shall the weak brother perish, for whom Christ died? But when ye sin so against the brethren, and wound their weak conscience, ye sin against Christ. Wherefore, if meat make my brother to offend, I will eat no flesh while the world standeth, lest I make my brother to offend.

Relationships Paramount

Paul is saying that our liberty in Christ is to be exercised by our love and not as a form of superiority. He is saying, "Everybody here has knowledge of the kind of city in which you have been living. It is a city of many gods — idol gods, where meat is first offered to these idols before it is consumed in the body. You have been saved from that. You know there are no idol gods. There is only one God. Your love in Jesus Christ has given you liberty and freedom, freedom from all that idol worship and ritual from which you have been saved. That liberty is to be exercised in love, and, therefore, if someone sees you at one of these feasts where meat is sacrificed to idols and that person is a Christian, he knows you have knowledge of the background, and he is offended. Get up and leave and do not offend that Christian brother." Paul says, "Do not do anything to make your brother stumble." Speaking personally I know there are some things I can do without dishonoring the Lord or breaking my own relationship with Christ, but they do not mean that much to me. The Body of Christ means more to me than my being privileged to indulge in certain things that are not wrong. I simply forego them for the glory of God because my relationships with Christ and my brother are paramount in my life.

I Corinthians 9:1-14

Am I not an apostle? am I not free? have I not seen Jesus Christ our Lord? are not ye my work in the Lord? If I be not an apostle unto others, yet doubtless I am to you: for the seal of mine apostleship are ye in the Lord. Mine answer to them that do examine me is this, Have we not power to eat and to drink? Have we not power to lead about a sister, a wife, as well as other apostles, and as the brethren of the Lord, and Cephas? Or I only and Barnabas, have not we power to forbear working?

Who goeth a warfare any time at his own charges? who planteth the vineyard, and eateth not of the fruit thereof? or who feedeth a flock, and eateth not of the milk of the flock? Say I these things as a man? or saith not the law the same also? For it is written in the law of Moses, Thou shalt not muzzle the mouth of the ox that treadeth out the corn. Doth God take care for oxen? Or saith he it altogether for our sakes? For our sakes, no doubt, this is written: that he that ploweth should plow in hope; and that he that thresheth in hope should be partaker of his hope.

If we have sown unto you spiritual things, is it a great thing if we shall reap your carnal things? If others be partakers of this power over you, are not we rather? Nevertheless we have not used this power; but suffer all things, lest we should hinder the gospel of Christ. Do ye not know that they which minister about holy things live of the things of the temple? and they which wait at the altar are partakers with the altar? Even so hath the Lord ordained that they which preach the gospel should live of the gospel.

Paul is speaking of his own special privileges in Christ, which he gladly lays aside so that he will not offend anybody or be a stumbling block to their serving the Lord. He says, "Look at my special privileges. Am I not an apostle? Don't I have the same liberty in Christ? Haven't I seen our Lord Jesus Christ? Don't I have power to eat and drink? Don't I have power to be married, to have a wife and to carry her around, even as the other apostles, including Peter? And don't I have a right to live of the gospel, or am I and Barnabas the only ones who should work with our hands while others who preach the gospel live of the gospel?"

He adds, "Certainly it is right that those who serve should be paid in order that they would live." He says, "Does a soldier go off to war and bear his own expenses? If a man plants, does he not share in the harvest?" Then he says, "Even the law of Moses says that you shall not put a muzzle on an ox that is treading out the wheat." Those who preach the gospel shall live of the gospel, he says, and refers to those Levites and others who worked in the service of God in the temple.

We know from Leviticus and other books of the Old Testament that the tithe originally went directly to the Levites because they were of the 12 tribes of Israel and were the only tribe which was not given a land inheritance in the Promised Land when the children of Israel had been brought there by Moses and Joshua. Therefore, as they carried on the services of God to help the people follow the Lord's ways and receive His blessings, they would actually live by the tithe of the other people.

The word "tithe" in the Bible means "tenth," and 10 is the number in the Bible for increase. People gave their tithe as a symbol of their faith in the power of God to increase their giving, and through that increase, those who ministered spiritual things to them also had their living, so there was an equality among them.

I Corinthians 9:15-23

> But I have used none of these things: neither have I written these things, that it should be so done unto me: for it were better for me to die, than that any man should make my glorying void. For though I preach the gospel, I have nothing to glory of: for necessity is laid upon me; yea, woe is unto me, if I preach not the gospel!
>
> For if I do this thing willingly, I have a reward: but if against my will, a dispensation of the gospel is committed unto me. What is my reward then? Verily that, when I preach the gospel, I may make the gospel of Christ without charge, that I abuse not my power in the gospel.
>
> For though I be free from all men, yet have I made myself servant unto all, that I might gain the more. And unto the Jews I became as a Jew, that I might gain the Jews; to them that are under the law, as under the law, that I might gain them that are under the law; to them that are without law, as without law, (being not without law to God, but under the law to Christ,) that I might gain them that are without law. To the weak became I as weak, that I might gain the weak: I am made all things to all men, that I might by all means save some. And this I do for the gospel's sake, that I might be partaker thereof with you.

Mastered by Jesus

Paul is saying that with all the privileges he had, he was not willing to use them solely for himself. At that time in Corinth he was not receiving any gifts for his own ministry. Although he said that the receiving of gifts and support was proper for any minister of the gospel, he worked with his own hands while he was there, he and Barnabas. He made a point that stands for the ages, saying, "The reason I am doing this is so you will understand what is in my heart. I am not preaching that somebody should give me something or that I should become wealthy or honored by the world. I am preaching because woe is unto me if I preach not the gospel."

He was referring to his Damascus road experience when he met Christ, his Lord. Christ had become his life. There was such a thrill, such a life-giving force, such an inward urge to share the good news of the gospel, that it consumed him. If he had to work with his hands he would do it. There were other places, such as Philippi, where they gave him offerings. He was saying that was proper, but on the other hand, he also was demonstrating times when he would not receive anything so that he could show them his motive. He had been mastered by Jesus and he wanted to see other men mastered by the Son of God. He knew he had a reward, a reward from the Lord. Even the Corinthians were his reward because they had accepted the gospel through him.

Paul said he would use different methods for different situations, including that of the Jews. He knew the Jews. He knew how to subordinate himself to them in order to better present Christ. He also knew the Gentiles. Whatever it took to get the gospel across, as long as it sprang from the love of God in Paul's heart, he would gladly do. When he says, "I became all things to all men that I might win some," he is not saying that he entered into their sins. He is saying he identified with them. He got down in the arena of their hurts, their needs, and let them see that he was a man trusting in Christ, who would meet all his needs and all their needs.

I know in my own life there is no way I can escape preaching the gospel. I, too, can say, "Woe is unto me if I preach not the gospel." I preached the gospel when I had to stand on the side of the road with my bag and my Bible, put my thumb out and thumb it 100 and 200 miles, preach a weekend, and be let out at the end of town near midnight on Sunday night and thumb it back to the city where my family lived and where I was going to the university. I can tell you one thing, if you are really called to preach, preach! But if you do not know whether you are called to preach, you had better find out. If you are full of doubts, get them settled one way or the other. That way, the glory of God will really flow through you to honor Christ and reach men for Him.

I Corinthians 9:24-27

Know ye not that they which run in a race run all, but one receiveth the prize? So run, that ye may obtain. And every man that striveth for the mastery is temperate in all things. Now they do it to obtain a corruptible crown; but we an incorruptible. I therefore so run, not as uncertainly; so fight I, not as one that beateth the air: but I keep under my body, and bring it into subjection: lest that by any means, when I have preached to others, I myself should be a castaway.

Win the Real Prize

Paul was fascinated by the athlete. When he saw the athlete submit himself wholly, daily, to the most rigorous discipline of his body and of his mind and spirit, it reminded him of what a Christian should do with his life. He said they run in a race, they compete in athletics, but only one receives the prize because he disciplined his life, he made a commitment to it. Yet, when he receives the prize, it is just a bunch of leaves put around his head, because that was what the prize was then. It was a corruptible crown. Today there are prizes of silver, gold, bronze or something else, but all of these also are corruptible. He says the crown we run for is an incorruptible one.

Paul says that he did not fight to lose, not as one that "beats the air." He went after the crown — the incorruptible crown. He conditioned his body to keep it in shape. Remember in I Corinthians 6 where he spoke about the Holy Spirit indwelling our bodies and making our bodies a temple of the Holy Spirit? Our bodies are very important, and we keep them under subjection to God along with our souls and our minds. He is saying that athletics in their ideal are good for us to study because there are many things about them that remind us of the Christian race.

Many times people talk about hell and the things you have to avoid or give up, and they talk about them in a way that turns us away from Christ. But there is another side, the side of sowing our seed and reaping a harvest. When we enter the race, it is not going to be like the races on this earth where only one can win — we are all going to win. What we win will not be corruptible but incorruptible, not temporal but eternal, and the prize is worth everything. He is pointing out that the prize of our Lord Jesus and heaven is going to be so great that we cannot afford to drop out of the race and miss the crown.

Many of these Corinthians were not going anywhere with Jesus. They were not in that race. They were messing up their lives. They were throwing their precious privileges away. When you get in the race for Christ, get in it and stay there. Get some discipline in your life. Get a goal. When someone asks you where you are going, tell them where you are going — you are going for Christ, and you are going to heaven and you are going to make something of your life. You are not going to waste it and let the devil have it. Let us pray.

Father, I pray that any desire we may have that is unlike God, or any sin that is trying to enter into our flesh would be faced squarely. And we will come against it by the power of our faith in Jesus Christ. Our desire is that our bodies shall be truly indwelt by the Holy Spirit, because we are God's property, and the devil

*has no part in us. And Father, we receive this through Jesus
Christ our Lord. Amen and amen.*

I Corinthians 10:1-11

Moreover, brethren, I would not that ye should be ignorant, how that
all our fathers were under the cloud, and all passed through the sea;
and were all baptized unto Moses in the cloud and in the sea; and
did all eat the same spiritual meat; and did all drink the same spiritual
drink: for they drank of that spiritual Rock that followed them: and
that Rock was Christ. But with many of them God was not well pleased:
for they were overthrown in the wilderness. Now these things were
our examples, to the intent we should not lust after evil things, as
they also lusted.

Neither be ye idolaters, as were some of them; as it is written, The
people sat down to eat and drink, and rose up to play. Neither let us
commit fornication, as some of them committed, and fell in one day
three and twenty thousand. Neither let us tempt Christ, as some of
them also tempted, and were destroyed of serpents. Neither murmur
ye, as some of them also murmured, and were destroyed of the
destroyer. Now all these things happened unto them for ensamples:
and they are written for our admonition, upon whom the ends of the
world are come.

Tempting God Dangerous

"You are getting over-confident, and I would like to take you back
to the Old Testament," Paul says, "and let you see some examples.
Our fathers (that meant the children of Israel) were under the cloud
by day and a pillar of fire by night. They passed through the Red
Sea. They were baptized into Moses' leadership. They had the manna
from heaven and drank of that rock which was a type of Christ
himself. But they got into murmuring. They went after idols. They
committed fornication. They sometimes acted as if it were child's
play. Then God stepped in and they understood they had tempted
God, they had pushed Him too far."

As Verse 9 said, "Neither let us tempt Christ, as some of them
also tempted, and were destroyed of serpents."

Some people today do not think God will do anything when people
continue doing wrong and abusing the things of God. Paul is saying,
"Do not be misled, for in one day several thousand people were
bitten by snakes and died because of their murmuring — murmuring
against God and murmuring against God's servant, Moses, who was
their leader. If we set aside the rights of God for our own so-called

rights, we are pushing God too far. We are tempting God."
That leads Paul to speak of temptation.

I Corinthians 10:12,13

> Wherefore let him that thinketh he standeth take heed lest he fall.
> There hath no temptation taken you but such as is common to man:
> but God is faithful, who will not suffer you to be tempted above that
> ye are able; but will with the temptation also make a way to escape,
> that ye may be able to bear it.

Temptation Not Unbearable

He is telling them they are going to be tempted. "However, do not
give in to that temptation; do not feel that you have to give in to
it." He says, "There is one thing you must bear in mind about
temptation: There is no unique temptation. Every temptation that
you face has already been faced by other people of God." He said,
"God is faithful. God is a faithful God. He is not going to permit you
to be tempted with something that you do not have the inner spiritual
strength to overcome, for in letting that temptation strike at you,
He has already made an escape route, and you can take that escape
route and you can bear it. You can overcome it."

This is a great word for you and me today. We simply have to
look for I Corinthians 10:13 and say as I say to myself:

"Oral, this temptation is not unique. The God I serve is faithful.
He is not going to let me be tempted beyond my ability. In every
temptation He is going to put a path through the mountain, an oasis
in the desert. He is going to show me a word in His Bible. Somebody
will come along and say something encouraging to me. I will get a
letter that will have someone's seed-faith in it that will help me pay
the bills. Or by praying in tongues and interpreting, God will give
me a word of knowledge, a word of wisdom, or some instruction
from Him on how to solve this. He just makes a way of escape, that's
all."

Therefore, Paul says, "Look for it. It will be there." As the old black
preacher who loved God so much said, "When God tells me to jump
through the wall, I jump — that is my business. And it is His business
to make the hole in the wall."

I Corinthians 10:14-22

> Wherefore, my dearly beloved, flee from idolatry. I speak as to wise
> men; judge ye what I say. The cup of blessing which we bless, is it
> not the communion of the blood of Christ? The bread which we break,

is it not the communion of the body of Christ? For we being many are one bread, and one body: for we are all partakers of that one bread. Behold Israel after the flesh: are not they which eat of the sacrifices partakers of the altar?

What say I then? that the idol is any thing, or that which is offered in sacrifice to idols is any thing? But I say that the things which the Gentiles sacrifice, they sacrifice to devils, and not to God: and I would not that ye should have fellowship with devils: Ye cannot drink the cup of the Lord, and the cup of devils; ye cannot be partakers of the Lord's table, and of the table of devils. Do we provoke the Lord to jealousy? are we stronger than he?

Now Paul starts bringing things to a head. He starts talking about the kinds of feasts in which the Corinthians were involved. One was the agape feast of the Holy Communion, and the others were the feasts ordinarily held in Corinth in honor of idol gods, idols inhabited by demons.

He is saying, "You cannot, on the one hand, sit down at the Lord's table and take the Communion and then go over to the table of devils and eat in the same way with them, for the fellowship is different. You sit down to take of the cup and the bread in fellowship with all of God's people of all ages in your worship of Jesus Christ. If you go over and sit down at the table of devils and try to have the same kind of fellowship with people around that table, people whose minds are moved upon by demon power, you are splitting your personality, you are dividing the Lord's presence in your life, because you cannot drink the cup of the Lord and the cup of devils. You cannot provoke the Lord to jealousy like this."

Why didn't he say this to other churches? Because they did not come from the same background. You cannot forget Corinth and the kind of city it was. And remember that Paul was, in effect, complimenting them by saying, "You have more strength of Christ in you than to let this kind of temptation overcome you."

Believers today have that same inner strength, however different our backgrounds. It really makes no difference. Christ is the one who is the central figure, and our fellowship with Him is the key issue. Paul is saying we have the power of the Holy Spirit, we have the inner strength, and we can do it.

I Corinthians 10:23-33

All things are lawful for me, but all things are not expedient: all things are lawful for me, but all things edify not. Let no man seek his own, but every man another's wealth. Whatsoever is sold in the shambles, that eat, asking no question for conscience sake: for the earth is the

Lord's, and the fulness thereof. If any of them that believe not bid you to a feast, and ye be disposed to go; whatsoever is set before you, eat, asking no question for conscience sake.

But if any man say unto you, This is offered in sacrifice unto idols, eat not for his sake that shewed it, and for conscience sake: for the earth is the Lord's, and the fulness thereof: conscience, I say, not thine own, but of the other: for why is my liberty judged of another man's conscience? For if I by grace be a partaker, why am I evil spoken of for that for which I give thanks? Whether therefore ye eat, or drink, or whatsoever ye do, do all to the glory of God. Give none offence, neither to the Jews, nor to the Gentiles, nor to the church of God: even as I please all men in all things, not seeking mine own profit, but the profit of many, that they may be saved.

Now read Verse 33, which is the last verse of Chapter 10, and then read the first verse of Chapter 11, because these two verses belong together.

I Corinthians 10:33,11:1

Even as I please all men in all things, not seeking mine own profit, but the profit of many, that they may be saved. Be ye followers of me, even as I also am of Christ.

Deity Over Diet

Paul is being extremely practical to us Christians. He says of himself that everything is all right for him to do, but that not all things are expedient or proper for him in his Christian witness, in order that he might edify other people. Therefore, there are certain things he will do and others he will not do. For example, he says, "You Christians here in Corinth are in a city where meat is sacrificed to idols and then often later sold in the marketplace. When you buy your meat, take it home and eat it. Or if you go out to eat and they serve meat, go ahead and eat it. However, if they tell you it was offered to an idol god, then do not eat it because it is going to offend someone who is weak in the faith." He says, "Be practical in these matters."

Paul says, "The earth is the Lord's and the fullness thereof." In effect, he is saying that meat that came from a lamb, a sheep, or from cattle is acceptable, so go ahead and eat it. But if it is involved with idol worship, then do not eat it for conscience' sake. He is saying, "There is nothing wrong with the meat itself. It is only wrong in what some people are going to do with it." There are Christian vegetarians who do not feel they should eat meat. Many of them are my close friends in the gospel. Paul says, "If you are going to be a vegetarian, be one. But do not condemn meat that comes from God's animals."

I know one of the dearest men of God in this world who, when he came to Christ, was taught that he should not eat meat, and he does not. But it never came between us. Why should it? We have fellowship in the Lord, not in the things we are eating or not eating.

"For the earth is the Lord's and the fullness thereof." When God made these things of the earth, He called them good. There is nothing wrong with corn, barley, hops, rye. Yet, people can take them and make them into whiskey, and people can be destroyed by it.

God also put the gold here and the silver. That does not mean we are to love them. We are to love God and to use gold and silver or money properly. That is what Paul is trying to say.

When Paul says, "Be ye followers of me, even as I also am of Christ," he is saying, "As long as you can look over my shoulder and see Jesus, follow me." And I say to you, you can follow Oral Roberts as long as you can look over his shoulder and see Jesus. If you cannot see Jesus, you stop. As long as you can see Jesus, then it does not matter whom you are following. You follow the people who follow Jesus because they become good examples for you. They become good leaders. But the leadership is in their obedience to Christ, so that Christ himself is seen to be number one.

I Corinthians 11:2-16

Now I praise you, brethren, that ye remember me in all things, and keep the ordinances, as I delivered them to you. But I would have you know, that the head of every man is Christ; and the head of the woman is the man; and the head of Christ is God. Every man praying or prophesying, having his head covered, dishonoureth his head. But every woman that prayeth or prophesieth with her head uncovered dishonoureth her head: for that is even all one as if she were shaven. For if the woman be not covered, let her also be shorn: but if it be a shame for a woman to be shorn or shaven, let her be covered.

For a man indeed ought not to cover his head, forasmuch as he is the image and glory of God: but the woman is the glory of the man. For the man is not of the woman; but the woman of the man. Neither was the man created for the woman; but the woman for the man. For this cause ought the woman to have power on her head because of the angels. Nevertheless neither is the man without the woman, neither the woman without the man, in the Lord.

For as the woman is of the man, even so is the man also by the woman; but all things of God. Judge in yourselves: is it comely that a woman pray unto God uncovered? Doth not even nature itself teach you, that, if a man have long hair, it is a shame unto him? But if a woman have long hair, it is a glory to her: for her hair is given her for a covering. But if any man seem to be contentious, we have no such custom, neither the churches of God.

Order, Not Hair, at Issue

At this point in Paul's letter to the church at Corinth, he has come across a problem that is troubling the Christians there. First, the Greeks prayed with their heads bare, both men and women, but the Jews were different. The Jewish man prayed with his head uncovered and the woman with her head covered, with a veil on. This could be traced back to creation. Second, Paul did not want a division over something that possibly could destroy the "inner purpose" of God in people's lives. In Verse 3, Paul is stating the created order of man. He says that God is the head of Christ, that Christ is the head of the man, and that man is the head of the woman. This is the order. Yet, Verse 11 says both man and woman belong to each other, can do nothing without each other, are equal partners, for Paul writes, "Neither is the man without the woman, neither the woman without the man, in the Lord."

He referred to the beginning when the woman wore a veil, a covering. It had nothing to do with how long her hair was, it was a covering. And this covering suggested that before her marriage she belonged to her father. When she was married, she had a veil that told the world she belonged to her husband. When she comes into the service of God she still is the glory of the man, and, therefore, she should pray with this veil on, or if she is prophesying aloud, she should do the same thing. Verse 5 says, "Every woman that prayeth or prophesieth," and that lets us know that women also prophesy along with men, and they do that publicly.

This is not as big an issue as it seems. Paul had to face a custom practiced in Corinth by the Jews and by the Greeks, but he was pointing to the created order so that God and Christ and man and woman formed the harmony of creation, of God's purpose, of His witness to the world. He was not trying to put man up too high or woman too low. He simply was saying this is the way God did it. When he came to Verse 15 about long hair and such, he said, "We do not want you to be contentious about this. There is no set law or custom in the churches of God," so it is not a "hair" problem or a question of how long is the woman's hair. It has to do with the created order and the way that we as human beings honor each other in the order that God has placed us.

I Corinthians 11:17-34

Now in this that I declare unto you I praise you not, that ye come together not for the better, but for the worse. For first of all, when ye come together in the church, I hear that there be divisions among you; and I partly believe it. For there must be also heresies among you, that they which are approved may be made manifest among you.

When ye come together therefore into one place, this is not to eat the Lord's supper. For in eating every one taketh before other his own supper: and one is hungry, and another is drunken. What? have ye not houses to eat and to drink in? or despise ye the church of God, and shame them that have not? What shall I say to you? shall I praise you in this? I praise you not.

For I have received of the Lord that which also I delivered unto you, That the Lord Jesus the same night in which he was betrayed took bread: and when he had given thanks, he brake it, and said, Take, eat: this is my body, which is broken for you: this do in remembrance of me. After the same manner also he took the cup, when he had supped, saying, This cup is the new testament in my blood: this do ye, as oft as ye drink it, in remembrance of me.

For as often as ye eat this bread, and drink this cup, ye do shew the Lord's death till he come. Wherefore whosoever shall eat this bread, and drink this cup of the Lord, unworthily, shall be guilty of the body and blood of the Lord. But let a man examine himself, and so let him eat of that bread, and drink of that cup. For he that eateth and drinketh unworthily, eateth and drinketh damnation to himself, not discerning the Lord's body.

For this cause many are weak and sickly among you, and many sleep. For if we would judge ourselves, we should not be judged. But when we are judged, we are chastened of the Lord, that we should not be condemned with the world. Wherefore, my brethren, when ye come together to eat, tarry one for another. And if any man hunger, let him eat at home; that ye come not together unto condemnation. And the rest will I set in order when I come.

The Importance of Communion

Paul now addresses one of the most important parts of our Christian experience. He starts talking about the Lord's Supper and how all of us in every age are to partake of it so that we can receive its supreme benefits in every part of our bodies, souls, and spirits.

He begins by saying to the Corinthian Church that they have missed the mark. They have gotten out of line. They have done some things which are contrary in the taking of the Lord's Supper, because he knows the Lord's Supper. He said, "The Lord gave it to me himself." In one of the revelations of Jesus Christ to Paul, He delivered to Paul exactly what He had said and done on the last night of His life when He was about to be nailed to the cross and His blood shed to fulfill the old covenant and to give the new covenant.

In the early churches, the Holy Communion was usually preceded by a common meal, which was called a "love feast" or "agape." The Christians came together with what we would call a potluck supper today. Different families would bring their food and put it on a common table. All of them would gather round and eat it and have fellowship together, and then they would take the Holy Communion. But the Corinthians had gotten away from that. Those who were more wealthy would bring more sumptuous food and the poor brought what they had. Eventually the wealthy got in one part of the building and had their food, and the poor ate in another section. There was no unity of the Body of Christ. This upset Paul because he knew that was not the way the Lord had given it to him. Paul was saying it was not necessary to have a big feast preceding the Lord's Supper.

There is something wonderful here, because in settling this issue with the Christians at Corinth concerning the Lord's Supper, Paul recorded for the first time since Jesus' death and resurrection His own words. They were about His own body and blood. Paul was deeply moved about the right Communion for every child of God, not only in Corinth but for every age, including ours. The Lord Jesus said to him, "On that last night, when I was betrayed, I took bread. And when I had given thanks I broke it and said, 'Take, eat. This is My body which is broken for you. And when you eat it remember Me.' And then I took the cup and I sipped of it and then I told them to sip of it and do it and remember Me. And every time they were to do it they were to remember Me. This cup is the New Testament in My blood, and it cost Me My life. It cost Me My life, Paul."

You can imagine the effect this personal revelation of Jesus to Paul had upon the apostle. Now he is remonstrating against those Christians who were taking it so lightly and not having a correct Communion. He said, "Some of you are doing it unworthily and you are receiving guilt and damnation into yourselves. Some of you are getting sick in ways you should not. In fact, some of you are dying prematurely."

Paul knew what he was talking about. He was talking about our risen Savior, our Lord who lives. He had given His life, but in paying that supreme price He came forth from the grave in newness of life, giving us a living Communion, so that when you and I take the bread into our mouths, we are taking Christ into our lives through our faith. This is a symbol of the Son of the living God. By our faith we take Him, His body and then His blood, or, saying it another way, we take His wholeness, His power of cleansing, His power of healing, His power of supplying our needs.

We take His very presence into our being because, number one, we are to do it often because we have needs often and, number two, we are to remember Jesus. He is the focal point, the key issue, the single source, the Son of God and the Lord of our lives. We are not to concentrate on the bread and the cup but upon Jesus. Everything revolves around Jesus. He is the Lord of our lives, and we remember Him.

He wanted to be remembered because He gave us the new covenant with its preferred position, a chain of blessing, its more abundant life, its eternal life, its indwelling of the Holy Spirit in our beings (including our bodies). He wanted us to remember Him. He did not say, "Remember an angel or a prophet or some church or the name of our denomination." He said, "You remember ME. Focus your thoughts, your faith upon ME, the Son of God. I am the Source of your total life and your total supply."

Then He said, "I want you to take the correct Communion by showing forth the cross, My death, until I come again." He wanted us to think about His death and resurrection, that He took our place. Then He wanted us to leap across the centuries and think about His second coming. Every time we have a correct Communion, we think of the coming of our Lord back to this earth to change things forever, to renovate this earth, to rid it of sin, to take up His rule and reign in Jerusalem, the Holy City, and become the Lord of all the earth. He said, "This is My body." Therefore, we are to think of Jesus' own physical body upon the earth, how free it was from sin and free from disease, how His mind was free from fear and torment, how He was in union with God. So He is saying, "Think of My own physical body, My own being upon this earth. As you eat and drink of the Communion, take of My health into your body. First, that will keep some sicknesses from ever attacking your body. And second, when sicknesses attack your body, you can experience My healing power." He says, "If you do this in a wrong way, by not discerning first of all My physical body and then second, all My believers who compose the Body of Christ, you are going to miss something. You are not going to make contact with that living power, the life of the Son of God. Without that some of you will be feeble. You will get sickly and you will die before your time." And in effect He is saying, "Some of you Corinthians have not thought about the key issue which is myself, My own body, and then the Body of Christ which is composed

270

of all believers." He is saying to us who believe in Him, "You are a believer and, therefore, you are a grain of that loaf of bread. You are part of it. You are part of every other believer who has ever lived, who now lives, or who shall come after you. You are part of a universal body of believers, and they are part of you."

When you approach the time to eat and drink of the Lord's Supper, look into your heart. It does not mean you have to be perfect, because if you are perfect, you will not ever take it. You come with a sense of your own unworthiness because none of us is worthy; however, there is a process of discernment. "You are to discern Me, My body, and My body of believers. You are to discern that you are in the Body of Christ, the Church against which the gates of hell shall never prevail. You are to get a sense of self-worth, of self-identity, of self-knowledge. As you take the Communion you are to feel like you are standing taller than a mountain. You are, in faith, to receive healing. You are in faith so that you can live out your life span and live it triumphantly, so discern."

If you do not discern the Lord's body, then you are just cutting yourself off from His flow of divine life for better health, for longer life, and for the Lord's personal closeness to you.

I remember coming home from a big tent crusade where I had preached in weather which was 38 to 40 degrees at night, praying for thousands of sick people and winning people to Christ. We had enormous crowds in the big tent. When I got home, my right shoulder and part of my neck were stiff. I supposed the cold air and all of that, along with the hard work, had caused it. I could not move my head, and I could barely move my shoulder. I was in excruciating pain. One of my dear friends in the gospel is Demos Shakarian, the founder of the Full Gospel Business Men's Fellowship International. He came to visit with me, and I said, "Demos, would you give me Holy Communion? My neck and my shoulder are stiff and so much in pain that I really need a healing." So Demos, who himself felt unworthy to give the elements, did so. And he said, "Brother Oral, this is our Lord's blood, and this is our Lord's body. It has life in it through your faith. You take it believing that God will loose your neck and your shoulder."

As I put the bread in my mouth and sipped of the cup, I turned my faith loose. A warmth came into my neck and my shoulder. I began to move my head, raise my shoulder. In a matter of minutes I was as normal as I possibly could be. The Lord had healed me through my faith in His body and blood.

Another time in one of the Oral Roberts University seminars, when we had several hundred people present, there was one person there in a wheelchair. This person had come, having had all the medical care and the laying on of hands, including the prayers of those there. One Sunday morning I was ministering the Holy Communion to the group, and I came to the part where we discern the Lord's body — that it was a healthy, whole body and, therefore, when we take the Communion we are to expect to be healed, to expect a miracle. This mother, sitting there in the wheelchair, believed the Lord as she heard me explain about taking a correct Communion, and when the bread touched her lips, we heard a commotion. We looked, and she was getting up out of the wheelchair and was walking down the aisle. She came upon the platform and said, "Oral Roberts, what you have been teaching is real. I have been in that wheelchair for several years. The Lord is healing me."

You see, that can happen also in forgiveness. We come to the Lord's table, and sometimes we are not just right with Him. We have done things we should not do, thought things we should not think, and we need a cleansing. Sometimes we need a restoration. Sometimes we need to get back into fellowship with our brothers and sisters in Christ. We can discern or grasp the meaning of Jesus' body and blood and by our faith bring ourselves into harmony with Jesus. Jesus will come so much alive in us that marvelous things will happen. Maybe a healing, maybe a reconciliation, maybe a cleansing; I cannot say exactly what will happen. But I know that something good will happen to you and me every time we take a correct Communion, and we ought to do it often because there is so much in Jesus for us.

I Corinthians 12:1-12

Now concerning spiritual gifts, brethren, I would not have you ignorant. Ye know that ye were Gentiles, carried away unto these dumb idols, even as ye were led. Wherefore I give you to understand, that no man speaking by the Spirit of God calleth Jesus accursed: and that no man can say that Jesus is the Lord, but by the Holy Ghost. Now there are diversities of gifts, but the same Spirit. And there are differences of administrations, but the same Lord. And there are diversities of operations, but it is the same God which worketh all in all.

But the manifestation of the Spirit is given to every man to profit withal. For to one is given by the Spirit the word of wisdom; to another the word of knowledge by the same Spirit; to another faith by the same Spirit; to another the gifts of healing by the same Spirit; to another the working of miracles; to another prophecy; to another discerning of spirits; to another divers kinds of tongues; to another the interpretation of tongues: but all these worketh that one and the selfsame Spirit, dividing to every man severally as he will. For as the body is one, and hath many members, and all the members of that one body, being many, are one body: so also is Christ.

Using Spiritual Gifts

Paul now begins the most powerful discussion of the manifestation of the power of God to set human beings free from sin, disease, demons, fear, and everything else that is negative in their lives. This is the most positive thing that the Apostle Paul could do in Corinth with the Christians. And with this part of his letter, he also sets the stage for Christians of all ages to understand that in the Church, in addition to preaching, teaching, praying, taking Holy Communion, and worshiping, there are manifestations of the Holy Spirit coming forth in what he calls "gifts," a better translation of which is "spirituals at work."

In Romans 15, Verses 18 and 19, Paul says, "For I will not dare to speak of any of those things which Christ hath not wrought by me, to make the Gentiles obedient, by word and deed." Notice that he says, by the "word" of God and then by the "deed" that accompanies the Word of God. Then he adds in Verse 19 what these deeds are: In addition to the preaching of the Word, there were mighty signs and wonders by the power of God. And that enabled him to fully preach the gospel of Christ.

In the second chapter of I Corinthians, Verses 3-5, Paul says this in a different way, although he is saying the same thing: "I was with you in weakness, and in fear, and in much trembling. And my preaching was not with enticing words of man's wisdom, but in demonstration of the Spirit and of power, or of results, that your faith should not stand in the wisdom of men, but in the power of God." Here Paul states his own inadequacies, his normal fears. But he went then into a deeper dimension of the Holy Spirit, into the mighty deeds, signs, and wonders, calling upon God to confirm His Word with signs following, and the miracles then brought the results. In this 12th chapter of I Corinthians, Paul is preparing to show these Christians at Corinth and Christians of all time that we must get into the gifts of the Holy Spirit, which are the manifestations of the Spirit in believers to go beyond what this world knows, what this world is able to do, and call upon our Lord to bring it into existence, into being, into action.

The Apostle Paul had dealt with the Holy Communion, its abuses, and its proper use. Now he deals with the gifts of the Spirit. He faces them head-on because they were at work in his own life, and he says that he wants them to remember that at one time they were carried away by dumb idols, which were given over to the power of demons, and to remember that no man speaking by the Spirit of God could call Jesus accursed. That is, in fact, what the Jews did. They thought that every man who was crucified was accursed. Paul wanted them to know that no man could call Jesus accursed and at the same time speak by the Spirit of God. Then he said, "I want to remind you that no man can call Jesus Lord except by the Holy Spirit." He is setting the stage for us to understand that God, the Holy Spirit, is active in our lives in the now.

Then he says there are varieties of gifts but the same Holy Spirit. There are differences of administration but the same Jesus. There are varieties of operations but the same God. He is talking about the Trinity at work in the power of the Holy Spirit, and that no matter what is done supernaturally in the Lord, it is really by the Trinity altogether. Paul then takes us back to the statement of Jesus, when He said that He was going to send us another Comforter, the Holy Spirit, who would testify of Jesus. So the whole work of the Holy Spirit is built around Jesus and a gift of the Spirit is just that much of Jesus, our Lord.

The Holy Spirit takes this characteristic of power or of knowledge or of love from Jesus, and He personally manifests that in the believers. There are nine "gifts" mentioned here in these 12 verses, and Paul says that this manifestation happens in every believer. And for what reason? To meet needs in people. That the work of God, the Body of Christ should profit. So approach your understanding of the gifts of the Spirit in the most positive way.

There is nothing divisive about the gifts of the Spirit. They're the purest, most positive outworkings of Jesus we can ever have. Now divisiveness is in people who get off the main line of God, who get out of the Spirit. And Paul is saying, "I do not want you uninformed about these gifts because the Holy Spirit is the agent through which the Father and the Son work, and you, as a believer, are going to have a manifestation of the Holy Spirit in one or more of these gifts in order to meet needs and to honor God."

Verse 11 lets us know that all these gifts come from the same Holy Spirit who works them as He wills. So do not think you can will one of these gifts into being. The Holy Spirit wills them into activity. Paul is talking about the Holy Spirit acting sovereignly or at His own will and His will alone so that you and I do not run around saying, "God, I want the gift of knowledge, I want the gift of wisdom, I want the gift of healing." It is the Holy Spirit who decides.

But you can know that the Holy Spirit is so active in your life that He will manifest one of these gifts or even more than one gift from time to time in and through your life. Therefore, as the Holy Spirit indwells us and we trust Him to reveal these things of Jesus in our lives, we can be assured that one or more of these gifts will be working in us and probably in line with our heart's desire. For example, the gift of healing works in and through me primarily because my whole nature is inclined toward the sick. Even before my conversion, I had a deep feeling for sick people. Those of us who are not medical doctors but who are believers and who pray for the sick have an inner feeling already toward the sick, and then the Holy Spirit manifests the gift of healing through us from time to time, and we find that our desire to see the sick healed is accelerated. We find that there is power flowing through us, the power of Jesus himself, and we are manifesting that much of Jesus.

What am I really saying? Let us start here with the first gift or manifestation that Paul refers to in Verse 8: "For to one is given by the Holy Spirit the word of wisdom." That is a word of wisdom, not just wisdom but wisdom which becomes a word, a "rhema."

For example, I was at the Berlin World Congress of Evangelism sponsored by Billy Graham in the 1960's. While I was there I kept the lowest profile possible because I was a guest, an invited guest, and I wanted to be in prayer and to be a part of it but not necessarily a public part. But one day a man came to me privately, a man who was a minister of the gospel from South India. He said, "Oral Roberts, when I received the invitation to come to this World Congress on Evangelism, I wanted to come because of Billy Graham and his leadership and to be a part of it. But I also learned that you were going to be in this congress and I had hoped to ask you a question which has been troubling me for many months."

I said, "What is your question?"

He said, "I am a minister, and in my church I have never prayed for the sick. I have not been taught that God heals the sick through believers or through a gift of healing. One day I was in my church study and a family rushed in with their little child who had had tetanus, whom they had taken to the hospital, and the doctors had said, 'You have come too late; the child is going to die.' They thrust this child into my arms and said, 'Pastor, pray.'" Then he said, "Oral Roberts, I, who had never prayed for the sick, found myself praying for this little boy, and God healed him."

I said, "Well, great!"

"Oh," he said, "but I have been troubled."

I said, "How in the world could you be troubled when God healed a little child who was dying of tetanus?"

He said, "I am troubled about whether I did right or not."

"What do you mean did you do right? Didn't the child live?"

"Oh, yes. In fact, it started a revival in my church. But you see, I have never prayed for the sick. My church does not believe that God heals the sick, and I am troubled. What I want to ask you is, did I do the right thing?"

The first thought that went through my mind was, "Of course, you did the right thing." But I did not say that. I paused a moment, and immediately the Holy Spirit manifested a word of wisdom for me to speak. This was a supernatural moving of the Holy Spirit in my life, in the same way that Jesus would have spoken to this man. You must remember that is what a gift of the Spirit is all about. It is that much of Jesus. The Spirit gave me this word of wisdom, which I spoke. I said, "You are asking the question, in praying for this child and God's healing him, did I do the right thing? Why don't you ask the little boy?"

Immediately the man said, "Why don't I ask the little boy? Why don't I ask the little boy? Yes! Why don't I ask the little boy?"

Then he just threw his arms around me and began to weep. "Why," he said, "if I ask the little boy, the very fact he was healed will answer my question."

That was a word of wisdom that the Holy Spirit gave me, but it was not for myself. It was given to me to minister to a person who was troubled with a deep question. The gift of the word of wisdom answered that. I have heard from this man over the years, and every time he reminds me of the word of wisdom that God let me say, "Why don't you ask the little boy?" And, by the way, during the rest of the Congress of Evangelism there in Berlin, this word began to be spoken, and before I realized it, person after person, delegate after delegate, began to say to me, "Why don't you ask the little boy?" And it became a blessing, a power of God to open our minds.

The next one is the gift of the word of knowledge by the same Holy Spirit. Think of Jesus' knowledge. Think of the way that men tried to trap Him in His words and could not. Think of the things He knew. All things were known by our Lord. Can you realize how limited your knowledge and my knowledge and the knowledge of others is? That does not mean we are not to use all the knowledge we have. God expects us to do that. God expects us to increase our knowledge in this world. He tells us to study, to learn, but there is a moment when all the knowledge of all the people in all the world fails. Then we are told here by the Apostle Paul that the Holy Spirit will manifest a word of knowledge that we can speak, and when we speak it, it becomes the word of knowledge to other people or to another person or to a situation. I do not want to speak of my own experiences so much, so I will just say that when this word of knowledge is spoken to a situation, it is as if Jesus was there saying the same words.

276

The next one is the gift of the working of faith by the same Holy Spirit. As a sinner, you have faith to become a Christian. People say, "Can a sinner have faith?" Certainly. If he does not have faith, he cannot ever be saved. God has dealt to every man the measure of faith. That is what Paul said in Romans 12. But, now, after we have believed on the Lord and become believers, we have faith to believe the Lord simply as believers. In addition, there is a faith that is God-faith. It is the faith that Jesus exercises himself and that can become a manifestation in us so that in a given situation our faith becomes a knowing. We know that we know that we know that we know. It is the absence of doubt by the Holy Spirit. In other words, the Holy Spirit just empties us of doubt and fills us with a knowing so that we know that we know that we know, and we then deliver that knowing in prayer for someone or in words to a situation, and it becomes a word of faith. It is not that we have that faith within ourselves; it is a manifestation of the Spirit of God in us so that for that moment it is just like Jesus standing there with a knowing of faith. And we speak it forth or manifest it in our hearts.

Then He speaks of the working of miracles. This is a very special gift by the Spirit of God. We look around us and see miracles every day. We see miracles in God's world, miracles in God's earth. We see miracles through man's ability, that is, man has tremendous breakthroughs. We see them on every side and we do not reject those things that man is creating by his own innate ability, his inborn creativity, his hard work. But Paul says over and beyond that which is innate is the power of the Spirit to work in the believer to manifest the gift of the working of miracles; that is, the divine order in its highest form now begins to operate.

I think of it in terms of myself. I was an unknown young preacher going to the university, pastoring a small church, when God began to manifest this gift of the working of miracles. I could never have done the mighty things I have done, such as acquiring a huge tent, the world's largest canvas tent cathedral (seating 12,000); ministering to people in 46 different countries; building a major university, fully accredited with seven graduate schools, including theology and medicine; and building the largest medical center on one base on the whole earth — over 2,000,000 square feet (about 50 acres) of floor space. All these things are miracles, because Oral Roberts could not do them with his own innate ability or his inborn creativity.

People say, "What a promoter Oral Roberts is." But I am not a good promoter at all if I am on my own. I am just me. But when the Spirit of God comes, then that moves people and it moves things. I could provide many other examples but in the interest of time let this suffice. Believe me, I am not special. I am not special in that God would just select me and manifest these gifts and not do it with any other person. In fact, Paul begins by saying in Verse 7, the manifestation of the Spirit is given to every man, to every believer. I believe one or more of these gifts works in all of us, whether we know it or not. Paul says, "I do not want you to be uninformed. In being informed about them you can welcome them and allow them to work through you."

I remember someone who was really against believing that the gifts of the Spirit are operative for us today in the Holy Spirit. He said, "Well, you take the gifts and I'll take the fruit." In Galatians, Paul speaks of the fruit of the Spirit: love, joy, peace, long- suffering, and so on. So, he says, "I will just take the fruits of the Spirit, and you take the gifts of the Spirit." But do you know what that is like? That is like saying, "Well, you take the train and I will take the track," or vice-versa.

I replied, "Well, I will take both fruit of the Spirit and gifts of the Spirit. I will take the train on the track. I want it all." Here is where Christians and the organized church have missed the boat. They do not understand the positive power of the gifts of the Spirit, and that if they are believers, the gifts of the Spirit are being manifested in them.

Some say, "What about the fruit of the Spirit?" That is something you do. That is something you grow, you mature in, in love, long-suffering. When we get to I Corinthians 13, we will be seeing the fruit of the Spirit. But now we are talking about the gifts of the Spirit, which are manifested by the Holy Spirit himself. It is His will, and these gifts are not for you and me as a singular, personal possession. These gifts are to work through us. We are like delivery people.

I will illustrate this with a story about a milkman. We used to have people who delivered milk to our doors, and we would say, "The milkman is coming." The man was not made out of milk, he was just bringing bottles of milk. He was the delivery man. So we are not possessors of the gifts; we are deliverers of the gifts. It is the person in need of the word of wisdom to whom we deliver it. It is the person in need of the word of knowledge to whom we deliver it. It is the person who is sick to whom we deliver a gift of healing, for God to work through that gift of healing and heal the person either through medicine or through prayer or the combination of both. It is the gift of healing, and that gift of healing works supernaturally upon the natural. Many believers do not understand that the supernatural gift of healing also works upon natural healing and that natural and supernatural are both God's. They belong to God and to God's people.

The next gift that is mentioned is the gift of prophecy or inspired utterance, an utterance created not by the mortal mind but by the Holy Spirit, then placed in our minds so we can speak forth in faith. That is an inspired utterance. I know that many in the Church believe that is just preaching, but I have heard a lot of preaching that was not inspired. I have heard a lot of preaching that did not say anything, and maybe I have done some of it myself. But I know when that inspiration comes. When I am speaking by inspiration prophetically, that is the gift of the power of prophecy to work through me or anyone else who is a believer.

Then there is the gift of discerning of spirits, the Spirit of God working in us in a situation so we can determine whether the spirit is of God or of a demon, a right spirit or a wrong spirit. And believe me, we have got to have this gift working in our services. In our activities, we have to know we are led by the Spirit of God and not by the spirit of the devil.

The eighth and ninth gifts are the gift of tongues, followed by the gift of interpretation of tongues. They are put together because they work together. In tongues, it is the Holy Spirit being manifested in your spirit as a believer, enabling you to pick up the problem or the need of another person and to take that need through tongues or through praying in the Spirit directly to the Father, and then getting the interpretation of the Father so you can speak in your own tongue, your own language, to that situation, bringing God's answer.

This is a sovereign work of the Holy Spirit. Not every believer is necessarily going to have the gift of tongues or the gift of the interpretation of tongues manifested in him or her. They may, for we are told expressly that the Spirit divides to every believer severally as He wills — not as I will, not as you will, but as the Holy Spirit wills. Before we get to I Corinthians 14, I want to say that the prayer language of the Spirit, which is personal, coming out of the power of the Spirit, is not a gift of tongues. Among those of us who are charismatic, I hear people time and time again saying, "God gave me the gift of tongues," and they are referring mostly to their own personal prayer language, or they do not seem to know the difference. We have got to learn the difference, and we will before we finish with the 14th chapter of this book.

Paul points out why there are different gifts by the same Spirit by comparing it with the parts of our bodies. There are parts of the body that are covered, such as the heart, lungs, kidneys, liver, and stomach. They must be better protected than the hand or the face or the head or the feet or other parts of the body. Paul compares that with the different believers through whom the Spirit manifests

279

various gifts of the Spirit. These nine gifts make up a whole, just as all the parts of your body make up your entire body.

Therefore, you cannot say that the gift of healing is greater than the gift of tongues, or the gift of tongues is greater than the gift of healing, or the gift of the word of knowledge is greater than the gift of prophecy, or the gift of discerning of spirits is greater than the gift of the working of miracles. It depends upon the function and the need. For example, you cannot say that your eyes are greater than your heart. That is what we are going to study next.

I Corinthians 12:13-31

For by one Spirit are we all baptized into one body, whether we be Jews or Gentiles, whether we be bond or free; and have been all made to drink into one Spirit. For the body is not one member, but many. If the foot shall say, Because I am not the hand, I am not of the body; is it therefore not of the body? And if the ear shall say, Because I am not the eye, I am not of the body; is it therefore not of the body? If the whole body were an eye, where were the hearing? If the whole were hearing, where were the smelling?

But now hath God set the members every one of them in the body, as it hath pleased him. And if they were all one member, where were the body? But now are they many members, yet but one body. And the eye cannot say unto the hand, I have no need of thee: nor again the head to the feet, I have no need of you. Nay, much more those members of the body, which seem to be more feeble, are necessary: And those members of the body, which we think to be less honourable, upon these we bestow more abundant honour; and our uncomely parts have more abundant comeliness.

For our comely parts have no need: but God hath tempered the body together, having given more abundant honour to that part which lacked: that there should be no schism in the body; but that the members should have the same care one for another. And whether one member suffer, all the members suffer with it; or one member be honoured, all the members rejoice with it. Now ye are the body of Christ, and members in particular. And God hath set some in the church, first apostles, secondarily prophets, thirdly teachers, after that miracles, then gifts of healings, helps, governments, diversities of tongues. Are all apostles? are all prophets? are all teachers? are all workers of miracles? have all the gifts of healing? do all speak with tongues? do all interpret? But covet earnestly the best gifts: and yet shew I unto you a more excellent way.

Spirit Manifests Gifts

In Verse 18, God says that He has set every one of our body members in its place as it hath pleased Him. The wondrous creation of the body is in front of us every day of our lives, and we see the inner workings of it and are always amazed how in multiplicity God can bring unity so that the various members of the body are working, those seen and unseen. And yet there is one movement of the entire physical being. This is the analogy He uses to show us how the various gifts of the Spirit work in multiplicity and yet with the aim toward unity, that He has placed them in His body — the Body of Christ, His militant Church upon the earth — as the working parts. Therefore, every part is as essential as the other, for without one part, the whole of the Body of Christ is weakened. With every gift of the Spirit working properly, the entire Body of Christ is fully alive, and as Paul said, "I have fully preached the gospel."

This means that the gospel is fully preached — the gospel of good news — and the world has its best chance to know about God, to receive His saving power and healing love and to become a member in the unity of His body. It is a wonderful thing God is talking about here, and just as you or I would not pass over our hand or our foot or an eye, simply saying, "The eye is divisive" or "The hand is divisive" — just as we would not do that, God is saying that He has set these gifts in the Body of Christ among its members. Therefore, Paul is saying to the Corinthian Christian, "Do not get carried away because one of you has working in him the gift of healing or a woman has the discerning of spirits working in her or some person of great renown has one or more of the gifts working in him or her. Do not say that you are something special or that you are inferior if you do not think that the gift the Spirit is manifesting through you is as prominent as that of someone else. That has nothing to do with it. The hand does not want to be the eye. The eye does not want to be the ear. The brain does not want to be the feet. The knees do not want to be the shoulders. The hips do not want to be the heart. One gift is not competing against another. We who are believers, through whom these gifts are manifested for us to deliver them to the needs of people, do not have any desire to work against one another or to feel higher or lower, greater or lesser. God is teaching us a lesson that we all belong to one another, and we are one."

We look about at the denominational world, and if someone should walk up and say, "Are you a believer?" and the answer is, "Yes," the next question is, "What church are you a member of?" And the moment a denominational name is called, immediately a mental picture is produced based upon background teaching and denominational orientation, and the result is usually a warm reception or a rejection based on prejudice. But we are not to prejudge a believer because he belongs to or does not belong to the denomination that we do, or has not joined one at all but perhaps is meeting with a group of believers in fellowship that does not have a denominational name.

So Jesus is talking through Paul to the Corinthians in order to talk to you and me, saying that He is the head, we are the body, and that the head and the body become the Body of Christ, the living Church upon the earth, the Church against which the gates of hell shall never be able to prevail, the Church militant — an organism set in the midst of a world dead to God. Each one of us, then, is delighted with the part that God has assigned unto us, and we do not judge it the way men do, we just receive it. Therefore, we are important, we are unique and irreplaceable. We are God's choice.

One of the things that Paul is trying to point out to us today as believers is that when one of us is suffering, the other should not say, "What in the world has he or she done? They must be getting what they deserve," or "They are bringing reproach upon us." What has actually happened is that the organized church is ruling out, in effect, suffering for Christ.

I personally know that to be true. I know that in the moments and in the periods when I have been the closest to God from the standpoint of obedience and delivering people by His power, there has been more opposition from fellow believers than from the secular world. When I hear of something good happening to you, I should be delighted. If I hear you are sick or someone is misrepresenting you or causing you harm of another nature, I should sorrow in my heart with you and pray for you and lift you up. When something happens to any of us, good or bad, the rest of us should suffer with that one or should rejoice with that one and refuse to listen to all the gossip or to some inferior person who is intimidated by the success of another Christian. We will not pay any attention to that person but will try to bring correction to such an individual and do it in a spirit of love.

Paul is saying that the thing that hurts our Savior the most and causes the greatest disruption in His body here on earth occurs when someone says about another, He is a Catholic, he is a Baptist, he is a Methodist, or he is a charismatic, or he does not belong to any church. What he is implying is, "Well, he is nobody in God."

But do you know that God looks at the heart? Most of us have been brought up in some particular denominational emphasis, more or less, and there are things in that emphasis that we may tend to exaggerate. But God is not overly concerned with that particular thing because He recognizes that "we have this treasure in earthen vessels." We are just plain old human beings. What God is looking for is a Christian, a believer who is trying to walk in the steps of Jesus, whether that person says, "I am a Catholic, I am a Baptist, I am a Methodist, I am a Pentecostal, I am a charismatic, I am nondenominational," or if he has just accepted Christ. Right here is where Jesus Christ is trying to get inside our hearts. I pray for the sick all over the nation and the world. I seldom ask a person about his denomination. I pray for Christians; I pray for sinners; I pray for people because they have needs. I pray because I am expressing the love of Christ. It is up to that person what to do with the benefits he receives through my prayers.

The most important thing concerning Oral Roberts and his relationship with God and with other believers and with this world is that I keep my eyes on Jesus and express my love in every way I know how, and I am a believer, a true believer, and I respect the particular part of the Body of Christ of which I am an ordained elder. When people go beyond what I am saying right here and what I am saying under the anointing of God, God is not pleased with the attitude that people are expressing in the name of Christ.

Christ is looking for reality in you and me as believers because He has set us in the body. As it says in Verse 18: "But now hath God set the members every one of them in the body, as it hath pleased him." We are in the Body of Christ but we have a denominational flavor about us, and often we let the particular denominational emphasis become the absolute truth, as though we alone have all the truth of God. That sort of thing breeds hatred, and soon the Body of Christ is not composed of true believers at all. It becomes just a bunch of backslidden people who are filled with hate, despising one another, and even rejoicing over another's misfortune. That is of the devil, not of God, and you and I should put our foot down right now and decide, "I am going to be a believer, a follower of Jesus Christ." Verse 27 is the absolute test: "Now ye are the body of Christ, and members in particular." Notice that: "You are." You are now the Body of Christ — not yesterday, not tomorrow — you are now the Body of Christ, and you are members in particular. You are individual members. You do not lose your individuality, but you merge your spirit into the entire body.

God speaks in Verse 28 of the rank of the gifts and callings of God. Notice this: "And God hath set some in the church: apostles, prophets, teachers, miracles, gifts of healings, helps, governments, diversities of tongues." This is probably the one verse that stands out above all others as far as the administration of God's work is concerned here on earth. He has set in the Church apostles, prophets, teachers, that is to say, men and women who are given the gifts of God to preach and teach the Word of God. Next, He set in the Church miracles, gifts of healings. That means He set the various gifts in the Church through which the mighty supernatural power of God accompanies the preaching of the Word and confirms it with signs following. Although this was written before Mark's gospel, we remember in the last verses of Mark's gospel that they went everywhere preaching, the Lord working with them confirming His Word with signs and wonders.

The Word, as it is preached and taught, must be confirmed by miracles, gifts of healings, and other gifts of the Spirit which bring forth the supernatural impact of God himself so that the Word becomes a living Word and the impact of the Word produces miracles of deliverance. The mighty power of God moves, and people feel it. They are changed and events are changed.

The third thing He mentions is helps and governments. First, we have the Word of God. Second, we have the gifts of the Spirit. And third, we have administration. In other words, we cannot have the work of God in the Body of Christ, His Church on earth, without administrators — men and women who carry on the business of the Church in an orderly way so that the preaching of the Word can go forth and the miracles and healings of the gifts of the Spirit can occur. So He has set in the Church helps and governments.

It seems to be the thing to do on earth among some denominations to choose administrators above those who are great preachers or teachers of the Word, above those who are workers of miracles and through whom the gift of healing is done. It often happens that the person selected to be in charge of God's work on earth is a person who cannot preach very well or who does not bring forth miracles or healings of the people. But here Paul has put everything in its rank: First, the Word of God; second, the confirming of it by signs and wonders; third, the administrators — those who help and govern; and, fourth, diversities of tongues, thereby showing the absolute necessity of communication with the Father and His confirmation, through tongues and interpretation, of what He is doing.

Stop now and rid your mind of prejudice, eliminate denominational emphasis, become like a little child, take this as Paul wrote it and, in effect, stand in the shoes of the Corinthian believers. He is saying, "Christians, the first thing that you must have are those apostles, prophets, teachers, and ministers of the gospel who give you the Word of God." Then he says the preaching and the teaching of the Word of God do not stand alone. No one can say that because he or she is strong in the Word of God in preaching and teaching, that is enough. The Word preached by itself is not enough.

Here is where the denominational world is falling apart. When we go to church, what do we hear? We hear the preaching and teaching of the Word if we are lucky. But Paul said that God also has set in the Church miracles, gifts of healings. These and other similar gifts are to follow the Word. That is to say, the anointed preaching and teaching of the Word produces faith in the hearts of people to believe in miracles and healings and other demonstrations of the Spirit of God. What church has that? Or if a local church has it, what denomination has it? Where are the miracles? Where are the healings?

Notice the third thing. He is saying to the believers, "You have to have the Word of God preached and taught to you. Second, it must always be confirmed with miracles and gifts of healings of the people and, third, you have to have people who can help it along, who can govern it, who can see that the way is prepared for the preaching and teaching of the Word in order for the Word to be confirmed with miracles and healings of the people.

"Fourth," he says, "you must stay in constant communication with God through tongues because tongues represents the Holy Spirit joining with your spirit in a divine-human reciprocity — your spirit and the Holy Spirit join together to communicate with God in ways that your intellect or your mind cannot." The interpretation of tongues comes back to confirm all that is being preached and taught in the Word, all the mighty workings of miracles and gifts of healings, and even confirms the authenticity of the people helping and governing. Paul placed that precisely as God inspired him. What God is looking for now are churches, individual groups of believers, who will do it just exactly as He said.

It is being done in certain instances. I know of charismatic churches where all four of these things are being carried out — never perfectly, of course, because we are human beings, but they are carrying them out in the rank and the order in which God has set them here in I Corinthians 12:28.

Verse 29 is very important because Paul asks some rhetorical questions with implied answers. He says, "In view of the Body having many members, many parts, and all these parts working together, such as apostles, prophets, miracles, gifts of healings, tongues, interpretation of tongues, they are supposed to work together and are each a part of the other or the whole." Then Paul asks, "Are all apostles? prophets? teachers?" The implication is no. Why not? Because what if all the Church was made up of apostles? Or if there were none in the Church except teachers? Or all were prophets? Just suppose that your body was made up of all toes or all heads?

285

So you would ask, "Oral Roberts, is all of you a head? Is all of you a hip?" The implication is no. Then he asks, "Are all workers of miracles?" The implication is no. Would every member in the Body be given the gift of the working of miracles so that that is all there would be in the church? "Do all have the gift of healing? Do all have the gift of tongues?" The implication is a flat no.

Notice he is speaking of the gift of tongues, not the prayer language of the Spirit that we will discuss in the 14th chapter. (The prayer language is dependent upon the will of the believer to release whenever he wishes, just as Paul did when he said, "I would that you all spoke with tongues, and I pray in tongues or speak in tongues more than all of you." That is a personal prayer language for one's private devotions, different from what Paul is talking about here.)

The 12th chapter concerns the gifts of the Spirit. One of those is the gift of tongues. That gift of tongues is sovereignly manifested through a believer by the will of the Spirit. The Spirit decides that. I could say, "I believe I will manifest the gift of tongues." I would not get anywhere unless the Spirit himself had willed that I do it. So, do all have a gift of tongues? Certainly not. That does not mean what some think it means. They mean to say, "Well, yes, there are gifts of tongues in the Church," but do not know any of them or where they are, and they will not allow them to work in the Church. It is an excuse to get rid of it.

The plain fact is that when Paul began this chapter, he said, "I would that you not be uninformed on the gifts of the Spirit." He is telling you to be informed on the gift of tongues. It, like a member of your body, say your arm, has a function. You do not use your arm unless your brain wills for you to use your arm. No one can manifest the gift of tongues unless the brain or the Spirit — the Spirit of the Body of Christ, the Holy Spirit — decides for that gift of tongues to be manifested, because it is a special gift. This gift is manifested for some but not for others.

Bear in mind, you should not run around saying, "I have the gift of tongues." Even if you pray in tongues 50 times a day, you should not say that, because praying in your private devotions with the prayer language of the Spirit is not the gift of tongues.

The gift of tongues is, of course, a gift of the Holy Spirit, and praying in the prayer language is a gift, but not in the same sense as the gift of tongues. Praying in the prayer language is the gift of the Holy Spirit working in your life. It is the Spirit himself. The gift of tongues working is like your leg working or your arm working. It is working because the brain says for it to work.

Verse 31 is a key verse to many people: "But covet earnestly the best gifts: and yet shew I unto you a more excellent way." Paul is saying to earnestly covet the gift that is best suited for your personality and for your caring heart. He says even when that is done and your proper gift is working in you, there is something more eternal. He says, "I show unto you a more excellent way," and it really means, "I show unto you a more eternal way."

In the light of time and eternity, there is something even greater than being an apostle, prophet, teacher, worker of miracles, one with the gift of healing, or one with the gift of tongues, gift of interpretation of tongues, or any other gift. Even though you are to earnestly desire that the gift best suited to you will be manifested in you by the Holy Spirit, yet there is something more eternal. Let us pray again.

> *I pray that beginning now as never before you will begin to release your prayer language of the Holy Spirit, that you will open yourself by your will so the Holy Spirit can manifest His gifts, any of the gifts, in and through your life. I pray that you will understand best what gift God wants to manifest through you and that the love you have for God will increase more and more so that the greater love you have, the more perfectly God can manifest the gifts of His Spirit through you. I am expecting this to happen in your life and for you to be fully charismatic in releasing these gifts and doing it through your will and the love you have in our heavenly Father. Thank You for it, Lord, through Jesus Christ our Master. Amen and amen.*

Now we are going to begin this great 13th chapter on agape love. We are going to get to Verse 13 where Paul talks about being face to face with God, when the gifts will no longer be necessary, when that which is eternal — divine love — will be there.

I Corinthians 13:1
> Though I speak with the tongues of men and of angels, and have not charity, I am become as sounding brass, or a tinkling cymbal.

Meaning of Agape Love

Read this verse as it really is: "Though I speak with the tongues of men and of angels, and have not Jesus . . ." Why should it read like that? The word "love" in the Greek is "agape" and means God's love rather than man's love or brotherly love or erotic or sexual love. Agape is the pure love of God who so loved the world — a world lost and undone and hating God — that He gave His only begotten Son. God gave the best thing He had for the worst thing of all. God loved in spite of the value of the object of His love. That is agape love. He loved the unlovable. He loved the ones who did not want to be loved by Him.

That is what Paul is speaking of now, the love that is not human, not earthly, but the love that is eternal. That is the way you have to interpret the last verse of the 12th chapter: "But covet earnestly the best gifts: and yet shew I unto you a more excellent (or eternal) way." Immediately he speaks of agape love, eternal love, that which cannot pass away.

Then he begins to compare. He says if he speaks in tongues, either of men or of the angels of God, and he does not have agape love or he does not have Jesus who will love even unlovely people through him, who will love and keep on loving despite what happens, he admits, "I am nothing. Why, I am like a sounding brass or a tinkling cymbal." Or as my father used to say, like a mule kicking in a tin barn. You know what that would sound like.

I Corinthians 13:2

> And though I have the gift of prophecy, and understand all mysteries, and all knowledge; and though I have all faith, so that I could remove mountains, and have not charity, I am nothing.

"And have not Jesus and His agape love ruling and reigning in my heart and motivating me in everything I do, I am a zero. I am a cipher." In no way is the Apostle Paul putting down any of the gifts of the Spirit. He is not putting down tongues, interpretation; he is not putting down prophecy; he is not putting down the word of knowledge; he is not putting down the gift of faith. He is just saying, "Folks, keep on earnestly coveting and desiring the best gifts or the gifts best suited for you, your personality, the way you are." But remember this: Without this eternal love, without Jesus ruling and reigning in your life, you could have all that and yet be like a mule kicking in a tin barn, just making a lot of noise. In fact, he said, in the eyes of God, you can be nothing.

Someone said to me, "Do you mean to say, Oral Roberts, that one could have the gifts of the Spirit and when he did not have agape love these gifts would still work?" They would certainly work in some way because Paul clearly states that the gifts and the callings of God are never recalled. Consider the gift of healing, which seems to work in me quite often. Healing is my tendency, my personality, the caring in my heart, my very disposition. It is natural that God would supernaturally manifest that gift of healing through me. Now let us say that I use it to the best of my knowledge, and then all of a sudden I get out of love, that I am no longer in direct fellowship with Jesus Christ. Does that gift leave me? I can continue to manifest that gift up to a certain point. Yes, it will finally leave me if I continue to disobey God, get out of the Spirit, or not follow Christ or manifest His eternal love. But it will never totally leave me.

As someone said, there are people in hell today who, though they could preach like an apostle or a prophet, are there because they got out of the love of God. They are still preaching. They are preaching in hell but getting no converts. They are preaching without that satisfaction that comes in preaching under the anointing of the Spirit in obedience to God. Doubtless there will be people in hell who spoke in tongues or who had great faith to move mountains, who, for one reason or another, got out of the eternal love of God, turned against God, and became apostates. We will talk about that in Hebrews, how an apostate is no longer redeemable and how that individual is in hell and still goes through all the motions of those gifts. They are absolutely nothing. It is all over with. And that can happen right here on earth too. But that is no excuse for us to turn away from the preaching of the Word, just because some minister of the gospel gets out of God's eternal love. There is no excuse for us to reject the tongues and interpretations of tongues because one person here and one person there will abuse that gift.

I remember when one of the great spiritual leaders of our time said to me the very moment I walked into his presence, "Oral, someone came out of the hills down here speaking in tongues, and what little interest I had went out the window." From that moment, that great spiritual leader became diametrically opposed to tongues and interpretation. Only recently has he opened his heart again and accepted tongues and interpretation. In all those years he suffered because he let somebody who abused the gifts of God turn him away from the Holy Spirit's gifts themselves.

I Corinthians 13:3

> And though I bestow all my goods to feed the poor, and though I give my body to be burned, and have not charity, it profiteth me nothing.

Whenever I mention the word "charity," remember it is agape love, the eternal love of God embodied in Jesus Christ. Every time I say charity, think of Jesus and His love.

I Corinthians 13:4-10

> Charity suffereth long, and is kind; charity envieth not; charity vaunteth not itself, is not puffed up, doth not behave itself unseemly,

seeketh not her own, is not easily provoked, thinketh no evil; rejoiceth not in iniquity, but rejoiceth in the truth; beareth all things, believeth all things, hopeth all things, endureth all things.

Charity never faileth: but whether there be prophecies, they shall fail; whether there be tongues, they shall cease; whether there be knowledge, it shall vanish away. For we know in part, and we prophesy in part. But when that which is perfect is come, then that which is in part shall be done away.

A Portrait of Jesus

When Paul tells what love will do, he is, in effect, giving us a portrait of our Lord Jesus Christ. And we would say Jesus suffered long. Jesus is kind. Jesus did not envy people. He was not puffed up in himself. He never behaved himself in an ungodly way. He did not seek His own, but He sought the welfare of others. He did not think evil of people nor rejoice in bad things happening to them. He rejoiced in the good, in the truth. Jesus bore all things. He believed that all things of God would endure. His hope was always strong. His endurance was strong. Jesus endured. Jesus never failed.

Then, Paul says, "But prophecies and tongues and knowledge are not going to have a place forever. They are just for here on earth. They are for the temporal world. They are for this moment of time that man lives upon the earth, and while we live here we do not have whole knowledge. We do not even have inspired utterances or prophecies in their completeness, only in part. But when that which is perfect is come, when the Lord comes, when we see Him face to face, then at that very moment all these things we have been talking about — the gifts of the Spirit — will have no further function." Can you see that?

I Corinthians 13:11

When I was a child, I spake as a child, I understood as a child, I thought as a child: but when I became a man, I put away childish things.

Paul is saying that when we are face to face with God, the things we only understand in part and with partial ability and knowledge will be looked upon as a little child who does not have all the knowledge or the consciousness of sin. But we will be mature.

I Corinthians 13:12

For now we see through a glass, darkly; but then face to face; now I know in part; but then shall I know even as also I am known.

Paul said, "Right now it is as if we are looking through a dark glass, a colored glass. It is hard to see through it. But when Jesus comes, then we will see Him face to face. While right now I know in part, later I will be known just as I am known by God. As God knows me, I will then be revealed through the way He sees things. I see things through a glass that is colored because I am human, but God does not have any colored glasses. He sees us as He sees us, and when that happens, things are going to be super."

I Corinthians 13:13
> And now abideth faith, hope, charity, these three; but the greatest of these is charity.

Paul speaks of the "now." He says, "And now, faith is here, hope is here, and love is here. Certainly love is here. All three are here. Faith to be believed, hope to be hoped, and love to be loved. But when it comes right down to it, the only one that is eternal is love." When we are face to face with God, we will no longer need to have faith. We will no longer need to have further hope because our hopes will be realized. What we believed and hoped for will have met us face to face. The agape love will remain because God is love.

Why does love remain? Why is it the greatest? Because it is the nature of God, and God is eternal. "Jesus Christ, the same yesterday, today, and forever." Love is a billion times greater than believing and hoping or anything in this world. There is only one thing that outshines all others in time and in eternity, and that is the nature of God — love, agape love.

"Now abideth faith and hope" — right here in this present world — and there is no substitute for them. You and I cannot live without our faith, because as we saw in the book of Romans, the just shall live by their faith.

The 11th chapter of Hebrews says, "Faith is the substance of things hoped for," so we have to have hope, hope in God. We also have to have that agape love in this present life, and thank God we can have it, are having it, will have it. What Paul is telling us is that we have an anchor that holds. What is that anchor? God's eternal love! His unchanging nature. The Christ who is the same yesterday, today, and forever, who is with you and me right now. And if we live on this earth tomorrow, He will be there. Praise God! It is great to be a believer.

I Corinthians 13:13, 14:1
> And now abideth faith, hope, charity, these three; but the greatest of

these is charity. Follow after charity, and desire spiritual gifts, but rather that ye may prophesy.

There is no interruption here. Paul is saying that the greatest thing of all is agape love, the very nature of God, His unchangeableness, His eternity within himself, and he says, "Follow after that. Follow after agape love, the very nature of God, the real Jesus. Follow after Him and desire spiritual gifts." Don't you see that having Jesus as agape love abiding in your heart now and forever does not eliminate the need for the gifts of the Spirit through which that love can flow? The gifts of the Spirit are not an appendix; they are the natural outflowing of agape love. Just as you have a track, you have to have a train. Just as you have a car, it has to have a motor.

Someone says, "I have Christ. I have His love." Great! But Paul says, "Desire spiritual gifts. Earnestly desire that God will, according to your nature, your personality, your inborn tendencies, manifest a gift of the word of knowledge, a gift of the word of wisdom, or a gift of faith, healing, working of miracles, discerning of spirits, prophecy, tongues, or interpretation of tongues. Or desire that in the nature of your calling and performance in your everyday life and career, be it the calling of an apostle, prophet, teacher, worker of miracles, one who brings healing to people, one who is able to help and govern in the work of God, or one who has some other gift, that you will have the love through which to act. Just as your breath has to have your human body through which to breathe, so love has to work through the gifts. So do not say, "You take the gifts and I will take the love." Or I should not say, "I will take the gifts and you take the love," or "I will take the love and you take the gifts." We take them together. That is the way God put them in order, for you and me as believers. When Paul opens I Corinthians 14 by saying, "Follow after charity, and desire spiritual gifts, but rather that ye may prophesy. For he that speaketh in an unknown tongue speaketh not unto men, but unto God" — talking about prophecy and about tongues — he is referring to their Corinthian background. Corinth was a spectacular type of city where the people sought after spectacular things. They were not a people of depth, and even though they had turned away from the sins of Corinth and had accepted Christ as their personal Savior and were now a group of believers in a church that Paul established in Corinth, they still reflected too much of their background. Paul was not calling their being believers into question. He was calling into question the fact that they had brought some of the background in which they had been reared as Corinthians.

It seems that speaking in tongues through the gift of tongues and its interpretation appealed particularly to these Corinthian believers. It seemed that it stood out to them as more desirous than the gift of the word of knowledge or the word of wisdom, or the gifts of faith, working of miracles, healings, or prophecy. So Paul says, "When you follow after charity or the agape love of Jesus Christ, and then you desire spiritual gifts for this agape love to flow through, do it by desiring first of all that you may prophesy, because prophecy is an inspired utterance to the minds of people, whereas the gift of tongues has an entirely different purpose." He says in Verses 2-5, "For he that speaketh in an unknown tongue . . . ." The word "unknown" is not in the original Scriptures.

I Corinthians 14:2-5

> For he that speaketh in an unknown tongue speaketh not unto men, but unto God: for no man understandeth him; howbeit in the spirit he speaketh mysteries. But he that prophesieth speaketh unto men to edification, and exhortation, and comfort. He that speaketh in a tongue edifieth himself; but he that prophesieth edifieth the church. I would that ye all spake with tongues, but rather that ye prophesied: for greater is he that prophesieth than he that speaketh with tongues, except he interpret, that the church may receive edifying.

Prophecy and Interpretation Valued

Paul now describes the necessity of prophecy or having inspired utterances that God might speak through us to the souls of men. He says that when one prophesies with this inspired utterance he is speaking directly to men for, one, their edification; two, that they may have an exhortation from God; and, three, that there may be the comfort of the Holy Spirit brought into their lives. Now you can see why prophecy is so valuable when you are in the presence of people.

"On the other hand," he says, "if you speak in tongues, you do not speak to men, you speak only to God." Notice the difference? In prophecy, you speak only to men. In tongues, you speak only to God. "He that speaketh in an unknown tongue speaks not unto men but unto God." It is a vertical experience rather than a horizontal one. When we prophesy or speak with inspired utterance, we are speaking horizontally, from me to you or you to me or from one of us to a congregation. We are speaking directly to men. But the moment we speak in tongues, we are speaking out of our spirits and in our spirits directly to our heavenly Father. Because it is our spirit speaking over our tongue, we are speaking in another tongue, a tongue that is not understood. It is not understood by the speaker of the tongue. If I speak in tongues, for example, I do not know what I am saying.

However, Paul says something very important here. When you speak in tongues, you are speaking in the spirit and you are speaking mysteries to the human mind. "Therefore, when we are with men," he says, "it is better for us to prophesy because we speak directly to them so that we might lift them up, instruct, and comfort them in the Lord. However, when you speak in tongues, you are speaking directly to God and you are edifying yourself. You are building up yourself."

Someone says, "Prophecy is for the Church and tongues is for the individual; therefore, one should not be selfish and want to speak in tongues." I beg to differ. It is time we recognize our own individuality and appreciate ourselves. Whoever taught us to hate ourselves?

Jesus said that we ought to love God and then love our neighbors as we love ourselves. Where did the old statement come from that we are to love God first, neighbors second, and ourselves third? That is not the way it reads. We love our neighbors as we love ourselves. We do not love our neighbors more than we love ourselves. If we did, we would not have any self-worth. We have to have self-worth in order to love anybody. When you speak in tongues to edify yourself, you ought to be praising God so you can instruct yourself, build yourself up on the inside to receive divine therapy. God gives us therapy from our spirit and God knows that we need it.

In Verse 5 Paul says he wishes all the Corinthian Christians spoke with tongues. Apparently some of them did and some of them did not. This is a very important point. There are entire denominations which have said, "No, we are not going to have tongue-speaking." Others say, "Yes, we are going to have it, period." Paul does not agree with either one. Paul says, "I would that you all spake with tongues, but rather, that you prophesied." "I would that you all spake with tongues" — he wished everybody did. In Verse 18 he says, "I thank my God I speak with tongues more than you all." There was a flow of tongues from Paul more than the flow of tongues from any other believer there in the Corinthian church. He wished everybody did. Then he stopped. He did not force tongues on anybody.

I am certainly not trying to force tongues on anybody. When we finish this chapter, I think you will see that by your will, you can release your prayer language of tongues to God and interpret back to your mind. I think you will see that because you are born again by the Holy Spirit and you have received the gift of the Holy Spirit as Peter said in Acts 2:38, because you have repented, you can release your prayer language at will. I do it every day of my life. Many times I release my prayer language, and I am praying in tongues, speaking in tongues to my heavenly Father. I am speaking in the Spirit, not with my mortal mind, using my own learned language, but with the language of the Holy Spirit. I do that often. I thank my God I do. I wish everybody would release his prayer language because, as a believer, the Holy Spirit indwells you, He indwells your body. You can, by the Holy Spirit, release tongues, or your prayer language to God, and Paul is wishing for this.

Praying in tongues is not a badge of whether you are saved or not. You are saved by the blood of Christ. It is not a badge of whether you are superior or not. In fact, when I pray in tongues it is because I am inferior. In Romans Paul said, "We know not what we should pray for as we ought." Paul included himself.

The greatest need in the world at important times in our lives as Christians is to know how to pray and to know how to get our prayers answered. If you do not know what to pray for, you do not know how to start. That is why praying in tongues is so important, by your will. As we will see in Verses 14 and 15, we can release our own personal, private devotional prayer language of tongues. That is our high privilege because we are born of the Spirit of God, and the Holy Spirit has given us himself as a gift.

Paul says when you are delivering the Word of God, he would rather you prophesy because it is far greater to prophesy than it is to speak in tongues, except when you also interpret. He is saying the number- one practice is to prophesy, that is, to give the inspired utterance of the Holy Spirit concerning the Word of God and what God is saying to His people. He says that is the most important thing of all, except when you are in church speaking in tongues AND interpreting the meaning so the church can understand what God is saying back through you. He is saying that the moment you speak in tongues AND have the interpretation, it is as great and proper and in place as much as prophecy is, because through the interpretation the tongue that has been spoken to God is now interpreted, not translated word for word, but interpreted back as God's response to the need in the Body of Christ. Therefore, people are edified, instructed, built up, just as they are in prophecy, except that a different methodology is used.

Another thing Paul is trying to instruct us about is that when we prophesy, it should have to do with people. We have to be with people. When we pray in tongues and edify ourselves, we do not have to be with anybody. We have it in our private devotions as we are alone with God, or driving along in the car, or walking, or sitting, or wherever we are. It is a very private, personal experience unless it then is interpreted and the interpretation carries it over from just edifying Oral Roberts and blessing me to being a great edification to those who hear the interpretation.

If I were praying in tongues alone, that would be fine for me. I would be edifying and uplifting myself in the Lord, which is very valuable to me as a Christian. But if I wanted that to edify the Body of Christ or any group of people in the Body of Christ, then I would have to interpret it into their language so they would understand what I was saying to God or what God was saying back to me or what God was saying to them through the tongues language I was using, which is a direct communication with God, or through the interpretation, which is a direct communication back from God to the prayer or the praise in tongues.

In the 14th chapter of I Corinthians where Paul uses the personal pronoun "I" and when he says "in the church" he is doing two things. He is speaking of himself as an individual or of you and me as individuals and our individual speaking in tongues, which is prayer or praise to God in tongues by our spirit, or he is speaking of a gift of tongues, which is for the Church and which requires interpretation.

I Corinthians 14:6-13

> Now, brethren, if I come unto you speaking with tongues, what shall I profit you, except I shall speak to you either by revelation, or by knowledge, or by prophesying, or by doctrine? And even things without life giving sound, whether pipe or harp, except they give a distinction in the sounds, how shall it be known what is piped or harped? For if the trumpet give an uncertain sound, who shall prepare himself to the battle? So likewise ye, except ye utter by the tongue words easy to be understood, how shall it be known what is spoken? for ye shall speak into the air.
>
> There are, it may be, so many kinds of voices in the world, and none of them is without signification. Therefore, if I know not the meaning of the voice, I shall be unto him that speaketh a barbarian, and he that speaketh shall be a barbarian unto me. Even so ye, forasmuch as ye are zealous of spiritual gifts, seek that ye may excel to the edifying of the church. Wherefore let him that speaketh in an unknown tongue pray that he may interpret.

Tongues, Prophecy Compatible

In Verse 5, Paul says, "I would that ye all spake with tongues, but rather that ye prophesied: for greater is he that prophesieth than he that speaketh with tongues, except he interpret, that the church may receive edifying." He is now dealing with interpretation. He began by saying that he would that they all spake with tongues. That was a private, personal, direct communication to God. That emanates from the spirit of the believer rather than from his mind. Rather than the believer having to take his mind and try to reason out what he is to pray for, how he is going to say it, how he is going to get the prayer through, he bypasses his mind or intellect momentarily and gets down deep into his spirit. He begins to pray with his spirit, as the Holy Spirit, who indwells him and lives within him, gives him the words to say by his spirit.

You may ask, "Can my spirit talk?" Certainly. Your spirit can talk better than your physical mouth can talk. Your physical being is often saying anyway what your spirit is saying. Sometimes it says what your intellect or your mind is saying. But to speak purely from God, you have to get into the spirit because you were made a spirit; you were made in the likeness and image of God. Your spirit, your inner man, your inner woman, is the most real part of your existence. That is where the spirit lives. He lives in your spirit. Both the Holy Spirit and your spirit dwell in your body — in your total personality.

Paul is saying he wishes that you all did this, but if you are in front of people, he would rather that you prophesy because you would be prophesying in inspired utterance in the language that people understand, unless you can interpret what you said in tongues. Once you interpret, it is the same as an inspired utterance that prophecy gives. Someone asks, "If prophecy is all that great, why do we have to speak in tongues to begin with?" It is because God set this in the Church. God gave the privilege to the believer to pray with his spirit in tongues. That is a different function from prophecy. Prophecy cannot take the place of speaking in tongues to God, nor can tongues take the place of prophecy. God is not using prophecy against tongues or tongues against prophecy. He simply is trying to tell us that speaking in tongues is to God. Remember in Verse 2 Paul says that when he speaks in tongues, he speaks not unto men but unto God. Then in Verse 3, when he prophesies, he speaks unto men. So speaking in tongues is to God, while prophesying is unto men.

However, when you interpret the tongue, then you are giving that interpretation to men. You have spoken in tongues to God in order to get your communication through and receive His response back, which you then give to the people. You say it as God gives it to you. You say it in their language that they may be edified corporately as a group, just as you are edified singularly or as an individual.

Then he says, "Brethren, when I, Paul, an individual Christian and spiritual leader, come to you speaking with tongues, there is no way I am going to use that as a teaching device. I am not going to speak in tongues to preach the gospel or to instruct you in the Lord. That is not the purpose of tongues." He says, "What will I do? I will come unto you speaking with tongues in order to profit you and I will do that by following the speaking in tongues by a revelation — that is a word of knowledge — or by prophesying or by doctrine."

He will either follow his tongues with that or he will not speak in tongues in public to them. But he will speak in public to them with a direct revelation from God in their language or a word of knowledge to impart to them or a prophecy, an inspired utterance to them, or a doctrine or a theology. He is simply saying he is not going to take the time of the church service to stand up there speaking in tongues, because it is not intended to be a teaching device. He is going to use other methods such as revelation, knowledge, prophesying, and doctrine.

Then Paul gives them an illustration of what he is trying to explain. He says, when you hear a musical instrument, it makes a distinct sound. He says that in the walled cities there were watchmen on the wall and when they saw an enemy army coming, they would blow the trumpet. There was a distinct sound to that trumpet that the people understood to mean an enemy was coming and, therefore, they should man their posts. Every voice in the world has a significant meaning, he says. Therefore, when you come together and speak in tongues to men, it throws them off, in the same way that the watchman on the wall, who, when he saw an enemy army coming, would blow his trumpet with a sound that was utterly foreign to the alarm people were accustomed to hearing to get themselves ready for battle. He is saying it is just as senseless and dangerous for that watchman to blow the wrong sound on his trumpet as it is for you to try to use tongues as a teaching device, because it does not fit, it is out of order. It does not give a specific message or direction from God.

The tongue in which you are praying is for you alone and you are praying it to God. But if it is a gift of tongues, one of the nine gifts of the Spirit, then as we will see later in this chapter, it must be interpreted or else the person must keep quiet. However, he is not required to stop praying in tongues because he can do that under his breath. Paul says in Verse 12, "You Corinthian Christians are very zealous with these spiritual gifts, but the main thing for you to bear in mind is that you have them for the high purpose of edifying or building up the work of God. Therefore, let him that speaketh in an unknown tongue pray that he may interpret."

Paul's whole thrust here in tongues, first, is to put tongues in their proper place as being spoken to God; and, second, if you have to deal with other people through those tongues, you do it through interpretation, not through the tongues themselves.

The real heart of this chapter is in Verses 13, 14, and 15, where Paul is speaking autobiographically or personally.

I Corinthians 14:13-15

> Wherefore let him that speaketh in an unknown tongue pray that he may interpret. For if I pray in an unknown tongue, my spirit prayeth, but my understanding is unfruitful. What is it then? I will pray with the spirit, and I will pray with the understanding also: I will sing with the spirit, and I will sing with the understanding also.

Inner-Self Prayer

The Apostle Paul, in entering into his own personal experience of releasing his prayer language, begins by saying interpretation is all-important. He says, "Here is the reason: If I pray in a tongue, it is my spirit praying. It is my inner self praying by the power of the Holy Spirit." In Romans 8:26,27, Paul explained what he is saying in I Corinthians 14:13-15. Here we repeat Romans 8:26,27 in which Paul says . . .

Romans 8:26,27

> Likewise the Spirit also helpeth our infirmities: for we know not what we should pray for as we ought: but the Spirit itself maketh intercession for us with groanings which cannot be uttered. And he that searcheth the hearts knoweth what is the mind of the Spirit, because he maketh intercession for the saints according to the will of God.

Holy Spirit Prayer

Paul is stating that when it comes time to pray, neither he nor we know what we should pray for as we ought, but the Holy Spirit knows, and immediately the Holy Spirit goes into action by helping us, helping our weaknesses. He does that by making intercession for us with groanings which cannot be uttered or in words too deep for the mind to understand or for the mind to say. It is an inexpressible expression. While the Spirit is expressing what is deep within us that our mind cannot bring up, we are told that the Holy Spirit is searching our hearts. He also is searching our hearts from the standpoint that He knows what the mind of the spirit is and that He intercedes according to the will of God.

Prayer is intercession to God. All of us would like to be better intercessors, to know better how to pray, but Paul says we do not know what to pray for as we ought, and this is why we refer to I Corinthians 14:13,14 to understand what Paul is saying to you and me on a personal basis. "Let him that speaketh in an unknown tongue pray that he may interpret." Now Paul is getting down to a personal basis. This particular verse, Verse 13, is not one that is limited only to the gift of tongues. The gift of tongues has to be followed by the gift of interpretation of tongues, but here he is speaking of a private devotional experience that every child of God can have. Every believer has the Holy Spirit. Every believer can release his prayer language, and when he does he himself can interpret it. Why? Verse 14 says, "For if I pray in an unknown tongue, my spirit prays, but my mind is unfruitful," or it does not understand what is going on.

Let me illustrate. Here I am, and I know that I am a spirit made in the image of God, and I live in a human body and I am connected, body and spirit, with my mind. Therefore, as I am born into the world, my parents begin to teach me words. They also teach me in school how to understand words, how to convey my thoughts in words, how to use my thinking or intellectual ability. It is not long, as I grow up as a child, a boy, and a man, before I learn that I have vast powers in my mind, but I also have severe limitations.

Let us say I go on and get converted, which is true, and I begin to pray to God with my mind and I am able to get through to some extent. Then, through the complexity of the world I live in and my own mental and intellectual limitations, I reach a point in my life where I simply do not know what to pray for as I ought. At that time the most important thing in my life is how to get my prayers answered. What must I do? Say words which are not prayers at all? No! Paul says, here is what to do. He tells me to pray in a tongue so that my spirit can pray. My spirit then will take over at the point where the limitations of my mind start. In other words, in Oral Roberts' mind, as he starts to pray and it begins to reach its limitations and the mind does not know what to pray for, all I have to do as a believer is to go down, down, down into my spirit, into my inner being where the Holy Spirit lives, and there I enter the Holy Spirit's prayer.

Romans 8:26,27 says the Holy Spirit is interceding for us. The Holy Spirit is searching our hearts. In other words, as I go down in my spirit to pray in tongues, the Holy Spirit is already there searching out what is in Oral Roberts' heart. He is seeking the inexpressible that my mind is unable to express. He is reaching down deep for those hurts and those needs and those hopes and aspirations that my mind cannot grasp. He picks them up and gives words to them, and then I speak them. I speak those words not in Oral Roberts' learned language but in the language of the Spirit. Please understand that the Holy Spirit is a person. Please understand that the Holy Spirit has a greater mind than any of us. He is able to speak, to articulate meaning better than any of us. Remember that He is doing this day and night as the intercessor for the believers, as He searches our hearts for those things that we are unable to bring up with our mortal minds. When He does this, He is giving wings to our prayers as He gives direction to them. He gives direction to prayers as well as meaning, and then He gives wings to prayers so they go up over our lips. We speak the words that the Spirit puts in us. We say them. The Holy Spirit cannot say them. He does not speak in tongues; we speak in tongues. We say them and they go directly to God. As you pray in the Spirit which is praying in tongues, you are praying directly to God.

There are no way stations between you and the heavenly Father when you pray in the Spirit. When you pray with your mind only, you are praying intellectually, and you reach a point where you do not know what to pray for as you ought. You have reached a way station. You have reached a point where you have to stop and you look around and say, "What will I do now?"

Most Christians I know who pray like that will either groan or sigh or get frustrated or sometimes just give up and on occasion get bitter and cynical. However, when you are praying in the Spirit, you get out of your intellectual limitations because the Holy Spirit has no limitations. Your spirit's self, your inner being, washed in the blood of Christ and filled with the Spirit, has no limitations. The limitations are in your flesh. The limitations are in your mind. That is why Paul said that your mind must be renewed by the Holy Spirit. Even though you are a converted person, a believer, your mind must be constantly renewed by the Holy Spirit, and Oral Roberts believes that much of that renewing of your mind by the Holy Spirit comes through the Spirit giving you words to say in His tongue.

As you speak in tongues you are bypassing your mind. You are setting it aside momentarily as an observer. And although your tongue is used, you are speaking words directly to God. Those words are Holy Spirit-inspired. Those words are part of the intercessory prayer of the Holy Spirit in your behalf. Now you have half a loaf. Speaking in tongues is half a loaf. This is one of the major points Paul is trying to tell us in I Corinthians 14, that speaking in tongues is not unto man but unto God. It is speaking in the Spirit. It is our spirit praying. It is our opening up our inner man and allowing the Holy Spirit to take our feelings and put words to them that we speak over our tongue to the heavenly Father. And we are edified, we are lifted up, we are given therapy. But that is only half a loaf. Where is the other half? He said in Verse 13 . . .

I Corinthians 14:13
> Wherefore let him that speaketh in an unknown tongue pray that he may interpret.

Pray for Interpretation

For example, if Oral Roberts prays in tongues and is getting inner therapy, let him pray that he may interpret back to his mind.

I Corinthians 14:14
> For if I pray in an unknown tongue, my spirit prayeth, but my understanding is unfruitful.

God's Response

My mind is not understanding, so the other half of the loaf is the interpretation. Interpretation of what? The interpretation of the tongue. When I pray in tongues, my spirit understands, but my mind does not; therefore, it is half a loaf. When I am able to interpret I am interpreting the tongue to Oral Roberts, back to myself, back to my mind. Why? Because I may bypass my mind momentarily in order for my spirit to pray in tongues, but I am not going to get out of my mind. I am not going to leave my mind. I am not going to put my mind aside all the time and just become an emotional person. I am a normal human being with a spirit, mind, and body. I am a whole person and, therefore, I must learn how to pray a whole-person prayer, and I begin that in my spirit. But I interpret back to my mind. When we interpret the tongue back to the mind, we have God's response. We now know what to pray for and what to pray for comes clearly back to the mind. Now read part of Verse 15 again.

I Corinthians 14:15
> What is it then? I will pray with the spirit, and I will pray with the understanding also: . . .

Spiritual Understanding

That means with Paul's own understanding in his mind. Paul is saying the same as I was saying, that when he prayed in tongues he was praying with the Spirit, and his mind did not understand. But when he interpreted back to his spirit, he was able to pray with understanding. As I said, Paul was able to pray with understanding, and understanding is the key. If you can just remember one word in the 14th chapter of I Corinthians and keep it in mind, remember the word "understanding." Concentrate on this because it is important to you.

Paul begins the 14th chapter by telling us to earnestly covet the gifts of the Spirit. He talks about one of them, tongues, and he says it is praying unto God. He talks about prophecy, which is speaking to people's understanding. He says prophecy is greater than tongues unless you have the interpretation of tongues. The interpretation of tongues gives an inspired utterance to the mind and gives understanding. We do not have understanding. We have this "treasure in earthen vessels." Paul made that statement, "We have this treasure in earthen vessels." But this earthen vessel does not understand. That is the constant thing I hear: "I do not understand God, I do not know how to get my prayers through." That is why God gave us the Holy Spirit which is the unlimited, invisible presence of our Christ coming back to live within us, making us His temple. It is through tongues and interpretation that we learn to understand.

The organized church as a whole has missed this, and the typical Christian does not pray in tongues, and those who pray in tongues seldom ever interpret back to themselves. Those who do not pray in tongues are having to start their prayers in their minds. Sometimes they also can pray in their own language in the Spirit. There is no doubt about that but it is so much harder. The most beautiful thing I can say to you now is that as you have repented of your sins and believed on the Lord, you have received the gift of the Holy Spirit. Go back and read Acts 2:38. Peter said you shall receive that gift when you have repented and been baptized into Jesus himself. You have the Holy Spirit. You can speak with the Spirit. You can speak in tongues, you can begin your prayer with the Spirit rather than with your mind. What am I trying to say? Let Paul say it to us again in Verse 15.

I Corinthians 14:15
     What is it then? I will pray with the spirit, . . .

The Spiritual Mainstream

The word "will" in the Greek is determine. I determine to pray with the Spirit or in tongues. Then Paul says, "And I will, I determine, to pray with the understanding also." Do you notice his two-way prayer system here? The prayer begins in his spirit and then ends in his mind. Most of us start praying with our mind and seldom ever get in our spirit. But Paul did not originate his prayers in his mind. He originated his prayers in his spirit because he was indwelt by the Holy Spirit and he was able to begin praying in tongues. He did not want to keep on praying in tongues hour after hour. He prayed in tongues, he got the prayer through to the Father, and then he prayed that he would interpret back to his intellect or his mind, his thinking processes.

Let me give you two or three examples. Before we built Oral Roberts University in Tulsa, Oklahoma, we had all these hundreds of vacant acres at the edge of the city of Tulsa. I did not have the money and I did not have the know-how to build a university. God had said, "Build Me a university. Build it on My authority and on the Holy Spirit." First, I did not know how to build a university. Second, I certainly did not know how to build God's university. My mind almost broke under it because I was commanded to do it and did not know how. Day after day I would go out on those acres and walk and pray, pray, pray. I was originating my prayers in my mind, "Dear God, help me, O God, show me how." One day I was out there praying, groaning, sighing, getting more frustrated, and all of a sudden my spirit became very strong. I felt the Holy Spirit moving in my spirit and I just raised my voice and I spoke in tongues. I spoke words that my mind had not created. You may ask, "Was that your first time?" That was the first time that I understood what I was doing. In other words, I was being edified. And that was half a loaf. But I did not practice praying in tongues. I had never been taught how. I had never really seen anybody anywhere who would pray in tongues and then stop and interpret and pray with their understanding, so I did not have any role model.

There on those bare grounds as I walked, the Spirit, coming up out of my belly as Jesus said the Holy Spirit would in John 7:38, just chose to let it happen. I began to speak and a few words came out of my mouth that I had not learned. There was a release in my spirit. Paul said that when you pray in tongues you edify yourself. I needed self-worth in that hour. I did not know how to build God's university, yet I had a command of God to do it. I was gradually losing my self-worth. Have you lost yours?

These words came up over my tongue, and when I finished saying them I felt enormously better, but the problem was still there. I only had half a loaf. I was really moving now in the Spirit, and I began to pray in English again. But the words were flowing. The understanding was there. It was almost instantaneous that my prayer with my mind, my intellect, which was in English, my own known language, was just starting to flow out of me rather than a groaning and a sighing. I no longer said, "O God, help me, how can I do this?" I was not saying that. I found myself praying with understanding, and the understanding touched me. I knew I could build God's university. I understood through interpretation of my tongue back to my mortal mind praying in English or with understanding, as Paul said. The whole thing opened to me.

Oral Roberts University stands in Tulsa on about 500 acres. Over 4,000 fine young men and women are studying in the undergraduate school and in seven graduate schools. Every building is paid for. But it is only by having the whole loaf that it could be done.

Paul says, "I will sing with the spirit, and I will sing with the understanding also." He used his will. It was not an emotional thing. Of course, we are emotional beings, and from that standpoint, there is emotion in it. But emotion neither causes it to happen nor carries it on nor brings the interpretation. It is our will. I came at this thing as Paul said, by my will. I do it today by my will. Therefore, I pray in tongues many times a day, every day of my life. But I always try to interpret.

A dear friend of mine who had just lost his wife came to me, knowing that Evelyn and I had lost members of our family. He said, "Oral, will you tell me what you and Evelyn did to get through it?"

I said, "You might not understand how we got through it if I told you, because it is so different from what is taught in the organized church, and yet it is totally scriptural."

He said, "Please, please help me, I am hurting."

I said, "We got to the place where our minds could not face up to it. When we would try to pray, we did not know how to pray or what to pray for, so we just sighed and hurt and groaned and wept. The fourth night after the loss of our oldest daughter, Evelyn said to me, 'Oral, hold me, I cannot make it through the night.' Here is what we did. I said, 'Evelyn, let us pray in the Spirit, because we have prayed in English until we have no more words to say.' We began to pray in the Spirit, and soon the tears running down our cheeks were not tears of despair but tears of joy. I began to interpret back to my mind and hers, and she began to interpret to her mind and also to my intellect, and we received inspired utterance that we spoke out as an interpretation to our minds. And then we began to pray in that inspired utterance. Suddenly we were praying with understanding. The interpretation let us know that Rebecca was telling Jesus all about us and what our needs would be and what her children's needs would be."

My friend, as he listened, said, "I have read your books and I have seen your videotapes and I have heard your teaching on the Holy Spirit and I saw that you did pray in tongues and interpret as part of your everyday life, but I did not understand until today what you meant. I do pray in tongues and I get a release, but I have not interpreted; therefore, I have not been praying with the understanding. I am going home and I am going to start praying in tongues frequently, and each time I am going to pray to interpret and I am going to get through this."

I said, "Yes, you will."

If you have begun praying in tongues, learn to interpret back to your mind because when you interpret, you are watering your mind, you are blossoming your mind. Your mind is receiving an input from on high, and, therefore, when you pray and think with understanding based upon tongues and interpretation, you advance yourself in your ability to think, to believe, to love, to do.

When I pray in tongues and interpret back to my mind, and through it pray in understanding or sing in understanding, my love just flows. It seems to actuate every sense that I have. My physical senses come alive but more than that, that sixth sense, that sixth dimension, that whole inner being of self is uplifted, made alive.

I tell you that speaking in tongues and interpretation of tongues when done together are not the periphery of the infilling of the Holy Spirit. They are the mainstream.

That which the organized church has failed to understand and has primarily forbidden to happen is the mainstream of renewing your mind in the Holy Spirit. If you will, through being a believer in our Lord Jesus Christ, use your will to release your prayer language, which is tongues. Then you pray to interpret it and that means when interpretation comes back, it comes back in your language, your known language, and you start praying in it. You just keep it up and soon you will be praying with the best understanding you have ever had in your life. If you will practice it daily, it will be like a muscle growing stronger. Now start reading scripture again at Verse 16.

I Corinthians 14:16-20

Else when thou shalt bless with the spirit, how shall he that occupieth the room of the unlearned say Amen at thy giving of thanks, seeing he understandeth not what thou sayest? For thou verily givest thanks well, but the other is not edified. I thank my God, I speak with tongues more than ye all; yet in the church I had rather speak five words with my understanding, that by my voice I might teach others also, than ten thousand words in an unknown tongue. Brethren, be not children in understanding: howbeit in malice be ye children, but in understanding be men.

Do Not Abuse Tongues

Paul is saying that if he is with a group of people, as in eating a meal with them, and he gives thanks in tongues, he has done it very well, but they have not understood a thing that he says. They have no understanding. So you see, again, understanding is the key. In Verse 18 he says, "I thank my God, I speak with tongues more than ye all. However, when I get in the church and I stand up to teach or preach, I would rather say five words with my understanding than ten thousand words in tongues."

Can you imagine Paul standing before a crowd and spending an hour saying ten thousand words in tongues and their not understanding a word of it? There is such a thing as being ridiculous, and that is what Paul is indicating here. He says, "When I come before the church, I am going to speak to their understanding through my understanding."

I Corinthians 14:21,22

In the law it is written, With men of other tongues and other lips will I speak unto this people; and yet for all that will they not hear me, saith the Lord. Wherefore tongues are for a sign, not to them that believe, but to them that believe not . . .

God is Supernatural

Paul is referring to Israel's backsliding and God's use of people of other nations speaking to Israel in tongues. But they were tongues not known by the children of Israel and they could not understand them. They could hear, but they could not understand. He is saying that tongues are a sign to them who believe not. That is, when you are trying to share with believers, do it with your understanding, not in tongues. However, if you are speaking in tongues and an unbeliever hears it, it becomes a sign to him, a sign that something supernatural is taking place, a sign that God is manifesting himself. Despite the unbeliever's unbelief, the supernatural is not ruled out. God still speaks supernaturally.

I Corinthians 14:22,23

Wherefore tongues are for a sign, not to them that believe, but to them that believe not: but prophesying serveth not for them that believe not, but for them which believe. If therefore the whole church be come together into one place, and all speak with tongues, and there come in those that are unlearned, or unbelievers, will they not say ye are mad?

Tongues Can Mislead

Picture what Paul is saying. There may be several hundred believers in one place, and they all individually at the same time start speaking in tongues. Then an unbeliever enters. He will think they are crazy.

I Corinthians 14:24,25

But if all prophesy, and there come in one that believeth not, or one unlearned, he is convinced of all, he is judged of all: and thus are the secrets of his heart made manifest; and so falling down on his face he will worship God, and report that God is in you of a truth.

Inspiration Brings Conviction

Many people believe that prophecy is either forthtelling or foretelling: that is, it is either proclaiming the gospel, preaching, or foretelling a future event. Possibly it does include both. But as Paul is speaking of prophecy here, it is an inspired utterance that does not originate in the mind. It originates through the Holy Spirit, and the mind picks it up and says it in words of understanding that people can receive, and, therefore, as the Word is given in understanding, it brings conviction to the hearts of the hearers, and those hearers are apt to repent and turn to God.

I Corinthians 14:26

How is it then, brethren? when ye come together, every one of you hath a psalm, hath a doctrine, hath a tongue, hath a revelation, hath an interpretation. Let all things be done unto edifying.

Balance in the Church

When we come together, every one of us has a psalm. We sing because they sang the psalms in the early church. We have a doctrine, a theology. Paul is talking about a part of the church service that is given over to the teaching and preaching of the Word, which is good theology. Then some speak in tongues in order to gather up the corporate needs. For example, when I pray in tongues as an individual, the Holy Spirit gathers up the deepest things inside my being, and I bring them up to the Father. But when I speak in a gift of tongues, which I can do only when the Spirit sovereignly allows me to do it, I am not speaking for Oral Roberts. The tongue, through the Spirit, is gathering up the inner needs of all present. It is a corporate gathering up of their needs and a corporate understanding that their needs are being expressed to the Father. The inexpressible is now being expressed in tongues. The next thing he says is a revelation. God is revealing something. Then there is an interpretation. In that way, we do everything to edify or strengthen, to build up the people of God.

It is as simple as it can be. We do not have to worry about how to run a church service. He tells us how to operate it. We sing in the Spirit and with the understanding. We preach and teach with the Spirit and with the understanding. We speak in tongues, and we get the interpretation and revelations of the word of knowledge and word of wisdom and other gifts of the Spirit from our heavenly Father, and so the church service is balanced.

I Corinthians 14:27,28

> If any man speak in an unknown tongue, let it be by two, or at the most by three, and that by course; and let one interpret. But if there be no interpreter, let him keep silence in the church; and let him speak to himself, and to God.

Disorder Insults God

Paul is saying that in the church service, if there is a corporate need that cannot be met by prophecy alone, there will be a person who will speak in a tongue and then a second person and, at the most, a third. Each follows the other and then each one is interpreted. Then if there is no interpretation, the speaker ceases. He is silent in the church. He does not open his mouth. But Verse 28 says, "Let him speak to himself, and to God." Let him revert back to his own personal prayer language.

Paul is saying that it is proper for one to speak in tongues on behalf of the whole group. But if there is no interpreter, he does not have to stop speaking in tongues, except aloud. He can continue silently, releasing his own personal prayer language by speaking to himself and to God. A gift of tongues is on behalf of a group. It has to have an interpreter to give the understanding of it to the audience.

The key word of this chapter is "understanding," getting God's point of view. Speaking in tongues with interpretation is scriptural, but there are some people, even though they are genuine, who do not use common sense, and besides, they can get rude. Just because one speaks in tongues does not make one an angel or perfect. One speaks in tongues because there is a need, not because one is superior.

I have had many personal experiences along this line, both as a young pastor in the early days and also as an evangelist in the midst of crowds of 15,000 and more people. I remember when a person would try to speak in tongues loudly in the midst of one of our very large crusade services, I simply would not permit it. Although I believe in and practice tongues and interpretation daily, I would not let that person, however sincere or genuine he was in his own personal experience, exercise bad judgment and reflect badly upon the work of God. Because the entire audience could not hear, it would cause nothing but confusion, and that is against the Word of God. The Word of God speaks of order, and I had to follow order. I was not against the person at all. I was not saying the person was not genuine. But I would be out of order. In a congregation, the Word of God must go forth uninterrupted. The preacher must preach and the teacher must teach.

There is a place in virtually every service, if the group is small enough, for speaking in tongues and interpretation or an inspired word of prophecy. We who are in leadership in the Church must take responsibility and a leadership role. I say this to charismatic people all over the world: Much of the opposition would leave if you and I would exercise order, good spirit, respect for people who do not understand speaking in tongues. Paul is trying to regulate one of the most precious things in the world.

In Acts 1:8 Jesus said, "Ye shall receive power, after that the Holy Spirit is come upon you." The word "power" in the Greek language is "dunamus," equal to our word "dynamite." Speaking in tongues and interpretation of tongues is dynamite, and you treat it carefully. It has a purpose. Use it correctly, and it will bless us individually; it will bless the Church. But if people lose their common sense and their respect for one another and use it out of order, the dynamite will be misused, and some good people will get hurt. As we finish the chapter, we see that Paul is saying to us, "Use wisdom."

I Corinthians 14:29-33

Let the prophets speak two or three, and let the other judge. If any thing be revealed to another that sitteth by, let the first hold his

310

peace. For ye may all prophesy one by one, that all may learn, and all may be comforted. And the spirits of the prophets are subject to the prophets. For God is not the author of confusion, but of peace, as in all churches of the saints.

Using One's Will

One of the most wonderful things Paul says in Verse 32 is that the spirit of those who speak in tongues or prophesy is subject to the speaker. One thing we must learn is that when the Holy Spirit comes up in our belly like a river, just like Jesus said, and we have this tremendous desire to speak in tongues, even in a public service, remember that it is subject to our will. Someone said, "But I cannot help it." Oh, yes, you can, unless you are saying that your emotions run wild with you. If you are like that, you ought to learn you have a will, and Paul is telling you to exercise your will. He says the Spirit is subject to the speaker. Here he says to the prophets — even to prophets — "When I am in a public meeting and I have a tremendous inner urge to speak aloud in tongues, I can do it or, by my will, I can refrain from doing it." I use my will all the time, and all of us must because our will is the deciding factor. Paul is telling us that we have the power to speak in tongues, but we also have the power not to speak in tongues at a certain time and to let our will be in charge. "For," he says, "God is not the author of confusion but of peace as in all churches of the saints."

Speaking in tongues was not original with the believers at Corinth and was not limited to them. Speaking in tongues was practiced throughout the early church. The early church began with speaking in tongues. It was part and parcel of their experience just as it is with many of us in the Church today and should be with every believer.

I Corinthians 14:34,35

Let your women keep silence in the churches: for it is not permitted unto them to speak; but they are commanded to be under obedience, as also saith the law. And if they will learn any thing, let them ask their husbands at home: for it is a shame for women to speak in the church.

Women's "Silence" Explained

Paul is referring to a practice of the Jewish people in which men would sit in one place in the synagogue or the church and the women in the other. Sometimes the women would sit in the back, and while the service was going on, they would start asking questions out loud or just start talking and interrupting the service. Paul referred to the law of Moses which strictly forbade that and also referred to a group of the believers among the Corinthians who were disorderly women. He said, in effect, "Ladies, when you have questions like this, do not ask them in the church service. It is fine to ask the questions, but wait until you get home. Talk it over with your husbands."

Certainly Paul was not against women speaking in the Church. We have just read in I Corinthians 11:5 that women are not condemned to silence in the Church. They can exercise the gift of prophecy; they can speak in public; and that was practiced throughout the early church. Paul is speaking to a specific instance here. As far as I am concerned, there is no difference between men and women in the presence of God. They are equal in their participation in God's service, both in their order. What Paul is saying to us in the now is, "Be a part of the flow of the Spirit without interrupting it."

I Corinthians 14:36-40

> What? came the word of God out from you? or came it unto you only? If any man think himself to be a prophet, or spiritual, let him acknowledge that the things that I write unto you are the commandments of the Lord. But if any man be ignorant, let him be ignorant. Wherefore, brethren, covet to prophesy, and forbid not to speak with tongues. Let all things be done decently and in order.

Allow Spiritual Workings

As Paul ends this 14th chapter, he is really ending Chapters 12, 13, and 14. In the beginning of Chapter 12, he said, "I would not have you uninformed, I would not have you ignorant concerning the gifts of God." Now he is coming to the end of that teaching, and he is telling them, "Do not think for a moment that you are a bunch of special people and that you know it all. I am giving you the commandments of God, and if you reject them you are rejecting the commandments of God." We ought also to know that. We ought to believe exactly what the 12th, 13th, and 14th chapters say. He gets into agape love, and then he begins to explain tongues and interpretation as well as prophecy. Everything he said is a commandment of the Lord. "But if you insist, then go ahead and be

312

uninformed." That is sort of a tongue-in-cheek saying by Paul. Then he said, "Just settle down and go ahead and desire the spiritual gifts, especially to give inspired utterances through prophecy. But while you are doing that, do not forbid speaking with tongues. Do not forbid these spiritual workings. Let all things be done decently and in order."

That is very good advice.

Chapter 15 is an entirely different kind of chapter. Paul talks about the physical body and the resurrection of that body after death. When Paul first established the church at Corinth, preaching the gospel to both the Jews and Greeks or Gentiles who lived there, the cornerstone of his preaching was the resurrection of Jesus from the dead. The Corinthians received the message and were established into a mighty and powerful church. Later, they began many puzzling practices. They lost some of their fervor. They brought much of their culture into the church, and Paul had to straighten them out.

It is a wonderful thing to study with Paul as he dealt with a group of human beings like you and me. Sometimes we think of the people of the early church as being super people, super Christians, so angelic, so heavenly minded. It is important to understand that they were flesh and blood. They had occasion to rise to heights of faith and also to descend to the depths of doubt. They went into things that were unlike the Lord, and Paul had to deliver them the very message that Christ had delivered to him to get them back on the road. It is much like what is happening today. You and I in the Church have the greatest heritage of all, yet we need to go back to the original sources of information about Christ, the Bible, the written Word of God.

Chapter 15 is about one of the most powerful subjects you and I can study: our bodies and our resurrection from the dead.

I Corinthians 15:1-11

Moreover, brethren, I declare unto you the gospel which I preached unto you, which also ye have received, and wherein ye stand; by which also ye are saved, if ye keep in memory what I preached unto you, unless ye have believed in vain.

For I delivered unto you first of all that which I also received, how that Christ died for our sins acccording to the scriptures; and that he was buried, and that he rose again the third day according to the scriptures: and that he was seen of Cephas, then of the twelve.

After that, he was seen of above five hundred brethren at once; of whom the greater part remain unto this present, but some are fallen asleep. After that, he was seen of James; then of all the apostles. And last of all he was seen of me also, as of one born out of due time.

For I am the least of the apostles, that am not meet to be called an apostle, because I persecuted the church of God. But by the grace of God I am what I am: and his grace which was bestowed upon me was not in vain; but I laboured more abundantly than they all: yet not I, but the grace of God which was with me. Therefore whether it were I or they, so we preach, and so ye believed.

The Gospel Defined

Paul is summing up the tremendous revival that he had had in Corinth when he came preaching the gospel of the death, the burial, and the resurrection of Christ, according to the Scriptures.

Paul related how Christ had been seen face to face after His resurrection by Peter, by the 12, by over 500 people at one time, some of whom were still alive at that hour, and finally by himself, Paul, as of one born out of due season. That is, Paul was not one of the 12 apostles but was born again after Jesus' resurrection. Jesus appeared to Paul in His resurrected form.

With all that, Paul said, "I am the least of the apostles. I am not even worthy to be called an apostle because I persecuted the Church of the living God." Then he said, "But I am what I am because the grace of God has come into my heart, and although I was not with the original apostles, yet I have outlaboured them and it is not I but the grace of God in me. It was this preaching that established you Corinthians in the Lord and caused you to believe on the Lord Jesus Christ."

I Corinthians 15:12-19

Now if Christ be preached that he rose from the dead, how say some among you that there is no resurrection of the dead? But if there be no resurrection of the dead, then is Christ not risen: and if Christ be not risen, then is our preaching vain, and your faith is also vain. Yea, and we are found false witnesses of God; because we have testified of God that he raised up Christ: whom he raised not up, if so be that the dead rise not.

For if the dead rise not, then is not Christ raised: and if Christ be not raised, your faith is vain; ye are yet in your sins. Then they also which are fallen asleep in Christ are perished. If in this life only we have hope in Christ, we are of all men most miserable.

Resurrection is Everything

When Paul delivered the gospel to these people in Corinth, the resurrection was the thing they held onto. Remember that they came out of the Greek culture and did not believe that the spirit of man continued to exist after it left the body. It merely faded away into infinity, up in the air somewhere with all the other spirits that were wandering around out there in space. Also, the Jewish Christians among them came from a group of people who were divided over the resurrection of the dead. They believed in "sheol," the Hebrew term for the original paradise where the souls of the righteous dead went. It was not a place they looked forward to seeing. Only those great people of faith such as Abraham looked beyond that and saw Jesus' day and were glad and rejoiced in it, knowing that Christ would abolish paradise. He would take it up into His own bosom when He went to heaven so He would be there to receive those Christians who died in the faith and receive their spirits unto himself, as we will see later where Paul says, "Absent from the body but present with the Lord."

The Corinthian Christians had both a Greek and a Jewish background. It seems that the Greeks and some of the Jews had begun to try to steal away their faith in the resurrection, and Paul says flatly, "If Christ be preached that He rose from the dead, then how say some of you that there is no resurrection of the dead? I came to you preaching that He is risen from the dead. How can you who heard my preaching, received it, were raised from the death of sins and trespasses, and were told that your body would be raised from the dead, how can you now say there is no resurrection of the dead?

"If there is no resurrection, then Jesus is not risen. If Jesus is not risen, all the preaching we have done is in vain, and your faith is in vain. And if He is not raised, you are still in your sins and those who have been converted to Christ and have now died, they have perished."

Then Paul adds these terse words: "If in this life only we have hope in Christ, we are of all men most miserable." In other words, if Christ is not risen from the dead, and there is no resurrection facing us at our death, then trying to have faith in Christ in this life will make us the most miserable people who ever lived.

During all these years that I have been preaching the gospel, I have met all types of Christians, some of them so miserable they could barely breathe, and I have often wondered why a born-again child of God who has the living Christ within him can be so wretched and miserable in his Christian experience. I have about concluded, as did Paul, that they really do not believe in the resurrection. It never occurs to them that there is a resurrection.

But I tell you flatly, Oral Roberts is not remotely interested in serving a dead Christ. I have devoted my life to the Lord. Whatever talents I had in this world to go places in the secular realm and be popular in the mainstream of humanity, I surrendered those to Jesus Christ. Whatever talents I have, they belong to Him and I have reached the place where I know I am God's property. I do not belong to Oral Roberts, I belong to God. The number-one desire of my heart is to obey Christ. Do you think if Christ were not raised from the dead and I did not have the absolute assurance that I, too, would be raised from the dead, that I would turn away from all the glittering things of this world and follow a dead Christ? Not on your life! The resurrection lives in me, and the greatest future I have is not on this earth. This is a proving ground. Sometime in the future, God will raise Oral Roberts' body from the dead, reunite my immortal spirit with my new body — and I will live forever.

I Corinthians 15:20-22

> But now is Christ risen from the dead, and become the firstfruits of them that slept. For since by man came death, by man came also the resurrection of the dead. For as in Adam all die, even so in Christ shall all be made alive. But every man in his own order: Christ the firstfruits; afterward they that are Christ's at his coming.

Christ the Guarantee

Paul said, "But now is Christ risen from the dead." Paul was a NOW preacher. Christ was alive in the NOW for him and Paul said of Christ, "He is the first to be raised from the dead in resurrected form." There were people whom Jesus raised from the dead while He was on earth, but they died again. His was the first resurrection and it is the guarantee that every Christian will be raised from the dead.

Paul traces death back to the fall of Adam. In Adam's transgression, we were all present organically, and through Adam's death we all die. But through the resurrection we are present spiritually and eternally and shall all live forevermore. Then he said, "There will be an order of the resurrection: Christ is the firstfruits, and then at His coming, the rest of us will be raised."

I Corinthians 15:24-29

> Then cometh the end, when he shall have delivered up the kingdom to God, even the Father; when he shall have put down all rule and all authority and power. For he must reign, till he hath put all enemies under his feet. The last enemy that shall be destroyed is death. For

he hath put all things under his feet. But when he saith all things are put under him, it is manifest that he is excepted, which did put all things under him.

And when all things shall be subdued unto him, then shall the Son also himself be subject unto him that put all things under him, that God may be all in all. Else what shall they do which are baptized for the dead, if the dead rise not at all? why are they then baptized for the dead?

Dealing With Death

One of the most powerful things engulfing the mind of the Corinthian Christians was the fact of death. Death was what Jesus came against. The death in sins and trespasses, the death of our mortal flesh. Paul states that there is an end coming to this present world system, which through Adam's fall brought death and in which death continues to reign, so that all of us are going to die physically. However, Jesus is going to put all enemies under His feet. He is going to reign until death itself is abolished, for He says that the last enemy that shall be destroyed is death. Death has taken such a powerful hold upon mortal lives that it will be the last thing the gospel will defeat. But, thank God, He has put even death under His feet.

As Paul is reasoning with the Corinthian Christians about the reality of the banishment of death, the resurrection from the dead, he says, "If you do not believe in the resurrection of the dead, then why have you adopted a silly practice of baptizing for the dead if the dead rise not at all? Why are the dead baptized by proxy?"

Instead of allowing a person to believe upon Jesus Christ, repent of his sins, receive the gift of the Holy Spirit, and in that powerful moment of experience changed from a sinner to a child of God, they had gotten involved in a bunch of catechisms. If they died before they made their so-called public profession, they had someone baptized for them — a proxy.

But God does not have any grandchildren. God has only sons and daughters. The first thing Peter said on the day of Pentecost — and he said it to the whole world — was "Whosoever shall call upon the name of the Lord shall be saved." And Paul said in the second book of Corinthians that "if any man be in Christ he is a new creature. Old things are passed away. All things have become new." In other words, when they came preaching the gospel they preached a gospel that would save your soul and deliver you from the power of sin, not by proxy but by a one-on-one relationship with Christ. When you come to Christ, you become a son or a daughter, not a granddaughter or grandson.

In reference to "proxy," we will see in Paul's writings, especially in II Corinthians, that he wanted them to pray for him, but he wanted it while he was alive, not after he died. There is no place in the Scriptures where we are taught to pray for people who are dead. It is in this life where we have our will, our choice to make our decisions for Christ or against Him. It is in this life where Paul has said that we believe in our hearts and confess with our mouths that Jesus is risen from the dead, that He is the Christ, not by proxy but personally, by you and me. Yes, I believe in praying one for another, but it is for people who are alive.

I Corinthians 15:30-33

And why stand we in jeopardy every hour? I protest by your rejoicing which I have in Christ Jesus our Lord, I die daily. If after the manner of men I have fought with beasts at Ephesus, what advantageth it me, if the dead rise not? let us eat and drink; for tomorrow we die. Be not deceived: evil communications corrupt good manners.

Beware Evil Communications

Paul is referring to an incident in Ephesus when all the city was rioting in an uproar in which his own life was almost snuffed out by beastlike men. He said, "What advantage did I have in going through all that persecution and almost being killed if the dead do not rise?" Then, sort of tongue-in-cheek, he says, "You people are saying, 'Let us eat and drink, for tomorrow we die.' Do not be deceived by that. Evil communications corrupt good manners." Good manners in this usage does not mean how to use your knife and fork or act in polite society; it means staying in the faith, following the good teachings of the gospel.

I Corinthians 15:34-49

Awake to righteousness, and sin not; for some have not the knowledge of God: I speak this to your shame. But some man will say, How are the dead raised up? and with what body do they come? Thou fool, that which thou sowest is not quickened, except it die: and that which thou sowest, thou sowest not that body that shall be, but bare grain, it may chance of wheat, or of some other grain: but God giveth it a body as it hath pleased him, and to every seed his own body.

All flesh is not the same flesh: but there is one kind of flesh of men, another flesh of beasts, another of fishes, and another of birds. There are also celestial bodies, and bodies terrestrial: but the glory of the celestial is one, and the glory of the terrestrial is another. There is one glory of the sun, and another glory of the moon, and another glory of the stars: for one star differeth from another star in glory. So also is the resurrection of the dead. It is sown in corruption; it is raised in incorruption.

It is sown in dishonour; it is raised in glory: it is sown in weakness; it is raised in power: it is sown a natural body; it is raised a spiritual body. There is a natural body, and there is a spiritual body. And so it is written, The first man Adam was made a living soul; the last Adam was made a quickening spirit.

Howbeit that was not first which is spiritual, but that which is natural; and afterward that which is spiritual. The first man is of the earth, earthy: the second man is the Lord from heaven. As is the earthy, such are they also that are earthy: and as is the heavenly, such are they also that are heavenly. And as we have borne the image of the earthy, we shall also bear the image of the heavenly.

Bodily Restoration

Paul answers the man who asks, "How are the dead raised up, and with what body do they come?" by referring to seed, a seed of corn or a seed of wheat, any kind of seed. He said, "That seed is, first of all, just a bare seed. When you plant it, it has to die in order to change nature and be raised up into newness of life or into a stalk in which it reproduces itself in a far more glorious fashion, but it is still the same seed. And so, when the body dies and is raised from the dead, it is the same order of body, just like a grain of wheat is the same order of seed, even though you see it waving in the fields there, ripe with the wheat grain. And so, at the resurrection, our bodies are the same bodies which have been changed like unto Jesus' body and have become glorious bodies and yet recognizable, identifiable, unique unto us. We will know as we are known but we will have an absolutely perfect body, just as Jesus has a perfect body."

If you are thinking about how death changes our physical bodies, you have a point, and Paul is trying to cover that point. He talks about death, how the body is so weakened and how sometimes it is scarcely recognizable, if recognizable at all. Then he says, "It is going to be changed, because the second Adam, Jesus Christ, is a quickening Spirit. He is going to change all the disfigurement, all the corruption, anything that was crippled, anything that was missing in the body. Everything is restored to it eternally."

I Corinthians 15:50-58

Now this I say, brethren, that flesh and blood cannot inherit the kingdom of God; neither doth corruption inherit incorruption. Behold, I shew you a mystery; We shall not all sleep, but we shall all be changed, in a moment, in the twinkling of an eye, at the last trump: for the trumpet shall sound, and the dead shall be raised incorruptible, and we shall be changed. For this corruptible must put on incorruption, and this mortal must put on immortality.

So, when this corruptible shall have put on incorruption, and this mortal shall have put on immortality, then shall be brought to pass the saying that is written, Death is swallowed up in victory. O death, where is thy sting? O grave, where is thy victory? The sting of death is sin; and the strength of sin is the law. But thanks be to God, which giveth us the victory through our Lord Jesus Christ. Therefore, my beloved brethren, be ye steadfast, unmoveable, always abounding in the work of the Lord, forasmuch as ye know that your labour is not in vain in the Lord.

Resurrection Emphasized

Paul says that flesh and blood, or the natural man, cannot inherit or even understand the kingdom of God, but that you who are born of the Spirit, you who are in Christ, even though there will be corruption in your body, you are going to rise into an incorruptible body. Then Paul issues the battle cry of the ages. He says, "I show you a mystery. We shall not all die, but we shall all be changed."

He is speaking of the Rapture, and he refers to that time when the trumpet will sound and those who have already died in Christ shall be raised up into incorruptibility, and those who are alive shall be caught up. And in that catching up death will be involved, because death is a change. Then Paul says, "O death, where is your sting? O grave, where is your victory?" He speaks of the death of death and of the life of life. "Therefore, Christians," he says, "I thank God for this victory we have in the Lord Jesus Christ; therefore, be strong, be steadfast, do not move about in your faith; do not listen to everybody coming along trying to take away your faith in the resurrection of our Lord, for your labour is not in vain even when the persecutions hit."

Paul was saying that he, too, had faced the uproar, the riots in Ephesus where his life was almost taken, but the resurrection keeps his eye on the Lord, for he says, "Our labour is not in vain." If we do not believe in the resurrection of the Lord, even if we become Christians, we likely will fall away when some persecution comes along. We will not endure. The resurrection is the rock of Christ's own resurrection and it is our guarantee of resurrection.

Chapter 16 is the last chapter of the magnificent letter that Paul wrote to the Corinthians. It takes an absolutely different form because it deals with the nitty-gritty of everyday life.

I Corinthians 16:1-24

Now concerning the collection for the saints, as I have given order to the churches of Galatia, even so do ye. Upon the first day of the week let every one of you lay by him in store, as God hath prospered him, that there be no gatherings when I come. And when I come, whomsoever ye shall approve by your letters, them will I send to bring your liberality unto Jerusalem. And if it be meet that I go also, they shall go with me. Now I will come unto you, when I shall pass through Macedonia: for I do pass through Macedonia. And it may be that I will abide, yea, and winter with you, that ye may bring me on my journey whithersoever I go.

For I will not see you now by the way, but I trust to tarry a while with you, if the Lord permit. But I will tarry at Ephesus until Pentecost. For a great door and effectual is opened unto me, and there are many adversaries. Now if Timotheus come, see that he may be with you without fear: for he worketh the work of the Lord, as I also do. Let no man therefore despise him: but conduct him forth in peace, that he may come unto me: for I look for him with the brethren.

As touching our brother Apollos, I greatly desired him to come unto you with the brethren: but his will was not at all to come at this time; but he will come when he shall have convenient time. Watch ye, stand fast in the faith, quit you like men, be strong. Let all your things be done with charity. I beseech you, brethren, (ye know the house of Stephanas, that is the firstfruits of Achaia, and that they have addicted themselves to the ministry of the saints,) that ye submit yourselves unto such, and to every one that helpeth with us, and laboureth. I am glad of the coming of Stephanas and Fortunatus and Achaicus: for that which was lacking on your part they have supplied.

For they have refreshed my spirit and yours: therefore acknowledge ye them that are such. The churches of Asia salute you. Aquila and Priscilla salute you much in the Lord, with the church that is in their house. All the brethren greet you. Greet ye one another with an holy kiss. The salutation of me Paul with mine own hand. If any man love not the Lord Jesus Christ, let him be Anathema Maranatha. The grace of our Lord Jesus Christ be with you. My love be with you all in Christ Jesus. Amen.

Love Stands the Test

Paul begins this chapter by reminding them of the brethren in Jerusalem whose goods have been spoiled because of their faith; that is, the persecutors have come and reduced them, taken away what they had. He reminds them of the offering, the seed-faith gift that they are to send by Paul or others to those believers in Jerusalem.

The second verse is extraordinary for our time. Paul says, "Upon the first day of the week let every one of you lay by him in store as God hath prospered him that there be no gatherings when I come." When he speaks of their offering, a special offering which they are laying aside to be taken to Jerusalem, he takes that occasion to say, "Upon the first day of the week, every Sunday, when you meet together in the Lord, let everybody give as God has prospered him so there will not have to be emergency letters or emergency calls upon you."

That really strikes home to Oral Roberts. Paul was an evangelist. Today, the evangelist, as he does his work, similar to Paul, opening up new areas, pioneering new grounds, reaching souls that no one else can reach, often is left out of the tithes and offerings. His work is set aside as though it is totally unimportant. And Paul is saying here, "When I come, I do not want to come on an emergency financial basis. I do not want to come and say, 'I am out of money, I must have so much money — go ahead and lay by in store, every week.'" This is what we have been saying to everybody in God's work, in the church, the local church. He wanted them to be regular in their giving, continuous and continual.

In the 15th verse, he points them to the house of Stephanas, who was the first one he had led to Christ in Asia. He and his people had become so addicted to giving to the Lord's work, they were cited by Paul as an example to the believers in Corinth. Again and again, we say to you, our partner, it is your continual and continuous giving that enables us not to approach you on an emergency basis. I teach that we give our tithes and offerings to God as our seed-faith. We give it to the whole of the Church, including apostles, prophets, evangelists, pastors and teachers — not just to the evangelist alone nor to the pastor alone nor to the teacher alone. This is a fallacy that some have developed in the Church that only one of the callings should receive the seed gifts of the people. As an evangelist, I would never assume that responsibility because I am concerned about the whole of the Church.

Paul ends his letter by talking about some of his friends. One was young Timothy. Timothy was sort of shy, but very able. He wanted to be sure that they would not despise him because he was young, but receive him and let him do his work for God. He also mentioned Apollos, that great preacher of whom he spoke in the early part of this letter. Then he mentions Aquila and Priscilla and their church in Ephesus from which he is writing this letter, as they send their great love.

In Verse 14 he had said, "Let all your things be done in love." His last words are, "I love you in Jesus Christ." The entire letter of I Corinthians is a letter of love. Love deals with life as it is. It deals with problems, realities. It does not escape reality at all, does not even attempt to. Some people get an idea of love to the effect that if you love them you will not correct them, you will not say anything to them of a hard nature. But love is the very spirit of Jesus, who is the Spirit of truth. Love stands the test. If we really love each other, we will be truthful to each other, faithful to each other, and stand by each other.

The Second
Epistle of Paul
the Apostle to the
Corinthians

The Second Epistle of Paul the Apostle to the
Corinthians

The letters of Paul were written on a material called papyrus, which was made by beating reeds together until they became a parchment. Sometimes these parchments were 20 to 30 feet long. A person would roll them up, put them under his arm, and personally deliver them as a letter. In this case, Paul had sent his close associate in the gospel, young Titus, to the believers in Corinth with a letter of reconciliation. Now remember, in I Corinthians, Paul was concerned with what he had heard about incest being committed by some of the members of the church. So he is now very concerned about the response he will get from his second letter.

This may be Paul's most personal letter of all because it reveals many personal things about him. We get terrific inner glimpses of Paul the man. In II Corinthians he vents himself and allows his emotions to come out. We see a man who reaches great heights of emotion as well as tremendous depths. We see him struggling with his emotions, trying to control them. And we see him as he does control them. In II Corinthians Paul talks about having almost been killed, of the sparing of his life in Asia, and of his thorn in the flesh in which he is both supernaturally touched and satanically attacked. It is in this book that he also talks about the laws of seed-faith.

Paul wrote II Corinthians before his third visit to the church. He had made a quick unscheduled second visit there which had been highly unsatisfactory as far as we can understand. And now he writes this second letter, promising them another visit that they might have a second benefit. The big problem in Corinth was that false teachers had come in claiming that Paul had swayed the Corinthian believers. They called into question his apostleship and his call to evangelism. The charge was that Paul was trying to separate the new Christian faith from the law of Moses and that he was not to be trusted. These false leaders also said Paul was powerful at a distance and his letters were indeed strong, but in person he really was not much at all, he really was not a good speaker, he lacked the authority of a real apostle because he was not one of the original 12. They even whispered that because Paul, unlike the Greeks, did not make a charge for his orations, he therefore was not worth listening to.

Paul replied that his own life of sufferings for Christ was the thing the Corinthians should look at. He said that when he comes this time he will show them the marks of a true apostle with wonders and signs accompanying his ministry, and he hopes that will silence his critics who are in doubt about his true apostleship. So Paul wrote this letter partly to counter the false accusations which had become a part of his thorn in the flesh. He wrote it not for his own self-interest but to protect the church in Corinth, which he had founded, from these false teachers.

I want you to note that from the very first words Paul is in a spirit of saying, "Let's hang in here together. I am a man who has faced trouble. I relate to the troubles you are having. I care for you. So let's get into this thing together because as we unite and stay together, we are going to win the victory through Jesus Christ."

II Corinthians 1:1-7

> Paul, an apostle of Jesus Christ by the will of God, and Timothy our brother, unto the church of God which is at Corinth, with all the saints which are in all Achaia: Grace be to you and peace from God our Father, and from the Lord Jesus Christ. Blessed be God, even the Father of our Lord Jesus Christ, the Father of mercies, and the God of all comfort; who comforteth us in all our tribulation, that we may be able to comfort them which are in any trouble, by the comfort wherewith we ourselves are comforted of God. For as the sufferings of Christ abound in us, so our consolation also aboundeth by Christ. And whether we be afflicted, it is for your consolation and salvation, which is effectual in the enduring of the same sufferings which we also suffer: or whether we be comforted, it is for your consolation and salvation. And our hope of you is stedfast, knowing, that as ye are partakers of the sufferings, so shall ye be also of the consolation.

The Comfort of the Spirit

Paul leaves nothing to conjecture. He flatly states, "I am an apostle of Christ and I am an apostle by the will of God." And then he mentions a word about his young brother in the Lord, Timothy, and says he is writing directly to the church at Corinth. He offers them the grace of God and begins to praise the Lord. Then he immediately deals with the comfort of the Spirit of God that they and he must have and all of us today must have.

In Verse 6 when he mentions his sufferings for Christ, he says, "It is for you." This is a very important point for you to grasp. Paul is saying, "I am not in this for myself only. I am not out here preaching to gain something for myself or get a big name. All my ministry exists because of you. It is for you. And as I am comforted by the Spirit of God when I suffer, I can comfort you with that same comfort of the Lord." Now that may sound like a new thought, but it really is not. For we who are Christians are coming against this world of sin and the devil's power. So there is conflict and suffering. But Paul is trying to say that there is a comfort within our sufferings with which we can comfort one another. He is reminding us that the closer we serve our Lord and the more the devil strikes us, the more of the comfort of the Holy Spirit we can have that will give us the compassion of Christ to minister.

II Corinthians 1:8-14

For we would not, brethren, have you ignorant of our trouble which came to us in Asia, that we were pressed out of measure, above strength, insomuch that we despaired even of life: but we had the sentence of death in ourselves, that we should not trust in ourselves, but in God which raiseth the dead: who delivered us from so great a death, and doth deliver: in whom we trust that he will yet deliver us; ye also helping together by prayer for us, that for the gift bestowed upon us by the means of many persons thanks may be given by many on our behalf. For our rejoicing is this, the testimony of our conscience, that in simplicity and godly sincerity, not with fleshly wisdom, but by the grace of God, we have had our conversation in the world, and more abundantly to you-ward. For we write none other things unto you, than what ye read or acknowledge; and I trust ye shall acknowledge even to the end; as also ye have acknowledged us in part, that we are your rejoicing, even as ye also are ours in the day of the Lord Jesus.

Prayer Changes Things

Paul reminds them of the terrible persecution that came against him in Ephesus where he thought he was literally going to be killed in the tumult. He says that God delivered him from so great a death. Then he paid them a tribute. He said, "You helped me because you prayed for me." That is a very important point. Paul was down there in Ephesus. He was at the moment when his soul would leave his body. At that very moment the Christians at Corinth got together and prayed. He is now telling them how much their prayers helped, that prayer changed things, and that many persons were involved in it.

II Corinthians 1:15-22

> And in this confidence I was minded to come unto you before, that ye might have a second benefit; and to pass by you into Macedonia, and to come again out of Macedonia unto you, and of you to be brought on my way toward Judaea. When I therefore was thus minded, did I use lightness? or the things that I purpose, do I purpose according to the flesh, that with me there should be yea yea, and nay nay? But as God is true, our word toward you was not yea and nay. For the Son of God, Jesus Christ, who was preached among you by us, even by me and Silvanus and Timotheus, was not yea and nay, but in him was yea. For all the promises of God in him are yea, and in him Amen, unto the glory of God by us. Now he which stablisheth us with you in Christ, and hath anointed us, is God; who hath also sealed us, and given the earnest of the Spirit in our hearts.

Paul is telling them, "I know that others said that I had the wrong motive and that when I say yes it is like saying no and when I say no it is like saying yes. But let me tell you, brethren, God is true and our word toward you was not yea and nay, because the Son of God is the guarantee of every promise of God." And when he preached the promises of God, Jesus Christ was saying, "Yea, amen, Paul. That's it, Paul. Give them the gospel. I stand by the Word of God that you are preaching." And then he said that God had anointed them, had sealed them, and had given them the earnest of the Spirit in their hearts. In other words, He had given them the down payment on all that they were going to get in heaven.

II Corinthians 1:23,24

> Moreover I call God for a record upon my soul, that to spare you I came not as yet unto Corinth. Not for that we have dominion over your faith, but are helpers of your joy: for by faith ye stand.

A chord is touched in Paul's soul. The things he had heard had upset him so much that had he come there in the spirit of heaviness, the Corinthians might have regretted it. The only reason he had not come at that time was so that he would not appear to be domineering. He only wanted to be their helper, a partner with them in their development as children of God so he could show them how to walk by faith.

II Corinthians 2:1-4

> But I determined this with myself, that I would not come again to you in heaviness. For if I make you sorry, who is he then that maketh me glad, but the same which is made sorry by me? And I wrote this same unto you, lest, when I came, I should have sorrow from them of whom I ought to rejoice; having confidence in you all, that my joy is the joy of you all. For out of much affliction and anguish of heart I wrote unto you with many tears; not that ye should be grieved, but that ye might know the love which I have more abundantly unto you.

Nowhere in the Scriptures do we see such emotion in Paul. Paul reminded them that out of much anguish of heart he had written them and even in writing he had shed many tears. He had been grieved and he only shed those tears that they might know agape love, the kind of love he had mentioned in I Corinthians 13. It was like a father and mother saying to their children, "We love you so much, why do you keep doing these things? Don't you know that we love you? You are so close to us. You are part of our lives. We brought you into the world and we have great hopes for you." Paul is saying in effect, "I founded you as a church. I led you to Christ. I am saying everything I am saying to you because I want you to walk in faith, to live in love, and to grow and mature as a child of God."

II Corinthians 2:5-11

> But if any have caused grief, he hath not grieved me, but in part: that I may not overcharge you all. Sufficient to such a man is this punishment, which was inflicted of many. So that contrariwise ye ought rather to forgive him, and comfort him, lest perhaps such a one should be swallowed up with overmuch sorrow. Wherefore I beseech you that ye would confirm your love toward him. For to this end also did I write, that I might know the proof of you, whether ye be obedient in all things. To whom ye forgive any thing, I forgive also: for if I forgave any thing, to whom I forgave it, for your sakes forgave I it in the person of Christ; lest Satan should get an advantage of us: for we are not ignorant of his devices.

Forgiveness is the Key

Paul had written to them before about some individual who apparently had a personal antagonism toward Paul and who had now gotten right. He was pleading for them to forgive this person and as they forgave, he would forgive also. Paul is urging them into the healing love of forgiveness so that Satan would not take advantage of them. Forgiveness is the key. When we forgive one another it means that we stop the intentions of the devil to divide and destroy us.

II Corinthians 2:12,13

> Furthermore, when I came to Troas to preach Christ's gospel, and a door was opened unto me of the Lord, I had no rest in my spirit, because I found not Titus my brother: but taking my leave of them, I went from thence into Macedonia.

Paul was saying that when he got over to Troas, God opened a great door to him for the preaching of the gospel. But in spite of that he had no rest in his spirit because he was looking for Titus to come back and to report to him.

II Corinthians 2:14-17

> Now thanks be unto God, which always causeth us to triumph in Christ, and maketh manifest the savour of his knowledge by us in every place. For we are unto God a sweet savour of Christ, in them that are saved, and in them that perish: to the one we are the savour of death unto death; and to the other the savour of life unto life. And who is sufficient for these things? For we are not as many, which corrupt the word of God: but as of sincerity, but as of God, in the sight of God speak we in Christ.

Now when Paul says he thanks God who causes us to triumph in Christ, the Corinthians know exactly what he is talking about. This is a reference to a Roman triumph. When a general of Rome went out to conquer a province, he had to conquer the land, destroy at least 5,000 people, and take as trophies the leaders of the country, the spoils of war, the defeated soldiers, and bring them all back to Rome. When the conquering general returned as a hero and entered the city, the conquered leaders led the way. Following them were the captives. And then came the priests swinging their bowls of incense, just filling the air with the smell of incense. Then came the general standing in his chariot with the scepter of Rome held in his hand. Behind him were his own soldiers shouting in triumph.

This is what Paul was referring to. Paul is saying that there is a mighty march of triumph going on. Christ is the leader of it and those of us who preach the gospel are like those priests with their bowls of incense. When the captives smelled the incense they smelled their own death. But to the conquerors it smelled of life.

Paul is saying that what we preach is a savour of death unto death or life unto life. To the ungodly our words are death because they refuse to listen to them and have faith. But to those who believe, our words are life and it is sufficient for all things, both in this world and the world to come.

II Corinthians 3:1-3

Do we begin again to commend ourselves? or need we, as some others, epistles of commendation to you, or letters of commendation from you? Ye are our epistle written in our hearts, known and read of all men: forasmuch as ye are manifestly declared to be the epistle of Christ ministered by us, written not with ink, but with the Spirit of the living God; not in tables of stone, but in fleshy tables of the heart.

A Walking Letter

A true believer is a letter of Christ walking around for people to read and understand. Therefore, you and I must be very careful in the way we live our lives for Christ. Christ is not to be just a word to us, or, as He is with many people, a byword or curse word. He is a living Savior who has written himself into our spirits, into our conversations, and into our activities.

II Corinthians 3:4-11

And such trust have we through Christ to Godward: not that we are sufficient of ourselves to think any thing as of ourselves; but our sufficiency is of God; who also hath made us able ministers of the new testament; not of the letter, but of the spirit: for the letter killeth, but the spirit giveth life. But if the ministration of death, written and engraven in stones, was glorious, so that the children of Israel could not stedfastly behold the face of Moses for the glory of his countenance; which glory was to be done away: how shall not the ministration of the spirit be rather glorious? For if the ministration of condemnation be glory, much more doth the ministration of righteousness exceed in glory. For even that which was made glorious had no glory in this respect, by reason of the glory that excelleth. For if that which is done away was glorious, much more that which remaineth is glorious.

Paul is talking here about the Ten Commandments and all the other restrictions and promises held before the people of Israel. Paul said that when Moses was reading the law, he had to put a veil over his face because the glory of God was so bright the people could not stand to look upon him. It was a glorious thing. However, as a system of law, it never worked. It never fulfilled what God had in mind. And therefore, when the Spirit of God would write His laws not upon paper but in the heart of man, that would be far more glorious than the glory that had to be shielded by a veil upon Moses' face.

II Corinthians 3:12-18

Seeing then that we have such hope, we use great plainness of speech: and not as Moses, which put a vail over his face, that the children of Israel could not stedfastly look to the end of that which is abolished: but their minds were blinded: for until this day remaineth the same vail untaken away in the reading of the old testament; which vail is done away in Christ. But even unto this day, when Moses is read, the vail is upon their heart. Nevertheless when it shall turn to the Lord, the vail shall be taken away. Now the Lord is that Spirit: and where the Spirit of the Lord is, there is liberty. But we all, with open face beholding as in a glass the glory of the Lord, are changed into the same image from glory to glory, even as by the Spirit of the Lord.

Here Paul is making the veil over Moses' face synonymous with the law. It is said that even today as the Jews read the law of Moses, a sort of veil is over their minds and they cannot understand what they read. They cannot see that the law was looking forward to the coming of the Christ. But Paul said it is not that way in the Christian faith because the Lord is the Spirit of liberty. Jesus has come to free us from the veil that blinds our minds. As a matter of fact, we go from glory to glory as the Spirit of God gives us understanding of the real Christ.

II Corinthians 4:1-6

Therefore seeing we have this ministry, as we have received mercy, we faint not; but have renounced the hidden things of dishonesty, not walking in craftiness, nor handling the word of God deceitfully; but by manifestation of the truth commending ourselves to every man's conscience in the sight of God. But if our gospel be hid, it is hid to them that are lost: in whom the god of this world hath blinded the minds of them which believe not, lest the light of the glorious gospel of Christ, who is the image of God, should shine unto them. For we preach not ourselves, but Christ Jesus the Lord; and ourselves your servants for Jesus' sake. For God, who commanded the light to shine out of darkness, hath shined in our hearts, to give the light of the knowledge of the glory of God in the face of Jesus Christ.

He Who Blinds the Mind

Here the Apostle Paul introduces the devil as being the one who blinds the minds of people so that they cannot see God. Paul calls the devil the god of this world. He is not the god of the earth because the "earth is the Lord's and the fullness thereof." He is the god of this present world that is carried on by people who do not recognize God as God but who live for themselves. They are not really aware of how the devil has blinded their eyes, their minds, and their understanding so that the gospel is hidden from them. You and I have to understand that the real workings of this present world are based upon the blinding power of the devil because he does not want the light of God to shine in the hearts of men.

II Corinthians 4:7-18

But we have this treasure in earthen vessels, that the excellency of the power may be of God, and not of us. We are troubled on every side, yet not distressed; we are perplexed, but not in despair; persecuted, but not forsaken; cast down, but not destroyed; always bearing about in the body the dying of the Lord Jesus, that the life also of Jesus might be made manifest in our body. For we which live are alway delivered unto death for Jesus' sake, that the life also of Jesus might be made manifest in our mortal flesh.

So then death worketh in us, but life in you. We having the same spirit of faith, according as it is written, I believed, and therefore have I spoken; we also believe, and therefore speak; knowing that he which raised up the Lord Jesus shall raise up us also by Jesus, and shall present us with you. For all things are for your sakes, that the abundant grace might through the thanksgiving of many redound to the glory of God. For which cause we faint not; but though our outward man perish, yet the inward man is renewed day by day. For our light affliction, which is but for a moment, worketh for us a far more exceeding and eternal weight of glory; while we look not at the things which are seen, but at the things which are not seen: for the things which are seen are temporal; but the things which are not seen are eternal.

The Treasure of God in Earthen Vessels

Paul was referring to the ancient lights which were made of clay and in which oil was poured. The oil inside the clay filled the room with light when the wick was lit. So he is saying that we have the light of God in our mortal flesh, or in his words, we have this treasure in earthen vessels. And because this light is in us we are not distressed. We may be perplexed from a mortal standpoint but by the Spirit we are not in despair.

You and I are always feeling in our physical bodies the conflict of having the treasure of God in these earthen vessels. Every day that we live death is working in our body. But the Spirit of God is giving us the power to live a triumphant life. Our outward man is perishing, yet the inward man is renewed day by day. We have to get a balance between the things that we see and the things we do not see, between the temporal and the spiritual, and between the fact that our physical being begins to die when we are born and the truth that our spirits are immortal. It is very important that no believer comes to the point that he thinks his body will have a glorification on this earth. He must remember that the glorification of his body is in the resurrection from the dead and that death is an appointment. I want to tell you, we can have all the health promised us in the atonement for this life through the stripes upon Jesus' back. But Paul and the entire list of Bible writers teach us that there is death. You need to know that, not to be discouraged but to face life. Face it like it is.

II Corinthians 5:1-9

> For we know that if our earthly house of this tabernacle were dissolved, we have a building of God, an house not made with hands, eternal in the heavens. For in this we groan, earnestly desiring to be clothed upon with our house which is from heaven: if so be that being clothed we shall not be found naked. For we that are in this tabernacle do groan, being burdened: not for that we would be unclothed, but clothed upon, that mortality might be swallowed up of life. Now he that hath wrought us for the selfsame thing is God, who also hath given unto us the earnest of the Spirit. Therefore we are always confident, knowing that, whilst we are at home in the body, we are absent from the Lord: (For we walk by faith, not by sight:) We are confident, I say, and willing rather to be absent from the body, and to be present with the Lord. Wherefore we labour, that, whether present or absent, we may be accepted of him.

There are times we lie down at night and we hurt so badly we feel like we might not get through the night. Or we wake up in the morning and hurt so much we feel we will not make it through the day. But Paul speaks of knowing that we have a resurrection coming. We know that we have a new home and a new body. We are walking by faith and seeing that which is eternal because we are confident that whether we are absent from this body and go on to be with the

Lord or we remain here in this present body until the day we die, we are still going to labor for Christ. We know we are still going to have His freedom of the Spirit and be victorious in Him.

II Corinthians 5:10,11

For we must all appear before the judgment seat of Christ; that every one may receive the things done in his body, according to that he hath done, whether it be good or bad. Knowing therefore the terror of the Lord, we persuade men; but we are made manifest unto God; and I trust also are made manifest in your consciences.

Everyone to be Judged

The Apostle Paul states succinctly that not only will all unbelievers be called before that judgment seat but also all believers. We who believe the Lord have been judged for our sins and through repenting of them have received His forgiveness and salvation. Therefore, that judgment is past. But the deeds done in our bodies after we become believers (the deeds that are done between believing in Christ and the time that our bodies die) will be dealt with as works. We exercise our choice every day as to how we are going to live for the Lord. We choose whether or not we put God first in our lives, our giving, our praying, our loving — in everything. So whatever we do after we have believed on Jesus and been born again is going to be brought before the judgment seat of Christ.

Those who say that there is no judgment of Christ are denying the word of Christ himself. They are lying to you. Our God of love is also a God of judgment. He has a system of eternal laws and He rules by that system of eternal justice. Right now this is an age of mercy but we will soon be at the time of the judgment when there will be justice. We need to think about that and let a healthy fear come in our hearts (not an unholy fear, but a respect for what we are going to face). Therefore, we need to bring our bodies and thoughts into subjection to Christ so that we give our very best and let Christ receive the glory.

II Corinthians 5:12-17

For we commend not ourselves again unto you, but give you occasion to glory on our behalf, that ye may have somewhat to answer them which glory in appearance, and not in heart. For whether we be beside ourselves, it is to God: or whether we be sober, it is for your cause. For the love of Christ constraineth us; because we thus judge, that if one died for all, then were all dead: and that he died for all, that they which live should not henceforth live unto themselves, but unto him which died for them, and rose again. Wherefore henceforth know we no man after the flesh: yea, though we have known Christ after the flesh, yet now henceforth know we him no more. Therefore if any man be in Christ, he is a new creature: old things are passed away; behold, all things are become new.

A New Person

Here Paul replies to the critics, "These people have said that I am beside myself. Well, maybe I am beside myself but if I am, then I am very sober because I am moved by the love of Christ. It pushes up from inside me because I know that Christ died for every one of us. At one time He was in human flesh. But He is no longer in human form. He is resurrected from the dead and is glorified forever. Therefore, if any man be in the glorified Christ, he too is risen from the dead and is alive unto God as a new person."

We can be changed in our inner man and become new creatures. We can be born again to such an extent that we are saved. We are translated out of the kingdom of darkness into that of light. And we have a new life. Don't you think it is time that we returned to the reality of the newborn life, of being truly made new creatures in Christ rather than just being church members and going there because it is the thing to do? And now I want to pray with you.

> *Heavenly Father, I know there are many people in the world who really do not know they are saved even after they have made efforts to be saved. The Holy Spirit has not witnessed to their spirits that they are children of God. I pray these, my partners, will know beyond the shadow of a doubt that Jesus Christ is their personal Savior. I pray they will have knowledge of this in such a manner that they will have the authority of the believer and will know that they know that they know that they are saved by the blood of Jesus and are new creatures in Him. Amen and amen.*

II Corinthians 5:18-21

And all things are of God, who hath reconciled us to himself by Jesus Christ, and hath given to us the ministry of reconciliation; to wit, that God was in Christ, reconciling the world unto himself, not imputing their trespasses unto them; and hath committed unto us the word of reconciliation. Now then we are ambassadors for Christ, as though God did beseech you by us; we pray you in Christ's stead, be ye reconciled to God. For he hath made him to be sin for us, who knew no sin; that we might be made the righteousness of God in him.

Ambassadors for Christ

When the Roman Empire conquered a province, they would send a number of ambassadors to that country to help them write a constitution, to show them what the Roman government was all about, and to enlist them into active participation in the Roman Empire. Against this background, Paul said that when we are reconciled to Christ we are commissioned as ambassadors for Him. In other words, we speak in His name, share what the kingdom of God is like, and help others into the body of active believers. Why? Because God made Jesus Christ to be sin for us.

Now the question arises, why was Christ made sin for us? Paul said Jesus did this that you and I might be made the righteousness of God. In other words, the cross did not just happen. It was not an afterthought. It was something planned from eternity past because God knew that man, whom He created in His own image, would exercise his choice and go away from Him. God gave man a choice because he was the highest order of created beings upon this earth. Man was created in the likeness of God who has the power of choice. So through man's choice, he can choose either to go away from God or to be reconciled to God and in some unfathomable way become the righteousness of God through Jesus Christ.

II Corinthians 6:1-4

We then, as workers together with him, beseech you also that ye receive not the grace of God in vain. (For he saith, I have heard thee in a time accepted, and in the day of salvation have I succoured thee: behold, now is the accepted time; behold, now is the day of salvation.) Giving no offence in any thing, that the ministry be not blamed: But in all things approving ourselves as the ministers of God . . .

Paul is saying that because Christ came to reconcile us and to send us as His ambassadors, we then should take notice that today is the time of salvation. Furthermore, as we live in the now of our lives we are not to do things to offend other people so that the ministry will not be blamed. He is speaking of ministers as everyone who has believed on Christ. And notice, Paul is saying that he is approved unto God by 26 different things.

II Corinthians 6:4-10

. . . in much patience, in afflictions, in necessities, in distresses, in stripes, in imprisonments, in tumults, in labours, in watchings, in fastings; by pureness, by knowledge, by longsuffering, by kindness, by the Holy Ghost, by love unfeigned, by the word of truth, by the power of God, by the armour of righteousness on the right hand and on the left, by honour and dishonour, by evil report and good report: as deceivers, and yet true; as unknown, and yet well known; as dying, and, behold, we live; as chastened, and not killed; as sorrowful, yet alway rejoicing; as poor, yet making many rich; as having nothing, and yet possessing all things.

The Battle Between the Devil and God

You know, when we become children of God one of the first things the devil tries to do is to deceive us concerning how easy it is supposed to be to be a child of God. I remember years ago a man I had led to Christ came to me a few weeks later and told me of the things he had been suffering. He said, "I thought when I got saved I wouldn't have to face these things. I didn't even have to face them before I was saved." I said, "Do you know why? You did not face them then because the devil already had you. When you are going downstream you do not have to do anything. But when you go against the current you have got to swim." I said, "Brother, the devil hates you. He sees he does not have you now but that God has you. The battle is not over you and me anyway, it is a battle between the devil and God. The devil wants to destroy God by destroying you and me."

Tears came down his cheeks as I talked to him. He said, "I am so glad I brought this thought to you because I could have lost my soul. I had the wrong idea about the Christian life." My friend, it is true that when you and I become Christians we face adversity. But I want you to know that the battle is between the devil and God and as long as we remain on God's side there is no way we can lose.

II Corinthians 6:11-18

O ye Corinthians, our mouth is open unto you, our heart is enlarged. Ye are not straitened in us, but ye are straitened in your own bowels. Now for a recompense on the same, (I speak as unto my children,) be ye also enlarged. Be ye not unequally yoked together with unbelievers: for what fellowship hath righteousness with unrighteousness? and what communion hath light with darkness? And what concord hath Christ with Belial? or what part hath he that believeth with an infidel? And what agreement hath the temple of God with idols? for ye are the temple of the living God; as God hath said, I will dwell in them, and walk in them; and I will be their God, and they shall be my people. Wherefore come out from among them, and be ye separate, saith the Lord, and touch not the unclean thing; and I will receive you, and will be a Father unto you, and ye shall be my sons and daughters, saith the Lord Almighty.

Separate But Not Withdrawn

Paul is saying, "My heart is so open to you because you are straightening out your lives from your very hearts, not only because I have been preaching to you but because you desire to do it yourselves. Now let me remind you (and he is reminding you and me the same way), do not be yoked up with people who reject God. Do not be in fellowship with those people whose habits and whose ways of life tend to drag you down into the cesspool of sin with them." He is referring to an Old Testament scripture in Deuteronomy where God said not to yoke up an ass and the oxen and make them plow together because they are so dissimilar they can never come together in unity. So Paul says to come out from that kind of world that totally rejects God.

Now do not misinterpret the statement, "Be ye separate and touch not the unclean thing" to suggest that you and I are not to go into every man's world or that we are so holy we withdraw into our own little church world and live as in a hothouse. We are to get out there and mix and mingle with this world, but by the very purity of our souls be separate from the impurity of their souls. We are to have the courage to be Christians as we do business with them, which we have to do. We do business with them on the grounds of our faith in God and the way of the Lord. And we stick with it, come what will.

Paul says in Verse 18 that when you do this, God will be a Father unto you and you will be as sons and daughters. This is a reference to the Old Testament when God told His people that when you separate yourself from the things of the world He will take responsibility for you. There is one thing for sure, friend and partner: When we put God first He puts us first in His love. He will take care of you and me.

II Corinthians 7:1-10
>Having therefore these promises, dearly beloved, let us cleanse ourselves from all filthiness of the flesh and spirit, perfecting holiness

in the fear of God. Receive us; we have wronged no man, we have corrupted no man, we have defrauded no man. I speak not this to condemn you: for I have said before, that ye are in our hearts to die and live with you. Great is my boldness of speech toward you, great is my glorying of you: I am filled with comfort, I am exceeding joyful in all our tribulation. For, when we were come into Macedonia, our flesh had no rest, but we were troubled on every side; without were fightings, within were fears.

Nevertheless God, that comforteth those that are cast down, comforted us by the coming of Titus; and not by his coming only, but by the consolation wherewith he was comforted in you, when he told us your earnest desire, your mourning, your fervent mind toward me; so that I rejoiced the more. For though I made you sorry with a letter, I do not repent, though I did repent: for I perceive that the same epistle hath made you sorry, though it were but for a season. Now I rejoice, not that ye were made sorry, but that ye sorrowed to repentance: for ye were made sorry after a godly manner, that ye might receive damage by us in nothing. For godly sorrow worketh repentance to salvation not to be repented of: but the sorrow of the world worketh death.

Paul said that when he arrived in Macedonia, his flesh had no rest. He was troubled on every side. Now, what was he talking about? Inside, Paul was worried that the letter he had written to the Corinthians might not have been just the right thing to do. You see, in his humanness he realized he might not have said everything under the inspiration of the Holy Spirit. Then he tells the Corinthians he has seen Titus, and Titus has given the great report of how delighted they were to receive the letter and be corrected. Then he said he was so happy he sent the letter because the right kind of sorrow, godly sorrow, had been produced in the Corinthian believers. Now, the only kind of sorrow in your heart that will lead you to God is the kind of sorrow you feel when you have done something against God. You have a God-consciousness about some wrong you did, and that is what makes for true repentance.

II Corinthians 7:11-16

For behold this selfsame thing, that ye sorrowed after a godly sort, what carefulness it wrought in you, yea, what clearing of yourselves, yea, what indignation, yea, what fear, yea, what vehement desire, yea, what zeal, yea, what revenge! In all things ye have approved yourselves to be clear in this matter. Wherefore, though I wrote unto you, I did it not for his cause that had done the wrong, nor for his cause that suffered wrong, but that our care for you in the sight of God might appear unto you. Therefore we were comforted in your comfort: yea, and exceedingly the more joyed we for the joy of Titus, because his spirit was refreshed by you all. For if I have boasted any thing to him of you, I am not ashamed; but as we spake all things to you in truth, even so our boasting, which I made before Titus, is found a truth. And his inward affection is more abundant toward you, whilst he remembereth the obedience of you all, how with fear and trembling ye received him. I rejoice therefore that I have confidence in you in all things.

It Isn't All Negative

Paul had been trying to set things straight in the Corinthian church, so now in receiving the good news he was thrilled and finally said, "I now have confidence in you in all things." I think we should have a great appreciation of the people at Corinth. If there had not been a group of people like this we would not have been able to face similar situations in our lives. In treating these matters so carefully, Paul is also treating the matters that we face in our religious lives today. In every denomination and in every local church there is both the good spirit of the Corinthian believers and the bad spirit of the Corinthian believers. There are the good things and the bad things, the spiritual and the unspiritual, the times when there are divisions and the times when there is great unity. So we need First and Second Corinthians. We need to learn about the truth of such a church. There is a lot to say in favor of these Corinthian believers and of any group today in a church where they are trying to set things straight.

II Corinthians 8:1-9

Moreover, brethren, we do you to wit of the grace of God bestowed on the churches of Macedonia; how that in a great trial of affliction the abundance of their joy and their deep poverty abounded unto the riches of their liberality. For to their power, I bear record, yea, and beyond their power they were willing of themselves; praying us with much entreaty that we would receive the gift, and take upon us the fellowship of the ministering to the saints. And this they did, not as we hoped, but first gave their own selves to the Lord, and unto us by the will of God. Insomuch that we desired Titus, that as he had begun, so he would also finish in you the same grace also. Therefore, as ye abound in every thing, in faith, and utterance, and knowledge, and in all diligence, and in your love to us, see that ye abound in this grace also. I speak not by commandment, but by occasion of the forwardness of others, and to prove the sincerity of your love. For ye know the grace of our Lord Jesus Christ, that, though he was rich, yet for your sakes he became poor, that ye through his poverty might be rich.

A year before this, Paul had asked the Corinthians to join all the other churches in taking up a special offering for the poor Christians of Jerusalem, many of whom had their goods spoiled or confiscated because of their testimony for Christ. Because the gospel had originated with those of Jerusalem, Paul felt that the Gentile Christians should share their financial bounty with them. So the churches in Macedonia, even though they faced very deep poverty themselves, gave out of their poverty because they had a depth of liberality in their spirits since Christ was living in them.

I want to tell you that these people first gave themselves to God and then gave of their earnings with a joyful heart. The grace of giving that is inherent in Christ our Savior is a grace of God to be developed in our lives.

II Corinthians 8:10-15

And herein I give my advice: for this is expedient for you, who have begun before, not only to do, but also to be forward a year ago. Now therefore perform the doing of it; that as there was a readiness to will, so there may be a performance also out of that which ye have. For if there be first a willing mind, it is accepted according to that a man hath, and not according to that he hath not. For I mean not that other men be eased, and ye burdened: but by an equality, that now at this time your abundance may be a supply for their want, that their abundance also may be a supply for your want: that there may be equality: as it is written, He that had gathered much had nothing over; and he that had gathered little had no lack.

I remember one of the scriptures of the Old Testament where God commanded that when we make vows, to perform those vows and when we say we are going to give something to Him, to do it. But here in the New Testament the emphasis is even greater because of our Lord Jesus Christ who laid aside everything to come down here among us that we might have everything. So He is our example of giving. I think this is a wonderful word of exhortation to you and me to do all the things that God has called us to do.

II Corinthians 8:16-24

But thanks be to God, which put the same earnest care into the heart of Titus for you. For indeed he accepted the exhortation; but being more forward, of his own accord he went unto you. And we have sent with him the brother, whose praise is in the gospel throughout all the churches; and not that only, but who was also chosen of the churches to travel with us with this grace, which is administered by us to the glory of the same Lord, and declaration of your ready mind: avoiding this, that no man should blame us in this abundance which is administered by us: providing for honest things, not only in the sight of the Lord, but also in the sight of men. And we have sent with them our brother, whom we have oftentimes proved diligent in many things, but now much more diligent, upon the great confidence which I have in you. Whether any do enquire of Titus, he is my partner and fellowhelper concerning you: or our brethren be enquired of, they are the messengers of the churches, and the glory of Christ. Wherefore shew ye to them, and before the churches, the proof of your love, and of our boasting on your behalf.

It is very impressive to me, and I hope to you also, that Paul continues to talk about the grace of giving. It is really a lost art among many of the people of God. And it is sad that many Christians believe that when they give, they really lose. You know, that is the devil's business to make people believe that lie. It is also the fault of us ministers of the gospel who do not always explain the grace of giving as Paul did or explain Malachi 3:10,11, about the tithes and offerings. I firmly believe, based upon the Holy Word of God, that as we give, God will bless us and rebuke the devourer for our sake.

II Corinthians 9:1-15

For as touching the ministering to the saints, it is superfluous for me to write to you: for I know the forwardness of your mind, for which I boast of you to them of Macedonia, that Achaia was ready a year ago; and your zeal hath provoked very many. Yet have I sent the brethren, lest our boasting of you should be in vain in this behalf; that, as I said, ye may be ready: Lest haply if they of Macedonia come with me, and find you unprepared, we (that we say not, ye) should be ashamed in this same confident boasting. Therefore I thought it necessary to exhort the brethren, and they would go before unto you, and make up beforehand your bounty, whereof ye had notice before, that the same might be ready, as a matter of bounty, and not as of covetousness. But this I say, He which soweth sparingly shall reap also sparingly; and he which soweth bountifully shall reap also bountifully.

Every man according as he purposeth in his heart, so let him give; not grudgingly, or of necessity: for God loveth a cheerful giver. And God is able to make all grace abound toward you; that ye, always

having all sufficiency in all things, may abound to every good work:
(As it is written, He hath dispersed abroad; he hath given to the poor;
his righteousness remaineth for ever. Now he that ministereth seed
to the sower both minister bread for your food, and multiply your
seed sown, and increase the fruits of your righteousness;) being
enriched in every thing to all bountifulness, which causeth through
us thanksgiving to God. For the administration of this service not
only supplieth the want of the saints, but is abundant also by many
thanksgivings unto God; whiles by the experiment of this ministration
they glorify God for your professed subjection unto the gospel of
Christ, and for your liberal distribution unto them, and unto all men;
and by their prayer for you, which long after you for the exceeding
grace of God in you. Thanks be unto God for his unspeakable gift.

The Secret of Succeeding in Life

Paul is trying to tell you and me how to make it in this world. He
says when you give, understand you are sowing a seed. Do not do
it just because there is a big need. Rather, think of your own need.
Think of the purpose within your heart because God sheds forth His
love in a special way in the heart of the person who cheerfully gives,
that is, the person who just cannot wait to sow his seeds of faith.
    Then Paul tells us three things. First, it is God who gives us seed
to sow. Now hear that. It is God who gives us seed to sow. If it is
time, it is God who gives us that time. If it is talent, then it is talent
that is God-given. Second, when you sow it, God multiplies it. But
if you do not sow it, God cannot multiply it. Third, God will increase
the fruit of your righteousness. In other words, fruit comes from
seed that is planted. There is no such thing as something for nothing.
    If I had only one thing to say to you I would tell you to get hold
of the truth that you give out of what God has already given you to
plant. And when you give, know in your heart that from those seeds
you are going to receive a harvest. Therefore, when you plant your
seed, do it with a purpose and with a focus. Focus it so that you do
not give grudgingly or out of necessity. In other words, give out of
your own need. Give out of your own hurt. Give out of your own
lack. I give you my word as an ordained evangelist and apostle that
God will increase your righteousness and multiply your seed sown.
    Paul ends this chapter by saying, "Thanks be unto God for His
unspeakable gift." He is saying thanks to God for the greatest seed
of all, the seed of His Son Jesus Christ that He planted to gain the
harvest of our souls' salvation. This is a great chapter. Read it often.
Make II Corinthians 9:10 a verse you study and apply daily to your

life. And now, I want to pray with you.

*Father, I bring these partners to You that they may understand
that You want to meet their needs and give them the money
they must have to live in this world and be triumphant witnesses
for Jesus Christ. I pray that they will understand that to reap,
we sow, and to receive, we give, and we give in the same spirit
that You gave Your only begotten Son. And I pray that these
partners will be freed up beginning now through knowing that
when they give, You are going to multiply that giving back in
the form of their own needs. I thank You for it through Jesus
Christ our Lord. Amen and amen.*

II Corinthians 10:1-18

Now I Paul myself beseech you by the meekness and gentleness of
Christ, who in presence am base among you, but being absent am
bold toward you: but I beseech you, that I may not be bold when I
am present with that confidence, wherewith I think to be bold against
some, which think of us as if we walked according to the flesh. For
though we walk in the flesh, we do not war after the flesh: (For the
weapons of our warfare are not carnal, but mighty through God to
the pulling down of strong holds;) casting down imaginations, and
every high thing that exalteth itself against the knowledge of God,
and bringing into captivity every thought to the obedience of Christ;
and having in a readiness to revenge all disobedience, when your
obedience is fulfilled.

Do ye look on things after the outward appearance? If any man
trust to himself that he is Christ's, let him of himself think this again,
that, as he is Christ's, even so are we Christ's. For though I should
boast somewhat more of our authority, which the Lord hath given us
for edification, and not for your destruction, I should not be ashamed:
that I may not seem as if I would terrify you by letters. For his letters,
say they, are weighty and powerful; but his bodily presence is weak,
and his speech contemptible. Let such an one think this, that, such
as we are in word by letters when we are absent, such will we be
also in deed when we are present. For we dare not make ourselves
of the number, or compare ourselves with some that commend
themselves: but they measuring themselves by themselves, and
comparing themselves among themselves, are not wise.

But we will not boast of things without our measure, but according
to the measure of the rule which God hath distributed to us, a measure
to reach even unto you. For we stretch not ourselves beyond our
measure, as though we reached not unto you: for we are come as far
as to you also in preaching the gospel of Christ: not boasting of things

347

without our measure, that is, of other men's labours; but having hope, when your faith is increased, that we shall be enlarged by you according to our rule abundantly, to preach the gospel in the regions beyond you, and not to boast in another man's line of things made ready to our hand. But he that glorieth, let him glory in the Lord. For not he that commendeth himself is approved, but whom the Lord commendeth.

Paul is remembering those hard months of reaching these Corinthians with the gospel of Jesus Christ. Through the gospel they had been rescued from every imaginable sin. They had been brought together and established in Christ before Paul went to further the gospel. Now, while he is ministering to others, groups of very polished, highly cultured speakers have come to the Corinthians from Jerusalem and other places. And although they had nothing to do with the winning of these Corinthians to Christ or the suffering that Paul experienced in birthing the new converts into the kingdom of God, they have literally taken over and denounced the great apostle who brought the gospel to Corinth.

So now Paul responds, "When I was among you I did not try to overwhelm you by oratory or by being so polished. Therefore, you say that when I was present among you I was weak, but when I write to you my letters are very strong. Well, let me remind you that when I come back I will be just as strong in person as I am in letter and I will not boast out of measure, but only according to the measure that God has given to me. And I want to tell you Corinthians, it is not the person who commends himself, but the one whom God commends who will make it."

II Corinthians 11:1-33

Would to God ye could bear with me a little in my folly: and indeed bear with me. For I am jealous over you with godly jealousy: for I have espoused you to one husband, that I may present you as a chaste virgin to Christ. But I fear, lest by any means, as the serpent beguiled Eve through his subtilty, so your minds should be corrupted from the simplicity that is in Christ.

For if he that cometh preacheth another Jesus, whom we have not preached, or if ye receive another spirit, which ye have not received, or another gospel, which ye have not accepted, ye might well bear with him. For I suppose I was not a whit behind the very chiefest apostles. But though I be rude in speech, yet not in knowledge; but we have been throughly made manifest among you in all things. Have I committed an offence in abasing myself that ye might be exalted,

348

because I have preached to you the gospel of God freely?

I robbed other churches, taking wages of them, to do you service. And when I was present with you, and wanted, I was chargeable to no man: for that which was lacking to me the brethren which came from Macedonia supplied: and in all things I have kept myself from being burdensome unto you, and so will I keep myself. As the truth of Christ is in me, no man shall stop me of this boasting in the regions of Achaia. Wherefore? because I love you not? God knoweth. But what I do, that I will do, that I may cut off occasion from them which desire occasion; that wherein they glory, they may be found even as we.

For such are false apostles, deceitful workers, transforming themselves into the apostles of Christ. And no marvel; for Satan himself is transformed into an angel of light. Therefore it is no great thing if his ministers also be transformed as the ministers of righteousness; whose end shall be according to their works. I say again, Let no man think me a fool; if otherwise, yet as a fool receive me, that I may boast myself a little. That which I speak, I speak it not after the Lord, but as it were foolishly, in this confidence of boasting. Seeing that many glory after the flesh, I will glory also.

For ye suffer fools gladly, seeing ye yourselves are wise. For ye suffer, if a man bring you into bondage, if a man devour you, if a man take of you, if a man exalt himself, if a man smite you on the face. I speak as concerning reproach, as though we had been weak. Howbeit whereinsoever any is bold, (I speak foolishly,) I am bold also. Are they Hebrews? so am I. Are they Israelites? so am I. Are they the seed of Abraham? so am I. Are they ministers of Christ? (I speak as a fool) I am more; in labours more abundant, in stripes above measure, in prisons more frequent, in deaths oft.

Of the Jews five times received I forty stripes save one. Thrice was I beaten with rods, once was I stoned, thrice I suffered shipwreck, a night and a day I have been in the deep; in journeyings often, in perils of waters, in perils of robbers, in perils by mine own countrymen, in perils by the heathen, in perils in the city, in perils in the wilderness, in perils in the sea, in perils among false brethren; in weariness and painfulness, in watchings often, in hunger and thirst, in fastings often, in cold and nakedness. Beside those things that are without, that which cometh upon me daily, the care of all the churches.

Who is weak, and I am not weak? who is offended, and I burn not? If I must needs glory, I will glory of the things which concern mine infirmities. The God and Father of our Lord Jesus Christ, which is blessed for evermore, knoweth that I lie not. In Damascus the governor under Aretas the king kept the city of the Damascenes with a garrison, desirous to apprehend me: and through a window in a basket was I let down by the wall, and escaped his hands.

Suffering for the Gospel

In Verse 2 Paul says, "I am jealous over you with godly jealousy: for I have espoused you to one husband, that I may present you as a chaste virgin to Christ." He is referring to the Jewish wedding where the bridegroom had friends who had a great trust committed to them. They were to watch over the bride, the young virgin, between her betrothal and the wedding to see that she would not lose her virginity but remain chaste for her husband. Paul is saying to the Corinthian believers, "Now Jesus Christ, the Bridegroom, has entrusted the commission to me to see that you remain a pure bride. And I am not going to stand by while these false teachers and preachers try to steal you away from the gospel with all their vain philosophies, bragging, and boasting."

Then he adds, "Concerning their boasting, this is not a commandment of the Lord, but I can boast too." Now, I would like to point out he does not say all these things to exalt himself. Rather, he is saying, "Those fools talk like fools and you suffer fools gladly. Well, I will just be a fool for a moment and let you hear a man that has really been through something for the glory of God." He was not trying to exalt himself through these sufferings. He was just pointing out the truth that from day one of his Christian life he seemingly had been set aside as one to suffer for the gospel of Jesus Christ.

Paul says, "Of the Jews five times received I forty stripes save one." The rule was that a person could be sentenced to receive 40 stripes, but the one who did the whipping could stop at 39 because of the fear of miscounting. If he struck the victim one extra time, a 41st time, then the victim would get to whip him 40 times. So they gave them 40 stripes save one. This happened to Paul five times. Usually the Jews would only whip a person once. But with the Christians all limits were off and the authorities let the Jews whip them as often as they wanted to. So he is saying, "They whipped me as much as they wanted to."

He added, "Three times was I beaten with rods." Now, that was a Roman custom, and as Paul was a Roman citizen, they had no legal right to do that to him. But they did it anyway. So you see, Paul did indeed have reason to boast.

II Corinthians 12:1-21

It is not expedient for me doubtless to glory. I will come to visions and revelations of the Lord. I knew a man in Christ above fourteen years ago, (whether in the body, I cannot tell; or whether out of the body, I cannot tell: God knoweth;) such an one caught up to the third heaven. And I knew such a man, (whether in the body, or out of the body, I cannot tell: God knoweth;)

How that he was caught up into paradise, and heard unspeakable words, which it is not lawful for a man to utter.

Of such an one will I glory: yet of myself I will not glory, but in mine infirmities. For though I would desire to glory, I shall not be a fool; for I will say the truth: but now I forbear, lest any man should think of me above that which he seeth me to be, or that he heareth of me. And lest I should be exalted above measure through the abundance of the revelations, there was given to me a thorn in the flesh, the messenger of Satan to buffet me, lest I should be exalted above measure. For this thing I besought the Lord thrice, that it might depart from me. And he said unto me, My grace is sufficient for thee: for my strength is made perfect in weakness.

Most gladly therefore will I rather glory in my infirmities, that the power of Christ may rest upon me. Therefore I take pleasure in infirmities, in reproaches, in necessities, in persecutions, in distresses for Christ's sake: for when I am weak, then am I strong. I am become a fool in glorying; ye have compelled me: for I ought to have been commended of you: for in nothing am I behind the very chiefest apostles, though I be nothing.

Truly the signs of an apostle were wrought among you in all patience, in signs, and wonders, and mighty deeds. For what is it wherein ye were inferior to other churches, except it be that I myself was not burdensome to you? forgive me this wrong. Behold, the third time I am ready to come to you; and I will not be burdensome to you: for I seek not yours, but you: for the children ought not to lay up for the parents, but the parents for the children. And I will very gladly spend and be spent for you; though the more abundantly I love you, the less I be loved. But be it so, I did not burden you: nevertheless, being crafty, I caught you with guile.

Did I make a gain of you by any of them whom I sent unto you? I desired Titus, and with him I sent a brother. Did Titus make a gain of you? walked we not in the same spirit? walked we not in the same steps? Again, think ye that we excuse ourselves unto you? we speak before God in Christ: but we do all things, dearly beloved, for your edifying. For I fear, lest when I come, I shall not find you such as I would, and that I shall be found unto you such as ye would not: lest there be debates, envyings, wraths, strifes, backbitings, whisperings, swellings, tumults: and lest, when I come again, my God will humble me among you, and that I shall bewail many which have sinned already, and have not repented of the uncleanness and fornication and lasciviousness which they have committed.

The Thorn and the Grace

In this 12th chapter we have the thorn and the grace. Paul begins by saying, "I have had visions and revelations of the Lord. In fact, 14 years ago I had an experience. I could not tell if my spirit was in my body or if it had left my body. Only God knows. But one thing I do know, I was caught up to the third heaven." (He is not referring to the cloudy heavens or to the starry heavens, but to the one we will all be in when our spirits finally leave our bodies.) While he was there, he heard words that cannot be simplified for man's understanding. God let him hear Him but said He would not permit him to reveal what he heard.

Therefore, the devil wanted to take advantage of that and cause Paul to become proud so he would lose it all. Paul states, "There was given to me a thorn in the flesh, the messenger of Satan, to buffet me lest I should be exalted above measure." The Greek word for "messenger" here is "angelos." It has never been translated as "disease" or "physical infirmity" but as "an angel of the devil." That does not mean this devil entered Paul. The flesh is the outward part of man. So the messenger, or angelos, would strike Paul, as it were, with his open hand.

When the messenger of Satan became the thorn in Paul's flesh and began to strike him wherever he went, Paul asked God three different times to make the thing depart from him. Each time God spoke back and said, "Paul, My grace is sufficient for thee. Every time this messenger of Satan hits you, look for My grace." And that is what Paul did every time the angel of the devil stirred people up against him and caused all kinds of persecutions and sufferings that God would not remove.

Some people have said that God gave Paul the thorn in the flesh; that is not true. What God gave him were revelations. What God gave him were visions. That is what God gave him. But He also knew that the human mind has a tendency to be exalted whenever there is something superior happening in a person. So he permitted the devil to send a demon to cause problems for Paul wherever he went so that in the end Paul would stay humble and true to Him.

Now, that thing was not in Paul. It was a demon of persecution whose purpose was to put Paul in a bad light, to cause the hatred of the world against him, to stir up the people, and to even stir up the elements against him.

I want you to understand the nature of a thorn in the flesh. It is something that comes against us for the rest of our lives because of the fact we have had an experience with God so great that it is likely to puff us up. So you and I cannot say we have a thorn in the flesh if we have not received something extraordinary from God or are doing something for Him.

But the most important thing I want to say about the Bible's teaching on the thorn in the flesh is that it made Paul painfully aware of his human limitations. It also made him acutely aware of the very present grace of God that was always there. Every time the thorn struck, the grace would come gushing out. And Paul could appropriate it and rise above his limitations to the extent that they were not a hindrance to doing what God had called him to do. So whatever you feel is a thorn in the flesh of your life, I want to remind you that it is there to reveal to you the glorious grace of God that is more than sufficient to enable you to do what God has called you to do.

II Corinthians 13:1-14

This is the third time I am coming to you. In the mouth of two or three witnesses shall every word be established. I told you before, and foretell you, as if I were present, the second time; and being absent now I write to them which heretofore have sinned, and to all other, that, if I come again, I will not spare: Since ye seek a proof of Christ speaking in me, which to you-ward is not weak, but is mighty in you. For though he was crucified through weakness, yet he liveth by the power of God.

For we also are weak in him, but we shall live with him by the power of God toward you. Examine yourselves, whether ye be in the faith; prove your own selves. Know ye not your own selves, how that Jesus Christ is in you, except ye be reprobates? But I trust that ye shall know that we are not reprobates. Now I pray to God that ye do no evil; not that we should appear approved, but that ye should do that which is honest, though we be as reprobates. For we can do nothing against the truth, but for the truth. For we are glad, when we are weak, and ye are strong: and this also we wish, even your perfection. Therefore I write these things being absent, lest being present I should use sharpness, according to the power which the Lord hath given me to edification, and not to destruction.

Finally, brethren, farewell. Be perfect, be of good comfort, be of one mind, live in peace; and the God of love and peace shall be with you. Greet one another with an holy kiss. All the saints salute you. The grace of the Lord Jesus Christ, and the love of God, and the communion of the Holy Ghost, be with you all. Amen.

Paul is saying, "I pray for you." This is one of the things he holds up in all his letters, no matter what he has said. Paul has been struggling to face the problems in the Corinthian church. He has had to speak sharply. He knows when he comes in person that he may have to do it even more. But there is one thing he wants to do above all else, and that is to pray for them, because he believes in the power of prayer.

And finally, he says in effect, "Brethren, I bless you. You are a tough group to deal with, but I love you. You have had to be put in your proper place, but I stand by you. You have needed the strongest teachings that I can give you, but I trust in you. And I wish God's best for you. I pray for you and I bless you, my brethren. Through the grace of the Lord Jesus Christ, God's love, and the communion that we have in the Holy Spirit, I bless you."

The Epistle of Paul the Apostle to the
Galatians

The Epistle of Paul
the Apostle to the
Galatians

Paul was just midway through his ministry when he wrote First
and Second Corinthians. Now, as we go on to the next four books,
Galatians, Ephesians, Philippians, and Colossians (all of which Paul
wrote from a prison cell in Rome), we are going to see him in the
latter part of his life after he has been through about everything you
can imagine. As we read these books we are going to catch the spirit
of the man and some of his personal experiences that we have not
yet seen.

The churches of Galatia were in the area known as Asia Minor.
The churches at Lystra, Iconium, Antioch of Pisidia, and Derbe
comprised a cluster of Galatian churches.

When Paul wrote this letter it was rather urgent, because the
Judaizers were on his trail. Everywhere he had been they showed
up to cancel out the grace of God he was teaching. Therefore,
Galatians is not a book of niceties. Paul got right to the point. So
while it is only six chapters long, it is very powerful.

Galatians 1:1-5
> Paul, an apostle, (not of men, neither by man, but by Jesus Christ,
> and God the Father, who raised him from the dead;) and all the
> brethren which are with me, unto the churches of Galatia: Grace be
> to you and peace from God the Father, and from our Lord Jesus Christ,
> who gave himself for our sins, that he might deliver us from this
> present evil world, according to the will of God and our Father: to
> whom be glory for ever and ever. Amen.

In Verse 3, Paul begins with the word "grace." You will notice that
the last word Paul uses in Galatians is grace, which means "the
unmerited favor of God."

Galatians 1:6-9

> I marvel that ye are so soon removed from him that called you into the grace of Christ unto another gospel: which is not another; but there be some that trouble you, and would pervert the gospel of Christ. But though we, or an angel from heaven, preach any other gospel unto you than that which we have preached unto you, let him be accursed. As we said before, so say I now again, If any man preach any other gospel unto you than that ye have received, let him be accursed.

"Accursed" to the Jew meant that something was so far from God that they would not have anything to do with it. So Paul is saying, "If anybody comes along and preaches a gospel other than the one we have delivered to you, have nothing to do with it because it is a perversion of the gospel."

Galatians 1:10-2:6

> For do I now persuade men, or God? or do I seek to please men? for if I yet pleased men, I should not be the servant of Christ. But I certify you, brethren, that the gospel which was preached of me is not after man. For I neither received it of man, neither was I taught it, but by the revelation of Jesus Christ.
>
> For ye have heard of my conversation in time past in the Jews' religion, how that beyond measure I persecuted the church of God, and wasted it: and profited in the Jews' religion above many my equals in mine own nation, being more exceedingly zealous of the traditions of my fathers.
>
> But when it pleased God, who separated me from my mother's womb, and called me by his grace, to reveal his Son in me, that I might preach him among the heathen; immediately I conferred not with flesh and blood: neither went I up to Jerusalem to them which were apostles before me; but I went into Arabia, and returned again unto Damascus. Then after three years I went up to Jerusalem to see Peter, and abode with him fifteen days. But other of the apostles saw I none, save James the Lord's brother. Now the things which I write unto you, behold, before God, I lie not. Afterwards I came into the regions of Syria and Cilicia; and was unknown by face unto the churches of Judaea which were in Christ: but they had heard only, That he which persecuted us in times past now preacheth the faith which once he destroyed. And they glorified God in me.
>
> Then fourteen years after I went up again to Jerusalem with Barnabas, and took Titus with me also. And I went up by revelation, and communicated unto them that gospel which I preach among the Gentiles, but privately to them which were of reputation, lest by any

means I should run, or had run, in vain. But neither Titus, who was with me, being a Greek, was compelled to be circumcised: and that because of false brethren unawares brought in, who came in privily to spy out our liberty which we have in Christ Jesus, that they might bring us into bondage; to whom we gave place by subjection, no, not for an hour; that the truth of the gospel might continue with you.

But of these who seemed to be somewhat, (whatsoever they were, it maketh no matter to me: God accepteth no man's person:) for they who seemed to be somewhat in conference added nothing to me.

Meditating Before God

Paul had seen his beloved Galatians ripped apart by the Judaizers who were accusing him. They were saying, "Who does Paul think he is? He is the man that persecuted the Christians. Now almost overnight he says he is a Christian and an apostle. But he was not even numbered among the original twelve and here he is trying to tell you Galatians what the real gospel is. He has left out the law of Moses and has made it by grace alone." Paul cuts right across everything by saying that he had met Christ who had given him a revelation, and after he received Christ he went off alone into the deserts of Arabia and meditated before God.

I believe Paul did his meditation and learning by two methods. I believe he spent time in the desert restudying the Old Testament and all the prophets. He knew them almost by heart anyway. But I also believe that the Holy Spirit, who lived in and had filled Paul, became his teacher. I believe that Paul's prayer language of the Spirit and the interpretation back to his mind played a far greater role than any of us have ever been taught or imagined.

Why would he pray in tongues? Well, the Holy Spirit through tongues brought the inner therapy he desperately needed. He never completely got over having persecuted the Church of the living Christ. There was a great wound and hurt in him that although he did it in ignorance, he still had persecuted the Church. So to have the Holy Spirit's therapy for such a horrible experience was absolutely necessary. Paul himself tells us in I Corinthians 14 that he that speaketh in a tongue edifieth himself. That is to say, the Holy Spirit reaches down deep inside us and there begins to give the therapy that we must have.

Galatians 2:7-10

> But contrariwise, when they saw that the gospel of the uncircumcision was committed unto me, as the gospel of the circumcision was unto Peter; (For he that wrought effectually in Peter to the apostleship of the circumcision, the same was mighty in me toward the Gentiles:) and when James, Cephas, and John, who seemed to be pillars, perceived the grace that was given unto me, they gave to me and Barnabas the right hands of fellowship; that we should go unto the heathen, and they unto the circumcision. Only they would that we should remember the poor; the same which I also was forward to do.

"In answer to the critics," he says, "I went back to the Christian leaders themselves and met with them personally. They gave us the right hand of fellowship. They told us to remember the poor, which we had already been doing. They and I agreed that Peter was called to be the apostle to the Jews and I was called to be the apostle to the Gentile world."

Galatians 2:11-21

> But when Peter was come to Antioch, I withstood him to the face, because he was to be blamed. For before that certain came from James, he did eat with the Gentiles: but when they were come, he withdrew and separated himself, fearing them which were of the circumcision. And the other Jews dissembled likewise with him; insomuch that Barnabas also was carried away with their dissimulation. But when I saw that they walked not uprightly according to the truth of the gospel, I said unto Peter before them all, If thou, being a Jew, livest after the manner of Gentiles, and not as do the Jews, why compellest thou the Gentiles to live as do the Jews?
>
> We who are Jews by nature, and not sinners of the Gentiles, knowing that a man is not justified by the works of the law, but by the faith of Jesus Christ, even we have believed in Jesus Christ, that we might be justified by the faith of Christ, and not by the works of the law: for by the works of the law shall no flesh be justified.
>
> But if, while we seek to be justified by Christ, we ourselves also are found sinners, is therefore Christ the minister of sin? God forbid. For if I build again the things which I destroyed, I make myself a transgressor. For I through the law am dead to the law, that I might live unto God. I am crucified with Christ: nevertheless I live; yet not I, but Christ liveth in me: and the life which I now live in the flesh I live by the faith of the Son of God, who loved me, and gave himself for me. I do not frustrate the grace of God: for if righteousness come by the law, then Christ is dead in vain.

Living by Faith

Paul says to the Galatians, "I even stood up to Peter and won on this very issue that we are talking about. For the life that I live in my human flesh I live by the faith I have in the Son of God who loved me and gave himself for me. I am not going to weaken the gospel by mixing it with the law of Moses which has been fulfilled."

Galatians 3:1-7

O foolish Galatians, who hath bewitched you, that ye should not obey the truth, before whose eyes Jesus Christ hath been evidently set forth, crucified among you? This only would I learn of you, Received ye the Spirit by the works of the law, or by the hearing of faith? Are ye so foolish? having begun in the Spirit, are ye now made perfect by the flesh? Have ye suffered so many things in vain? if it be yet in vain. He therefore that ministereth to you the Spirit, and worketh miracles among you, doeth he it by the works of the law, or by the hearing of faith? Even as Abraham believed God, and it was accounted to him for righteousness.

Know ye therefore that they which are of faith, the same are the children of Abraham.

Paul was concerned about the inroads the Judaizers were making among his beloved Galatians. He says, "I want to ask you a question. When you received the Holy Spirit, was I up there talking to you about the law of Moses, or was I preaching the Word of God to you? And as you heard it, did you believe? The miracles that have been done through you and among you, were those done by the works of the law or by the hearing of faith? Do you not know that it is we who are of faith who are the real children of Abraham?"

Galatians 3:8-18

And the scripture, foreseeing that God would justify the heathen through faith, preached before the gospel unto Abraham, saying, In thee shall all nations be blessed. So then they which be of faith are blessed with faithful Abraham. For as many as are of the works of the law are under the curse: for it is written, Cursed is every one that continueth not in all things which are written in the book of the law to do them.

But that no man is justified by the law in the sight of God, it is evident: for, The just shall live by faith. And the law is not of faith: but, The man that doeth them shall live in them. Christ hath redeemed us from the curse of the law, being made a curse for us: for it is written, Cursed is every one that hangeth on a tree: that the blessing of Abraham might come on the Gentiles through Jesus Christ; that we might receive the promise of the Spirit through faith.

Brethren, I speak after the manner of men; Though it be but a man's covenant, yet if it be confirmed, no man disannulleth, or addeth thereto. Now to Abraham and his seed were the promises made. He saith not, And to seeds, as of many; but as of one, And to thy seed, which is Christ. And this I say, that the covenant, that was confirmed before of God in Christ, the law, which was four hundred and thirty years after, cannot disannul, that it should make the promise of none effect. For if the inheritance be of the law, it is no more of promise: but God gave it to Abraham by promise.

Paul is talking about a special orientation here that began with Abraham. Abraham, by his faith, was running forward toward God to obey Him and go where God told him to go. So he is saying, "If your orientation is to the law of Moses, you are looking back over your shoulder at sin that is trying to catch up with you while you are running from it. But, if you are in the Christian faith, you're looking forward to God the same way that Abraham did."

Galatians 3:19-29

Wherefore then serveth the law? It was added because of transgressions, till the seed should come to whom the promise was made; and it was ordained by angels in the hand of a mediator. Now a mediator is not a mediator of one, but God is one. Is the law then against the promises of God? God forbid: for if there had been a law given which could have given life, verily righteousness should have been by the law. But the scripture hath concluded all under sin, that the promise by faith of Jesus Christ might be given to them that believe.

But before faith came, we were kept under the law, shut up unto the faith which should afterwards be revealed. Wherefore the law was our schoolmaster to bring us unto Christ, that we might be justified by faith. But after that faith is come, we are no longer under a schoolmaster. For ye are all the children of God by faith in Christ Jesus. For as many of you as have been baptized into Christ have put on Christ. There is neither Jew nor Greek, there is neither bond nor free, there is neither male nor female: for ye are all one in Christ Jesus. And if ye be Christ's, then are ye Abraham's seed, and heirs according to the promise.

Passing From Childhood Into Adulthood

In virtually every culture there is a period of time when a child passes from childhood into adulthood. Paul is saying that the law of Moses is like that. In our childhood, when God could not deal with us any other way, He gave us the law of Moses so we would learn we were sinners and understand that we needed a Redeemer. But when we moved into adulthood, that is the point where Christ came and fulfilled the law of Moses. He became the sacrifice once and for all and opened the kingdom of God so that we could enter into a life of faith and go from childhood into adulthood.

Paul adds that now we are on Christ's side of things, all differences are immaterial. We no longer look at people as Jews or Greeks, as slaves or free, as male or female, but as human beings. For we are all the children of God by faith in Jesus Christ.

Galatians 4:1-11

> Now I say, That the heir, as long as he is a child, differeth nothing from a servant, though he be lord of all; but is under tutors and governors until the time appointed of the father. Even so we, when we were children, were in bondage under the elements of the world: but when the fulness of the time was come, God sent forth his Son, made of a woman, made under the law, to redeem them that were under the law, that we might receive the adoption of sons. And because ye are sons, God hath sent forth the Spirit of his Son into your hearts, crying, Abba, Father. Wherefore thou art no more a servant, but a son; and if a son, then an heir of God through Christ.
>
> Howbeit then, when ye knew not God, ye did service unto them which by nature are no gods. But now, after that ye have known God, or rather are known of God, how turn ye again to the weak and beggarly elements, whereunto ye desire again to be in bondage? Ye observe days, and months, and times, and years. I am afraid of you, lest I have bestowed upon you labour in vain.

Paul tells them that he has a great fear lest he has spent his labor in vain for them, because it looks as if they have gone back to their childhood. They cling to the law by observing the different feasts and years: the sabbath year, the seventh year, and the year of jubilee. Paul is fearful that they will slip back into legalism which will bring about the destruction of the faith that has come into their hearts.

Galatians 4:12-5:1

> Brethren, I beseech you, be as I am; for I am as ye are: ye have not injured me at all. Ye know how through infirmity of the flesh I preached the gospel unto you at the first. And my temptation which was in my

363

flesh ye despised not, nor rejected; but received me as an angel of God, even as Christ Jesus.

Where is then the blessedness ye spake of? for I bear you record, that, if it had been possible, ye would have plucked out your own eyes, and have given them to me. Am I therefore become your enemy, because I tell you the truth? They zealously affect you, but not well; yea, they would exclude you, that ye might affect them. But it is good to be zealously affected always in a good thing, and not only when I am present with you.

My little children, of whom I travail in birth again until Christ be formed in you, I desire to be present with you now, and to change my voice; for I stand in doubt of you. Tell me, ye that desire to be under the law, do ye not hear the law? For it is written, that Abraham had two sons, the one by a bondmaid, the other by a freewoman. But he who was of the bondwoman was born after the flesh; but he of the freewoman was by promise.

Which things are an allegory: for these are the two covenants; the one from the mount Sinai, which gendereth to bondage, which is Agar. For this Agar is mount Sinai in Arabia, and answereth to Jerusalem which now is, and is in bondage with her children. But Jerusalem which is above is free, which is the mother of us all. For it is written, Rejoice, thou barren that bearest not; break forth and cry, thou that travailest not: for the desolate hath many more children than she which hath an husband.

Now we, brethren, as Isaac was, are the children of promise. But as then he that was born after the flesh persecuted him that was born after the Spirit, even so it is now. Nevertheless what saith the scripture? Cast out the bondwoman and her son: for the son of the bondwoman shall not be heir with the son of the freewoman. So then, brethren, we are not children of the bondwoman, but of the free. Stand fast therefore in the liberty wherewith Christ hath made us free, and be not entangled again with the yoke of bondage.

A Spiritual Illustration

Paul is saying several things here. First, he is saying, "If you cannot accept all the things that I am explaining to you, then just remember who I am. Remember my relationship with you and that I travailed for your birth. I brought the gospel to you and am willing to do it again."

Then he gave them an illustration about the birth of Ishmael and of Isaac. You remember that Abraham and Sarah could not have children because of her barrenness. God had promised them that they would bear a son, and through him the seed of Abraham would spread over the world to be a light to the nations. But as they grew older and they approached the time when even Abraham might not be productive, Sarah suggested that she give him her bondwoman, Hagar, and let him procreate a child through her. That would be the son of promise. Abraham did that and Ishmael was born.

Later, however, God revived Abraham and Sarah's bodies in their old age and Sarah bore the child Isaac to fulfill the promise of God. As Ishmael and Isaac grew up together, it was not long before Ishmael began to persecute Isaac, who was the son of promise. Because of this, Sarah told Abraham to cast out the bondwoman and her son, and Abraham obeyed. Therefore, it was through Isaac then that the seed of Abraham was produced.

Paul picks up on this and compares Hagar and her son Ishmael to Mount Sinai and the giving of the law. He says, "As Ishmael persecuted Isaac and the law is persecuting the gospel of Jesus Christ, do you not understand that you are free, you are not the children of the bondwoman, but of the free? So stand therefore in the freedom that you have in Christ. It is Christ who makes you free, who untangled you from the yoke of bondage and brought you into faith."

Galatians 5:2-26

Behold, I Paul say unto you, that if ye be circumcised, Christ shall profit you nothing. For I testify again to every man that is circumcised, that he is a debtor to do the whole law. Christ is become of no effect unto you, whosoever of you are justified by the law; ye are fallen from grace. For we through the Spirit wait for the hope of righteousness by faith. For in Jesus Christ neither circumcision availeth any thing, nor uncircumcision; but faith which worketh by love. Ye did run well; who did hinder you that ye should not obey the truth? This persuasion cometh not of him that calleth you.

A little leaven leaveneth the whole lump. I have confidence in you through the Lord, that ye will be none otherwise minded: but he that troubleth you shall bear his judgment, whosoever he be. And I, brethren, if I yet preach circumcision, why do I yet suffer persecution? then is the offence of the cross ceased. I would they were even cut off which trouble you. For, brethren, ye have been called unto liberty; only use not liberty for an occasion to the flesh, but by love serve one another. For all the law is fulfilled in one word, even in this; Thou shalt love thy neighbour as thyself. But if ye bite and devour one another, take heed that ye be not consumed one of another. This I say then, Walk in the Spirit, and ye shall not fulfil the lust of the flesh.

For the flesh lusteth against the Spirit, and the Spirit against the flesh: and these are contrary the one to the other: so that ye cannot do the thing that ye would. But if ye be led of the Spirit, ye are not under the law. Now the works of the flesh are manifest, which are these; Adultery, fornication, uncleanness, lasciviousness, idolatry, witchcraft, hatred, variance, emulations, wrath, strife, seditions, heresies, envyings, murders, drunkenness, revellings, and such like: of the which I tell you before, as I have also told you in time past, that they which do such things shall not inherit the kingdom of God. But the fruit of the Spirit is love, joy, peace, longsuffering, gentleness, goodness, faith, meekness, temperance: against such there is no law. And they that are Christ's have crucified the flesh with the affections and lusts. If we live in the Spirit, let us also walk in the Spirit. Let us not be desirous of vain glory, provoking one another, envying one another.

Paul says, "I do not mean to say that Christ's freedom gives you license to do anything you want to do. You are ruled by love and you are to love your neighbor as yourself. If you interpret giving up circumcision and getting into faith as a license to do your own thing, then you are going to get entangled in the works of the flesh: adultery, fornication, uncleanness, idolatry, witchcraft, murders, drunkenness, and all these things. But if you live in the Spirit and walk in the Spirit, you will produce the fruit of the Spirit: love, joy, peace, longsuffering, gentleness, goodness, faith, meekness, and temperance. And against the fruit of the Spirit there is no law."

We are coming to the very key issue. But before we do, I want to stop and pray because it takes the power of God to change us so that we can grow the fruit of the Spirit.

> *Heavenly Father, it is Your Holy Spirit who indwells us and who enables us to grow in our love for You, our joy in Christ, our peace in the midst of this world; longsuffering when we are struck on every side; gentleness when it is our tendency not to be gentle; goodness in the midst of the devil's activity to make us bad and to do bad things; faith rather than fear or unbelief; meekness so that we depend upon You; and temperance so we are balanced in our lives. We are believing You today that we have the faith to produce these fruits as Your Spirit works with our spirit to grow them. Father, we are determined that we are going to grow the fruit of the Spirit in our lives every day through Your help. Amen and amen.*

Galatians 6:1-10

Brethren, if a man be overtaken in a fault, ye which are spiritual, restore such an one in the spirit of meekness; considering thyself, lest thou also be tempted. Bear ye one another's burdens, and so fulfil the law of Christ. For if a man think himself to be something, when he is nothing, he deceiveth himself. But let every man prove his own work, and then shall he have rejoicing in himself alone, and not in another. For every man shall bear his own burden. Let him that is taught in the word communicate unto him that teacheth in all good things. Be not deceived; God is not mocked: for whatsoever a man soweth, that shall he also reap. For he that soweth to his flesh shall of the flesh reap corruption; but he that soweth to the Spirit shall of the Spirit reap life everlasting. And let us not be weary in well doing: for in due season we shall reap, if we faint not. As we have therefore opportunity, let us do good unto all men, especially unto them who are of the household of faith.

Do Not Be Like the Judaizers

Paul is reminding the Galatians that the Judaizers had come in and set them into ranks and classes by saying, "Those of you who do what we say are better than those who do not do what we say." So Paul states, "That is not right. For when one of you has a fault or you fall into something that is unlike God, you do not lord it over the person but come to him in the spirit of meekness, considering yourself that you too might be tempted. In other words, bear one another's burdens. Instead of criticizing one another, pick each other up and feel that it is your own burden and that you are sitting where he sits and feeling what he feels. For do not be deceived. You really cannot mock God. For whatever a man sows that is what he is going to reap. If he sows after his flesh he will reap corruptible things. But if he sows after the Spirit, it will be of the Spirit that he reaps. And if it seems like a long time before your harvest comes, do not get discouraged because there is a due season for every seed to be harvested."

Galatians 6:11-18

Ye see how large a letter I have written unto you with mine own hand. As many as desire to make a fair shew in the flesh, they constrain you to be circumcised; only lest they should suffer persecution for the cross of Christ. For neither they themselves who are circumcised keep the law; but desire to have you circumcised, that they may glory in your flesh. But God forbid that I should glory, save in the cross of our Lord Jesus Christ, by whom the world is crucified unto me, and I unto the world. For in Christ Jesus neither circumcision availeth any thing, nor uncircumcision, but a new creature. And as many as walk according to this rule, peace be on them, and mercy, and upon the Israel of God. From henceforth let no man trouble me: for I bear in my body the marks of the Lord Jesus. Brethren, the grace of our Lord Jesus Christ be with your spirit. Amen.

Paul had been dictating this letter to a secretary as was his custom. But as he came to the end of it, he took the pen in his own hand and said, "Now look at how large the letters are I am writing. I want you to know that I am writing this and closing it with my own handwriting in letters big enough for you to see. And I want you to know and understand that the cross and the resurrection are what the gospel is all about."

Then he concludes by saying, "Brethren, the grace (or the unmerited favor) of our Lord Jesus Christ be with your spirit." That is Paul's last word to the Galatians — grace. And I believe that is an appropriate way to end this book. For grace is the only word that really matters.

The Epistle of Paul the Apostle to the
Ephesians

The Epistle of Paul
the Apostle to the
Ephesians

Many Bible scholars believe that Paul's letter to the Christians at Ephesus is the greatest letter he ever wrote. They believe it contains the core of all he taught and that it is the highest expression of God's revelation to Paul for the people who follow Jesus Christ. I am very excited about this book myself. I do not believe, however, that we can begin the book of Ephesians at Chapter 1 and Verse 1 and understand what Paul was writing for that time and for our time today. I believe we have to go back to the 19th chapter of Acts to see that the Ephesian church was an openly charismatic church.

I believe that all the churches in the early church of the First Century were charismatic and that they operated under the power of the Holy Spirit through the gifts of the Spirit and the fruit of the Spirit. I believe that was the h:ghest aim of all those who accepted Jesus Christ. When Paul wrote his letters, however, he had to write to the individual churches at their level of understanding. For example, the Corinthians had come out of a corrupt background and their level of understanding of the charismatic power of God was not as high. Therefore, Paul had to deal with the Corinthian church in a manner that they could understand and thereby rise to the heights of the charismatic power of God working in and through their lives. When Paul wrote to the Galatians, he had to deal with faith as the power greater than the law of Moses. But when he wrote to the Ephesians, he had the greatest opportunity to fully express himself without having to deal with serious flaws. There was a need among the Ephesians for greater unity, but it was not comparable to the need in most of the other churches to whom Paul wrote letters.

I want you to notice in the 19th chapter of Acts that when Paul came to Ephesus, he found certain disciples, 12 in number, who were worshiping God and looking forward to the coming of the

Messiah. Immediately, however, he discerned that the power of the Holy Spirit was not working in them. So he asked, "Have you received the Holy Spirit since you believed?" They said they had not even heard if there was a Holy Spirit. When he asked them to give an account of their spiritual relationship with God, they referred him back to John the Baptist. Paul accepted that but added that there was something more. He told them the Messiah had come in the person of Jesus Christ. When they heard that, they believed on Jesus and were baptized in His name. Paul then laid his hands on them, the Holy Spirit fell on all 12 of them, and they immediately released their prayer language.

These charismatic people, although only 12 in number, began to move in the gifts and the fruit of the Holy Spirit and became the nucleus upon which the whole Ephesian church was built. And when they came together, they created tremendous things by their faith. For example, in Acts 19:11 we read that God wrought special miracles by the hands of Paul so that from his body handkerchiefs and aprons were taken to the sick, and diseases departed from them and evil spirits went out of them. The Ephesian church understood that Paul was so filled with the Holy Spirit that points of contact could be taken from his anointed body, laid upon the sick, and the Spirit would help the people release their faith.

Following that manifestation of the Spirit in Ephesus, Paul's ministry and that of the charismatic Christians became so powerful that the Jews and Greeks who possessed books of magic gathered and burned them because they learned that the name of Jesus could not be used magically. Later, there was a mob scene in which Paul was accused of interrupting the worship of the goddess Diana whom millions of people worshiped. But the Spirit of God moved and delivered Paul from their hands. We are told that he spent over two years there, so he knew the Ephesians person by person and group by group. When he departed, he left a thriving charismatic church moving in the gifts and fruit of the Holy Spirit. So as he sits there in a Roman prison, chained to a guard, his mind goes back to the beloved ones in Ephesus that he led to Christ and established in the faith. His heart is overflowing.

Ephesians 1:1

> Paul, an apostle of Jesus Christ by the will of God, to the saints which are at Ephesus, and to the faithful in Christ Jesus: . . .

When Paul wrote to people, he wrote to them as an apostle. Here he includes not only the Ephesians but all who are faithful in Christ

372

Jesus.

Ephesians 1:2-8

Grace be to you, and peace, from God our Father, and from the Lord Jesus Christ. Blessed be the God and Father of our Lord Jesus Christ, who hath blessed us with all spiritual blessings in heavenly places in Christ: according as he hath chosen us in him before the foundation of the world, that we should be holy and without blame before him in love: having predestinated us unto the adoption of children by Jesus Christ to himself, according to the good pleasure of his will, to the praise of the glory of his grace, wherein he hath made us accepted in the beloved.

In whom we have redemption through his blood, the forgiveness of sins, according to the riches of his grace; wherein he hath abounded toward us in all wisdom and prudence . . .

Paul is saying that God has a plan for all of us and that plan includes a holy life lived by divine love because we have been adopted by Christ into the family of God. You recall that the family of God was the Jewish nation, the descendants of Abraham. But now Jesus himself has adopted us and given us the full rights and privileges of a child of God.

Ephesians 1:9-23

Having made known unto us the mystery of his will, according to his good pleasure which he hath purposed in himself: that in the dispensation of the fulness of times he might gather together in one all things in Christ, both which are in heaven, and which are on earth; even in him: in whom also we have obtained an inheritance, being predestinated according to the purpose of him who worketh all things after the counsel of his own will: that we should be to the praise of his glory, who first trusted in Christ.

In whom ye also trusted, after that ye heard the word of truth, the gospel of your salvation: in whom also after that ye believed, ye were sealed with that holy Spirit of promise, which is the earnest of our inheritance until the redemption of the purchased possession, unto the praise of his glory.

Wherefore I also, after I heard of your faith in the Lord Jesus, and love unto all the saints, cease not to give thanks for you, making mention of you in my prayers, that the God of our Lord Jesus Christ, the Father of glory, may give unto you the spirit of wisdom and revelation in the knowledge of him: the eyes of your understanding

373

being enlightened; that ye may know what is the hope of his calling, and what the riches of the glory of his inheritance in the saints, and what is the exceeding greatness of his power to us-ward who believe, according to the working of his mighty power, which he wrought in Christ, when he raised him from the dead, and set him at his own right hand in the heavenly places, far above all principality, and power, and might, and dominion, and every name that is named, not only in this world, but also in that which is to come: and hath put all things under his feet, and gave him to be the head over all things to the church, which is his body, the fulness of him that filleth all in all.

The Name Above All Names

Paul is telling you and me that while we have access to the wisdom and the knowledge of mortal man, we also have access to the wisdom of the deep things of God. And as we harmonize that wisdom with the written Word of God, we have a wisdom and knowledge that is not found in the books of this world or in the mouths of people.

Paul then tells you and me where Christ is. He says that God raised Christ from the dead and actually set Him down at His right hand far above all principalities, powers, mights, and dominions. Far above all Satan's powers and kingdoms Jesus has been elevated. The name of Jesus is above every name that is named. Therefore, we ought to focus our faith on the one whose name is above everything. Jesus' name is above every sin. His name is above every disease. Jesus' name is above every demon. Jesus' name is above all fear. The name of Jesus is above all our needs. Jesus' name is above every opposing force. Jesus' name is so great that God says, "I have put all things under His feet."

Jesus Christ of Nazareth is the head of God's Church, the Body of Christ, and that is where you and I are today. We are under that name. That name is in our hearts. The Holy Spirit has witnessed to our spirits that the name of Jesus lives in us. I want to pray with you concerning the name of Jesus being above everything that is named in this world and the world to come.

> *Father, I know that any power of the devil that is attacking us spiritually is under the name of Jesus. Anything attacking us mentally is under the dominion of our Savior. Any sickness or disease afflicting our bodies is under the name of Jesus. Any financial problem, family trouble, or anything that is coming*

*against us, is under the name that is above every name, the
mighty incomparable name of our Savior, Jesus Christ of
Nazareth.*

*And partner, as you release your faith in Christ, I pray that
the name of Jesus will deliver you from the crown of your head
to the soles of your feet and that God will heal you. I believe
this, and I stand in agreement with you that it is happening right
now and will continue to happen in your life. I believe it through
Jesus Christ and I accept His name above everything that is
named in this world and the world to come. Amen and amen.*

Ephesians 2:1-10

And you hath he quickened, who were dead in trespasses and sins;
wherein in time past ye walked according to the course of this world,
according to the prince of the power of the air, the spirit that now
worketh in the children of disobedience: among whom also we all
had our conversation in times past in the lusts of our flesh, fulfilling
the desires of the flesh and of the mind; and were by nature the
children of wrath, even as others.

But God, who is rich in mercy, for his great love wherewith he
loved us, even when we were dead in sins, hath quickened us together
with Christ, (by grace ye are saved;) and hath raised us up together,
and made us sit together in heavenly places in Christ Jesus: that in
the ages to come he might shew the exceeding riches of his grace in
his kindness toward us through Christ Jesus.

For by grace are ye saved through faith; and that not of yourselves:
it is the gift of God: not of works, lest any man should boast. For we
are his workmanship, created in Christ Jesus unto good works, which
God hath before ordained that we should walk in them.

Paul is reminding them and us that God quickened us while we
were dead in sin. Here, the word "sins" is the Greek word "himartia."
It means "missing the mark." The word "trespasses" is the Greek
word "paratoma," which means "slipping or falling from the truth."
These two words are combined to describe our death in sin. In other
words, we slipped, missed the mark, and have completely failed. It
is like walking a treacherous road in the darkest of nights without
a light.

When Paul says we were dead in trespasses and sins, he in effect
says that sin is a killer. Sin kills innocence. It kills ideals. And it kills
the will so that the will becomes weak and in bondage to the devil.

But we who were once dead in trespasses and sins have been

quickened, or raised up, so that we are delivered from the power of the devil. We are delivered from death because God who is rich in mercy reached down and raised us up just as He raised Christ from the dead and set Him at His right hand. In like manner, God sets us down in heavenly places in Christ Jesus. He is really saying that the Christian has two addresses, one on the earth and the other in heaven. He has two citizenships, one here in some nation, and the other in heaven.

Ephesians 2:11-22

> Wherefore remember, that ye being in time past Gentiles in the flesh, who are called Uncircumcision by that which is called the Circumcision in the flesh made by hands; that at that time ye were without Christ, being aliens from the commonwealth of Israel, and strangers from the covenants of promise, having no hope, and without God in the world: but now in Christ Jesus ye who sometimes were far off are made nigh by the blood of Christ. For he is our peace, who hath made both one, and hath broken down the middle wall of partition between us; having abolished in his flesh the enmity, even the law of commandments contained in ordinances; for to make in himself of twain one new man, so making peace; and that he might reconcile both unto God in one body by the cross, having slain the enmity thereby: and came and preached peace to you which were afar off, and to them that were nigh. For through him we both have access by one Spirit unto the Father.
>
> Now therefore ye are no more strangers and foreigners, but fellowcitizens with the saints, and of the household of God; and are built upon the foundation of the apostles and prophets, Jesus Christ himself being the chief corner stone; in whom all the building fitly framed together groweth unto an holy temple in the Lord: in whom ye also are builded together for an habitation of God through the Spirit.

Unity Through Christ

Paul tells the Ephesian Gentiles that they were once aliens from the family of God and strangers from the covenants. They were without Christ and had no hope. But now through the price of the blood of Christ, the Gentiles who believed have been made one because Christ broke down the middle wall that divided Jew from Gentile.

Paul is speaking of the temple in Jerusalem that had several courts, one leading to the other. The outer courtyard was the court of the

Gentiles, and there was a wall between it and the next courtyard, the court of the women of Israel. That courtyard was separated by a wall from the court of the Israelites, which was likewise separated by a wall from the court of the priests. Just over the wall from that courtyard was the Holy of Holies where the high priest went to take the blood and place it on the mercy seat so that God could roll back the people's sins for another year. When the Gentiles came to Jerusalem, even as proselytes to the Jewish faith, they could only stand in the court of the Gentiles. If they tried to get beyond that courtyard, there was a wall and the penalty of death.

Paul declares, however, that the blood of Christ has broken down that wall. Christ abolished it in His flesh on the cross. He set aside the enmity between Gentiles and Jews and made us one with God as our Father, the Holy Spirit as our Comforter, and Christ as our Redeemer. We are now brothers and sisters in Jesus Christ. For we are built upon the foundation of the apostles and prophets, and Jesus Christ himself is the chief cornerstone who fashions the building together as a holy temple of God. Jesus brings His people together, both Jew and Gentile, as the habitation of God through the Holy Spirit. It is not a temple made with hands. It is the habitation of God built through our faith in Jesus Christ who is the cornerstone of that new building.

Ephesians 3:1-19

For this cause I Paul, the prisoner of Jesus Christ for you Gentiles, if ye have heard of the dispensation of the grace of God which is given me to you-ward: how that by revelation he made known unto me the mystery; (as I wrote afore in few words, whereby, when ye read, ye may understand my knowledge in the mystery of Christ) which in other ages was not made known unto the sons of men, as it is now revealed unto his holy apostles and prophets by the Spirit; that the Gentiles should be fellowheirs, and of the same body, and partakers of his promise in Christ by the gospel: whereof I was made a minister, according to the gift of the grace of God given unto me by the effectual working of his power.

Unto me, who am less than the least of all saints, is this grace given, that I should preach among the Gentiles the unsearchable riches of Christ; and to make all men see what is the fellowship of the mystery, which from the beginning of the world hath been hid in God, who created all things by Jesus Christ: to the intent that now unto the principalities and powers in heavenly places might be known by the church the manifold wisdom of God, according to the eternal purpose which he purposed in Christ Jesus our Lord: in whom we have boldness and access with confidence by the faith of him.

Wherefore I desire that ye faint not at my tribulations for you, which is your glory. For this cause I bow my knees unto the Father of our Lord Jesus Christ, of whom the whole family in heaven and earth is named, that he would grant you, according to the riches of his glory, to be strengthened with might by his Spirit in the inner man; that Christ may dwell in your hearts by faith; that ye, being rooted and grounded in love, may be able to comprehend with all saints what is the breadth, and length, and depth, and height; and to know the love of Christ, which passeth knowledge, that ye might be filled with all the fulness of God.

A Matter of the Heart

The old Jewish way of praying was to stand and raise the hands to God. But here is a Jew by the name of Paul who is so in awe of the glory of God that he bows his knees. He just had to get down on his knees and pray. Let me point out, though, that Paul is not establishing a one-and-only way to pray, because prayer is from the heart and spirit. You can pray lying down, sitting down, standing up, walking, running, or riding. It depends on the condition of your heart.

Ephesians 3:20,21
> Now unto him that is able to do exceeding abundantly above all that we ask or think, according to the power that worketh in us, unto him be glory in the church by Christ Jesus throughout all ages, world without end. Amen.

Paul is saying that God is in us to help us achieve above all we can ask or think. Can you imagine what you can ask for? Can you conceive of what you can think? Far above that, God's Spirit will explode inside you and give you the ability to think and to ask. And I say that it is about time you and I did it.

As we begin reading the fourth chapter of Ephesians, I would like to remind you that Paul has dealt with the great eternal truths of God in the first three chapters. He is now going into the practical applications of those truths on the basis of how to be united together with our brothers and sisters in Christ. I would also like to point out that Paul brought this gospel of Christ's unity into a totally

378

disunited world. True, the Roman army had captured the civilized world and made a forced peace. But there was no real unity. The world was absolutely divided and racial prejudice was rampant. The Greeks were the learned people and they despised everyone else. The Romans conquered the Greeks and made them slaves. The Jews considered themselves the chosen people of the world. But there was a new group, the Christians, who sprung up and were trying to exhibit a new kind of love to the world.

There are four different Greek terms for the word "love." One is "eros," the love of a man for a woman. There is "philia," brotherly love. There is "storgy," family love. And then there is "agape," the pure and undefiled love of God that loves regardless of the value, or lack of value, a person may have. This is the type of love that Paul talked about, for it is the only love that could bring unity to a world of prejudice and hatred. And Paul began to speak of that kind of love and unity which was new in the world. And therefore, as we read this fourth chapter, we're going to learn how to bring ourselves under the control of God as His property, not belonging to ourselves.

Ephesians 4:1-8

> I therefore, the prisoner of the Lord, beseech you that ye walk worthy of the vocation wherewith ye are called, with all lowliness and meekness, with longsuffering, forbearing one another in love; endeavouring to keep the unity of the Spirit in the bond of peace. There is one body, and one Spirit, even as ye are called in one hope of your calling; one Lord, one faith, one baptism, one God and Father of all, who is above all, and through all, and in you all.
>
> But unto every one of us is given grace according to the measure of the gift of Christ. Wherefore he saith, When he ascended up on high, he led captivity captive, and gave gifts unto men.

Paul begins this chapter by saying he is the Lord's prisoner. In other words, he is God's property and is controlled by Him. Paul in turn tells the Ephesians, and us today, to come under the same control of God. My friend, there is a control of God over our lives to the extent that even a whisper from Him into our souls will turn us around. Just a word inside us or a scripture that speaks to our hearts can cause us to check ourselves and remember we are God's property and do not belong to ourselves.

Therefore, we should endeavor to unite with one another. We should play down our differences and lift up our sameness, our agreements, and the areas where we are alike in the Lord. For

Ephesians says there is only one body and one Spirit. And because there is only one body and one Spirit, we serve one Lord by one faith through one baptism and follow one God who is the Father of us all.

Ephesians 4:9-13

(Now that he ascended, what is it but that he also descended first into the lower parts of the earth? He that descended is the same also that ascended up far above all heavens, that he might fill all things.)

And he gave some, apostles; and some, prophets; and some, evangelists; and some, pastors and teachers; for the perfecting of the saints, for the work of the ministry, for the edifying of the body of Christ: till we all come in the unity of the faith, and of the knowledge of the Son of God, unto a perfect man, unto the measure of the stature of the fulness of Christ.

Christ's Gifts and the Ministry Callings

Notice in Verse 9 that when Jesus ascended He had first descended into the lower parts of the earth. In Luke 16:26 we studied how that before Christ's death and resurrection there was a place called Hades, or hell, located somewhere in the lower parts of the earth. All the souls of those who died, including those who had faith in the coming Messiah and those who did not, went there. St. Luke describes it as being divided with an inseparable gulf. On one side was paradise where the souls of the righteous went, people like Abraham, Isaac, and Jacob. On the other side was hell, the place of torment. Those in paradise could not pass into hell and those in hell could not pass into paradise. Those who died and went to hell were without hope. But those who died and went to paradise had hope of the coming Messiah.

So when Christ shed His blood at Calvary and rose from the dead, there was a moment before He ascended to His Father in heaven that He first descended to the lower parts of the earth. There He proclaimed His victory. In effect He said to Abraham and the others, "I am the Messiah, I have shed My blood for the sins of the people, I have died, I have been raised from the dead, I am King of Kings and Lord of Lords, and I have come to gather you up so that when I ascend you are going with me."

I thank God that in one matchless moment of history Jesus gathered up the souls of the righteous dead and up He went far above all kingdoms, powers, and principalities of the devil to the city of God. And with those righteous souls He swept into the presence of God, sat down at the Father's right hand, and broke out the gifts. He broke out the gifts of the Holy Spirit and began to pour them down upon His people. Hallelujah!

When Jesus ascended with the souls of the righteous dead, He abolished the part of Hades called paradise. So since His ascension, when a Christian's body dies, his soul does not go into paradise, the upper part of Hades. But immediately, in the twinkling of an eye, his soul leaves his mortal flesh and is in the presence of the heavenly Father. There it awaits the resurrection of the body from the dead when Jesus returns the second time.

Paul also says in this passage that God has given gifts in the form of apostles, prophets, evangelists, pastors, and teachers — the five ministry callings under which all other callings are placed. Paul establishes them as set in the Church by God. He says each of these five callings is absolutely sacred, divine, unalterable, and eternally ordained of God. I want to look at these callings one by one.

The word "apostle" is a Jewish word that originated from the action of the Sanhedrin. The Sanhedrin was composed of 70 learned Jewish men who were the governing body of the Jews. When they had a special task to be carried out they gave it to a person called an "apostilos." Backed by the full force of the Sanhedrin, he was to perform his special mission. The Christians took the word "apostle" from this and said that an apostle had to have seen Jesus and been a witness of His resurrection. An apostle today is a person who has been given a specific mission, a divine calling that is usually worldwide and certainly church-wide. So the effect of an apostle's ministry is felt everywhere.

A prophet is set in the Church the same way an apostle is. Whether the prophet is a man or a woman, he or she is given revelational knowledge based on the written Word of God. The Holy Spirit reveals to their spirits knowledge that must be shared. People hear that knowledge and have to judge it by the Word. So everyone who is a prophet is happy to submit his prophecy to those who are called of God. The third calling is that of the evangelist. He or she is the person who usually speaks to people who do not know Christ. We would think of the evangelist as a Marine who goes in first and softens up the area for the infantry to follow. And, of course, it is the pastors and teachers who follow to shepherd those won to Christ.

Notice the first three callings — apostles, prophets, and evangelists — touch the whole of the Church while the pastor and teacher are more on a local level. What is the reason? Verse 12 says it is for the perfecting of the saints. In other words, the ministry

callings are to instruct the people of God on this earth until we all
come to unity and until we all get to heaven.

Ephesians 4:14-16

> That we henceforth be no more children, tossed to and fro, and carried
> about with every wind of doctrine, by the sleight of men, and cunning
> craftiness, whereby they lie in wait to deceive; but speaking the truth
> in love, may grow up into him in all things, which is the head, even
> Christ: from whom the whole body fitly joined together and compacted
> by that which every joint supplieth, according to the effectual working
> in the measure of every part, maketh increase of the body unto the
> edifying of itself in love.

This is a beautiful word to Christians today that growing in Christ
is a continual process. When we are born again we are babes in
Christ. And we grow up by learning the Word of God — not just one
or two isolated scriptures, but the whole Bible.

Ephesians 4:17-24

> This I say therefore, and testify in the Lord, that ye henceforth walk
> not as other Gentiles walk, in the vanity of their mind, having the
> understanding darkened, being alienated from the life of God through
> the ignorance that is in them, because of the blindness of their heart:
> who being past feeling have given themselves over unto
> lasciviousness, to work all uncleanness with greediness.
>
> But ye have not so learned Christ; if so be that ye have heard him,
> and have been taught by him, as the truth is in Jesus: that ye put off
> concerning the former conversation the old man, which is corrupt
> according to the deceitful lusts; and be renewed in the spirit of your
> mind; and that ye put on the new man, which after God is created in
> righteousness and true holiness.

This 23rd verse is an important verse in the Word of God. For
God created man as a spirit with a mind and a body as the
instrumentalities of that spirit. But through the fall of man, the spirit
was relegated to a rank lower than the mind. So men are ruled by
their minds rather than by their hearts. Therefore, Paul says we need
a renewal in the spirit of our minds. That is, we need to put our
minds in proper relationship with our spirits.

The renewing of the spirit of our minds is absolutely important to our life in Christ. We cannot ignore our minds. But neither can we live solely by our minds. We must live in our spirits and then renew our minds by praying in the Spirit and interpreting back to our minds the response of God.

I want to pray with you now that you may be renewed in that area of your life where you are having negative thoughts, bad memories, or are not able to get control in the way that you must.

> *Father, You have told us to be renewed in the spirit of our minds. That tells us that our minds do not exist in and of themselves, but are backed by the spirit. Lord, we need our minds renewed today because things come against us, thoughts arise in our hearts, old memories bring in bitterness. So we are trusting You to give us Your deliverance.*
>
> *Dear partner, I am asking God to strengthen you, to deliver you, to renew and recover you so you can think straight, believe right, and follow God knowing that you know that you know that you are following our heavenly Father into victory. Thank You, Father, for hearing us pray through Jesus Christ. Amen and amen.*

Ephesians 4:25-28

Wherefore putting away lying, speak every man truth with his neighbour: for we are members one of another. Be ye angry, and sin not: let not the sun go down upon your wrath: neither give place to the devil. Let him that stole steal no more: but rather let him labour, working with his hands the thing which is good, that he may have to give to him that needeth.

Paul flatly says to put away lying and tell the truth. Why? Because we are members of one another and when we lie or cheat, we break the unity of the Body of Christ. He says to go ahead and be angry, but not to get violently mad so that we sin. We are not to let the devil rule over us through our anger.

Ephesians 4:29-5:8

Let no corrupt communication proceed out of your mouth, but that which is good to the use of edifying, that it may minister grace unto the hearers. And grieve not the holy Spirit of God, whereby ye are sealed unto the day of redemption. Let all bitterness, and wrath, and anger, and clamour, and evil speaking, be put away from you, with all malice: and be ye kind one to another, tenderhearted, forgiving one another, even as God for Christ's sake hath forgiven you.

Be ye therefore followers of God as dear children: and walk in love, as Christ also hath loved us, and hath given himself for us an offering and a sacrifice to God for a sweetsmelling savour. But fornication, and all uncleanness, or covetousness, let it not be once named among you, as becometh saints; neither filthiness, nor foolish talking, nor jesting, which are not convenient: but rather giving of thanks.

For this ye know, that no whoremonger, nor unclean person, nor covetous man, who is an idolater, hath any inheritance in the kingdom of Christ and of God. Let no man deceive you with vain words: for because of these things cometh the wrath of God upon the children of disobedience.

Be not ye therefore partakers with them. For ye were sometimes darkness, but now are ye light in the Lord: walk as children of light:....

The background against which Paul was talking was Roman immorality. The Romans were the most debauched, covetous, and idolatrous people in the world. They were known for their partying throughout the empire. So Paul was speaking to the Ephesian Christians to not follow the Romans, but to be followers of God and to walk in the purity of love. He was saying, "While you are renewing the spirit of your mind, renew your body as sacred before God and indwelt by the Holy Spirit."

Ephesians 5:9-33

(For the fruit of the Spirit is in all goodness and righteousness and truth;) proving what is acceptable unto the Lord.

And have no fellowship with the unfruitful works of darkness, but rather reprove them. For it is a shame even to speak of those things which are done of them in secret. But all things that are reproved are made manifest by the light: for whatsoever doth make manifest is light. Wherefore he saith, Awake thou that sleepest, and arise from the dead, and Christ shall give thee light.

See then that ye walk circumspectly, not as fools, but as wise, redeeming the time, because the days are evil. Wherefore be ye not unwise, but understanding what the will of the Lord is. And be not drunk with wine, wherein is excess; but be filled with the Spirit; speaking to yourselves in psalms and hymns and spiritual songs, singing and making melody in your heart to the Lord; Giving thanks always for all things unto God and the Father in the name of our Lord Jesus Christ; submitting yourselves one to another in the fear of God.

Wives, submit yourselves unto your own husbands, as unto the

Lord. For the husband is the head of the wife, even as Christ is the head of the church: and he is the saviour of the body. Therefore as the church is subject unto Christ, so let the wives be to their own husbands in every thing.

Husbands, love your wives, even as Christ also loved the church, and gave himself for it; that he might sanctify and cleanse it with the washing of water by the word, that he might present it to himself a glorious church, not having spot, or wrinkle, or any such thing; but that it should be holy and without blemish.

So ought men to love their wives as their own bodies. He that loveth his wife loveth himself. For no man ever yet hated his own flesh; but nourisheth and cherisheth it, even as the Lord the church: for we are members of his body, of his flesh, and of his bones.

For this cause shall a man leave his father and mother, and shall be joined unto his wife, and they two shall be one flesh. This is a great mystery: but I speak concerning Christ and the church. Nevertheless let every one of you in particular so love his wife even as himself; and the wife see that she reverence her husband.

Paul is speaking here about Christian marriage. And he is talking about how marriage had degenerated by the time Christ came. When we read the historical records of the Roman Empire of this time, we see there were as many as 20 divorces a man or woman would have.

In order to understand what Paul is saying, we have to begin with his reference to the relationship that Christ has with His Church and the relationship the Church has with Christ. First of all, Christ so loved the church that He gave himself for it that He might cleanse it and then present it to himself without soil, disfigurement, spot, wrinkle, or any such thing. Second, the Church should be in submission and obedience to Him so they can actually become one. Christ and His Church should be one because the head cannot exist without a body, and the body cannot exist without a head.

So he is saying, "Wives, submit yourselves to your husbands in the same way the Body of Christ submits herself to her head, Christ the Lord." To the husbands he is saying, "Love your wife just as Christ loves the Church, His body, and gave himself for it. You give yourself for your wife, no matter what the cost is, just as Christ did not count the cost when He gave himself for His Church."

That is the relationship that the husband is to have with the wife and the wife with the husband. We hear a lot today about wives submitting to their husbands, as though that is all there is to it. But let me tell you, friend, that can only happen when it is coupled with the husband's love. His love must be as strong and as tender as Christ's love. Therefore, Paul is pointing to the ideal. And whether we ever reach its fullness or not, we have something to strive for that is worth everything. That means the marriage is a success.

Ephesians 6:1-4

> Children, obey your parents in the Lord: for this is right. Honour thy father and mother; which is the first commandment with promise; That it may be well with thee, and thou mayest live long on the earth.
> And, ye fathers, provoke not your children to wrath: but bring them up in the nurture and admonition of the Lord.

Again we have to understand the background upon which Paul wrote this scripture. In the Roman Empire, children were not considered as highly as they are today. If the child was born a girl, they would often just throw her into the ocean or put her up for adoption. If it was a boy, they would bring him to the father and if he looked upon him with favor, the son was allowed to live. If not, they would take the little boy out and kill him. It is hard for us to understand how this could take place in the human race. But the people of the Roman Empire had become so idle in the fact that they had conquered the world, they really wanted to follow their orgiastic parties. Therefore, children were a hindrance and were not wanted. As a matter of fact, history tells us that at one time in Rome there were more orphans than there were children who were accepted by their parents. So naturally those children that did live saw all this going on and it made them not want to obey their parents.

When we fathers and mothers have Jesus Christ living in our hearts, we are going to love our children and care for them. We are going to care enough for them to discipline and back it up with our love.

Notice that Paul says, "That it may be well with thee, and thou mayest live long on the earth." Psychologists tell us the greatest incidences of mental illness and crime can be traced back to unhealthy relationships in the home. So it is still true today that if as children we treat our parents in an honorable way and as parents we treat our children in the ways of the Lord, our lives will be much more pleasant, enjoyable, and long.

I would like to say a word of encouragement to you. Sometimes there are things that happen beyond our understanding. So when you do everything you know to do — you honor the Lord and you honor your children — but somehow it does not work out well with one or more of them, please do not carry a load of guilt. It will only hurt you in the end. And to the young people I say, when you too have done everything you know to honor your parents in the Lord but somehow it does not turn out right, I do not want you to lay a load of guilt on yourself either. Paul is giving us the ideal here, so you and I are to strive for it. It may not be easy but it can be done. At least we can give it our best so when we stand before God we can say, "Lord, I gave You my best."

Ephesians 6:5-9

Servants, be obedient to them that are your masters according to the flesh, with fear and trembling, in singleness of your heart, as unto Christ; not with eyeservice, as menpleasers; but as the servants of Christ, doing the will of God from the heart; with good will doing service, as to the Lord, and not to men: knowing that whatsoever good thing any man doeth, the same shall he receive of the Lord, whether he be bond or free.

And, ye masters, do the same things unto them, forbearing threatening: knowing that your Master also is in heaven; neither is there respect of persons with him.

Service From the Heart

What does this scripture mean to you and me today? It means this: Under Christ we render service as unto the Lord — not with eye service as menpleasers, but as the servants of Christ who do the will of God from the heart. So this scripture applies to anybody who works for wages or who employs other people (the same as it does to husbands and wives). The bottom line is this: Whatever we do, we do not do it with eye service, but as the servants of Christ doing the will of God from the heart.

Ephesians 6:10-20

Finally, my brethren, be strong in the Lord, and in the power of his might. Put on the whole armour of God, that ye may be able to stand against the wiles of the devil. For we wrestle not against flesh and blood, but against principalities, against powers, against the rulers of the darkness of this world, against spiritual wickedness in high places.

Wherefore take unto you the whole armour of God, that ye may be able to withstand in the evil day, and having done all, to stand. Stand therefore, having your loins girt about with truth, and having on the breastplate of righteousness; and your feet shod with the preparation of the gospel of peace; above all, taking the shield of faith, wherewith ye shall be able to quench all the fiery darts of the wicked.

And take the helmet of salvation, and the sword of the Spirit, which is the word of God: praying always with all prayer and supplication in the Spirit, and watching thereunto with all perseverance and supplication for all saints; and for me, that utterance may be given unto me, that I may open my mouth boldly, to make known the mystery of the gospel, for which I am an ambassador in bonds: that therein I may speak boldly, as I ought to speak.

The Weapons of Spiritual Warfare

My friend, the Word of God makes it clear that there are unseen forces in this world, demons that do not have human bodies. The world without Christ lies in the power of these unseen forces. So there is only one way to successfully fight against them, and that is to take upon us the whole armor of God.

Paul lays out seven pieces of that armor. He says to gird your loins with truth. Truth is a reference to Jesus Christ, for Christ said, "I am the truth." When he speaks of the breastplate of righteousness, he is referring to the piece of armor on the Roman soldier that went from his shoulders to just below his waist. It covered the heart and other vital organs. When you know in your heart you are rightly related to God, that is righteousness to you. It is the breastplate that covers the vital organs of your being.

Then Paul says to shod your feet with the gospel. Romans, Chapter 1, declares the gospel is the power of God that carries us in all our actions. "Above all," he says, "take the shield of faith to quench all the fiery darts of the wicked one, the devil." Darts were arrows dipped in pitch, set on fire, and shot against the Roman shield which was made of two layers of wood. So when they struck a shield of wood, the fire would be put out and the dart would fall off. Many times the shield itself would be scarred, but the soldier would have been protected. That is exactly what faith is. It is a shield against the fiery darts of the wicked one who comes against us with temptations, trials, tribulations, misunderstandings, oppressions, and sickness. Faith is the weapon that puts out the fire.

Paul calls the helmet on the soldier's head salvation. In other words, we have got to be saved by the grace of God. But salvation is more than an act. It is a process that we live every day. For it is in our heads that the devil seeks entrance for his thoughts. It is in our heads where our minds are either controlled or not controlled. So Paul is saying that we must have a renewing of the spirit of our minds, as part of our salvation, to bring our thoughts into captivity to Jesus Christ.

Then Paul says to take the sword of the Spirit which is the Word of God. The Roman sword was a two-edged sword, so he compares it to the Word of God. One edge is to deal with sin, the other to deal with salvation. One edge is against disease, and the other is to bring forth health. One edge is against death, and the other is to bring forth life. One edge is against hell, the other brings forth heaven. That is the sword of the Spirit.

Finally, the seventh piece of armor is mentioned in Verse 18. It is praying in the Spirit, what I call the prayer language of the Spirit. Many Christians never put on this last piece of armor, but I believe it is one of the most effective weapons God has given to us for the spiritual war we are fighting.

Ephesians 6:21-24

> But that ye also may know my affairs, and how I do, Tychicus, a beloved brother and faithful minister in the Lord, shall make known to you all things: whom I have sent unto you for the same purpose, that ye might know our affairs, and that he might comfort your hearts.
>
> Peace be to the brethren, and love with faith, from God the Father and the Lord Jesus Christ. Grace be with all them that love our Lord Jesus Christ in sincerity. Amen.

Paul is in Rome, he is in jail, and he is bound with chains. But he is still ardent in his faith and loving toward all Christians everywhere. He says, "Tychicus is beloved and faithful. He will tell you all about my affairs and comfort your hearts."

Ephesians is a triumphant letter. It is a tribute to the spirit of Christ in Paul and the spirit of Paul himself. That spirit, the spirit of victory through Christ, rings in our hearts even to this day.

The Epistle of Paul the Apostle to the
Philippians

The Epistle of Paul
the Apostle to the
Philippians

The church at Philippi was born in the midst of terrible tribulation and persecution (Acts 16:6-40 gives the exciting account of the exploits that led to the birth of the Philippian church). Therefore, Paul had the warmest affection for them as he sat and wrote this letter. Chained to a soldier in a Roman prison, he remembered the beloved brothers and sisters in Christ at Philippi. It was a nostalgic moment in his life. His heart grew tender as he began to write, remembering that Epaphroditus, a dear brother in the Lord, had just come to him with a letter from the Philippian Christians. They told him of their condition and sent gifts of money and supplies for his physical welfare. Paul remembered all that as he began to pen his words.

Philippians 1:1-11

Paul and Timotheus, the servants of Jesus Christ, to all the saints in Christ Jesus which are at Philippi, with the bishops and deacons: Grace be unto you, and peace, from God our Father, and from the Lord Jesus Christ.

I thank my God upon every remembrance of you, always in every prayer of mine for you all making request with joy, for your fellowship in the gospel from the first day until now; being confident of this very thing, that he which hath begun a good work in you will perform it until the day of Jesus Christ: even as it is meet for me to think this of you all, because I have you in my heart; inasmuch as both in my bonds, and in the defence and confirmation of the gospel, ye all are partakers of my grace.

For God is my record, how greatly I long after you all in the bowels of Jesus Christ. And this I pray, that your love may abound yet more and more in knowledge and in all judgment; that ye may approve

393

things that are excellent; that ye may be sincere and without offence till the day of Christ; being filled with the fruits of righteousness, which are by Jesus Christ, unto the glory and praise of God.

Paul says he and Timothy are writing to all the saints. The word "saints" in the Bible does not necessarily mean someone who is so holy that no one else can even get near him. Rather, it is taken from the word "different." So Paul is writing to people who are different — not eccentric or odd, but different from the norm. That does not mean they have reached the highest level of perfection, but that they are people who are different in their dedication to truly become followers of Jesus Christ.

Philippians 1:12-20

But I would ye should understand, brethren, that the things which happened unto me have fallen out rather unto the furtherance of the gospel; so that my bonds in Christ are manifest in all the palace, and in all other places; and many of the brethren in the Lord, waxing confident by my bonds, are much more bold to speak the word without fear.

Some indeed preach Christ even of envy and strife; and some also of good will: the one preach Christ of contention, not sincerely, supposing to add affliction to my bonds: but the other of love, knowing that I am set for the defence of the gospel.

What then? notwithstanding, every way, whether in pretence, or in truth, Christ is preached; and I therein do rejoice, yea, and will rejoice. For I know that this shall turn to my salvation through your prayer, and the supply of the Spirit of Jesus Christ, according to my earnest expectation and my hope, that in nothing I shall be ashamed, but that with all boldness, as always, so now also Christ shall be magnified in my body, whether it be by life, or by death.

The Apostle Paul is reminding them of the severe persecution he endured while in Philippi, the same kind he is going through now in Rome. But he says the chains around him are known of even in the palace of Caesar. (He is referring particularly to the praetorian guards, a group of specially trained soldiers who are in effect the bodyguards of Caesar.) In other words, the things that have happened to him have not been negative, but have turned out to extend the gospel.

Philippians 1:21-30

For to me to live is Christ, and to die is gain.

But if I live in the flesh, this is the fruit of my labour: yet what I shall choose I wot not. For I am in a strait betwixt two, having a desire to depart, and to be with Christ; which is far better: nevertheless to abide in the flesh is more needful for you.

And having this confidence, I know that I shall abide and continue with you all for your furtherance and joy of faith; that your rejoicing may be more abundant in Jesus Christ for me by my coming to you again.

Only let your conversation be as it becometh the gospel of Christ: that whether I come and see you, or else be absent, I may hear of your affairs, that ye stand fast in one spirit, with one mind striving together for the faith of the gospel; and in nothing terrified by your adversaries: which is to them an evident token of perdition, but to you of salvation, and that of God.

For unto you it is given in the behalf of Christ, not only to believe on him, but also to suffer for his sake; having the same conflict which ye saw in me, and now hear to be in me.

The burdens that Paul bore, the pains that struck his body, and the loneliness he endured all came crashing against him like a tidal wave as he sat chained in that Roman cell. And he cried out that he really would like to go home. He had a desire to leave his body to be with Christ, which would be much better for him. But in the midst of that painful experience, faith took hold again and he shouted, "For me to live is Christ and to die is gain." If he was killed, death would release him into the direct presence of Jesus Christ. But if he lived, he would simply have more of Jesus in this life. And that is where Paul found himself — in this life.

Philippians 2:1-11

If there be therefore any consolation in Christ, if any comfort of love, if any fellowship of the Spirit, if any bowels and mercies, fulfil ye my joy, that ye be likeminded, having the same love, being of one accord, of one mind. Let nothing be done through strife or vainglory; but in lowliness of mind let each esteem other better than themselves. Look not every man on his own things, but every man also on the things of others.

Let this mind be in you, which was also in Christ Jesus: who, being in the form of God, thought it not robbery to be equal with God: but made himself of no reputation, and took upon him the form of a servant, and was made in the likeness of men: and being found in fashion as a man, he humbled himself, and became obedient unto death, even the death of the cross.

Wherefore God also hath highly exalted him, and given him a name which is above every name: that at the name of Jesus every knee

should bow, of things in heaven, and things in earth, and things under
the earth; and that every tongue should confess that Jesus Christ is
Lord, to the glory of God the Father.

Verses 6-11 may be the greatest statement Paul made in the 13
books of our Bible that he wrote. For he is describing what we know
as the incarnation. He says Jesus was equal with God by divine right,
but He left heaven and took upon himself the form of a human being.
And as a man He became obedient unto death, that is, He became
the perfect instrument to go to the cross and die for our sins.

Because Jesus humbled himself and became a man He was able
to feel what man feels — He hungered, He thirsted, He wept, He
agonized, He laughed, He rejoiced, He sorrowed, He went to the
depths of despair, and He experienced the heights of joy and glory.
And in His humanity He showed us what the Father is like. He showed
us that the Father cares, the Father feels, and the Father enters into us.

Philippians 2:12-24

Wherefore, my beloved, as ye have always obeyed, not as in my
presence only, but now much more in my absence, work out your
own salvation with fear and trembling. For it is God which worketh
in you both to will and to do of his good pleasure.

Do all things without murmurings and disputings: that ye may be
blameless and harmless, the sons of God, without rebuke, in the midst
of a crooked and perverse nation, among whom ye shine as lights in
the world; holding forth the word of life; that I may rejoice in the day
of Christ, that I have not run in vain, neither laboured in vain.

Yea, and if I be offered upon the sacrifice and service of your faith,
I joy, and rejoice with you all. For the same cause also do ye joy, and
rejoice with me.

But I trust in the Lord Jesus to send Timotheus shortly unto you,
that I also may be of good comfort, when I know your state. For I
have no man likeminded, who will naturally care for your state. For
all seek their own, not the things which are Jesus Christ's. But ye
know the proof of him, that, as a son with the father, he hath served
with me in the gospel. Him therefore I hope to send presently, so
soon as I shall see how it will go with me. But I trust in the Lord that
I also myself shall come shortly.

I know that some people use the statement, "Work out your own
salvation with fear and trembling," to place emphasis upon works
as if there is no faith or a single act through which we enter into
the kingdom of God. On the other hand, I know that some take this
passage as proof there are things they need to work at. But Paul is

saying both belong together and one without the other is not complete. Yes, we do enter the kingdom of God through an act of faith, but once we enter, there are things for us to do. Faith and works must go hand in hand.

Philippians 2:25-30

Yet I supposed it necessary to send to you Epaphroditus, my brother, and companion in labour, and fellowsoldier, but your messenger, and he that ministered to my wants. For he longed after you all, and was full of heaviness, because that ye had heard that he had been sick. For indeed he was sick nigh unto death: but God had mercy on him; and not on him only, but on me also, lest I should have sorrow upon sorrow.

I sent him therefore the more carefully, that, when ye see him again, ye may rejoice, and that I may be the less sorrowful. Receive him therefore in the Lord with all gladness; and hold such in reputation: because for the work of Christ he was nigh unto death, not regarding his life, to supply your lack of service toward me.

The Gamblers

There was a group in the early church called the gamblers. This was not a word they called themselves, but a word the world used in describing them as Christians. They were called gamblers because they went to visit the sick wherever they were. Regardless of whether the sick were in prison or had diseases that were contagious, the gamblers went to them with the gospel. They went with love and care in their hearts and with faith and prayer to bring deliverance. Epaphroditus could very well have been a part of this group because Paul says, "For the work of Christ he was nigh unto death, not regarding his life."

I feel like pausing and praying a healing prayer with you because you may have something torturing your life if you have been doing good things and putting your life on the line for Christ.

Father, in the name of our Savior and Lord, Jesus Christ of Nazareth, I pray for these my friends and partners who are going through something because of the work of God. They have reached out and they have been giving, serving, loving, and doing for You. Have mercy as You did upon Epaphroditus and raise them up and set them free. And Father, supply their needs in Jesus' name. I receive that with them beginning this very day. Amen and amen.

Philippians 3:1-9

> Finally, my brethren, rejoice in the Lord. To write the same things to you, to me indeed is not grievous, but for you it is safe. Beware of dogs, beware of evil workers, beware of the concision. For we are the circumcision, which worship God in the spirit, and rejoice in Christ Jesus, and have no confidence in the flesh.
>
> Though I might also have confidence in the flesh. If any other man thinketh that he hath whereof he might trust in the flesh, I more: circumcised the eighth day, of the stock of Israel, of the tribe of Benjamin, an Hebrew of the Hebrews; as touching the law, a Pharisee; concerning zeal, persecuting the church; touching the righteousness which is in the law, blameless.
>
> But what things were gain to me, those I counted loss for Christ. Yea doubtless, and I count all things but loss for the excellency of the knowledge of Christ Jesus my Lord: for whom I have suffered the loss of all things, and do count them but dung, that I may win Christ, and be found in him, not having mine own righteousness, which is of the law, but that which is through the faith of Christ, the righteousness which is of God by faith: . . .

Paul is coming to the end of his letter to the Philippians. And he reminds them that we Christians are true Jews because we worship God in the Spirit and not merely by the works of the law. Our rejoicing is not in the things of the law but in Christ Jesus the risen Lord. He says to have no confidence in the fleshly things of this world but to have confidence in Christ Jesus the Son of God. Then he gives his own credentials and says he has canceled them out of his life because it is only through Jesus that he has the joy of the Lord.

Philippians 3:10-14

> That I may know him, and the power of his resurrection, and the fellowship of his sufferings, being made conformable unto his death; if by any means I might attain unto the resurrection of the dead.
>
> Not as though I had already attained, either were already perfect: but I follow after, if that I may apprehend that for which also I am apprehended of Christ Jesus. Brethren, I count not myself to have apprehended: but this one thing I do, forgetting those things which are behind, and reaching forth unto those things which are before, I press toward the mark for the prize of the high calling of God in Christ Jesus.

Looking back over his life, Paul stands up and says, "The thing I want most of all in my life is to know Jesus and to know Him in the power of His resurrection." You see, Paul looked upon the resurrection of Jesus Christ as an event that had happened, that was going to happen beyond death, and that was happening every day as Christ's resurrection touches our lives in the now.

Then he says, "Dear beloved Philippians, I want you to know there is one thing Paul does. Forgetting all my pedigree and my so-called glorious past, I reach forth to all those things that are before me. For the battle is not over yet. The last chapter of the book has not been written. The glory is yet to come, so I am pressing and putting my life on the line because I look forward to receiving the prize of the high calling of God in Jesus Christ."

Philippians 3:15-21

Let us therefore, as many as be perfect, be thus minded: and if in any thing ye be otherwise minded, God shall reveal even this unto you. Nevertheless, whereto we have already attained, let us walk by the same rule, let us mind the same thing.

Brethren, be followers together of me, and mark them which walk so as ye have us for an ensample. (For many walk, of whom I have told you often, and now tell you even weeping, that they are the enemies of the cross of Christ: whose end is destruction, whose God is their belly, and whose glory is in their shame, who mind earthly things.)

For our conversation is in heaven; from whence also we look for the Saviour, the Lord Jesus Christ: who shall change our vile body, that it may be fashioned like unto his glorious body, according to the working whereby he is able even to subdue all things unto himself.

Paul wanted the Philippians to follow him rather than the enemies of the gospel of Christ. There were many people coming into the Philippian church under the guise of being apostles, prophets, evangelists, pastors, and teachers. But they created great division. So Paul said, "Pay attention to whom you are following."

Philippians 4:1-13

Therefore, my brethren dearly beloved and longed for, my joy and crown, so stand fast in the Lord, my dearly beloved. I beseech Euodias, and beseech Syntyche, that they be of the same mind in the Lord.

And I intreat thee also, true yokefellow, help those women which laboured with me in the gospel, with Clement also, and with other my fellowlabourers, whose names are in the book of life. Rejoice in the Lord alway: and again I say, Rejoice.

Let your moderation be known unto all men. The Lord is at hand. Be careful for nothing; but in every thing by prayer and supplication with thanksgiving let your requests be made known unto God. And the peace of God, which passeth all understanding, shall keep your hearts and minds through Christ Jesus.

Finally, brethren, whatsoever things are true, whatsoever things are honest, whatsoever things are just, whatsoever things are pure, whatsoever things are lovely, whatsoever things are of good report; if there be any virtue, and if there be any praise, think on these things. Those things, which ye have both learned, and received, and heard, and seen in me, do: and the God of peace shall be with you.

But I rejoiced in the Lord greatly, that now at the last your care of me hath flourished again; wherein ye were also careful, but ye lacked opportunity. Not that I speak in respect of want: for I have learned, in whatsoever state I am, therewith to be content. I know both how to be abased, and I know how to abound: every where and in all things I am instructed both to be full and to be hungry, both to abound and to suffer need. I can do all things through Christ which strengtheneth me.

Many people have not been taught how to use their faith. So when things go wrong they lean back and say, "This must be what God wants, so I will just tough it out." But this is not what Paul is saying. He is saying, "I have learned to be content in whatever situation I am in because Christ will strengthen me. His grace will abound and take me through this. In fact, I can do anything because Christ strengthens me."

Philippians 4:14-19

Notwithstanding ye have well done, that ye did communicate with my affliction. Now ye Philippians know also, that in the beginning of the gospel, when I departed from Macedonia, no church communicated with me as concerning giving and receiving, but ye only. For even in Thessalonica ye sent once and again unto my necessity. Not because I desire a gift: but I desire fruit that may abound to your account.

But I have all, and abound: I am full, having received of Epaphroditus the things which were sent from you, an odour of a sweet smell, a sacrifice acceptable, well-pleasing to God. But my God shall supply all your need according to his riches in glory by Christ Jesus.

God's Abundant Provision

Paul has just stated how he has been hungry and alone, suffered, and done without. Now he tells the Philippians that because of their giving he has all — he abounds and is full. He is saying, "Folks, you have really loaded me down. I have so much that I am abounding in everything I need." (Isn't that the way it should be?) Then he says, "What you have sent is the basis upon which you will receive. From the seeds you have planted you will reap a harvest. Your giving is like a sweet smelling sacrifice that is pleasing to God."

When Paul came to Verse 19, I believe all the angels in heaven must have bent down to listen to him say, "But my God shall supply all your need according to his riches in glory by Christ Jesus." He is saying, "My heavenly Father knows your needs. Through His inexhaustible wealth He is going to supply them. He is going to take care of you just as He has taken care of me."

Philippians 4:20-23

> Now unto God and our Father be glory for ever and ever. Amen.
> Salute every saint in Christ Jesus. The brethren which are with me greet you. All the saints salute you, chiefly they that are of Caesar's household. The grace of our Lord Jesus Christ be with you all. Amen.

When Paul said, "The saints in Caesar's household send you their greeting," you could almost hear the gasps of amazement from the Philippian Christians. This is a little phrase that he inserted but it is bigger than the mountains. Even Caesar's household could not escape Paul's testimony in that dark Roman prison. For the soldiers who came in contact with him felt the influence of Christ and many were converted. They then went back to their positions in the household of Caesar and spread the Word. And a fellowship of Christians sprang up in the palace itself. My friend, never think you are alone as a child of God or that your witness for Him does not count. What a glorious way to end Philippians and get ready for Colossians.

The Epistle of Paul
the Apostle to the
Colossians

The Epistle of Paul
the Apostle to the
Colossians

The Colossian church was not established by Paul in person, but the Colossians were greatly influenced by his ministry. For while he was in Ephesus, about a hundred miles away, the Word tells us that all the people in the surrounding area heard the gospel. That certainly included the city of Colosse.

Paul had sent Epaphras the evangelist into the regions of Laodicea and Colosse to preach the gospel. Epaphras probably became the pastor of the Colossian church. Later, he went to Rome where Paul was in prison and told him that trouble was brewing in Colosse. There was a heresy that was about to split the church apart. So Paul dictated a letter to be read aloud to the brethren of the Colossian church. And this is what he wrote.

Colossians 1:1-11

Paul, an apostle of Jesus Christ by the will of God, and Timotheus our brother, to the saints and faithful brethren in Christ which are at Colosse: Grace be unto you, and peace, from God our Father and the Lord Jesus Christ.

We give thanks to God and the Father of our Lord Jesus Christ, praying always for you, since we heard of your faith in Christ Jesus, and of the love which ye have to all the saints. For the hope which is laid up for you in heaven, whereof ye heard before in the word of the truth of the gospel; which is come unto you, as it is in all the world; and bringeth forth fruit, as it doth also in you, since the day ye heard of it, and knew the grace of God in truth: as ye also learned of Epaphras our dear fellowservant, who is for you a faithful minister of Christ; who also declared unto us your love in the Spirit.

For this cause we also, since the day we heard it, do not cease to pray for you, and to desire that ye might be filled with the knowledge of his will in all wisdom and spiritual understanding; that ye might walk worthy of the Lord unto all pleasing, being fruitful in every good work, and increasing in the knowledge of God; strengthened with all might, according to his glorious power, unto all patience and longsuffering with joyfulness . . .

When Paul received the news from Epaphras that trouble was brewing among the Colossians, he said he did not cease to pray for them. He prayed that they might walk worthy of the calling of God and be strengthened so they could endure with patience, longsuffering, and the joy of God in their hearts.

Colossians 1:12-14

Giving thanks unto the Father, which hath made us meet to be partakers of the inheritance of the saints in light: who hath delivered us from the power of darkness, and hath translated us into the kingdom of his dear Son: in whom we have redemption through his blood, even the forgiveness of sins: . . .

Paul is getting ready to face the heresy head-on. He begins to talk about the body of Jesus and His blood shed on the cross through which we have forgiveness of sins.

Colossians 1:15-17

Who is the image of the invisible God, the firstborn of every creature: for by him were all things created, that are in heaven, and that are in earth, visible and invisible, whether they be thrones, or dominions, or principalities, or powers: all things were created by him, and for him: and he is before all things, and by him all things consist.

Paul is dealing with a group of people who have accepted Christ, are organized into a local church, are full of the joy of the Lord, but have been invaded by those who deny the physical incarnation of Jesus Christ. He points out that Jesus is equal with the Father. And through that equality He is part of the invisible God who created the whole universe. For by Him all things are created that are in heaven and on earth, whether they are visible or invisible. Jesus Christ, the Son of God who took on human form, is the agent of cohesion in the universe. He holds the universe together to be a cosmos, rather than a chaos.

Colossians 1:18-23

And he is the head of the body, the church: who is the beginning, the firstborn from the dead; that in all things he might have the preeminence. For it pleased the Father that in him should all fulness dwell; and, having made peace through the blood of his cross, by him to reconcile all things unto himself; by him, I say, whether they be things in earth, or things in heaven.

And you, that were sometime alienated and enemies in your mind by wicked works, yet now hath he reconciled in the body of his flesh through death, to present you holy and unblameable and unreprovable in his sight: if ye continue in the faith grounded and settled, and be not moved away from the hope of the gospel, which ye have heard, and which was preached to every creature which is under heaven; whereof I Paul am made a minister . . .

Paul is telling us that the peace we can have in this world comes through the blood of the body of Jesus who died on the cross. Through that blood God can reconcile all things unto himself. And while that includes the reconciliation of you and me to our heavenly Father, it also includes those things of creation that got out of their created order through man's rebellion against God.

Colossians 1:24-29

Who now rejoice in my sufferings for you, and fill up that which is behind of the afflictions of Christ in my flesh for his body's sake, which is the church: whereof I am made a minister, according to the dispensation of God which is given to me for you, to fulfil the word of God; even the mystery which hath been hid from ages and from generations, but now is made manifest to his saints: to whom God would make known what is the riches of the glory of this mystery among the Gentiles; which is Christ in you, the hope of glory: whom we preach, warning every man, and teaching every man in all wisdom; that we may present every man perfect in Christ Jesus: whereunto I also labour, striving according to his working, which worketh in me mightily.

Completing Christ's Sufferings

The Apostle Paul says he rejoices in his own personal sufferings for the Christians at Colosse because it fills up or completes the sufferings of Christ. My friend, this is what you and I are called to do. We are called to stand up for God. The devil does not like that and the world is against it. So through their striking at us, we are filling up the sufferings of Christ in our own flesh for Jesus' sake and for the sake of His Church.

Colossians 2:1-7

For I would that ye knew what great conflict I have for you, and for them at Laodicea, and for as many as have not seen my face in the flesh; that their hearts might be comforted, being knit together in love, and unto all riches of the full assurance of understanding, to the acknowledgement of the mystery of God, and of the Father, and of Christ; in whom are hid all the treasures of wisdom and knowledge.

And this I say, lest any man should beguile you with enticing words. For though I be absent in the flesh, yet am I with you in the spirit, joying and beholding your order, and the stedfastness of your faith in Christ. As ye have therefore received Christ Jesus the Lord, so walk ye in him: rooted and built up in him, and stablished in the faith, as ye have been taught, abounding therein with thanksgiving.

Even though Paul had never seen the Christians at Colosse, he was praying for them and believing with them. As a matter of fact, he was there with them in the spirit. So how can he be in prison in Rome and yet at the same time be with the Colossians in the spirit? That is the wonder of the mystery he is talking about. We can uplift and be in the spirit with one another as we go through our struggles.

Colossians 2:8-15

Beware lest any man spoil you through philosophy and vain deceit, after the tradition of men, after the rudiments of the world, and not after Christ. For in him dwelleth all the fulness of the Godhead bodily. And ye are complete in him, which is the head of all principality and power: in whom also ye are circumcised with the circumcision made without hands, in putting off the body of the sins of the flesh by the circumcision of Christ: buried with him in baptism, wherein also ye are risen with him through the faith of the operation of God, who hath raised him from the dead.

And you, being dead in your sins and the uncircumcision of your flesh, hath he quickened together with him, having forgiven you all trespasses; blotting out the handwriting of ordinances that was against us, which was contrary to us, and took it out of the way, nailing it to his cross; and having spoiled principalities and powers, he made a shew of them openly, triumphing over them in it.

Paul is telling the Jewish Christians who have been depending on their circumcision that there is a new kind of circumcision not made with hands. It is in the body of Jesus Christ that was nailed to the cross. He is saying, "You have been baptized into Him, so you are risen from your sins. Your faith is now in God and all the things that were against you have been blotted out — even your sins have been nailed to the cross. They too were crucified with Christ."

Colossians 2:16-23

Let no man therefore judge you in meat, or in drink, or in respect of an holyday, or of the new moon, or of the sabbath days: which are a shadow of things to come; but the body is of Christ.

Let no man beguile you of your reward in a voluntary humility and worshipping of angels, intruding into those things which he hath not seen, vainly puffed up by his fleshly mind, and not holding the Head, from which all the body by joints and bands having nourishment ministered, and knit together, increaseth with the increase of God.

Wherefore if ye be dead with Christ from the rudiments of the world, why, as though living in the world, are ye subject to ordinances, (Touch not; taste not; handle not; which all are to perish with the using;) after the commandments and doctrines of men? Which things have indeed a shew of wisdom in will worship, and humility, and neglecting of the body; not in any honour to the satisfying of the flesh.

Paul is referring to the false teachers who came into Colosse with their doctrine that the people should hold onto the law of Moses, count Jesus as only equal to an angel, and allow the things of the Gentile world to be part of their worship and way of life. Paul says, "Not so. Do not be deceived by people like this. You are dead to the things of this world. All the things they tell you — touch not, taste not, handle not — are a mere shadow of that which was to come. And that which was to come has come — Jesus Christ of Nazareth. He is the Head. So keep your mind on Him."

Colossians 3:1-10

If ye then be risen with Christ, seek those things which are above, where Christ sitteth on the right hand of God. Set your affection on things above, not on things on the earth. For ye are dead, and your life is hid with Christ in God.

When Christ, who is our life, shall appear, then shall ye also appear with him in glory. Mortify therefore your members which are upon the earth; fornication, uncleanness, inordinate affection, evil concupiscence, and covetousness, which is idolatry: for which things' sake the wrath of God cometh on the children of disobedience: in the which ye also walked some time, when ye lived in them.

But now ye also put off all these; anger, wrath, malice, blasphemy, filthy communication out of your mouth. Lie not one to another, seeing that ye have put off the old man with his deeds; and have put on the new man, which is renewed in knowledge after the image of him that created him: ...

409

Paul is a great theologian and preacher, but he is also a very practical man in Christ. He is saying, "God will not do certain things for you. He will not bring under subjection the passions of your spirit, mind, and body. You have to do that yourself. He will give you the strength and power to do it. But you must exercise that and do the work yourself." I want to stop and pray that we will.

Father, I thank You for the Son of the living God, Jesus Christ, who lives in us. For in Him we have the strength to stop doing and saying the things that are obscene and unlike You. Help us, Lord, because we are trusting in You and are determined to be clean and free, through Jesus Christ our Savior. Amen and amen.

Colossians 3:11

Where there is neither Greek nor Jew, circumcision nor uncircumcision, barbarian, Scythian, bond nor free: but Christ is all, and in all.

This is one of the great statements in the Word of God. It strikes at the root of all prejudice. If we are in Christ, we are no longer to be ruled by prejudice. We are to be ruled by the unprejudice of Jesus Christ who lives in us.

Colossians 3:12-25

Put on therefore, as the elect of God, holy and beloved, bowels of mercies, kindness, humbleness of mind, meekness, longsuffering; forbearing one another, and forgiving one another, if any man have a quarrel against any: even as Christ forgave you, so also do ye.

And above all these things put on charity, which is the bond of perfectness. And let the peace of God rule in your hearts, to the which also ye are called in one body; and be ye thankful.

Let the word of Christ dwell in you richly in all wisdom; teaching and admonishing one another in psalms and hymns and spiritual songs, singing with grace in your hearts to the Lord. And whatsoever ye do in word or deed, do all in the name of the Lord Jesus, giving thanks to God and the Father by him.

Wives, submit yourselves unto your own husbands, as it is fit in the Lord. Husbands, love your wives, and be not bitter against them.

Children, obey your parents in all things: for this is well pleasing unto the Lord. Fathers, provoke not your children to anger, lest they be discouraged. Servants, obey in all things your masters according to the flesh; not with eyeservice, as menpleasers; but in singleness of heart, fearing God.

And whatsoever ye do, do it heartily, as to the Lord, and not unto men; knowing that of the Lord ye shall receive the reward of the inheritance: for ye serve the Lord Christ. But he that doeth wrong shall receive for the wrong which he hath done; and there is no respect of persons.

Paul speaks of the reciprocal obligations of the family. He tells us that if we do everything as unto God rather than men, the relationships we have in our families and with those connected to us will work out, and we will receive a reward from our heavenly Father.

Colossians 4:1-4

Masters, give unto your servants that which is just and equal; knowing that ye also have a Master in heaven.

Continue in prayer, and watch in the same with thanksgiving; withal praying also for us, that God would open unto us a door of utterance, to speak the mystery of Christ, for which I am also in bonds: that I may make it manifest, as I ought to speak.

I want you to notice that Paul did not ask prayer to be freed from prison, but for the ability to speak the gospel and for the opportunity to do God's work.

Colossians 4:5-18

Walk in wisdom toward them that are without, redeeming the time. Let your speech be alway with grace, seasoned with salt, that ye may know how ye ought to answer every man.

All my state shall Tychicus declare unto you, who is a beloved brother, and a faithful minister and fellowservant in the Lord; whom I have sent unto you for the same purpose, that he might know your estate, and comfort your hearts; with Onesimus, a faithful and beloved brother, who is one of you. They shall make known unto you all things which are done here.

Aristarchus my fellowprisoner saluteth you, and Marcus, sister's son to Barnabas, (touching whom ye received commandments: if he come unto you, receive him;) and Jesus, which is called Justus, who are of the circumcision. These only are my fellowworkers unto the kingdom of God, which have been a comfort unto me.

Epaphras, who is one of you, a servant of Christ, saluteth you, always labouring fervently for you in prayers, that ye may stand perfect and complete in all the will of God. For I bear him record, that he hath a great zeal for you, and them that are in Laodicea, and them in Hierapolis. Luke, the beloved physician, and Demas, greet you.

Salute the brethren which are in Laodicea, and Nymphas, and the church which is in his house. And when this epistle is read among you, cause that it be read also in the church of the Laodiceans; and that ye likewise read the epistle from Laodicea. And say to Archippus, Take heed to the ministry which thou hast received in the Lord, that thou fulfil it.

The salutation by the hand of me Paul. Remember my bonds. Grace be with you. Amen.

The Gospel Moving Out

As I close my teaching on Colossians, I would like to point out that Paul mentions more Gentiles than Jews. More and more, the gospel is moving toward the Gentile world. It is moving into areas where the common person, who was not known as an apostle, could be a strong witness for Christ. God is using more and more people other than the Peters, Johns, Andrews, and the Pauls.

The First Epistle of
Paul the Apostle to the
Thessalonians

The First Epistle of
Paul the Apostle to the
Thessalonians

Thessalonica was a city heavily involved with Greek culture. Now known as Salonica, Thessalonica had a natural harbor that linked Rome with the East. Paul entered this great port city after he was expelled from Philippi. When he arrived in Thessalonica, he taught in the synagogue three straight Sabbaths. (Luke tells us about this in Acts 17.) He had such success preaching the gospel of Jesus Christ that the Jews in the synagogue were enraged. They raised so great a struggle against Paul, he had to be smuggled out of the city to a nearby town called Berea, where they were more open to God and to searching the Scriptures for themselves.

What happened in Thessalonica, however, was important to Christianity becoming a world religion. For Paul faced six crucial problems in his dealings with the Thessalonians. First, he faced the questions of the second coming of Christ and what caused the people to think it was so eminent that they stopped working and just sat around waiting for Jesus to come. Second, the Thessalonians worried about those who had already died in Christ. If Christ's coming was so eminent, what was going to happen to those who had died in Christ before them? Third, there was a tremendous concern about the Greek influence of democracy which created a tendency in the Thessalonians to despise lawful authority. Fourth, there was a danger of the Thessalonian Christians going back to idol gods and immorality. Fifth, there was a group in the city that accused Paul of preaching for what he could get out of it. And sixth, divisions within the church had developed.

The letters to the Thessalonians were written from Athens, where Paul went after he left Berea. The apostle was so concerned about the Thessalonians that he sent Timothy from Athens to find out the facts and report back to him. When Timothy returned he came with both bad and good news. It was in that spirit that Paul wrote these important letters — letters that are valuable to you and me in the now of our Christian experience.

I Thessalonians 1:1-4

Paul, and Silvanus, and Timotheus, unto the church of the Thessalonians which is in God the Father and in the Lord Jesus Christ: Grace be unto you, and peace, from God our Father, and the Lord Jesus Christ.

We give thanks to God always for you all, making mention of you in our prayers; remembering without ceasing your work of faith, and labour of love, and patience of hope in our Lord Jesus Christ, in the sight of God and our Father; knowing, brethren beloved, your election of God.

When Paul mentions Silvanus, he is referring to Silas, who took the place of Barnabas in Paul's missionary team beginning with the second missionary journey. It is Paul, Silas, and Timothy to the church of the Thessalonians which is in God and in the Lord Jesus Christ. In other words, God is the very atmosphere in which the Thessalonian believers live and exist.

This is a powerful point for you and me to consider and receive. We are in God. We are in our Lord Jesus Christ with the power of the Holy Spirit. And we are living in a new atmosphere.

I Thessalonians 1:5-10

For our gospel came not unto you in word only, but also in power, and in the Holy Ghost, and in much assurance; as ye know what manner of men we were among you for your sake. And ye became followers of us, and of the Lord, having received the word in much affliction, with joy of the Holy Ghost: so that ye were ensamples to all that believe in Macedonia and Achaia.

For from you sounded out the word of the Lord not only in Macedonia and Achaia, but also in every place your faith to God-ward is spread abroad; so that we need not to speak any thing.

For they themselves shew of us what manner of entering in we had unto you, and how ye turned to God from idols to serve the living and true God; and to wait for his Son from heaven, whom he raised from the dead, even Jesus, which delivered us from the wrath to come.

A Cherished Word

In the Old Testament "beloved" was a word used by the Jews to speak of great men of God, such as Moses and Solomon. But Paul uses it for the lowest of Gentiles who only recently had come into the kingdom of Jesus Christ. He calls them beloved and says they know they are chosen of God.

Then he says, "Our gospel came not unto you in word only. It was not mere rhetoric. It was the power of the Holy Spirit with great assurance."

I Thessalonians 2:1-7

For yourselves, brethren, know our entrance in unto you, that it was not in vain: but even after that we had suffered before, and were shamefully entreated, as ye know, at Philippi, we were bold in our God to speak unto you the gospel of God with much contention.

For our exhortation was not of deceit, nor of uncleanness, nor in guile: but as we were allowed of God to be put in trust with the gospel, even so we speak; not as pleasing men, but God, which trieth our hearts.

For neither at any time used we flattering words, as ye know, nor a cloak of covetousness; God is witness: nor of men sought we glory, neither of you, nor yet of others, when we might have been burdensome, as the apostles of Christ.

But we were gentle among you, even as a nurse cherisheth her children: . . .

Paul is saying, "I could have come to you as a mighty apostle of the Lord Jesus Christ. But I did not use such credentials, for I was not seeking the glory of men. I was as concerned about you as a mother nursing her newborn child."

I Thessalonians 2:8-10

So being affectionately desirous of you, we were willing to have imparted unto you, not the gospel of God only, but also our own souls, because ye were dear unto us. For ye remember, brethren, our labour and travail: for labouring night and day, because we would not be chargeable unto any of you, we preached unto you the gospel of God.

Ye are witnesses, and God also, how holily and justly and unblameably we behaved ourselves among you that believe: . . .

Today when a minister of the gospel goes out as a missionary, he is usually supported by churches and other groups. But at that time, there were no Christian churches to speak of in the Gentile world. Paul therefore worked with his own hands to support himself.

I Thessalonians 2:11-16

> As ye know how we exhorted and comforted and charged every one
> of you, as a father doth his children, that ye would walk worthy of
> God, who hath called you unto his kingdom and glory.
>
> For this cause also thank we God without ceasing, because, when
> ye received the word of God which ye heard of us, ye received it not
> as the word of men, but as it is in truth, the word of God, which
> effectually worketh also in you that believe.
>
> For ye, brethren, became followers of the churches of God which
> in Judaea are in Christ Jesus: for ye also have suffered like things of
> your own countrymen, even as they have of the Jews: who both killed
> the Lord Jesus, and their own prophets, and have persecuted us; and
> they please not God, and are contrary to all men: forbidding us to
> speak to the Gentiles that they might be saved, to fill up their sins
> alway: for the wrath is come upon them to the uttermost.

This was not easy for Paul to say about his own Jewish brethren
whom he loved so much. He was even willing to be accursed himself,
that they might be saved. But he could not overlook the fact that
they had killed the Lord, eliminated the prophets, and forbidden
him to speak to the Gentiles so they could be saved.

I Thessalonians 2:17-20

> But we, brethren, being taken from you for a short time in presence,
> not in heart, endeavoured the more abundantly to see your face with
> great desire. Wherefore we would have come unto you, even I Paul,
> once and again; but Satan hindered us. For what is our hope, or joy,
> or crown of rejoicing? Are not even ye in the presence of our Lord
> Jesus Christ at his coming? For ye are our glory and joy.

Leaping Over the Devil's Roadblocks

Paul is already missing the new Christians at Thessalonica. He
wants to be with them again face to face. But when he has tried to
go to them, he has been hindered by the devil. The Greek word used
here for "hinder" means "roadblock." The apostle is saying the devil
threw up a roadblock. But let me remind you that although Paul
was hindered, he was not stopped. He was able to get this personal
letter, through the hands of young Timothy, to the Christians at
Thessalonica so they could hear it read and be lifted up in the Lord
as if Paul himself were there.

My friend, you do not have to let the devil stop you. You can leap over his roadblocks by your faith, your determination to obey God, and your belief that God is good.

I Thessalonians 3:1-10

Wherefore when we could no longer forbear, we thought it good to be left at Athens alone; and sent Timotheus, our brother, and minister of God, and our fellowlabourer in the gospel of Christ, to establish you, and to comfort you concerning your faith: that no man should be moved by these afflictions: for yourselves know that we are appointed thereunto.

For verily, when we were with you, we told you before that we should suffer tribulation; even as it came to pass, and ye know. For this cause, when I could no longer forbear, I sent to know your faith, lest by some means the tempter have tempted you, and our labour be in vain.

But now when Timotheus came from you unto us, and brought us good tidings of your faith and charity, and that ye have good remembrance of us always, desiring greatly to see us, as we also to see you: therefore, brethren, we were comforted over you in all our affliction and distress by your faith: for now we live, if ye stand fast in the Lord.

For what thanks can we render to God again for you, for all the joy wherewith we joy for your sakes before our God; night and day praying exceedingly that we might see your face, and might perfect that which is lacking in your faith?

In the early church, individuals who came to Christ made such an abrupt change from the way other people were living that they were immediately pounced upon by the devil and by other people. So when individuals came to Christ, they were quickly taught to expect the tempter to come and strike against them. They were also taught that people would misunderstand them. The new convert, therefore, had to know how to possess himself in sanctification and be set apart for the glory of God. When Timothy arrived in Thessalonica he discovered good news — the new Christians were doing exactly that.

I Thessalonians 3:11-13

Now God himself and our Father, and our Lord Jesus Christ, direct our way unto you. And the Lord make you to increase and abound in love one toward another, and toward all men, even as we do toward you: to the end he may stablish your hearts unblameable in holiness

> before God, even our Father, at the coming of our Lord Jesus Christ with all his saints.

Paul is beginning to edge toward the moment when he will deal with the number-one struggle the Thessalonians are facing: how to conduct themselves toward the coming of the Lord Jesus Christ. He says he wants them to increase in love so they will be established in a holy life before God. And he reminds them that when the Lord Jesus comes, He will complete that holiness in their lives. Meanwhile, he wants them to start looking for the coming of the Lord Jesus Christ in a realistic way.

I Thessalonians 4:1-12

> Furthermore then we beseech you, brethren, and exhort you by the Lord Jesus, that as ye have received of us how ye ought to walk and to please God, so ye would abound more and more.
>
> For ye know what commandments we gave you by the Lord Jesus. For this is the will of God, even your sanctification, that ye should abstain from fornication: that every one of you should know how to possess his vessel in sanctification and honour; not in the lust of concupiscence, even as the Gentiles which know not God: that no man go beyond and defraud his brother in any matter: because that the Lord is the avenger of all such, as we also have forewarned you and testified.
>
> For God hath not called us unto uncleanness, but unto holiness. He therefore that despiseth, despiseth not man, but God, who hath also given unto us his holy Spirit.
>
> But as touching brotherly love ye need not that I write unto you: for ye yourselves are taught of God to love one another. And indeed ye do it toward all the brethren which are in all Macedonia: but we beseech you, brethren, that ye increase more and more; and that ye study to be quiet, and to do your own business, and to work with your own hands, as we commanded you; that ye may walk honestly toward them that are without, and that ye may have lack of nothing.

Paul is telling them to reach deeper depths of love. But love in itself is not enough. For we live in a real world where we must be calm and be engaged in honest labor.

The word has reached Paul that these Thessalonians have become so carried away with the coming of Christ that they quit working and started sponging off of society. So he is saying, "If you really love, you have to put your love into action. You have to study to be quiet and calm about the coming of the Lord. Develop a Christian walk of work, honesty, and integrity toward all people. And if you do, you will lack nothing."

I Thessalonians 4:13-18

But I would not have you to be ignorant, brethren, concerning them which are asleep, that ye sorrow not, even as others which have no hope. For if we believe that Jesus died and rose again, even so them also which sleep in Jesus will God bring with him.

For this we say unto you by the word of the Lord, that we which are alive and remain unto the coming of the Lord shall not prevent them which are asleep.

For the Lord himself shall descend from heaven with a shout, with the voice of the archangel, and with the trump of God: and the dead in Christ shall rise first: then we which are alive and remain shall be caught up together with them in the clouds to meet the Lord in the air: and so shall we ever be with the Lord. Wherefore comfort one another with these words.

The Promise of the Rapture

Paul is holding out the promise of the rapture. It is a promise that at any moment, when the Lord so chooses, He will raise our loved ones who have died in Him. And in the next split second, if we are physically living at that moment, He will catch us up out of this world and we will be gone. We will leave to be with Jesus wherever He is.

That is the ultimate of serving Jesus. It is why we try to walk so closely with the Lord every day. For the greatest reward of all is to be caught up to be with our Lord Jesus Christ and never be separated from Him again. Let me tell you, friend, we are on the winning side.

I Thessalonians 5:1-11

But of the times and the seasons, brethren, ye have no need that I write unto you. For yourselves know perfectly that the day of the Lord so cometh as a thief in the night. For when they shall say, Peace and safety; then sudden destruction cometh upon them, as travail upon a woman with child; and they shall not escape.

But ye, brethren, are not in darkness, that that day should overtake you as a thief. Ye are all the children of light, and the children of the day: we are not of the night, nor of darkness. Therefore let us not sleep, as do others; but let us watch and be sober. For they that sleep

sleep in the night; and they that be drunken are drunken in the night.

But let us, who are of the day, be sober, putting on the breastplate of faith and love; and for an helmet, the hope of salvation. For God hath not appointed us to wrath, but to obtain salvation by our Lord Jesus Christ, who died for us, that, whether we wake or sleep, we should live together with him. Wherefore comfort yourselves together, and edify one another, even as also ye do.

The point Paul is making is that since we know Christ is coming, but we do not know the exact hour, we have to be ready as though He were coming the very next minute. On the other hand, we have to keep working with our lives because He might not come in our lifetime or for a thousand years.

I Thessalonians 5:12-24

And we beseech you, brethren, to know them which labour among you, and are over you in the Lord, and admonish you; and to esteem them very highly in love for their work's sake. And be at peace among yourselves.

Now we exhort you, brethren, warn them that are unruly, comfort the feebleminded, support the weak, be patient toward all men. See that none render evil for evil unto any man; but ever follow that which is good, both among yourselves, and to all men.

Rejoice evermore. Pray without ceasing. In every thing give thanks: for this is the will of God in Christ Jesus concerning you. Quench not the Spirit. Despise not prophesyings. Prove all things; hold fast that which is good. Abstain from all appearance of evil. And the very God of peace sanctify you wholly; and I pray God your whole spirit and soul and body be preserved blameless unto the coming of our Lord Jesus Christ. Faithful is he that calleth you, who also will do it.

I believe Paul's key thought in this passage is Verse 18 where he says, "In every thing give thanks." He does not say, "For everything give thanks," because we cannot give thanks for everything. But we can give thanks in the midst of everything because Christ lives in us. Friend, when we strip it all away, the only thing that really counts in this world is — are we saved? Is Christ living in us? Are we prepared for the coming of the Lord? If not, I pray you will take the time right now to stop and invite the Lord into your life. He will fill you with the joy of His presence and enable you to give thanks in the midst of everything.

I Thessalonians 5:25,26
>Brethren, pray for us. Greet all the brethren with an holy kiss.

At that time, greeting the brethren with a holy kiss was kissing the person on each cheek, or a double embrace. What is really meant in this scripture is to be affectionate in Christ toward one another.

I Thessalonians 5:27,28
>I charge you by the Lord that this epistle be read unto all the holy brethren. The grace of our Lord Jesus Christ be with you. Amen.

Paul ends this letter with the word "amen." Amen means "let it be" or "let it come to pass." Paul is saying, "Let everything I have said to you in this letter come to pass." I echo the words of the great apostle by saying I too am looking forward to the second coming of our Lord Jesus Christ. Amen. Let it come to pass.

The Second Epistle of
Paul the Apostle to the
Thessalonians

The Second Epistle of
Paul the Apostle to the
Thessalonians

After finishing I Thessalonians, Paul felt a great urgency to write a second letter to his beloved Thessalonian brothers and sisters in Christ. The battle was still raging inside them, for they were still concerned about the second coming of Christ. They had heard about the catching away of the saints, and their questions were answered about the dead in Christ. But there were still many unanswered questions about the man of sin, called the Antichrist, who will be the devil incarnate just as God's Son was incarnated by God himself.

In I Thessalonians Paul covered the first phase of the second coming of Christ, the rapture. This is when our Lord Jesus Christ will call His people up from the grave and from among the living. It is a catching away to himself in the clouds. In II Thessalonians, Paul talks about the second phase of our Lord's return, the revelation. This is when He will reveal himself as He returns to the earth with the saints. Every eye will see Him, every tongue will confess His name, and every knee will bow before Him. Paul begins this second letter to the Thessalonians with a tremendous word of encouragement, after which he immediately goes into an explanation of the second return of Christ in the revelation.

II Thessalonians 1:1-5

Paul, and Silvanus, and Timotheus, unto the church of the Thessalonians in God our Father and the Lord Jesus Christ: Grace unto you, and peace, from God our Father and the Lord Jesus Christ.

We are bound to thank God always for you, brethren, as it is meet, because that your faith groweth exceedingly, and the charity of every one of you all toward each other aboundeth; so that we ourselves glory in you in the churches of God for your patience and faith in all your persecutions and tribulations that ye endure: which is a manifest

427

> token of the righteous judgment of God, that ye may be counted
> worthy of the kingdom of God, for which ye also suffer . . .

The Thessalonian Christians were suffering for something greater than themselves. They were suffering for the kingdom of God.

II Thessalonians 1:6-9

> Seeing it is a righteous thing with God to recompense tribulation to
> them that trouble you; and to you who are troubled rest with us,
> when the Lord Jesus shall be revealed from heaven with his mighty
> angels, in flaming fire taking vengeance on them that know not God,
> and that obey not the gospel of our Lord Jesus Christ: who shall be
> punished with everlasting destruction from the presence of the Lord,
> and from the glory of his power . . .

Paul is saying it is a righteous thing for God to take notice of the tribulation that comes against His people and for Him to punish the persecutors. In fact, when the Lord is revealed from heaven — the second phase of His return — everyone who does not know God and has not accepted the gospel of Jesus Christ will be punished with everlasting destruction. And that destruction is banishment from the presence of the Lord and the glory of His power.

Partner, that really is what hell is. It is no longer having access to the presence of God. It is being banished forever with no further opportunity to glimpse or experience the power of God.

II Thessalonians 1:10-2:5

> When he shall come to be glorified in his saints, and to be admired
> in all them that believe (because our testimony among you was
> believed) in that day.
>
> Wherefore also we pray always for you, that our God would count
> you worthy of this calling, and fulfil all the good pleasure of his
> goodness, and the work of faith with power: that the name of our
> Lord Jesus Christ may be glorified in you, and ye in him, according
> to the grace of our God and the Lord Jesus Christ.
>
> Now we beseech you, brethren, by the coming of our Lord Jesus
> Christ, and by our gathering together unto him, that ye be not soon
> shaken in mind, or be troubled, neither by spirit, nor by word, nor
> by letter as from us, as that the day of Christ is at hand.
>
> Let no man deceive you by any means: for that day shall not come,
> except there come a falling away first, and that man of sin be revealed,
> the son of perdition; who opposeth and exalteth himself above all
> that is called God, or that is worshipped; so that he as God sitteth in

the temple of God, shewing himself that he is God. Remember ye not, that, when I was yet with you, I told you these things?

Signs of Christ's Return

Paul tells the Christians at Thessalonica there are two things they should remember: the coming of the Lord Jesus Christ and the fact we will be gathered to Him. He says, "Therefore, hold these in your mind so you will not be shaken, troubled, or discouraged."

Then he says, "Here is something for you to watch out for. First, the day of Christ's second coming will not take place until there is a time of mass backsliding among God's people. Second, the son of perdition, the Antichrist, will be revealed before Christ returns. This man will exalt himself above all that is worshiped. As a matter of fact, he will enter the great temple of God and take his seat as if he were God."

II Thessalonians 2:6,7

And now ye know what withholdeth that he might be revealed in his time. For the mystery of iniquity doth already work: only he who now letteth will let, until he be taken out of the way.

The word "letteth" means "prevent." So Paul is saying there is someone preventing the rise of the Antichrist.

II Thessalonians 2:8-12

And then shall that Wicked be revealed, whom the Lord shall consume with the spirit of his mouth, and shall destroy with the brightness of his coming: even him, whose coming is after the working of Satan with all power and signs and lying wonders, and with all deceivableness of unrighteousness in them that perish; because they received not the love of the truth, that they might be saved.

And for this cause God shall send them strong delusion, that they should believe a lie: that they all might be damned who believed not the truth, but had pleasure in unrighteousness.

Paul says that in due time the wicked one, the Antichrist, will be consumed by the Lord Jesus Christ and destroyed with the brightness of His coming. But he also says the Antichrist will have the power to do signs and lying wonders. As the incarnate son of the devil, he will be able to deceive those who have rejected the Lord. In fact, the Lord will allow a strong delusion to overtake those who have turned from Him so that when they follow the Antichrist they will actually think they are following God. They will be eternally damned because they choose to turn their backs on God and His Son.

This is a frightening thing to think about, but it should not frighten you and me, because we know that we know that we know Jesus Christ as our Lord and Savior. He is our Redeemer. And we will be caught up to be with Him when He returns to this earth.

II Thessalonians 2:13,14

> But we are bound to give thanks alway to God for you, brethren beloved of the Lord, because God hath from the beginning chosen you to salvation through sanctification of the Spirit and belief of the truth: whereunto he called you by our gospel, to the obtaining of the glory of our Lord Jesus Christ.

How are we chosen by God? We are chosen by our belief of the truth. God presents the truth to us to believe or disbelieve. Our believing of it causes us to be chosen, whereby we receive the gospel and obtain the presence of Christ in our lives.

II Thessalonians 2:15-17

> Therefore, brethren, stand fast, and hold the traditions which ye have been taught, whether by word, or our epistle. Now our Lord Jesus Christ himself, and God, even our Father, which hath loved us, and hath given us everlasting consolation and good hope through grace, comfort your hearts, and stablish you in every good word and work.

Partner, I want to pray with you as we end this chapter.

> *Father, we thank You for the beautiful revelation of the gospel through Your servant, Saint Paul. We are grateful we have the Apostle Paul as one of our teachers as we look forward to the coming of the Lord Jesus to catch us up from this world to be with You forever. We thank You for the comfort that gives our hearts and for the renewed determination we feel inside us to stabilize our Christian lives and obey You. Thank You, Father, through Jesus Christ. Amen and amen.*

II Thessalonians 3:1-11

> Finally, brethren, pray for us, that the word of the Lord may have free course, and be glorified, even as it is with you: and that we may be delivered from unreasonable and wicked men: for all men have not faith.

But the Lord is faithful, who shall stablish you, and keep you from evil. And we have confidence in the Lord touching you, that ye both do and will do the things which we command you. And the Lord direct your hearts into the love of God, and into the patient waiting for Christ.

Now we command you, brethren, in the name of our Lord Jesus Christ, that ye withdraw yourselves from every brother that walketh disorderly, and not after the tradition which he received of us. For yourselves know how ye ought to follow us: for we behaved not ourselves disorderly among you; neither did we eat any man's bread for nought; but wrought with labour and travail night and day, that we might not be chargeable to any of you: not because we have not power, but to make ourselves an ensample unto you to follow us.

For even when we were with you, this we commanded you, that if any would not work, neither should he eat. For we hear that there are some which walk among you disorderly, working not at all, but are busybodies.

In no way is Paul referring to handicapped people who do not have the ability to work. He is talking about those who refuse to work when they have the ability. Some of the Thessalonians had forsaken their work and were sitting around waiting for the coming of the Lord. So Paul is saying, "That is not living an orderly Christian life. You are not working and making use of your life. Your priorities are not straight. You are to be orderly minded people."

II Thessalonians 3:12-18

Now them that are such we command and exhort by our Lord Jesus Christ, that with quietness they work, and eat their own bread.

But ye, brethren, be not weary in well doing. And if any man obey not our word by this epistle, note that man, and have no company with him, that he may be ashamed. Yet count him not as an enemy, but admonish him as a brother.

Now the Lord of peace himself give you peace always by all means. The Lord be with you all. The salutation of Paul with mine own hand, which is the token in every epistle: so I write. The grace of our Lord Jesus Christ be with you all. Amen.

Paul is saying that after he dictated this letter, he took a pen in his own hand and added something like a P.S. "This is my signature. I am doing this by my own hand. Do not pay attention to other letters that claim to be sent from me, because they are not. Here is how you can tell: I add my own signature at the end."

As we leave the letters to the Thessalonians, we can look back and see many wonderful things about the coming of the Lord. We see how to conduct ourselves as we patiently wait and continue our work. We see we face persecution and are in constant struggle with the forces of the devil because he is against God and His people. We see that in the Church there will be some who have known the Lord who will fall away and become apostates. And when that happens and reaches its climax, it will signal the rising of the Antichrist. But in the midst of that, we see that the Lord himself will come — first in a rapture, or catching away of His people, and then to be revealed to the world.

I would like to point out that we have completed our reading and teaching of Paul's letters to the churches which began with the church at Rome.

The First Epistle
of Paul the Apostle to
Timothy

The First Epistle
of Paul the Apostle to
Timothy

Paul met Timothy on his first missionary journey. Timothy was the son and grandson of two fine women, Eunice and Lois. He was the son, however, of a mixed marriage. His mother was Jewish and his father was Greek. In his hometown of Lystra, Timothy came in direct contact with the saving grace of the Lord Jesus Christ and he accepted Christ as his personal Savior. It was not long until Paul saw that Timothy was bright and enthusiastic and asked him to join his missionary group. The young Timothy became a co-laborer with Paul.

Over the years as they traveled and established churches together, Paul counted Timothy as his own son. He entrusted great responsibility to Timothy to carry his messages to churches where serious situations existed. Timothy always came through. He came through with great difficulty, however, because he was not naturally courageous. He was nervous in personality and often had to be encouraged. But he had a deep inner strength and a strong faith in Jesus Christ that helped him to carry out faithfully the missions Paul entrusted to him.

Timothy was called of God to be an evangelist. Over the years he was a dedicated evangelist and a minister of the gospel. As Paul neared the end of his life he sat down and wrote very personal letters to Timothy. He gave his fellow evangelist and co-laborer in the gospel great Christian advice — advice that you and I can still use today.

I Timothy 1:1-4

Paul, an apostle of Jesus Christ by the commandment of God our Saviour, and Lord Jesus Christ, which is our hope; unto Timothy, my own son in the faith: Grace, mercy, and peace, from God our Father

435

and Jesus Christ our Lord.

As I besought thee to abide still at Ephesus, when I went into Macedonia, that thou mightest charge some that they teach no other doctrine, neither give heed to fables and endless genealogies, which minister questions, rather than godly edifying which is in faith: so do.

In effect, Paul is saying, "Timothy, you tell the people to get over their passion for pedigree and to be concerned about living the Christian life. For there is no substitute for their own personal relationship with Jesus Christ — not their heritage, their pedigree, or their genealogy. Those things may have some value, but that is not what the gospel is all about. Christianity is a relationship with a person — Jesus Christ of Nazareth. That is what counts."

I Timothy 1:5-11

Now the end of the commandment is charity out of a pure heart, and of a good conscience, and of faith unfeigned: from which some having swerved have turned aside unto vain jangling; desiring to be teachers of the law; understanding neither what they say, nor whereof they affirm.

But we know that the law is good, if a man use it lawfully; knowing this, that the law is not made for a righteous man, but for the lawless and disobedient, for the ungodly and for sinners, for unholy and profane, for murderers of fathers and murderers of mothers, for manslayers, for whoremongers, for them that defile themselves with mankind, for menstealers, for liars, for perjured persons, and if there be any other thing that is contrary to sound doctrine; according to the glorious gospel of the blessed God, which was committed to my trust.

Paul is instructing Timothy to counteract the false teaching of particular teachers who wanted to bring the Christians back under the law of Moses. He is reminding Timothy that the law of Moses had two great purposes: one, to reveal the sinfulness of the people and show them they could not save themselves, and two, to show the people they needed a Redeemer.

I Timothy 1:12-14

And I thank Christ Jesus our Lord, who hath enabled me, for that he counted me faithful, putting me into the ministry; who was before a blasphemer, and a persecutor, and injurious: but I obtained mercy, because I did it ignorantly in unbelief. And the grace of our Lord was exceeding abundant with faith and love which is in Christ Jesus.

436

Paul is reminded of his own miraculous conversion. His heart swells in gratitude as he thanks God for saving him and putting him in the ministry, even though he had blasphemed the name of Jesus, persecuted the Church, and injured many of the Christians. He had done all these things thinking he was doing right. But when he had a vision of the Lord on the Damascus road, it opened his mind. He saw that what he had done in his ignorance and unbelief was a terrible thing against God, himself, the Church, and Christian people.

I Timothy 1:15-20

This is a faithful saying, and worthy of all acceptation, that Christ Jesus came into the world to save sinners; of whom I am chief. Howbeit for this cause I obtained mercy, that in me first Jesus Christ might shew forth all longsuffering, for a pattern to them which should hereafter believe on him to life everlasting.

Now unto the King eternal, immortal, invisible, the only wise God, be honour and glory for ever and ever. Amen.

This charge I commit unto thee, son Timothy, according to the prophecies which went before on thee, that thou by them mightest war a good warfare; holding faith, and a good conscience; which some having put away concerning faith have made shipwreck: of whom is Hymenaeus and Alexander; whom I have delivered unto Satan, that they may learn not to blaspheme.

Church Discipline

Paul mentions two men, Hymenaeus and Alexander, whom he has delivered unto Satan so they would learn not to blaspheme. In the letters to the churches, Paul states that when brothers or sisters do something like this, we are to go to them personally, privately, and in a loving way to try to help them. If they refuse, we are to take a second person with us to try to help. If they still refuse, we are to take them before the whole body of believers. If they refuse the help of the entire body of believers, they are to be set apart and denied participation with those who believe in Jesus Christ, because they have rejected the Lord.

Hymenaeus and Alexander, having turned away from the faith, were taken through all these stages and they still refused to be reconciled to the faith. Therefore, they were exposed to the devil without the protective covering of other believers surrounding them so they would learn and quickly return to their faith in Jesus Christ.

I Timothy 2:1-8

> I exhort therefore, that, first of all, supplications, prayers,
> intercessions, and giving of thanks, be made for all men; for kings,
> and for all that are in authority; that we may lead a quiet and peaceable
> life in all godliness and honesty. For this is good and acceptable in
> the sight of God our Saviour; who will have all men to be saved, and
> to come unto the knowledge of the truth.
>
> For there is one God, and one mediator between God and men, the
> man Christ Jesus; who gave himself a ransom for all, to be testified
> in due time. Whereunto I am ordained a preacher, and an apostle, (I
> speak the truth in Christ, and lie not;) a teacher of the Gentiles in
> faith and verity. I will therefore that men pray every where, lifting up
> holy hands, without wrath and doubting.

What are holy hands? I believe Paul means that we as believers
should live as close to God as we know how. We should keep our
consciences clear so that when we come to God our hands are, in
effect, holy as they are lifted to Him.

I Timothy 2:9,10

> In like manner also, that women adorn themselves in modest apparel,
> with shamefacedness and sobriety; not with broided hair, or gold, or
> pearls, or costly array. But (which becometh women professing
> godliness) with good works.

Paul is not saying that women are not to dress well or take care
of themselves. He is saying, "Do not live primarily for dress and
outward show. Make Christ and doing His good works the aim of
your life."

I Timothy 2:11-15

> Let the woman learn in silence with all subjection. But I suffer not a
> woman to teach, nor to usurp authority over the man, but to be in
> silence. For Adam was first formed, then Eve. And Adam was not
> deceived, but the woman being deceived was in the transgression.
> Notwithstanding she shall be saved in childbearing, if they continue
> in faith and charity and holiness with sobriety.

Many of the Jewish people in Ephesus had been saved and had
carried over to the Christian church one of the practices of their
synagogues. In the synagogues, men would sit in one area while
women would sit in another. Women were not allowed to participate
in the Jewish service. They were to merely observe. But while the

service was going on, the women would talk and gossip among themselves.

So Paul is telling Timothy to instruct the Ephesian women to learn in silence. Rather than using the Christian church service as a time of catching up on the news and gossiping, they are to sit quietly, listen, and learn.

I Timothy 3:1-7

This is a true saying, If a man desire the office of a bishop, he desireth a good work. A bishop then must be blameless, the husband of one wife, vigilant, sober, of good behaviour, given to hospitality, apt to teach; not given to wine, no striker, not greedy of filthy lucre; but patient, not a brawler, not covetous; one that ruleth well his own house, having his children in subjection with all gravity; (For if a man know not how to rule his own house, how shall he take care of the church of God?) not a novice, lest being lifted up with pride he fall into the condemnation of the devil. Moreover he must have a good report of them which are without; lest he fall into reproach and the snare of the devil.

Paul is telling Timothy something in this chapter he already knows. There are to be three different types of spiritual leaders set in the Church: elders, deacons, and bishops. There may be two or three dozen elders in a large church, but only one bishop, or administrator, of all that happens in the church. Paul goes on to describe the characteristics of bishops and deacons.

I Timothy 3:8-14

Likewise must the deacons be grave, not doubletongued, not given to much wine, not greedy of filthy lucre; holding the mystery of the faith in a pure conscience. And let these also first be proved; then let them use the office of a deacon, being found blameless.

Even so must their wives be grave, not slanderers, sober, faithful in all things. Let the deacons be the husbands of one wife, ruling their children and their own houses well. For they that have used the office of a deacon well purchase to themselves a good degree, and great boldness in the faith which is in Christ Jesus. These things write I unto thee, hoping to come unto thee shortly . . .

In those days there were no welfare systems as we have today in many of the modern governments. The church had to take care of its own people. So, one of the main tasks of the deacons was to go each week in groups of two to the homes of the church families and find out how they were getting along. As you know, many of the

439

early Christians lost their jobs because they became Christians. Others were ostracized by society and thus were thrown upon the mercy of the church. The deacons would ascertain who was in need and how the church could help.

Therefore, deacons had to be honest men. They had to be careful how they conducted themselves because they knew what was happening in the various homes. They knew the financial standing of the homes. They knew the private matters of the families. And they could not divulge that information to people who did not need to know. They had to be fair, honest, trustworthy leaders.

I Timothy 3:14-4:6

These things write I unto thee, hoping to come unto thee shortly: but if I tarry long, that thou mayest know how thou oughtest to behave thyself in the house of God, which is the church of the living God, the pillar and ground of the truth. And without controversy great is the mystery of godliness: God was manifest in the flesh, justified in the Spirit, seen of angels, preached unto the Gentiles, believed on in the world, received up into glory.

Now the Spirit speaketh expressly, that in the latter times some shall depart from the faith, giving heed to seducing spirits, and doctrines of devils; speaking lies in hypocrisy; having their conscience seared with a hot iron; forbidding to marry, and commanding to abstain from meats, which God hath created to be received with thanksgiving of them which believe and know the truth. For every creature of God is good, and nothing to be refused, if it be received with thanksgiving: for it is sanctified by the word of God and prayer.

If thou put the brethren in remembrance of these things, thou shalt be a good minister of Jesus Christ, nourished up in the words of faith and of good doctrine, whereunto thou hast attained.

Paul is pointing out to Timothy that the closer we get to the rising of Antichrist, the more Satan will reveal himself through his evil spirits. Also, as sin reaches its climax, men will be more vulnerable. They will be willing to believe the doctrines of devils rather than the doctrine of God. They will speak lies and hypocrisy. And they will no longer have a sensitivity to the Spirit of God, because their consciences will be seared. Like cattle branded with a branding iron, the devil's mark will be on them.

I Timothy 4:7-10

But refuse profane and old wives' fables, and exercise thyself rather unto godliness. For bodily exercise profiteth little: but godliness is profitable unto all things, having promise of the life that now is, and of that which is to come. This is a faithful saying and worthy of all acceptation. For therefore we both labour and suffer reproach, because we trust in the living God, who is the Saviour of all men, specially of those that believe.

Paul admits there is some profit in the training of our bodies. But he says there is something even more profitable: the training of the eternal part of ourselves. Being godly is profitable both now and in the world to come.

I Timothy 4:11-16
> These things command and teach. Let no man despise thy youth; but be thou an example of the believers, in word, in conversation, in charity, in spirit, in faith, in purity. Till I come, give attendance to reading, to exhortation, to doctrine.
>
> Neglect not the gift that is in thee, which was given thee by prophecy, with the laying on of the hands of the presbytery. Meditate upon these things; give thyself wholly to them; that thy profiting may appear to all. Take heed unto thyself, and unto the doctrine; continue in them: for in doing this thou shalt both save thyself, and them that hear thee.

Counsel to Youth

In those days a person was not considered mature until he was around 40 years of age. Timothy may have been 35 or 40 years old, but he became a co-laborer with Paul in the gospel at an unusually early age. He had no doubt been self-conscious about his youth, and that had carried over.

So in steps Paul. The great apostle tells Timothy he can counteract his self-consciousness by making a decision to be an example to the believers in the manner of his conversation and the depth of his love. He tells Timothy to show the people his faith by his works — by the signs and wonders that accompany those who live in faith and purity.

I Timothy 5:1-10
> Rebuke not an elder, but intreat him as a father; and the younger men as brethren; the elder women as mothers; the younger as sisters, with all purity.
>
> Honour widows that are widows indeed. But if any widow have children or nephews, let them learn first to shew piety at home, and to requite their parents: for that is good and acceptable before God.

Now she that is a widow indeed, and desolate, trusteth in God, and continueth in supplications and prayers night and day. But she that liveth in pleasure is dead while she liveth. And these things give in charge, that they may be blameless. But if any provide not for his own, and specially for those of his own house, he hath denied the faith, and is worse than an infidel.

Let not a widow be taken into the number under threescore years old, having been the wife of one man, well reported of for good works; if she have brought up children, if she have lodged strangers, if she have washed the saints' feet, if she have relieved the afflicted, if she have diligently followed every good work.

Family Care

By the time this letter was written, the Church had an official register of widows and precise standards for their care. There were many widows in those days. There were also many older women who had never married who required special care. And the Church, under the leadership of men like Paul and Timothy, was doing what it could to provide for them as members of God's family of believers on earth.

I Timothy 5:11-18

But the younger widows refuse: for when they have begun to wax wanton against Christ, they will marry; having damnation, because they have cast off their first faith. And withal they learn to be idle, wandering about from house to house; and not only idle, but tattlers also and busybodies, speaking things which they ought not.

I will therefore that the younger women marry, bear children, guide the house, give none occasion to the adversary to speak reproachfully. For some are already turned aside after Satan.

If any man or woman that believeth have widows, let them relieve them, and let not the church be charged; that it may relieve them that are widows indeed.

Let the elders that rule well be counted worthy of double honour, especially they who labour in the word and doctrine. For the scripture saith, Thou shalt not muzzle the ox that treadeth out the corn. And, The labourer is worthy of his reward.

I remember when I was a young boy growing up on a farm, how my father would take my brother Vaden and me in a wagon to gather in the corn. Papa never put a muzzle on the horses while they pulled the wagon down through the rows of corn. So, each horse would take a bite of corn now and then to keep himself strong for the work he was engaged in.

That is what Paul is saying in this passage. Those who are in the ministry, who give their time and strength to it, are to be sustained by those they minister to. And the elders who work especially hard are to receive more.

I Timothy 5:19-23

Against an elder receive not an accusation, but before two or three witnesses. Them that sin rebuke before all, that others also may fear. I charge thee before God, and the Lord Jesus Christ, and the elect angels, that thou observe these things without preferring one before another, doing nothing by partiality.

Lay hands suddenly on no man, neither be partaker of other men's sins: keep thyself pure. Drink no longer water, but use a little wine for thy stomach's sake and thine often infirmities.

Paul instructs Timothy to be very careful when he lays hands on someone to ordain him. For if he has not prepared himself properly, he will not be able to carry out their work in a mature way. He also admonishes Timothy to use a little wine so his physical body could adjust to the water of the area he is in. He knows Timothy is a young man with stomach problems that are easily aggravated by bad water. Although total abstinence from alcohol is recommended, the body's health must come first.

I Timothy 5:24-6:2

Some men's sins are open beforehand, going before to judgment; and some men they follow after. Likewise also the good works of some are manifest beforehand; and they that are otherwise cannot be hid.

Let as many servants as are under the yoke count their own masters worthy of all honour, that the name of God and his doctrine be not blasphemed. And they that have believing masters, let them not despise them, because they are brethren; but rather do them service, because they are faithful and beloved, partakers of the benefit. These things teach and exhort.

Living Under Slavery

Slavery in those days was widespread. It was more economic than racial. There were as many as 60 million slaves in the Roman Empire. So when you think about the Christian church being the tiniest of minorities, it would have been fatal for them to have risen up against the Romans. What could they do? The only thing they could do was try to lead the slaves and masters to Jesus Christ and put them together as brothers so they would treat one another with equal respect.

I Timothy 6:3-10

> If any man teach otherwise, and consent not to wholesome words, even the words of our Lord Jesus Christ, and to the doctrine which is according to godliness; he is proud, knowing nothing, but doting about questions and strifes of words, whereof cometh envy, strife, railings, evil surmisings, perverse disputings of men of corrupt minds, and destitute of the truth, supposing that gain is godliness: from such withdraw thyself.
>
> But godliness with contentment is great gain. For we brought nothing into this world, and it is certain we can carry nothing out. And having food and raiment let us be therewith content.
>
> But they that will be rich fall into temptation and a snare, and into many foolish and hurtful lusts, which drown men in destruction and perdition. For the love of money is the root of all evil: which while some coveted after, they have erred from the faith, and pierced themselves through with many sorrows.

Paul is not teaching that as Christians we are not to have our needs met or prosper in the things of God. He is saying to love people and use things, not love things and use people. For when we love God first, we can love everything else all we want to. That gives us balance with everything else in the world.

Paul does warn, however, that people who lust to be rich are in a dangerous position because when they lust for money, it becomes the root of all evil. It becomes a seed they plant. And when that seed matures, it brings forth a harvest of spiritual death. So it is the lust, or the love, for money that Paul is condemning.

I Timothy 6:11-19

> But thou, O man of God, flee these things; and follow after righteousness, godliness, faith, love, patience, meekness. Fight the good fight of faith, lay hold on eternal life, whereunto thou art also called, and hast professed a good profession before many witnesses.
>
> I give thee charge in the sight of God, who quickeneth all things, and before Christ Jesus, who before Pontius Pilate witnessed a good confession; that thou keep this commandment without spot, unrebukeable, until the appearing of our Lord Jesus Christ: which in his times he shall shew, who is the blessed and only Potentate, the King of kings, and Lord of lords; who only hath immortality, dwelling

in the light which no man can approach unto; whom no man hath seen, nor can see: to whom be honour and power everlasting. Amen.

Charge them that are rich in this world, that they be not highminded; nor trust in uncertain riches, but in the living God, who giveth us richly all things to enjoy; that they do good, that they be rich in good works, ready to distribute, willing to communicate; laying up in store for themselves a good foundation against the time to come, that they may lay hold on eternal life.

Wealth in the Early Church

Do not think the Christians in the early church were only poor people. Many of them were wealthy. And Paul did not condemn them for their wealth. He simply said to not be proud or put riches in the place of God, the true source. Rather, use wealth to do good.

I Timothy 6:20,21

O Timothy, keep that which is committed to thy trust, avoiding profane and vain babblings, and oppositions of science falsely so called: which some professing have erred concerning the faith. Grace be with thee. Amen.

Paul is giving Timothy a beautiful closing word by saying, in effect, "Timothy, you have to ask the right questions. Do not be like the false teachers with their so-called oppositions of science who ask such questions as, 'What if there is no God? What if the Word of God is not true? And what if the gospel Paul preached is false?' You just ask questions like, 'How can we love one another more deeply? How can we make the greatest contribution with our lives? And how can we uplift Jesus even better?' If you ask questions like these, Timothy, you will be on the right track." The apostle then closes his first letter to his son in the faith with one of his favorite words: grace.

The Second Epistle of
Paul the Apostle to
Timothy

The Second Epistle of
Paul the Apostle to
Timothy

In this letter, Paul talks about his life. We learn much about him that we did not know before. We also learn many things about the young man Timothy. In addition, we learn how to avoid certain evils in the world, how to strengthen our faith, and how to come to a moment of triumph in our own Christian experiences that will carry us all the way through.

II Timothy 1:1-5

Paul, an apostle of Jesus Christ by the will of God, according to the promise of life which is in Christ Jesus, to Timothy, my dearly beloved son: Grace, mercy, and peace, from God the Father and Christ Jesus our Lord.

I thank God, whom I serve from my forefathers with pure conscience, that without ceasing I have remembrance of thee in my prayers night and day; greatly desiring to see thee, being mindful of thy tears, that I may be filled with joy; when I call to remembrance the unfeigned faith that is in thee, which dwelt first in thy grandmother Lois, and thy mother Eunice; and I am persuaded that in thee also.

A Heritage of Faith

Paul is saying, "Timothy, the kind of faith you have is the kind that has no ifs, maybes, or hope sos. It is a knowing faith. It is a faith that stood the trials of the devil. It is a faith that was handed down to you, but one you have personally accepted by trusting in Jesus Christ your Lord."

II Timothy 1:6-11

Wherefore I put thee in remembrance that thou stir up the gift of God, which is in thee by the putting on of my hands. For God hath not given us the spirit of fear; but of power, and of love, and of a sound mind.

Be not thou therefore ashamed of the testimony of our Lord, nor of me his prisoner: but be thou partaker of the afflictions of the gospel according to the power of God; who hath saved us, and called us with an holy calling, not according to our works, but according to his own purpose and grace, which was given us in Christ Jesus before the world began, but is now made manifest by the appearing of our Saviour Jesus Christ, who hath abolished death, and hath brought life and immortality to light through the gospel: whereunto I am appointed a preacher, and an apostle, and a teacher of the Gentiles.

Stirring Up the Gift Inside Us

This is so wonderful for you and me today because our gift also seems to lie low sometimes. But the gift of God is in us and we can stir it up. We can get it moving. So many times I have seen this happen in my life and in other people's lives. I have met people who were so near the point of letting the gift of God leave their lives forever that I just had to stop, point out this particular scripture, and show them they were not alone in their feelings. For God knows our humanity. He knows we are flesh and blood. And He is there to help us stir up the gift inside us.

Paul reminds Timothy that fear has no place in the Christian's life because God does not give us the spirit of fear. I want you to know there are three types of fear. The first is the right kind of fear. It is the fear of God, or the reverential respect for our Lord. The second is the normal fear we all experience in our daily living. It is a healthy respect for danger that keeps us from running in front of a speeding car or jumping from a tremendous height. The third type of fear is the spirit of fear. It is what Paul is talking about. It is a fear from the devil that tries to take over our lives and master us. But Paul says there is something greater than the spirit of fear: the Spirit of the living God inside us.

II Timothy 1:12-18

For the which cause I also suffer these things: nevertheless I am not ashamed: for I know whom I have believed, and am persuaded that he is able to keep that which I have committed unto him against that day.

Hold fast the form of sound words, which thou hast heard of me,
in faith and love which is in Christ Jesus. That good thing which was
committed unto thee keep by the Holy Ghost which dwelleth in us.

This thou knowest, that all they which are in Asia be turned away
from me; of whom are Phygellus and Hermogenes.

The Lord give mercy unto the house of Onesiphorus; for he oft
refreshed me, and was not ashamed of my chain: but, when he was
in Rome, he sought me out very diligently, and found me. The Lord
grant unto him that he may find mercy of the Lord in that day: and
in how many things he ministered unto me at Ephesus, thou knowest
very well.

Paul flatly says the first two people are traitors. They simply are
troublemakers of the worst sort. But he says he wants God to
remember and give mercy to Onesiphorus and his family because
he was the one who sought him out in prison.

In those days that was not a safe thing to do. It was not safe to
inquire if a particular person was in prison, because the authorities
could put you in prison for trying to find out. But Onesiphorus was
not ashamed of the chain that rattled on Paul's hand. He sought him
out and when he found him, he ministered to his needs. So Paul
prayed the Lord would grant Onesiphorus mercy in that day.

II Timothy 2:1-10

Thou therefore, my son, be strong in the grace that is in Christ Jesus.
And the things that thou hast heard of me among many witnesses,
the same commit thou to faithful men, who shall be able to teach
others also.

Thou therefore endure hardness, as a good soldier of Jesus Christ.
No man that warreth entangleth himself with the affairs of this life;
that he may please him who hath chosen him to be a soldier. And if
a man also strive for masteries, yet is he not crowned, except he
strive lawfully.

The husbandman that laboureth must be first partaker of the fruits.
Consider what I say; and the Lord give thee understanding in all things.

Remember that Jesus Christ of the seed of David was raised from
the dead according to my gospel: wherein I suffer trouble, as an evil
doer, even unto bonds; but the word of God is not bound. Therefore
I endure all things for the elect's sakes, that they may also obtain the
salvation which is in Christ Jesus with eternal glory.

Paul gives Timothy a tremendous statement of his situation. He
says, "Remember, Jesus Christ was raised from the dead according
to my gospel, and that is the reason that I am in trouble with people

who do not believe. They say I am an evildoer. But let me tell you, Timothy, while they may be able to bind my body, they cannot bind the Word of God. They can throw me into prison, but there are no bars that can bind God's eternal Word. Therefore, I endure all things for the sake of the elect that they may obtain salvation through Jesus Christ."

II Timothy 2:11-18

It is a faithful saying: For if we be dead with him, we shall also live with him: if we suffer, we shall also reign with him: if we deny him, he also will deny us: if we believe not, yet he abideth faithful: he cannot deny himself.

Of these things put them in remembrance, charging them before the Lord that they strive not about words to no profit, but to the subverting of the hearers.

Study to shew thyself approved unto God, a workman that needeth not to be ashamed, rightly dividing the word of truth. But shun profane and vain babblings: for they will increase unto more ungodliness. And their word will eat as doth a canker: of whom is Hymenaeus and Philetus; who concerning the truth have erred, saying that the resurrection is past already; and overthrow the faith of some.

The Word of Truth

Rightly dividing the word of truth is like a stonemason who cuts stone in a particular way to make it fit with other stones in a building. The word of truth is essentially contained in the Word of God, but it also spreads out through the whole universe. For there is some truth in nearly everything. Therefore, you and I have to know the truth of God so we can divide out things that are erroneous. And we can only do that as we study, apply ourselves, and ask God for even greater ability to know His truth.

II Timothy 2:19-21

Nevertheless the foundation of God standeth sure, having this seal, The Lord knoweth them that are his. And, Let every one that nameth the name of Christ depart from iniquity.

But in a great house there are not only vessels of gold and of silver, but also of wood and of earth; and some to honour, and some to dishonour. If a man therefore purge himself from these, he shall be a vessel unto honour, sanctified, and meet for the master's use, and prepared unto every good work.

Paul is saying this in line with what he has just said about those who rightly divide the word of truth and those who do not. For there are leaders in the Church who are like gold. They are able to purge themselves from the things of this world and teach the eternal truths of God. But there are those who are not like gold at all. They do not have the truth. They are weak. They are not able to divide the Word of God correctly. And they have not purged themselves from the things of this world. Therefore, we ought to take notice of them and only listen to the ministers of the gospel who preach the real Word of God.

II Timothy 2:22-26

Flee also youthful lusts: but follow righteousness, faith, charity, peace, with them that call on the Lord out of a pure heart. But foolish and unlearned questions avoid, knowing that they do gender strifes.

And the servant of the Lord must not strive; but be gentle unto all men, apt to teach, patient, in meekness instructing those that oppose themselves; if God peradventure will give them repentance to the acknowledging of the truth; and that they may recover themselves out of the snare of the devil, who are taken captive by him at his will.

It is so easy as a young person to rise and fall with the feelings of passion, to have hate one moment and love the next. But Paul says there is something better to do. He says to follow after love and flee anything that is not of love and peace. In other words, the peace of God can take the place of changing passions.

II Timothy 3:1-5

This know also, that in the last days perilous times shall come. For men shall be lovers of their own selves, covetous, boasters, proud, blasphemers, disobedient to parents, unthankful, unholy, without natural affection, trucebreakers, false accusers, incontinent, fierce, despisers of those that are good, traitors, heady, highminded, lovers of pleasures more than lovers of God; having a form of godliness, but denying the power thereof: from such turn away.

Marks of the Last Days

Paul tells Timothy outright that troubled times are ahead. For as Christ's second coming nears, evil will intensify in the world. He lists a number of things that will be wrong and he says they will all end as we enter the last days.

Then he talks about the Church and says there will be people who will love pleasure more than they love God. They will have a form of godliness but will deny the real power of God. He says to turn away from such people. I really cannot improve on what Paul is saying, for this is a perfect description of the last days we are living in today.

II Timothy 3:6-15

For of this sort are they which creep into houses, and lead captive silly women laden with sins, led away with divers lusts, ever learning, and never able to come to the knowledge of the truth. Now as Jannes and Jambres withstood Moses, so do these also resist the truth: men of corrupt minds, reprobate concerning the faith. But they shall proceed no further: for their folly shall be manifest unto all men, as theirs also was.

But thou hast fully known my doctrine, manner of life, purpose, faith, longsuffering, charity, patience, persecutions, afflictions, which came unto me at Antioch, at Iconium, at Lystra; what persecutions I endured: but out of them all the Lord delivered me. Yea, and all that will live godly in Christ Jesus shall suffer persecution. But evil men and seducers shall wax worse and worse, deceiving, and being deceived.

But continue thou in the things which thou hast learned and hast been assured of, knowing of whom thou hast learned them; and that from a child thou hast known the holy scriptures, which are able to make thee wise unto salvation through faith which is in Christ Jesus.

Persecuted But Victorious

Paul is reminding Timothy that everyone who lives a godly life in Christ Jesus will suffer persecution. There is no way that we as true Christians can escape persecution. I personally believe that the closer we live to God and the more we are determined to do His work and be obedient to His calling, the more the devil opposes us and causes people to come against us. Sometimes, they do not even know why they come against us. But I also believe that we are victorious through Jesus Christ our Lord. We may be persecuted from time to time, but we are winners when all is said and done.

II Timothy 3:16-4:8

All scripture is given by inspiration of God, and is profitable for doctrine, for reproof, for correction, for instruction in righteousness: that the man of God may be perfect, thoroughly furnished unto all good works.

454

I charge thee therefore before God, and the Lord Jesus Christ, who shall judge the quick and the dead at his appearing and his kingdom; Preach the word; be instant in season, out of season; reprove, rebuke, exhort with all longsuffering and doctrine.

For the time will come when they will not endure sound doctrine; but after their own lusts shall they heap to themselves teachers, having itching ears; and they shall turn away their ears from the truth, and shall be turned unto fables. But watch thou in all things, endure afflictions, do the work of an evangelist, make full proof of thy ministry.

For I am now ready to be offered, and the time of my departure is at hand. I have fought a good fight, I have finished my course, I have kept the faith: henceforth there is laid up for me a crown of righteousness, which the Lord, the righteous judge, shall give me at that day: and not to me only, but unto all them also that love his appearing.

Praise God for Paul

I personally praise God for Paul. He never lost his confidence. He sometimes temporarily despaired that his life would end prematurely, but he never gave up the fight. And his life did not end until he finished the plan God had for him.

We too will finish our lives someday. Partner, our lives are not necessarily in the number of our years, but in the way we obey God. This is very touching to me because someday we will finish our course on this earth and go to be with the Lord in heaven. We will look back at this tiny planet and say, "I was there for a brief moment. There were high moments and there were low moments. But I held steady. And from this heavenly vantage point, earth was but a passing moment in the eternity of my life."

II Timothy 4:9-13

Do thy diligence to come shortly unto me; for Demas hath forsaken me, having loved this present world, and is departed unto Thessalonica; Crescens to Galatia, Titus unto Dalmatia. Only Luke is with me. Take Mark, and bring him with thee: for he is profitable to me for the ministry. And Tychicus have I sent to Ephesus.

The cloak that I left at Troas with Carpus, when thou comest, bring with thee, and the books, but especially the parchments.

Paul is coming to the end of his very personal letter to Timothy and to those of us in the faith. He is talking about his close co-laborers in the gospel. He tells Timothy to bring Mark with him when he comes because Mark "is profitable to me for the ministry." This is one of the great lines of the Bible because Mark was the "quitter." He was the man who left Paul on his first missionary journey when the going got tough and the persecutions started. But something happened to Mark. Peter became interested in him and was able to touch young Mark in a way that Paul could not.

According to the best records available, Mark was around 40 years old when this letter was written. But when he quit he was a teenager. So at the time he just had not grown up yet. He had not found himself. And all those inner teenage conflicts had not been resolved.

Partner, this speaks so well to you and me today. For God always has someone to help us when we are up and when we are down. If we are just listening and sensitive, God will send someone for us.

II Timothy 4:14,15

Alexander the coppersmith did me much evil: the Lord reward him according to his works: of whom be thou ware also; for he hath greatly withstood our words.

Apparently, Alexander was an informant who gave false information about Paul that contributed to the persecution that came against him. In this particular instance, Paul says the Lord will reward this man according to his deeds.

That is still true today. The best thing we can do is leave the vengeance to God. For He alone is able to stand its power. If we take vengeance on others, vengeance will destroy us.

II Timothy 4:16-22

At my first answer no man stood with me, but all men forsook me: I pray God that it may not be laid to their charge. Notwithstanding the Lord stood with me, and strengthened me; that by me the preaching might be fully known, and that all the Gentiles might hear: and I was delivered out of the mouth of the lion.

And the Lord shall deliver me from every evil work, and will preserve me unto his heavenly kingdom: to whom be glory for ever and ever. Amen.

Salute Prisca and Aquila, and the household of Onesiphorus. Erastus abode at Corinth: but Trophimus have I left at Miletum sick.

Do thy diligence to come before winter. Eubulus greeteth thee and Pudens, and Linus, and Claudia, and all the brethren. The Lord Jesus Christ be with thy spirit. Grace be with you. Amen.

This passage shows how personal the relationships were between the Christians in the early church. It is a reminder that we are to recognize and appreciate one another as brothers and sisters in Christ.

I would like for us to pray together as we close the second letter to Timothy.

> *Father, we thank You for Paul. We thank You that we have the opportunity to be taught by him and that his words to Timothy are also addressed to us. And we thank You that we can live our lives in the same faith of taking You at Your Word, that we can know there is a crown of righteousness laid up for us also, and that something good awaits us at every turn of the road. Bless this my friend and partner and be very close. Through Jesus Christ I pray and I believe. Amen and amen.*

The Epistle
of Paul to
Titus

The Epistle
of Paul to
Titus

When a situation arose that was tough to handle, Paul always tried to find the right person for the job. Such was the case with the nation of Crete. Crete was a Mediterranean island whose people were known throughout the Roman Empire as a quarrelsome, hard-to-handle people. Therefore, since those on the island who accepted Jesus Christ came from such an unruly people, they carried some of the Cretian characteristics with them into the Church. They needed sound, practical advice on how to live the Christian life.

Titus, the young Greek, was the man for the hour. He had been led to Christ and personally taught by Paul in the doctrines of Jesus Christ. He had helped Paul take up the collections among the Macedonian churches for the poor saints in Jerusalem. He was there in Jerusalem when Paul was put in prison and eventually shipped off to Rome to stand before Caesar. He had been sent by Paul with special messages and help for the Corinthian church to lead them in the grace of giving. He was a faithful, dependable, practical Christian man.

More than any other book that Paul wrote, the book of Titus deals with the practical issues of daily Christian living. It is a book for developing strong Christian character.

Titus 1:1-11

Paul, a servant of God, and an apostle of Jesus Christ, according to the faith of God's elect, and the acknowledging of the truth which is after godliness; in hope of eternal life, which God, that cannot lie, promised before the world began; but hath in due times manifested his word through preaching, which is committed unto me according to the commandment of God our Saviour; To Titus, mine own son after the common faith: Grace, mercy, and peace, from God the Father and the Lord Jesus Christ our Saviour.

> For this cause left I thee in Crete, that thou shouldest set in order the things that are wanting, and ordain elders in every city, as I had appointed thee: if any be blameless, the husband of one wife, having faithful children not accused of riot or unruly.
>
> For a bishop must be blameless, as the steward of God; not selfwilled, not soon angry, not given to wine, no striker, not given to filthy lucre; but a lover of hospitality, a lover of good men, sober, just, holy, temperate; holding fast the faithful word as he hath been taught, that he may be able by sound doctrine both to exhort and to convince the gainsayers.
>
> For there are many unruly and vain talkers and deceivers, specially they of the circumcision: whose mouths must be stopped, who subvert whole houses, teaching things which they ought not, for filthy lucre's sake.

There were certain characteristics that Titus was to look for before he ordained elders and bishops. They should be men who were faithful, gentle, of strong character, and not given to wine, making decisions too quickly, or coming to blows with people. They should be men who had led their own families to God, were hospitable, cared for people, were sober, just, holy, and temperate — men who held fast the faithful Word of God as they were taught.

Paul was getting very practical about the kind of Christian character he wanted his ministers to have.

Titus 1:12-16

> One of themselves, even a prophet of their own, said, The Cretians are alway liars, evil beasts, slow bellies. This witness is true. Wherefore rebuke them sharply, that they may be sound in the faith; not giving heed to Jewish fables, and commandments of men, that turn from the truth.
>
> Unto the pure all things are pure: but unto them that are defiled and unbelieving is nothing pure; but even their mind and conscience is defiled. They profess that they know God; but in works they deny him, being abominable, and disobedient, and unto every good work reprobate.

One of the things Paul points out to Timothy is that to people who have a wicked mind and are unbelievers, nothing is pure. Their consciences are defiled. But to the pure all things are pure.

Let me give you an example. There are people who are so sexually oriented that everything they hear or think about has a sexual connotation. Others are so absorbed by money that they put a financial slant on everything they hear, do, or think. But if a person is earnestly serving God, he can talk about anything he wants to and his mind never has all these innuendos. He thinks pure things. He is straightforward and single-minded in his thinking.

Titus 2:1-6

> But speak thou the things which become sound doctrine: that the aged men be sober, grave, temperate, sound in faith, in charity, in patience. The aged women likewise, that they be in behaviour as becometh holiness, not false accusers, not given to much wine, teachers of good things; that they may teach the young women to be sober, to love their husbands, to love their children, to be discreet, chaste, keepers at home, good, obedient to their own husbands, that the word of God be not blasphemed. Young men likewise exhort to be sober minded.

Paul begins by outlining the qualifications in character and disposition for elders and bishops. Then he turns to the older men, the older women, the younger women, and the younger men, and he lays out the character traits for them in the Christian faith. So he is speaking of people who are not ministers of the gospel.

Titus 2:7,8

> In all things shewing thyself a pattern of good works: in doctrine shewing uncorruptness, gravity, sincerity, sound speech, that cannot be condemned; that he that is of the contrary part may be ashamed, having no evil thing to say of you.

Paul is saying to Titus, "You be the example. You be the pattern of good works for the people of Crete. Then as they are around you, they will be touched and influenced by your Christian character."

Titus 2:9-15

> Exhort servants to be obedient unto their own masters, and to please them well in all things; not answering again; not purloining, but shewing all good fidelity; that they may adorn the doctrine of God our Saviour in all things.
>
> For the grace of God that bringeth salvation hath appeared to all men, teaching us that, denying ungodliness and worldly lusts, we should live soberly, righteously, and godly, in this present world; looking for that blessed hope, and the glorious appearing of the great God and our Saviour Jesus Christ; who gave himself for us, that he might redeem us from all iniquity, and purify unto himself a peculiar people, zealous of good works. These things speak, and exhort, and rebuke with all authority. Let no man despise thee.

463

I believe Paul is urging Titus to tell the Christians in Crete that Christianity is distinctively different. It is a radical approach to life because it brings people into purity. Why? It is a direct personal relationship with a personal God.

Titus 3:1-7

Put them in mind to be subject to principalities and powers, to obey magistrates, to be ready to every good work, to speak evil of no man, to be no brawlers, but gentle, shewing all meekness unto all men. For we ourselves also were sometimes foolish, disobedient, deceived, serving divers lusts and pleasures, living in malice and envy, hateful, and hating one another.

But after that the kindness and love of God our Saviour toward man appeared, not by works of righteousness which we have done, but according to his mercy he saved us, by the washing of regeneration, and renewing of the Holy Ghost; which he shed on us abundantly through Jesus Christ our Saviour; that being justified by his grace, we should be made heirs according to the hope of eternal life.

Obedience to the Law

The people of Crete were an unruly group of people. So Paul told Titus to instruct the Cretian Christians to be subject to the principalities and powers, to obey the law, and be ready to do every good work, because Christian service begins in being subject to the laws of the land.

Titus 3:8-13

This is a faithful saying, and these things I will that thou affirm constantly, that they which have believed in God might be careful to maintain good works. These things are good and profitable unto men.

But avoid foolish questions, and genealogies, and contentions, and strivings about the law; for they are unprofitable and vain. A man that is an heretic after the first and second admonition reject; knowing that he that is such is subverted, and sinneth, being condemned of himself.

When I shall send Artemas unto thee, or Tychicus, be diligent to come unto me to Nicopolis: for I have determined there to winter. Bring Zenas the lawyer and Apollos on their journey diligently, that nothing be wanting unto them.

Paul is saying that Titus will soon leave Crete. He tells him that others will be coming to take his place. Paul also urges Titus to come before winter because he needs him.

Titus 3:14,15

And let ours also learn to maintain good works for necessary uses, that they be not unfruitful. All that are with me salute thee. Greet them that love us in the faith. Grace be with you all. Amen.

Our heavenly Father, we thank You for Paul's letter to Titus. We thank You for the information he gave on how to develop strong Christian character, have healthy faith, and be loving toward all people. For we need to learn how to be practical in our Christian walk in this present world.

My dear partner, I pray God will bless you, strengthen you, and help you to be strong in your Christian character and practical in your walk with Christ in this present world. I pray this through Jesus Christ our Lord. And I expect it to happen. Amen and amen.

The Epistle
of Paul to
Philemon

The Epistle
of Paul to
Philemon

Philemon is a tender yet dramatic letter concerning three men. First, there is Paul, the apostle and evangelist. Second, there is Philemon, a wealthy slave owner whom Paul led to Christ many years before. And third, there is Onesimus, the slave who is owned by Philemon and who is one of the 60 million slaves in the Roman Empire.

This Onesimus had thrown off his bonds, robbed his master, and fled to Rome, the melting pot of the world. There, he hoped to escape in the thronging multitudes and forever be free from slavery. But while in Rome, he met Paul and was led to Christ by the apostle. So the letter to Philemon is a touching epistle that reveals the heartbeat of Paul as he reaches out to Philemon, a fellow Christian, on behalf of Onesimus, the former slave and now Christian brother.

Philemon 1-6

Paul, a prisoner of Jesus Christ, and Timothy our brother, unto Philemon our dearly beloved, and fellowlabourer, and to our beloved Apphia, and Archippus our fellowsoldier, and to the church in thy house: Grace to you, and peace, from God our Father and the Lord Jesus Christ.

I thank my God, making mention of thee always in my prayers, hearing of thy love and faith, which thou hast toward the Lord Jesus, and toward all saints; that the communication of thy faith may become effectual by the acknowledging of every good thing which is in you in Christ Jesus.

Paul has been hearing of the love and faith of Philemon as far away as Rome. So he tells him that he has heard something very special about him. He has heard about his communication, or giving.

Paul prays that the giving of Philemon's faith may become effectual in every good thing and be returned to him through Jesus Christ. This is a beautiful statement of seed-faith giving and receiving.

Philemon 7

> For we have great joy and consolation in thy love, because the bowels of the saints are refreshed by thee, brother.

Paul tells Philemon that it brings him great joy to see this tender and deep love transcend all human standards of the world. For Philemon is involved in Christian giving and receiving. He is involved in refreshing the people of God. He stands as a strong bulwark for the Lord.

Philemon 8-12

> Wherefore, though I might be much bold in Christ to enjoin thee that which is convenient, yet for love's sake I rather beseech thee, being such an one as Paul the aged, and now also a prisoner of Jesus Christ.
>
> I beseech thee for my son Onesimus, whom I have begotten in my bonds: which in time past was to thee unprofitable, but now profitable to thee and to me: whom I have sent again: thou therefore receive him, that is, mine own bowels: . . .

Useless to Useful

It is interesting that Onesimus' name means "profitable" in Greek. Paul uses that meaning to make a play on the term. He says, "Philemon, in the past this slave was unprofitable. But now he is profitable to you and to me. I have sent him to you. So I ask you to receive him just as you would receive me." You see, Paul believes that in Christ the useless person is made useful. And the unworthy is made worthy.

Philemon 13-16

> Whom I would have retained with me, that in thy stead he might have ministered unto me in the bonds of the gospel: but without thy mind would I do nothing; that thy benefit should not be as it were of necessity, but willingly.
>
> For perhaps he therefore departed for a season, that thou shouldest receive him for ever; not now as a servant, but above a servant, a brother beloved, specially to me, but how much more unto thee, both in the flesh, and in the Lord?

Paul desires to retain Onesimus. The change in him through the power of Christ is remarkable. But he knows that according to the law, Onesimus has to return to his owner. He asks Philemon, however, to consider Onesimus no longer as a slave, but as a brother in Christ.

Philemon 17-20

> If thou count me therefore a partner, receive him as myself. If he hath wronged thee, or oweth thee ought, put that on mine account; I Paul have written it with mine own hand, I will repay it: albeit I do not say to thee how thou owest unto me even thine own self besides. Yea, brother, let me have joy of thee in the Lord: refresh my bowels in the Lord.

Paul Not Poor

Evidently Paul has financial resources. For he tells Philemon, "If Onesimus owes you a lot of money, I will repay it. However, I would like to remind you of what you owe me. You owe me your own soul because I led you to Christ. So refresh my heart and receive this slave back as a beloved brother, knowing that whatever he owes you, I will repay."

Philemon 21,22

> Having confidence in thy obedience I wrote unto thee, knowing that thou wilt also do more than I say. But withal prepare me also a lodging: for I trust that through your prayers I shall be given unto you.

Paul takes it for granted that Philemon has received the message in his heart, so he tells him he is going to come by for a visit and expects to see him. Then he ends the letter by mentioning five of his co-laborers.

Philemon 23-25

> There salute thee Epaphras, my fellowprisoner in Christ Jesus; Marcus, Aristarchus, Demas, Lucas, my fellowlabourers. The grace of our Lord Jesus Christ be with your spirit. Amen.

The Meaning of Freedom

I want you to look at these two men. One of them is in prison. His hands are bound at the wrists. He does not have the freedom

471

to walk around. The other is a slave no longer in chains. There are no bonds on his body. He is not in prison. And yet, both men are free.

The Bible teaches that freedom does not depend on outward circumstances, but on what is inside our hearts. It depends on having a new relationship with Jesus Christ and being a new creature in Him.

Paul never would have asked to send Onesimus to Philemon had not both men tasted of the unsearchable riches and the unlimited freedom that is in Jesus Christ. They both knew that regardless of the physical circumstances, we are free indeed when we have experienced the liberating power of Jesus Christ. May you and I experience that freedom today and every day of our lives.